SCOTTISH HISTORY SOCIETY

FIFTH SERIES

VOLUME 3

====

Miscellany XI

Miscellany

of the Scottish History Society

ELEVENTH VOLUME

★

★

EDINBURGH
printed for the Scottish History Society *by*
PILLANS & WILSON LTD., EDINBURGH
1990

British Library Cataloguing-in-Publication Data:
A catalogue record for this book is available
from the British Library

ISBN 0 906245 12 5

Printed in Great Britain

CONTENTS

═══

A generous contribution from the
Carnegie Trust for the Universities of Scotland
towards the cost of producing this volume
is gratefully acknowledged by the
Council of the Society

T. I. Rae

THOMAS IAN RAE, 1926-1989

A memoir by Professor Ian B. Cowan

Thomas Ian Rae was born in Norwich on 9 June 1926. He received his early education at Knox Academy in Haddington and, after his move to Hawick, the High School there. In these formative years he conceived a strong love for the Borders which was to remain with him for the rest of his life. Called to active service during the closing years of World War Two, Ian, after a six-month Services short course at Oxford, served at sea in the Royal Navy from 1944 until 1947.

This disruption in his life brought to a premature end his plans to study physics. Instead he entered the University of St Andrews to read for a degree in medieval and modern history, in which he graduated with first-class honours in 1951 after an active undergraduate career in which his principal extra-curricular interest revolved around the Kate Kennedy Club which he helped to revive.

An academic life appeared in the offing and, indeed, his initial career took him in this direction with appointments as an assistant in the history departments at Glasgow and St Andrews universities, in both of which he was held in high regard by staff and students alike. Assistantships in those years were, however, even for the most gifted, terminable, poorly paid appointments; but inclination, rather than uncertainty over future prospects, appears to have dictated his decision in August 1955 to join the Department of Manuscripts in the National Library of Scotland. Quickly adapting himself to his new role, he rejected an opportunity to return to academic life in 1962 and thereafter devoted his life to his chosen profession.

Academia was not, however, abandoned. Two terms as a research fellow at the Folger Library in 1963 and the Huntington Library in 1969 were followed in 1970 by a temporary return to the University of St Andrews in which he deputised for Ronald Cant, during his absence in America, in teaching a senior honours class once a week. The students

who attended that class remember him as a dedicated and articulate teacher who quickly gained their affection and respect.

Thereafter, with the exception of an honorary fellowship to study 'The Scottish Origin Legend' in the Institute for Advanced Studies in the Humanities at the University of Edinburgh in 1976/77, Ian stuck to his last, giving unstinting service to his department, which not only occasioned frequent visits to London, but also encompassed trips as far afield as Australia. His period of office saw the acquisition of an enormous and valuable range of manuscripts relating to modern Scottish history. Readers' needs, however, were never neglected and queries were readily answered in person or by correspondence. Indeed, such was his dedication to his duties that he had frequently to be persuaded to take his annual leave entitlement. His fellowship at the University of Edinburgh was one means of ensuring that a period of outstanding leave was profitably utilised.

Within the milieu of the National Library, one of his major contributions to the work of the Department of Manuscripts, of which he became Keeper in October 1972, was to reorganise the regular publication of volumes of the Department's Catalogue. Between 1982 and 1989, four volumes appeared, the last posthumously; the experience he gained in this way was of direct benefit to the historical organisations he worked for, especially the Scottish History Society. He is remembered in the Library as a gentle and popular colleague, one whose unflamboyant but enthusiastic support of the Library always appeared better in committee than in public, and whose advice was regularly sought by colleagues and outsiders on a wide variety of subjects.

Such a full professional life might have sufficed for many, but Ian's service in other fields far exceeded the call of duty. Although essentially a sixteenth-century historian, he was a founder member of the Scottish Medievalists' Conference in 1957, the year in which he acted as treasurer for its progenitor, the Balfour of Denmilne conference. A regular attender at the Medievalists' annual conferences, he saw membership of the group swell from a handful of young, ambitious historians to over 150 young and (eventually) not so young enthusiasts. Personally supportive of many of its ventures, he contributed to its highly successful *Historical Atlas of Scotland, c.400-c.1600.*

When it was suggested in 1962 that a biennial Scottish Historical

Conference might be mounted, he willingly offered his services as honorary secretary; and when the organising committee was given formal status in 1972 as the Scottish Historical Conference Trust, he became one of the trustees. This duty was, however, far from nominal; Ian was not only actively concerned in the organisation of most of its meetings, but also acted as a speaker, tour guide and general factotum when the occasion demanded.

In other fields he was equally active. As a contributor to the *Scottish Historical Review* it was natural that he should be asked to become a member of the Company of Scottish History when that body was established in 1966 to publish the *Review*. In this latter capacity he served as a director of the company from 1971 to 1974, and four years later, in a time of growing crisis which threatened the future of the journal, he accepted the post of chairman. As such he acted with a tireless enthusiasm coupled with reassuring unflappability. Without his commonsense and practical outlook the journal might well have foundered. On his retiral from the chairmanship in 1984, the *Review* was again on course, the finances consolidated and the future secure.

He was also a member of the council of the Scots Ancestry Research Society, a position offered almost *ex officio* to the Keeper of Manuscripts in the National Library. Characteristically, he did much more than was strictly required of him, and latterly was deeply involved with the finances of the Society, and with the search for new and better premises.

Other learned societies also sought his services. As a member of the Council of the Scottish Record Society, Ian confined his interest to regular attendance at meetings over several years; but his services to the Scottish History Society were herculean. A member of Council from 1965, he became honorary secretary in 1969 and immediately immersed himself not only in the routine administration of the Society, but also in the promotion of a major membership campaign.

His primary concern was, however, with publications, initiating and checking proposals and seeing volumes through the press. Countless editors have attested to his helpfulness in bringing their texts to final publication. Whether he was cajoling or cosseting them, Ian's devotion to his task never failed to win their admiration and gratitude. Ultimately, however, the dual responsibilities of the secretary became too great and he reluctantly proposed that a new position of Publications Secretary should be created. Characteris-

tically, he opted for this demanding post which he occupied from 1976 until his death.

In this period his duties expanded rather than contracted. With rising publication costs, new methods of production had to be sought; many hours were spent considering means of achieving this. Long discussions with Constables (1982) Ltd. were held, only to be thwarted by the liquidation of a firm which, as T. & A. Constable, had served the Society for a hundred years. The collapse occurred half-way through the printing of the Society's centenary volume, *Acts of the Lords of the Isles*; it not only brought plans for a new format to a premature end, but also posed serious financial and production problems for the Society. Single-handed, Ian not only rescued the plates of the volume in progress but also retrieved the considerable stock of past publications and transported them in a hired van to safety in Glasgow.

The difficulties, however, had only begun. In the aftermath of the crisis, few printers were prepared to accept a half-finished volume which, with a production run of only 850 copies, had little financial appeal. After many fruitless negotiations, Ian reached a successful agreement with Messrs Pillans & Wilson, Edinburgh, who undertook to complete the centenary volume and to print future editions. A fruitful partnership was thus entered into and a new style and format quickly agreed.

This arrangement placed new responsibilities upon the publication secretary, as editors now had to submit their texts upon disc with printing commands already entered. Strict supervision was required. The requisite instructions had to be given and the compatibility of discs with computers had to be assessed, while edited discs had to be checked for accuracy. All these tasks Ian performed on his own Amstrad in what, for him, became a labour of love. Many unrecorded hours must have been spent at this task, which came to fruition in the birth of the new Fifth Series of publications.

With this accomplished, Ian might have been forgiven if he had retired from office, but although he occasionally discussed this possibility, he clearly saw that day as some way off. Two days before he died, he organised the final details for the distribution of the latest volume, *Letters of George Lockhart of Carnwath*, and plans were already advanced for subsequent volumes.

The new Fifth Series is in itself a fitting memorial to Ian's devotion to

the Scottish History Society. The financial savings brought by these changes have not only averted a crisis in the Society's affairs, but have allowed it to face the future with some confidence. All societies depend upon the dedication and conscientiousness of their officials, and in these qualities Ian was never found wanting. Indeed, in all his efforts for the furtherance of Scottish historical studies, he demonstrated an intense loyalty to a cause for which he received too little personal recognition.

If Ian's technical ability and administrative skills were his more obvious characteristics, his claims to scholarship were equally valid. If not a prolific writer, he was meticulous in research. His 1961 Ph.D thesis was published as *The Administration of the Scottish Frontier, 1513-1603* (Edinburgh, 1966), and remains the standard work on its subject. Although no other major works followed, there was a co-edition with John Imrie and W.D. Ritchie of the *Selkirk Burgh Court Book, 1503-1545* (Scottish Record Society, 1960-9), and he edited *The Union of 1707: its impact on Scotland* (Glasgow, 1974), a volume arising from the 1972 Scottish Historical Conference. Articles appeared on 'Edinburgh Castle, 1751-53', *Book of the Old Edinburgh Club*, xxxii (1966), 54-107; 'The Scottish antiquarian tradition', *Scottish Antiquaries and Historians* (Abertay Historical Society Publications, no. 16, 1972); 'Historical scepticism in Scotland before David Hume', *Studies in the Eighteenth Century II*, ed. D.F. Brissenden (Canberra, 1973); 'The political attitudes of William Drummond of Hawthornden', *The Scottish Tradition*, ed. G.W.S. Barrow (Edinburgh, 1974); and 'The historical writing of Drummond of Hawthornden', *Scottish Historical Review*, lxiv (1975), 22-62. All were scholarly and perceptive. For the Scottish History Society he edited 'The beginning and the end of the Lewis Chemical Works, 1857-1874, by D. Morison', *Scottish Industrial History Miscellany* (1978); he also wrote the introduction to a new edition of *The Statistical Account of Scotland, 1791-1799* for the Eastern Borders (vol. iii, Wakefield, 1979), both dealing with a somewhat later period than most of his work. The latter work, on the Borders, was undoubtedly a labour of love, as was his posthumously-published article on 'The origins of the Advocates' Library', *For the Encouragement of Learning: Scotland's National Library, 1689-1989*, eds. Patrick Cadell and Ann Matheson (HMSO, 1989).

Reviews in various journals, but mainly for the *Scottish Historical Review*, were equally well informed. His main contribution to that

journal was undoubtedly the annual 'List of Articles in Scottish History', published under his editorship between 1960 and 1980. When he relinquished that task, the tradition of such a compilation was well established. For a time he also contributed to the *Annual Bibliography of British and Irish History*, published under the auspices of the Royal Historical Society.

He was never happier than with friends and acquaintances, to whom he was unfailingly loyal and kind. Most lunchtimes would find him with a small, but well-established, coterie in the Edinburgh University Staff Club, while visits to his three sons and a growing number of grandchildren were a source of pride and enjoyment.

Nevertheless, Ian's life was very much that of the National Library. Although he might have retired at sixty, he continued for three further years in order to complete his innovatory work on the Catalogue of Manuscripts. Though the prospect of retirement at the end of 1989 initially brought him some misgivings, he nevertheless came to terms with the thought. In addition to furthering publications of the Scottish History Society, the completion of the *Selkirk Burgh Court Book* and a co-edition of the Cupar Town Council Minutes all beckoned, while the prospect of spending more time with his grandchildren also appealed. Retirement might have proved to be as busy as his fruitful working life. Sadly, it was not to be. On his way to give a lecture in London on 7 July 1989, Ian died suddenly and prematurely, leaving a gap in Scottish historical studies which will be hard indeed to fill.

A PLEA ROLL OF EDWARD I'S ARMY
IN SCOTLAND, 1296

edited by C.J. Neville, PH.D

INTRODUCTION

In the twenty-fourth year of the reign of King Edward of England,
Easter Day fell on the day of the Annunciation of our Lady. On the
Wednesday in Easter week, being the twenty-eighth day of March,
the before named King Edward passed the river Tweed with 5000
armed horse and 30000 footmen...[1]

So began a contemporary account of the opening campaign of the War
of Independence, a campaign which ended some five months later with
the formal submission of representatives of the Scottish baronage and
landholding ranks to the crown of England. Edward I's conquest of the
kingdom of Scotland in 1296 was a watershed in Anglo-Scottish
relations, celebrated by English chroniclers and mourned by Scottish
observers. Pierre de Langtoft saw it as the fulfilment of Merlin's
prophecies:

Now are the two waters united in one
Which have been separated by great mountains;
And one realm made of two different kingdoms
Which used to be governed by two kings....

---

[1] J. Stevenson (ed.), *Documents Illustrative of the History of Scotland, 1286-1306* (2 vols., Edinburgh,
1870), ii, 25. This fourteenth-century French manuscript is also printed in *Instrumenta Publica*, ed. T.
Thomson (Bannatyne Club, 1834), 177-80, and appears also in *Bannatyne Miscellany*, i, eds. W. Scott
and D. Laing (1827), 271-82, together with an early sixteenth-century English translation, 264-70.

There is neither king nor prince of all the countries
Except king Edward, who has thus united them;
Arthur had never the fiefs so fully.[2]

For John of Fordun, on the other hand, looking back on the events of
the 1290s from a late fourteenth-century perspective, the submission of
the earls, barons and other landholders signalled the tragic conclusion
to a decade of political turmoil in Scotland which had begun with the
death of King Alexander III in 1286: 'how worthy of tears, and how
hurtful, his death was to the kingdom of Scotland, is plainly shown
forth by the evils of after times'.[3]

The campaign of 1296 remains of importance for several reasons. For
political historians its significance lies in the fact that it signalled the
commencement of open hostilities which would characterise relations
between the kingdoms of England and Scotland for three hundred years
and more; as such it has received extensive historiographical study. It
has likewise been commented upon by military historians, for seldom
until modern times has one nation been overrun and apparently
subjugated by another in such a brief span of time. In the late 1290s
Edward I already boasted an impressive record as a military leader, but
the swiftness of his victory in the spring and summer of 1296 was noted
with respect even by those who were already his ardent admirers.[4]

The campaign is noteworthy for still another reason, for it generated
a valuable and all-too-rare administrative document. The army plea roll
transcribed and edited below records the details of nearly two hundred
offences allegedly committed by members of the English expeditionary

---

[2] *The Chronicle of Pierre de Langtoft*, ed. T. Wright (2 vols., Rolls Ser., 1868), ii, 265, 267. For a
discussion of poems which praised Edward I's victory in 1296, see R.M. Wilson, *The Lost Literature of
Medieval England* (London, 1952), 201-6, and L. Stones, 'English chroniclers and the affairs of
Scotland, 1286-1296', in *The Writing of History in the Middle Ages: Essays Presented to Richard William
Southern*, eds. R.H.C. Davis and J.M. Wallace-Hadrill (Oxford, 1981), 335-43; A. Gransden,
'Propaganda in English medieval historiography', *Journal of Medieval History*, i (1975), 367, 369.
[3] *Johannes de Fordun Chronica Gentis Scotorum*, ed. W.F. Skene (The Historians of Scotland, i,
Edinburgh, 1871), 309; *John of Fordun's Chronicle of the Scottish Nation*, trans. F.J.H. Skene (The
Historians of Scotland, iv, Edinburgh, 1872), 304.
[4] The itinerary of Edward I's progress through Scotland states with disarming simplicity that Edward
'conquered the realm of Scotland, and searched it, as is above written, within twenty-one weeks, and
no more': Stevenson (ed.), *Documents*, ii, 31. See also the succinct account of the campaign of 1296 in
Flores Historiarum, ed. H.R. Luard (3 vols., Rolls Ser., 1890), iii, 97-8.

force which occupied Scotland between late March and mid-September 1296. The paucity of extant Exchequer accounts relating to such crucial military matters as provisions, stores and household expenditures for the campaign of 1296 is well known, and has been lamented by historians,[5] but the survival of the plea roll goes some way towards compensating for the loss of these materials. If historians remain unable to determine precisely the numbers of cavalry and infantry men who fought in Scotland, they are nonetheless rewarded in a host of other areas. The roll casts light on a variety of army-related matters, from practical affairs such as watch-keeping duties and muster-taking, to more domestic aspects of army life, which are only rarely glimpsed from such a great distance in time. These include gambling, fighting and booty sharing. The document also reveals something of the manner in which ingenious commanders and common foot-soldiers alike sought out comfortable quarters and entertained themselves away from their own homes.

The careful recording of the names of both defendants and plaintiffs makes it possible, in conjunction with other contemporary source materials, both public and private, to construct brief biographies of several hundred of the fighting men in the English army. The picture which emerges is one of an expedition which drew on all levels of English, Welsh and Irish society, from the ranks of the greatest feudal lords to those of the poorest villagers. Finally, the roll transcribed here is noteworthy because the judgments rendered by the court and the procedures used to submit suspects to trial provide legal historians with valuable insight into the workings of military law in a period which is otherwise almost devoid of reliable source material.

The document classified in the Public Record Office, London, as E39/93/15 (Exchequer Scottish Documents) consists of nine large parchment membranes of differing sizes, measuring from 119 cm to 173 cm, each written front and dorse. A torn fragment sewn to the foot of membrane 1 suggests that the clerk who was ultimately responsible for the roll in the form in which it has come down to us was William Beccles, clerk of the king's Wardrobe. Although the fragment is badly damaged, the following words may still be read:

---

[5] M. Prestwich, *War, Politics and Finance under Edward I* (Totowa, N.J., 1972), 51, 94.

Rot.

Edwardi R.

liberatum in Garderoba apud Twedemuth

per dominum Willelmum de Beccles clericum Comitis Marescal...[6]

William de Beccles was certainly present in Berwick at the conclusion of the campaign in August 1296, for on the last day of that month he paid over to Roger le Bigod, Marshal of England, the sum of £50, 'as part of the fee due to him by the king for his service in the king's army in Scotland'.[7] Other internal evidence, however, suggests that Beccles was not solely responsible for the final version of the roll. Membranes 1r to 4d and 7r to 9d are written in one hand, while another clerk wrote the intervening membranes, 5r to 6d.[8] The entries numbered 75 and 85 below include several words penned in as additions to the original text in a contemporary, but again different, hand. In the former the words indicate that a second deliberation or discussion of the case occurred after its initial hearing at Roxburgh on 10 May; in the latter, the words were added to correct an omission made by the clerk who had drafted that section of the roll. Similarly, in no. 54, several scored-out words show that a pardon granted to the defendant was subsequently rescinded, while in no. 84 a large space was left blank in the manuscript for the recording of a decision which was never set down. No. 146 refers to a second attempt on the part of a plaintiff to secure a favourable decision in a plea of trespass. The organisation of the roll, then, suggests a series of collations: one by a clerk who travelled around Scotland in the company of the king and the marshal, charged with collecting notes on army pleas as they were heard in a dozen different locations, who then drew these up in final form (membranes 1r-4d, 7r-9d); another whose task was to record gaol delivery proceedings where these were held (membranes 5r-6d); and a third, perhaps William de Beccles, who added his own emendations to the final version of the roll.

Equally revealing evidence of the composite nature of the final version of the document is found in its internal organisation, which does not correspond precisely to the chronological progress of

[6] Transcripts of the contents of E39/93/15 are reproduced here by permission of H.M. Stationery Office.

[7] PRO, E101/684/50 (1), calendared in *Calendar of Documents Relating to Scotland* [CDS], v (supplementary, 1106-1516), eds. G.G. Simpson and J.D. Galbraith (Edinburgh, n.d.), no. 156.

[8] I am grateful to Professor Geoffrey Barrow for his opinion on the handwriting in the roll.

Edward's army on the expedition. Army pleas heard at Wark on 21 March, Berwick on 4 April and Roxburgh on 10 May are enrolled first (membranes 1r-4d), followed by a series of gaol delivery trials held in several Scottish towns between 17 May and 8 August (membranes 5r-6d) which, as noted above, were recorded by a different clerk. This format is similar to contemporary records of visitations of the Eyre south of the border, in which cases of trespass and other pleas were set down in the rolls separately from crown pleas, and was probably intended deliberately to recall these other rolls.

Finally, the formulaic and, at times, monotonous recording of a majority of the cases suggests that the roll represents a condensed version of a series of more extensive notes. Unusual incidents of trespass and cases of alleged felony are described with careful attention to detail. The *minutiae* of more mundane incidents are omitted, and they are often subsumed under the general category of 'trespass'. Here, too, the clerks who drew up the roll consciously imitated the editorial practice of their fellows who compiled Eyre rolls.

There seems little doubt that the roll was drawn up shortly after Edward's return to Berwick in the last days of August 1296. Indeed, the record of two of the last pleas heard there suggests strongly that it was drafted in its final form on Thursday 28 August. In no. 179, the settlement of John de Roddom vs. John Sampson was postponed until the following day, when a jury was to be assembled by the sheriff of Northumberland. In no. 184, final deliberation of Hugh Despenser's case against the same John Sampson was likewise delayed, this time until the following Monday, 1 September, again in order that a jury of men who had cognisance of the alleged incident might be convened. The final verdict of neither case is recorded on the roll. But by 28 August Edward I was tremendously occupied with other, more pressing, concerns. On this and subsequent days he was called upon to preside over the assembly which he had summoned at Berwick to receive and record the oaths of fealty proffered by several hundred defeated Scotsmen. The army plea roll was probably hurriedly submitted to the royal Wardrobe and forgotten there in the days which ensued.

The existence of PRO E39/93/15 has been known to historians for many years, but it has never been printed and translated in its entirety. An eighteenth-century transcript is included among various

Hardwicke family papers now in the British Library;[9] another, dating probably from the nineteenth century, is to be found among the Advocates' Manuscripts housed in the National Library of Scotland.[10] Both contain numerous editorial errors, though they have been used in this edition to fill in gaps when words or letters are illegible in the original document. Excerpts from E39/93/15 were translated by Joseph Bain in the late nineteenth century and included in his *Calendar of Documents relating to Scotland*.[11] These were selected chiefly for their anecdotal value, and do not reflect the prevalence in the document of cases enrolled merely as 'pleas of trespass'.[12] The roll is cited briefly in two histories of the fourteenth-century Court of Chivalry, and reference to its existence is made in more recent historical works, notably by Michael Prestwich, in his examination of the administration of war in the reign of Edward I.[13] But little attention is paid in any of these works to its value as a source of information concerning army life. Maurice Keen likewise notes the existence of the roll in his study of the origins of the constable's court in England (where it is misdated to 1294-95), but he dismisses it because it sheds little light on the procedures which he argues were developed for use in military tribunals in the fourteenth century.[14]

Despite the short shrift it has been given by scholars, the plea roll contains much of value as a source of legal and military history. In first place, it shows clearly that the notion of military law, as both a complement to, and an extension of, English common law, was very much in existence in the closing years of the thirteenth century. In times of war common law principles became peripatetic, capable of expression wherever the persons of the king and his highest officials travelled, within the kingdom of England proper, or outwith its traditional boundaries. When John Lovel, who acted as deputy marshal

---

[9] British Library, Additional MS 35,822.

[10] National Library of Scotland, Advocates' MS [Adv. MS] 17.1.19.

[11] *CDS*, ii, no. 822.

[12] Those entries from the original document that were calendared by Bain in *CDS*, ii, no. 822, are noted in the edition below.

[13] L. W. Vernon Harcourt, *His Grace the Steward and Trial of Peers* (London, 1907), 362-3; G. D. Squibb, *The High Court of Chivalry* (Oxford, 1959), 11; E.F.M. Powicke, *The Thirteenth Century, 1216-1307* (Oxford, 1954), 615n; Prestwich, *War, Politics and Finance*, 107n, 115n, 167.

[14] M. Keen, 'The jurisdiction and origins of the constable's court', in *War and Government in the Middle Ages: Essays in Honour of J.O. Prestwich*, eds. J. Gillingham and J.C. Holt (Cambridge, 1984), 165 and n.

of the army on the expedition of 1296 (no. 165), heard and ruled on accusations of spying, homicide, larceny, robbery and other war-related crimes levelled against Scotsmen (nos. 89, 95 and 98), he acted on the authority which he wielded as a representative of the English crown in territory considered subject to that crown. It was under similar authority that he also undertook to prosecute English soldiers for offences allegedly committed against Scotsmen (nos. 134 and 136). Geoffrey Barrow has argued that although the theoretical justification for Edward I's war against Scotland lay in the rebellion of his vassal King John, he was nevertheless aware that until Balliol had formally resigned his kingdom, he was in a 'curious' position, constitutionally and legally. The forced resignation did not, in fact, take place until July 1296, and Barrow suggests that Edward's actions between the fall of Berwick in late March and the first week of July belie his uncertainty as to his constitutional position.[15] Certainly, no legal niceties troubled his military justices. From the time the army moved to relieve Wark Castle in March until its triumphant return to Berwick in August, the deputy marshal exercised the prerogative of his office as if no boundary existed between Edward I's hereditary possessions and those he would claim *de jure* only after 10 July. Scotsmen and Englishmen alike (as well as Irishmen and Welshmen) brought their complaints before him, or were adjudged according to the rules, regulations and traditions inherent in his office.

The later thirteenth century in England was a crucial period in the development of substantive law and, more generally, of legal procedure – civil, criminal and, as the army plea roll shows, military. One of the many striking features of the document is the tremendous development in the judicial powers of the marshal which it attests. This official had cognisance no longer merely of matters arising from organisation and discipline within the king's household, but now of all matters concerning discipline within the royal host and of relations

[15] G.W.S. Barrow, *Robert Bruce and the Community of the Realm of Scotland* (3rd edn., Edinburgh, 1988), 73. Cf. M. Prestwich, 'Colonial Scotland: the English in Scotland under Edward I', in *Scotland and England, 1296-1815*, ed. R.A. Mason (Edinburgh, 1987), 6-7. On the events surrounding Balliol's resignation, see E.L.G. Stones and M.N. Blount, 'The surrender of King John of Scotland to Edward I in 1296: some new evidence', *Bulletin of the Institute of Historical Research* [*BIHR*], xlviii (1975), 94-106, and M. Prestwich, 'The English campaign in Scotland in 1296, and the surrender of John Balliol: some supporting evidence', *BIHR*, xlix (1976), 135-8.

between soldiers and non-combatants.[16] In the reign of Edward I, too, royal justices were beginning to distinguish with increasing confidence between offences which were considered felonious and those defined as trespass.[17] Plucknett defined the latter as a 'varied assortment of torts', and noted that they were brought to court by means of a variety of actions, notably the still ill-defined procedures of complaint (*querela*), writs of trespass and actions of *quare*.[18] The roll demonstrates clearly the broad scope in the concepts of tort and trespass posited by Plucknett. The entries range from straightforward cases of debt to cases in which the defendant was not accused of the felonious offence of larceny, but was said rather to have 'illegally withheld', 'taken and withheld' or 'taken and led away' the plaintiff's animals or goods.[19] Other goods were said to have been 'alienated', 'illegally taken' or 'taken and carried off'.[20] Injuries to the person pursued by means of the actions noted above include accusations of illegal imprisonment or attachment, assault and injury.[21] The problems which late thirteenth-century lawmakers continued to experience in treating the thorny

[16] The functions of the marshal in the twelfth and thirteenth centuries are discussed in J.O. Prestwich, 'The military household of the Norman kings', *English Historical Review* [*EHR*], xcvi (1981), 1-35. For the late thirteenth and fourteenth centuries, see Keen, 'The jurisdiction and origins of the constable's court'. Keen's article does much to clarify Squibb's confusion with respect to the powers of the marshal and constable in this period.

[17] On the history of the action of trespass in the development of legal procedure, see T.F.T. Plucknett, *A Concise History of the Common Law* (4th edn., London, 1948), 349-53, 428-31; F. Pollock and F.W. Maitland, *The History of English Law Before the Time of Edward I* (3rd edn., 2 vols., Cambridge, 1968), ii, 511-28; S.F.C. Milsom, 'Trespass from Henry III to Edward III', *Law Quarterly Review*, lxxiv (1958), 195-224, 407-36, 561-90. More recently, see M.S. Arnold (ed.), *Select Cases of Trespass from the King's Courts, 1307-1399* (2 vols., Selden Soc., 1985), i, pp. ix-lxxxv, and *The Roll of the Shropshire Eyre of 1256*, ed. A. Harding (Selden Soc., 1981), pp. xxxii-lviii. The best recent study of the development of the law of felony in the late thirteenth and early fourteenth centuries is H.N. Schneebeck, 'The Law of Felony in Medieval England from the Accession of Edward I until the Mid-Fourteenth Century' (University of Iowa PhD dissertation, 1973).

[18] Plucknett, *Concise History of the Common Law*, 431.

[19] Pleas of 'trespass' only: nos. 15, 16, 21, 25, 26, 29, 32, 39, 54, 66, 69, 72, 77, 137, 138, 145, 148, 150, 156, 166 and 171. Complaints: nos. 4, 5, 6, 7, 11, 27, 33, 35, 36, 43, 46, 47, 61, 64, 67, 79, 81, 84, 90, 91, 108, 112, 147, 153, 154 and 158. Debt: nos. 3, 34, 42, 53, 75, 78 and 174. Illegally withheld: nos. 9, 19, 20, 31, 38, 44, 48, 53, 56, 62, 63, 70, 73, 78, 120, 159 and 170. Took and withheld: nos. 143 and 144. Took and led away: nos. 110, 113, 127, 161, 176, 179, 183 and 184. Led away: no. 37.

[20] Alienated: nos. 58, 82, 160, 162, 164, 167 and 169. Illegally took: nos. 22 and 57. Took and carried off: nos. 8, 30, 59, 68, 71, 152, 157, 163, 175, 176, 177, 178, 179 and 182. Other property-related suits include a charge relating to the wounding of the deputy marshal's destrier, no. 121; illegal ejection, no. 28; breaking lodgings, nos. 51 and 185; and the illegal attachment of goods, no. 93.

[21] Illegal imprisonment: nos. 57 and 152. Illegal attachment of persons: no. 18. Assault: nos. 83, 142, 151, 172 and 173. Injury: nos. 68, 142, 151, 172 and 173.

question of intent in incidents of robbery are clearly shown in a number of cases which were heard as a result of several different actions, and which were punished sometimes as trespasses, but at other times as felonies.[22]

The judicial sessions held on the campaign of 1296 also tried suspects on a wide variety of criminal charges. These trials were held in sessions of gaol delivery, as distinct from tribunals convened to hear pleas of trespass in the army; on each of the nine occasions when they were held the clerk who drafted this portion of the roll differentiated their status clearly.[23] Regrettably, no specific commissions of gaol delivery have survived for the campaign, but it seems likely that these must have been issued. The marshal was empowered by virtue of his office to judge cases involving life and limb, but because the judicial procedures adopted were those current at common law, specific commissions to deliver town gaols of suspected criminals were required. Moreover, the scope of the felonious and treasonable offences which were heard and determined was sufficiently broad as to necessitate the authority of commissions as extensive as those of gaol delivery. The presence on the expedition of Chief Justice Sir Roger Brabazon[24] probably ensured the observation of these legal requirements; indeed, Brabazon himself may have joined army officials on the bench at these tribunals.

The gaol delivery sessions closely resembled in form and content those convened in this period south of the border. The justices heard accusations and appeals of robbery and larceny. Predictably, most of these involved horses, harness and other war gear; they illustrate, incidentally, the casual fashion in which some of the king's mounted troops made arrangements for fulfilling their military service requirements. The presence in the king's army of men charged with 'numerous larcenies, robberies, arsons, homicides and other misdeeds', and the details of more than a dozen trials for murder, similarly underline the violent tenor of life in the ranks. With few exceptions the victims of these deadly encounters were not residents of the newly

---

[22] Nos. 1, 98, 122, 125 and 140. Felony: nos. 41, 87, 130, 133, 139 and 141. On the question of intent as it related to robbery, see Plucknett, *Concise History of the Common Law*, 422-3; Pollock and Maitland, *History of English Law*, ii, 493-4; Schneebeck, 'Law of Felony', 527-48.

[23] Sessions of gaol delivery were held at Roxburgh on 17 May, Edinburgh on 12 June, Stirling on 19 June, Clunie on 28 June, Forfar on 5 July, Aberdeen on 18 July, Elgin on 28 July, Kildrummy on 1 August, and Perth on 8 August. These sessions are enrolled in E39/93/15 at mm. 5r, 5d, 6r, 6d.

[24] No. 30. Sir Roger secured a pardon for two men amerced for a false plea of trespass.

conquered Scottish territories, but members of the royal expedition, often Welshmen.[25]

Unsettling as were their circumstances, these sorts of criminal activities were not frequent. Of more interest to historians are those incidents which constituted treason, and which were therefore of special concern to the king and his military officers. Two Scotsmen, John de Salton and John the porter, were charged by the marshal with being 'spies of the Scottish king and enemies of the [English] king', while William de Chester was also accused of being a spy.[26] Two accusations of firing granges and houses (and, in one case, churches and houses) in England, and one of breaking prison, were reserved to royal officials presiding over sessions of gaol delivery, for these were offences considered treasonable (nos. 88, 99 and 114). When two Scotsmen confessed to the marshal that they had held a public ceremony in which they solemnly excommunicated King Edward, they were similarly committed to trial before royal agents who were empowered by the most authoritative of commissions (no. 115).

Curiously, the one felonious offence which one would expect members of a conquering army to commit, the crime of rape, was not the subject of a single trial in the pleas heard in 1296. In part this may have been a reflection of the state of flux which had until recently characterised the status of the offence,[27] but its absence from the roll must surely be due chiefly to a reluctance on the part of women victims to confront a military court with a charge so difficult to prove.[28]

The verdicts returned and the sentences imposed on convicted felons

---

[25] Two exceptions are the case of Richard de Leeds, a resident of Perth, who was killed while in pursuit of a horse stolen from his house, and a boy, John, allegedly killed by a Welshman: nos. 127 and 132.

[26] Nos. 89 and 118. See also nos. 1 and 40, where two other charges of spying were dealt with by the deputy marshal.

[27] For changes in the methods of prosecuting rape, see J.B. Post, 'Ravishment of women and the Statutes of Westminster', in *Legal Records and the Historian*, ed. J.H. Baker (Royal Hist. Soc., Studies in History, 1978), 150-64; B.A. Hanawalt, 'Women before the law: females as felons and prey in fourteenth-century England', in *Women and the Law: A Social Historical Perspective*, ed. D.K. Weisberg (2 vols., Cambridge, Mass., 1982), i, 181-6; J.M. Carter, 'The status of rape in thirteenth-century England, 1218-1275', *International Journal of Women's Studies*, vii (1984), 248-59; B.A. Hanawalt, *Crime and Conflict in English Communities, 1300-1348* (Cambridge, Mass., 1979), 104-7; R. Kittel, 'Rape in thirteenth-century England: a study of the common-law courts', in *Women and the Law*, ed. Weisberg, ii, 103-4.

[28] On the difficulties involved in prosecuting cases of alleged rape, see J.M. Carter, 'Rape in medieval English society: the evidence of Yorkshire, Wiltshire and London, 1218-76', *Comitatus*, xiii (1982), 51-3; Hanawalt, 'Women before the law', 183-4, and Schneebeck, 'Law of Felony', 482-6.

demonstrate the determination of juries and justices to deal harshly with men whose violence was considered unacceptable even by army standards. Two of the entries, nos. 177 and 184, reveal that the jurors who were summoned to the sessions were not local people, but rather men in the king's immediate entourage and in the army at large, who had first-hand knowledge of the circumstances surrounding alleged incidents. Altogether, some one hundred suspects were dealt with at the nine sessions of gaol delivery; together they were charged with almost fifty felonies. Twelve of these men – more than 10 per cent – were sentenced to hang, and three others (including the king's two excommunicators) escaped the noose only because of their clerical status (nos. 115 and 136). Their offences were clearly of the most serious sort. A gang of seven men was put to death because its members had set off on a raid through English lands and set fire there to churches and houses (no. 99). Brawls within the ranks were to be expected, but the conviction of an English soldier for the murder of a Welshman demonstrated the disapproval of army authorities (no. 111). Similarly, when a soldier deliberately lured his opponent to his death he was adjudged guilty and sentenced to hang (no. 135). Capital punishments were also handed down to an Irishman who burgled the home of a Scotsman in Forfar, and to a man who committed blasphemy by robbing a church (nos. 123 and 133). Both these incidents represented open challenges to authority: the former to the conventions of war proclaimed by the king's marshal, the latter to holy mother church. The final sentence of hanging was imposed on a soldier who broke prison.[29] The wide variety of offences for which verdicts of guilty were returned suggests that justices and juries alike were prepared to make examples of serious offenders.

The procedures followed in the numerous judicial sessions held in the spring and summer of 1296 were those used at common law. A century later the Court of Chivalry, presided over by the constable of England and the earl marshal, would boast a procedural system substantially different from that of the common law,[30] but the rules and regulations

---

[29] No. 114. The law permitted the immediate execution, without need for a trial, of suspected felons who broke prison: J.G. Bellamy, *Crime and Public Order in England in the Later Middle Ages* (London, 1973), 178; R.B. Pugh, *Imprisonment in Medieval England* (Cambridge, 1968), 224-31.
[30] Keen, 'The jurisdiction and origins of the constable's court', and Vernon Harcourt, *His Grace the Steward*, 362-99.

adopted on the Scottish campaign were virtually identical to those in contemporary sessions of the Eyre. Terms of imprisonment were imposed in some twenty-eight instances, and the awarding of damages in a half dozen cases reflected a growing trend found in England.[31] Amercements were levied on defeated parties in some 105 cases, ranging in amount from 6d to one mark. It is not possible to assess with confidence the sum total of the monies raised in this manner, because in some thirty cases in which the amercement was pardoned, either on the intervention of the marshal, constable or some other army official, or because the party was too impoverished to pay, the marginalia do not specify the amounts forgiven. Furthermore, the sums enrolled were not always the same as those actually collected.[32] But from those entries which do note clearly that amercements were levied and duly paid, it would appear that the judicial sessions held in Scotland raised only £116, a paltry sum compared to the cost of the expedition.

Perhaps the chief interest of the roll lies in the plentiful information it reveals about the conditions of life in a large medieval army. Edward I's expeditionary force consisted of some 25,000 infantry men and several hundred mounted troops,[33] and drew on musters ordered from England, Wales and Ireland.[34] The general responsibility for quartering this large number of men fell on the marshal and constable, though their deputies co-ordinated the myriad of arrangements which were made as

[31] Damages awarded: nos. 14, 31, 62, 73, 149 and 164. Damages ranged from the small sum of 6d to the unusual amount of 40s. On the growth of actions for damages in the reign of Edward I, see Pollock and Maitland, *History of English Law*, ii, 524-6.

[32] A. Harding, *The Law Courts of Medieval England* (London, 1973), 68; Bellamy, *Crime and Public Order*, 190-1; *Crown Pleas of the Wiltshire Eyre, 1249*, ed. C.A.F. Meekings (Wiltshire Arch. and Nat. Hist. Soc., 1961), 106-15.

[33] This estimate is offered in Prestwich, *War, Politics and Finance*, 93-4, and, more recently, in M. Prestwich, *Edward I* (London, 1988), 470. In this later work, Prestwich cites an Exchequer document (PRO, E159/69 m 11d) printed in Stevenson (ed.), *Documents*, ii, 20-1, and corrects Stevenson's error of transcription. See also J.H. Ramsay, 'The strength of English armies in the middle ages', *EHR*, xxix (1914), 222.

[34] *Parliamentary Writs and Writs of Military Summons*, ed. F. Palgrave (2 vols., Record Comm., 1827), i, 275-8; Prestwich, *War, Politics and Finance*, 84, 94. The Irish contingent did not join the king's expedition until June: *The Chronicle of Walter of Guisborough*, ed. H. Rothwell (Camden Soc., 1957), 279; J.H. Lydon, 'An Irish army in Scotland, 1296', *The Irish Sword*, v (1962), 184-7. The roll also notes the presence in the army of Gascons, Flemings and Scotsmen, the latter recruited chiefly from the border counties, which were occupied and garrisoned after the capture of Berwick.

the army made its frequent halts around the kingdom.[35] Problems inevitably arose, ranging from incidents of violence committed by grudging Scotsmen against troops billeted in their homes, to more tiresome quarrels among English captains for possession of the most comfortable accommodation. Incidents of the latter sort were dealt with firmly by the king's officials. When, for example, Sir Ralph de Bleyou complained that three soldiers had unjustly taken advantage of his offer to accommodate them for one night, the culprits were fined 1s each – the equivalent of a full day's pay (no. 19). Similarly, when William de Beyrmor attempted to double-cross John Gichard with respect to arrangements which the two had made for the former's lodgings in Roxburgh, Beyrmor was amerced at 12d, and was further required to pay damages of 5s (no. 73). When he subsequently attempted to launch a counter-suit against Gichard the deputy marshal amerced him again, and compelled him to make his peace with Gichard (no. 81).

A more potentially unsettling situation occurred in Arbroath between the agents of Fulk FitzWarin and the earl of Hereford in late June and early July 1296, when goods secured by Gilbert de Lindsay for the use of the earl were carried off by FitzWarin, then forcibly recovered by Lindsay. The deputy marshal's requirement that both men's complaints be put to arbitration revealed his unwillingness to favour either of the contenders, and his wish to avoid dissension between two powerful tenants of the crown (nos. 160 and 161). The deputy marshal himself, John Lovel, was involved in a dispute with a fellow Englishman over the ownership of a sum of money discovered in lodgings in Berwick, a dispute which degenerated into a much more serious quarrel within just a few weeks (nos. 146 and 165). When a scuffle broke out in Berwick at the end of the campaign between Gilbert de Umfraville, son of the earl of Angus, and the king's agent, Hugh de

---

[35] *Liber Quotidianus Contrarotulatoris Garderobiae*, ed. J. Nichols (Soc. of Antiquaries, 1787), 201ff. The military duties of these officials are briefly described in Prestwich, 'The military household of the Norman kings', 21; G.H. White, 'The household of the Norman kings', *Transactions of the Royal Historical Society* [*TRHS*], 4th ser., xxx (1948), 149-53; Prestwich, *War, Politics and Finance*, 263, n. 3. On 29 June 1296 Gilbert de Lindsay rode ahead of the king's army to Arbroath where, acting as marshal for the earl of Hereford, constable of England, he made arrangements for the lodging of the earl's company: no. 160.

Lowther, steps were taken immediately to settle the contention between the parties.[36]

The administrative difficulties involved in victualling an army the size of Edward I's 1296 expedition were enormous.[37] As in the Welsh wars of the previous decade, troops were victualled according to a variety of arrangements. The men who rode as members of the king's household, or who were assigned to garrison captured fortresses, were kept supplied with goods brought from England by sea or overland by royal purveyors operating out of Carlisle and, later, Berwick, as well as with foodstuffs obtained locally through the king's right of prise. Inevitably, disputes arose between royal agents and the people from whom they obtained victuals, and the plea roll includes several such incidents. William de la Pole, for example, was sued for trespass by the English merchant Robert Scot for refusing to pay 44s owed for a quantity of beer (no. 174). More serious were the charges of regrating and forestalling flour and other victuals brought against several English officers and their men at the delivery of Roxburgh gaol; all those involved were amerced (nos. 101, 102 and 103).

Most soldiers, however, were expected to fend for themselves in the matter of victuals, for the king was under no obligation to supply food to men who were paid wages.[38] Some probably carried a few days' or weeks' worth of food with them from home. This was especially true of the contingents from the northern English border counties. Otherwise, they had to buy food in local markets, and here, too, disputes arose. The roll records several charges of debt arising from victualling arrangements, others in which the plaintiff sued for non-delivery of animals and goods purchased and duly paid for, and still others in which the defendant was charged with refusal to pay for goods.[39]

It was not unusual for even the greatest of Edward's magnates to

---

[36] *Calendar of Close Rolls* [*CCR*], *1288-1296*, 488-9.

[37] For a general discussion of the victualling of Edward I's Scottish expeditions, see Prestwich, *War, Politics and Finance*, 114-28, and M. Prestwich, 'Victualling estimates for English garrisons in Scotland during the early fourteenth century', *EHR*, lxxxii (1967), 346-53. For sea-going victualling arrangements, see also W. Stanford Reid, 'Sea power in the Anglo-Scottish war, 1296-1328', *Mariners' Mirror*, xlvi (1960), 7-13.

[38] Prestwich, *War, Politics and Finance*, 114.

[39] General pleas of debt: nos. 3, 34, 42, 53 and 78. Non-delivery of goods: nos. 52, ewes; 70, ewes. Refusal to pay for goods: nos. 55, sheep's carcasses; 168, animals; 174, beer; 181, oxen, cows, calves and mares.

attempt outright plunder and pillage under the guise of victualling. At
the sessions convened at Roxburgh on 10 May 1296, Robert de
Bamburgh complained that the earl marshal's bailiff, Hugh Thorold,
'falsely imprisoned him, attached 119 of his sheep, and wilfully drove
them off, to Robert's damage of 40s and more'. The bailiff countered by
claiming that Robert had himself stolen the animals from Patrick earl of
March, and that Thorold had not stolen them but, acting in his capacity
of bailiff, had rather attached them and had demanded sureties that
Robert would duly appear to answer the earl's man with respect to the
charge. In the end, Thorold forfeited his attempt to keep the animals by
failing to appear before the court on the day set for adjudication, and
Robert recovered possession (no. 57). A similar attempt at plunder
occurred later in the campaign, when Walter de Huntercumbe was
accused of stealing animals from a moor near Aberdeen (no. 183), and a
highly ironic incident occurred in early July when 966 animals, the
booty of Hugh Despenser, were seized by two English soldiers while
on their way south in England (no. 184). Incidents of plundering and
pillaging also took place on a smaller scale among the king's foot
soldiers, but were ignored by army commanders, who acknowledged
the right of every man to acquire spoils on campaign.[40]

But when these activities contravened direct royal prohibitions, or
when they caused serious dissension in the ranks, they were more
closely scrutinised. When one soldier was charged with plundering
lands that had been placed under the king's peace, he made no attempt
to deny his action, but pleaded successfully that he had done it before
the proclamation of the peace had been made (no. 126). More
troublesome were the disputes which sometimes took place among
thieves during the sharing of booty: the Welshman Owen Montgomery made himself notorious for his attempts to double-cross his
associates in the division of spoils.[41]

The maintenance of good relations among the troops was a crucial
concern in an army as large and as varied as that of 1296, for while
altercations with the conquered Scots might be expected, internal

[40] One entry in the roll, no. 50, mentions the formation of a company for plundering the king's
enemies.
[41] Owen de Montgomery's attempts to retain an unfair share of despoiled goods were the subject of
two separate charges: nos. 74 and 80. He was charged with the more general offence of trespass by
some of his companions on three other occasions: nos. 43, 66 and 67.

conflicts seriously undermined the morale of the troops. The marshal acted decisively when brawls broke out among soldiers: the parties were first required to make amicable agreements with each other, then were fined the stiff sum of 1s each, five times the daily wage of the average infantryman (nos. 104, 105 and 106). More widespread trouble erupted in Edinburgh when the army was quartered there in June. The Welsh forces clashed with their English fellows, and the deputy marshal's destrier was wounded in the melee. The culprit responsible for the horse's wounds was dispatched to prison, not merely because of the senior status of the plaintiff, but as an example to all potential trouble-makers.[42]

More problematic still to army commanders were offences which represented a challenge to their authority, because these endangered the very success of the campaign. Overall command of the army fell to the marshal and the constable, but they depended heavily for the effective deploying of troops and manoeuvring of men upon a host of subordinate officials - millenars, centenars and vintenars, and the marshals and constables of individual noble contingents. Acts of insubordination were not tolerated. When some soldiers were charged with refusal to obey a centenar, each was fined the equivalent of five days' pay,[43] and when several others refused or failed in their duty to perform watch and ward at night, they too were harshly dealt with (nos. 17, 23 and 116).

The symbol of the marshal's authority, the royal banner, was not merely a thing of pomp and show; it was the visible expression of the power vested in this official by the king, and was to be accorded respect.[44] Alebinus de Whelton, who had the temerity to ride ahead of the banner of the constable and marshal as the army approached the town of Clunie, was immediately seized 'as one who had shown contempt for the king's precept'. He compounded his offence by subsequently escaping from the custody of the marshal's officials, and for this offence forfeited his two horses and was committed indefinitely

[42] No. 121. Violent confrontations between Welsh and English soldiers plagued the expedition; they were at the centre, for example, of at least six charges of homicide. See nos. 109, 111, 117, 119, 132 and 135.

[43] No. 13. Another man's failure to go on foray as ordered resulted in his imprisonment: see no. 23.

[44] The symbolic and legal significance of banners and other devices is discussed in M. Keen, *The Laws of War in the Later Middle Ages* (London, 1965), 105-8, 111, and M. Keen, 'Treason trials under the law of arms', *TRHS*, 5th ser., xii (1962), 92-5.

to prison (no. 165). When two other soldiers displayed the ill grace of departing from under the marshal's banner in order to plunder the village through which they were passing, they too were committed to prison.[45]

The army of 1296 included men of all sorts. There were representatives of the most influential ranks of society,[46] humbler craftsmen and the landless poor. A list of soldiers identified in the document according to their civilian occupations includes Thomas the barber, Elias the shepherd, Alan the carter, Simon the chapman, Robert the cook, Gilbert the collier, Henry the forester, Roger Hirdman, Augustine the mercer, John the taverner and Adam, Ralph and William the tailors. Some men were undoubtedly called upon to use their skills in the service of the expedition: such men included Aymer the baker, William and John the armourers, William the carpenter, John the cook, John the smith, Elie le Ferur, Adam the king's harper and, perhaps most important, given wartime conditions, Nicholas and Master Thomas the physicians. The clerks who appear frequently in the roll provided scribal services in recording debt, loan and purchase agreements, and chaplains celebrated mass, blessed the troops and heard their confessions.

Most of the fighting men remain, to modern observers, merely names; they disappear from royal records of any sort after the return of the army to England in the autumn of 1296. But for several hundred men it is possible to construct a brief history of royal service both preceding and following the campaign of 1296. For such men war against the king's enemies, in Scotland and elsewhere, was evidently both honourable and profitable.

Sir Robert Darcy and Sir William de Huntercumbe were typical of the hundreds of lesser noblemen who spent several years in royal service. As a young man Darcy accompanied Edward I north during negotiations relating to the Great Cause, and in 1295 served the king in Wales. In the spring of 1296, as a reward for his efforts in Scotland, he was restored without penalty to his father's lands in Lincolnshire,

---

[45] No. 10. Desertion from the army, which would become a serious problem in Edward I's later campaigns in Scotland, does not appear to have been widespread in 1296. See Prestwich, *War, Politics and Finance*, 95-9.

[46] A partial list of the noble contingent in the expedition of 1296 may be found in *Parliamentary Writs*, i, 275-8.

which he had entered illegally following the older man's death. He was in Scotland with John earl of Warenne in 1297, when he was knighted, and returned there to fight at Falkirk in 1298, then again in 1300. In 1306 Darcy was again in the king's service in occupied Scotland, this time under Aymer de Valence, but lack of remuneration had caused him by then to tire of his duties. In October 1306 his lands were taken into the king's hands because he had deserted the army, 'in the contempt of the king and to the retarding of the king's business'.[47]

Sir Walter de Huntercumbe served the king in Wales in the campaigns of the 1280s, and was in Wales again in the spring of 1295, after a journey to Gascony in the royal service in the autumn of 1294. On the expedition of 1296 he travelled in the company of John de Warenne, earl of Surrey, and after the conquest of Scotland was appointed keeper of the castle of Edinburgh and the sheriffdoms of Edinburgh, Linlithgow and Haddington. He remained there until 1298, when he fought at the battle of Falkirk, but was relieved of the custody of Edinburgh Castle towards the end of that year. He was appointed a captain in Northumberland in 1299, and from then until his death around 1313 he divided his time equally between his landed interests in Northumberland and a variety of duties north of the border. Huntercumbe's frequent absences from his lands cost him a great deal. In 1307 he petitioned Edward I for permission to retain the scutage raised from his tenants, reminding the king that he had been 'in all the Scottish wars until the present'.[48]

Lesser men, such as Griffin ap Rees, Robert de Neketon and William de Denton, served in a less illustrious, but equally steadfast capacity. The Welshman ap Rees was a soldier in Scotland in 1296, then fought in Gascony in 1297.[49] Neketon returned to Scotland with the king in 1298, and was still a member of the garrison of Newcastle-on-Ayr in

[47] Calendar of Patent Rolls [CPR], 1281-1292, 440; CPR, 1292-1301, 54, 293; CCR, 1288-1296, 410, 480; PRO, SC1/21/58; H. Gough (ed.), Scotland in 1298 (London, 1888), 48; PRO, C42/2/21/8; Calendar of Fine Rolls, 1272-1307, 543; PRO, E101/13/16 m 16.
[48] Gough (ed.), Scotland in 1298, 24, 136, 249; CPR, 1292-1301, 202, 249, 387; PRO, E370/1/10; CDS, ii, nos. 997, 1014, 1036, 1351, 1356, 1374, 1413; CDS, v, nos. 155, 273, 291, 480; C. Moor, Knights of Edward I (5 vols., Selden Soc., 1929-32), ii, 252-3; J.E. Morris, The Welsh Wars of Edward I (Oxford, 1968), 70-1, 159, 210, 213; Book of Prests of the King's Wardrobe for 1294-5, ed. E.B. Fryde (Oxford, 1962), pp. xxviii, xlviii and n., pp. 149-50.
[49] CPR, 1292-1301, 335.

1301-02.[50] Denton served in Gascony under the earl of Lincoln in 1297, and for his service was pardoned his involvement in the death of a man.[51] The professional biographies of other, equally 'typical', men reveal similar patterns of service.

Among the several thousand common folk who joined the expedition, a few are identifiable as criminals, pardoned on condition that they perform military service in Scotland. Edward I's recruitment of convicted felons, outlaws and fugitives, later to become notorious, had begun on a large scale two years earlier at the time of his campaign to Gascony.[52] By 1296 the immense resources represented by the gaols and byways of England as recruitment grounds were openly acknowledged by the king when he empowered Sir Roger Brabazon

> to receive from persons in prison or outlaws at large charged with homicides, robberies, or other crimes, or from the friends of such, sufficient mainprise that they will forthwith go on the king's service to Scotland and remain there at the king's wages, during pleasure, and after their return take their trial if appealed: and after such mainprise being testified by the said Roger before the chancellor, they are to have letters of pardon of the king's suit.[53]

Some men took advantage of the offer immediately and enlisted as soldiers;[54] others were able to appeal successfully to the king's ongoing mercy with respect to crimes they committed after the army had

---

[50] Gough (ed.), *Scotland in 1298*, 27, 166; *CCR, 1296-1302*, 228, 276; *CPR, 1292-1301*, 390, 442; PRO, C47/22/3(26).

[51] *CPR, 1292-1301*, 354.

[52] N.D. Hurnard, *The King's Pardon for Homicide Before A.D. 1307* (Oxford, 1969), 247-8.

[53] *CPR, 1292-1301*, 186 (8 March 1296). A proclamation to this effect was issued to the kingdom at large on 11 April 1296: Stevenson (ed.), *Documents*, ii, 38-9.

[54] The northerner Lambert de Burgh, for example, had been at large on bail since 1288, for a murder: *CCR, 1288-1296*, 1. William the carter had been in York gaol in 1294 for a similar offence: *CPR, 1292-1301*, 117. John le Fraunceis of Derbyshire was an outlaw as late as December 1295, though he subsequently served the king in the campaigns of 1296 and 1298: *CCR, 1288-1296*, 293, 351, 408; Gough (ed.), *Scotland in 1298*, 188. John le Husser had been in gaol in Buckinghamshire for receiving thieves and other alleged trespasses as late as August 1295: *CPR, 1292-1301*, 138. On the eve of the army's departure for Scotland, the king's suit against Roger de Beauchamp and some two dozen others for the death of a man was respited, for 'the king wishes to show them favour because they are setting out on his service for Scotland': *CCR, 1288-1296*, 475. Beauchamp was still serving the king in Scotland some four years later: Gough (ed.), *Scotland in 1298*, 20, 33; F. Palgrave (ed.), *Documents and Records Illustrating the History of Scotland* (London, 1837), i, 213.

B

crossed into Scotland.[55] A few soldiers traded on their loyal record of service on the campaign of 1296 when, in subsequent years, they too sought refuge under the expedient of royal pardons.[56]

The presence of women in the army plea roll is not unusual, for no medieval army travelled without the variety of services which women provided.[57] Some wives followed their husbands: Richard le Seler and his wife Margery, for example, brought a suit against a Scotsman at the sessions held in Roxburgh on 10 May.[58] Others perhaps hoped to scratch a respectable living by working as cooks, laundresses or servants for the troops;[59] still others became the unwary victims of the dangers which accompanied the presence of fighting men in a conquered town.[60] Most, however, were probably camp followers and prostitutes. Sometimes they joined their companions in their boisterous escapades.[61] The dangers which might befall a woman involved in such a precarious relationship are illustrated in the case of Maud de

[55] On 28 July 1296, at Elgin, Alan Bloyou was pardoned the death of a fellow soldier 'for services in the Scottish war': *CPR, 1292-1301*, 193. The Welshman William de Crakehale was outlawed, then pardoned, at Berwick in August 1296 for the wilful killing of John Page: *CPR, 1292-1301*, 195.

[56] See, for example, William de Denton, pardoned on 17 June 1298; Richard de Hereford, pardoned on 8 September 1298; William de Chester, pardoned on 15 September 1298; Robert Roland, pardoned on 5 November 1298; Simon le Chamberlain, knight, pardoned on 10 November 1298, and Ralph the tailor, pardoned after several years' service, including the campaign of 1296, on 16 October 1301: *CPR, 1292-1301*, 354, 358, 359, 371, 374, 614.

[57] Indeed, the fact that the names of only fifteen women appear on the roll is surprising; this is surely not an accurate representation of their numbers on the expedition. On the role of women in medieval armies, see B.C. Hacker, 'Women and military institutions in early modern Europe: a reconnaissance', *Signs*, vi (1981), 646-54; B.S. Anderson and J.P. Zinsser (eds.), *A History of Their Own* (2 vols., New York, 1988), i, 362; P. Contamine, *War in the Middle Ages*, trans. M. Jones (Oxford, 1984), 241.

[58] No. 47. Simon de Blye and his wife Sybil were named in a suit of trespass in a curious case, no. 152. Augustine le Mercer and his wife Agnes, Scots, appeared as defendants at the sessions of 10 May 1296: no. 85.

[59] Agnes the laundress laid a charge of assault and robbery against two English women at the sessions held in Roxburgh on 10 May 1296: no. 68. Christine the laundress was a defendant in a suit of trespass heard at Perth: no. 145.

[60] One unidentified woman was robbed of beer and milk: no. 86. A Scotswoman who had taken refuge in a church while the army passed through the town of Clunie laid charges against two soldiers when the church was broken into and her possessions carried off: no. 122. The husband of a resident of Perth was killed by an English soldier when he attempted to retrieve a stolen horse: no. 127. Another resident of Perth was robbed of some beer by an Englishman who was accompanied by a notorious Scottish thief: no. 136. These examples illustrate the indifference of medieval soldiers to the rules of conduct proscribing attacks on women and other non-combatants. See C.T. Allmand, 'The war and non-combatant', in *The Hundred Years War*, ed. K. Fowler (London, 1971), 289-90.

[61] See, for example, nos. 2, 68, 142 and 152.

Blackburnshire. She was successful in a suit of trespass brought against a soldier in the early stages of the campaign, but was later sued in turn by the man and accused of stealing 3s worth of cloth (nos. 14 and 45). Women, then, appear in the plea roll both as plaintiffs and defendants and, in one very curious entry, as recipients of the blessings of a dubious cleric (no. 152). Even children were not untouched by the passage of an enemy host: at least one boy was killed when the army halted in Elgin, while another, who seems to have followed his father on the expedition, attempted unsuccessfully to launch an appeal against his father's murderer (nos. 132 and 124).

The unique nature of the army plea roll is a matter of great interest to historians. It is an invaluable source for a wide variety of information concerning army life in the medieval period; it offers much useful evidence concerning an expedition which is otherwise ill-represented in surviving record materials, and it contributes to a clearer understanding of the relationship between common law and military law procedures in the late thirteenth century. Finally, it goes some way towards illuminating an event that has hitherto been overlooked in the history of the English invasion of Scotland. In no. 47 (dated 10 May) reference is made to the recent 'making of peace in Roxburgh'. Clearly, the allusion is to a specific event, and Geoffrey Barrow has suggested that it signals a formal surrender to Edward I by James the Steward who, until that time, had been entrusted with the custody of Roxburgh Castle. If the fortress was indeed handed over to the English forces, and the Steward admitted to Edward's peace, then it indicates that Balliol, who did not formally surrender until July, was deprived of one of his most important supporters in the crucial weeks which ended in his own submission.[62]

Editorial notes

In the later thirteenth century the royal clerks who drafted the final versions of judicial rolls had for some decades been practising a series of editorial conventions of their own. For example, a plea of denial such as *X venit et defendit vim et injuriam et totum de verbo in verbum* was contracted to *X venit et defendit vim et injuriam etc*;[63] *X adjudicatur prisona quousque*

---

[62] This interpretation, for which I am indebted to Professor Barrow, goes some way towards explaining the otherwise ambiguous documents found in *CDS*, ii, nos. 737, 739 and 740.

[63] Or, commonly, *vim et injuriam quando etc.*

finem fecerit was rendered as *X adjudicatur prisona quousque etc*; and *X ponit se super patriam* became simply *X ponit se*. These contractions are reproduced in the Latin text of this edition. Grammatical contractions, however, notably suffixes denoting declensions, have been extended. A suspension is indicated by the use of an apostrophe. Any added textual matters, and words supplied by conjecture, have been placed between square brackets. Minor errors of spelling, such as *atachiatus* for *attachiatus*, have been corrected, but attention is drawn in square brackets to more serious scribal errors. The writer emended his own text on occasion. Interlineations and corrections are indicated by the use of backward and forward slashes, \thus/, or otherwise signalled in square brackets. Repetitive Latin words, such as *predictus* and *inde*, are not translated when they would be tiresomely superfluous in the English text.

The authors of the roll only occasionally distinguished between the letters 'c' and 't', and never between 'u' and 'v' or 'i' and 'j'. In most of these cases modern usage has been adopted. The vagaries of the clerks' use of punctuation marks have been ignored, and modern punctuation has been adopted in an effort to ensure clarification of long sentences. Proper names have been accorded capital initial letters. Where capital letters occur in common nouns in the original text, other than in words which begin sentences, they have been removed.

Marginal notes, in abbreviated form, appear beside all but a handful of the entries on the roll. In these, *suspendatur* is noted as a stylised 'S', *misericordia* as *mia, condonatur* as the stylised symbol ' $\wp$ ', *et cetera* as *et*, and so on. These have been extended and placed in brackets at the end of each entry. Monetary sums appear consistently in the text in their abbreviated form, that is, *li* for *libra*, *s* for *solidus*, *d* for *denarius* and *ob* for *obolum*. These have been extended in transcriptions of the marginalia, but left intact in the textual entries. The symbol for the conjunction *et* has been extended throughout.

Place names and personal names were enrolled by the clerks without any regard for consistency. In rendering Welsh and Scottish names in particular, they appear to have been guided by purely phonetic principles. Where identification of such names is possible they have been modernised.

I wish to acknowledge the financial assistance of the Social Sciences and Humanities Research Council of Canada in the preparation of this

piece. I wish also to thank Professor Geoffrey Barrow, whose attention to detail, editorial skills and knowledge of the period of the English invasion were generously offered, and which proved immensely helpful.

C.J.N.

Placita excercitus domini regis apud Werk die mercurii proxima post dominicam in Ramis Palmarum anno regni regis E. vicesimo quarto.

1. Willelmus de Wytyngham attachiatus fuit per Johannem de Wygeton militem apud Dalton et per ipsum liberatur prisone quia dictum fuit quod fuit insidiator regni Scocie et quod subtraxit se extra patriam ubi habet terram ne deserviret domino regi in guerra sua contra Scottos. Et quod est de affinitate Johannis Redecomyn inimici domini regis Anglie. Et Willelmus venit et dicit ad sectam domini regis quod in nullo est culpabilis et de hoc ponit se. Et juratores dicunt quod per sacramentum suum quod bonus est et fidelis et in nullo super sibi inpositum est culpabilis. Ideo quietus.

2. Alicia de Wllore Thomas de Lung et Johannes Andreu de Presteven queruntur de Johanne de Thweyt et Ricardo de Houcleye Matheo de Kyklor et Johanne de Sutton de placito roberie. Et eadem Alicia et alii non sunt prosecuti. Ideo ipsa et plegii sui de prosequendo videlicet Willelmus le Rus et Robertus le Espernor in misericordia. Et alii ad sectam eorum sunt quieti. Et ad sectam regis dicunt quod \non/ sunt culpabiles\et/ de hoc ponunt se. Et juratores dicunt super sacramentum suum quod predictus Johannes et alii in nullo sunt culpabiles. Ideo inde quieti.   (misericordia xii denariorum)

Placita exercitus domini regis apud Berewyk die mercurii proxima post clausum Pasche anno regni Regis E. vicesimo quarto.

3. Matheus de Ridemane miles recognoscit se teneri Johanni filio Marmaduk militi in x libris solvendas ad festum Pentecostes proximo futurum.   (recognicio)

4. Rogerus de Pedwardyn miles de comitiva Gilberti de Gaunt queritur de Radulpho Paynel. Postea concordati sunt et idem Rogerus ponit se. Et fecit finem. Et condonatur per marescallum.
                                    (misericordia condonatur)

Pleas of the king's army at Wark on Wednesday next after Palm Sunday in the 24th year of the reign of King E[dward] [21 March 1296].

1. William de Whittinghame was attached by John de Wigton knight at Dalton, and sent to prison, because it was said that he was a Scottish spy, and that he withdrew from the country where he held lands in order to avoid serving in the king's army against the Scots. And [it was said] that he is of the affinity of John 'Red' Comyn, the enemy of the king of England. William comes and says at the suit of the king that he is not guilty and he puts himself [on the country]. The jurors say on oath that he is a good and loyal man, and is is no wise guilty of the offences with which he is charged. Therefore [he is] acquitted. [*CDS*, ii, no. 822, p. 189.]

2. Alice de Wooler, Thomas de Lung and John Andreu de Prestfen bring a suit of robbery against John de Thwayt, Richard de Hocclyve, Matthew de Kyklor and John de Sutton. Alice and the others have not prosecuted. Therefore she and her sureties for prosecuting, namely William le Rus and Robert le Espernor, [are] in mercy. The others are acquitted of their suit. At the suit of the king they say that they are not guilty and they put themselves [on the country]. The jurors say on their oath that John and the others are in no wise guilty. Therefore [they are] acquitted.   (amercement 12 pence)

Pleas of the king's army at Berwick on Wednesday next after the Sunday following Easter, in the 24th year of the reign of King E[dward] [4 April 1296].

3. Matthew de Redman knight acknowledges that he owes to John son of Marmaduke knight, £10, to be paid at the feast of Whitsun next.
(recognisance)

4. Roger de Petwardyn knight, of the company of Gilbert de Gaunt, brings a suit against Ralph Paynel. Later they are agreed and Roger puts himself [on the country]. He has made a fine. [The amercement is] pardoned by the marshal.   (amercement pardoned)

5. Jacobus de Stafford queritur de Roberto de Umframville de comitiva Johannis Wak. Et Robertus non venit ideo etc. Et quod preceptum est quod [sic] idem Robertus distringatur ad respondendum dicto Jacobo. Condonatur ad instanciam J. Wak.   (misericordia condonatur)

6. Johannes de Keludon et Robertus de Neketon queruntur de Johanne de Thetbotle de comitiva Walteri de Huntercumbe. Et idem Johannes manucaptus per Walterum non venit. Ideo preceptum est quod dictus Johannes attachietur per corpus.

7. Symon le Chaumbreleyn et Osbertus Motegan queruntur de Thoma de Burnham. Postea concordati sunt per licenciam. Et predicti Symon et Osbertus ponunt se per manucaptionem Henrici de Bayuse militis. [Et deliberantur?] per J. de Segrave.   (misericordia condonatur)

8. Robertus de Maners Nicholaus de Poterton et Henricus de Neuland attachiati sunt ad respondendum Henrico de Rye de placito transgressionis. Et unde queritur quod predictus Robertus et alii venerunt die veneris in septimana Pasche ad hospicium dicti Henrici in Berewyk et bona sua de predicto hospicio inventa ad valenciam xx marcarum ceperunt et asportaverunt et alia enormia ei intulerunt ad grave dampnum ipsius Henrici etc.

Et predicti Robertus et alii dicunt quod de hospicio dicti Henrici nulla bona asportaverunt sed dicunt quod in predicto hospicio prius quam dictus Henricus tanquam in suo hospicio proprio intraverunt. Et hoc petunt quod inquiratur. Et predictus Henricus similiter. Et juratores dicunt super sacramentum suum quod predicti Robertus et alii de bonis predicti Henrici nichil asportaverunt prout queritur nec in domo sua intraverunt. Ideo consideratum est quod predicti Robertus et alii eant inde quieti. Et predictus Henricus in misericordia. Et condonatur per ipsum marescallum ad instanciam episcopi de Dunelm'.
          (misericordia condonatur)

9. Comes Warenne per attornatum suum optulit se versus Thomam Havard in placita transgressionis. Et unde queritur quod predictus Thomas injuste detinet unum equum nigrum et unum sementerium oneratum de x solidos panis quod cepit die veneris in septimana Pasque

5. James de Stafford brings a suit against Robert de Umfraville, of the company of John Wake. Robert does not come, therefore, etc. It is ordered that Robert be distrained to answer James. [The amercement is] pardoned at the instance of J[ohn] Wake.   (amercement pardoned)

6. John de Kellowden and Robert de Neketon bring a suit against John de Thetbotle, of the company of Walter de Huntercumbe. John, who is mainprised by Walter, does not come. Therefore it is ordered that he be attached in his person.

7. Simon the chamberlain and Osbert Motegan bring a suit against Thomas de Burnham. Later they are agreed by licence. Simon and Osbert put themselves [on the country] by mainprise of Henry de Bayouse knight. [They are delivered?] at the instance of J. de Segrave.
                                                    (amercement pardoned)

8. Robert de Maners, Nicholas de Potterton and Henry de Newland are attached to answer Henry de Rye on a plea of trespass. Whereon he complains that on Friday in Easter Week [30 March] Robert and the others came to his lodgings in Berwick, took and carried away goods of his that they found there to the value of 20 marks, and committed other outrages against him to his great damage etc.

Robert and the others say that they did not carry off any goods from Henry's lodgings, but they say that they entered the lodgings before Henry himself [had returned there]. They ask for enquiry to be made, as does Henry. The jurors say on their oath that Robert and the others did not carry off any of Henry's goods as he complains, nor that they entered his house. Therefore it is considered that Robert and the others are acquitted and that Henry [is] in mercy. [The amercement is] pardoned by the marshal at the instance of the bishop of Durham.
                                                    (amercement pardoned)

9. The earl of Warenne by his attorney presented himself against Thomas Havard in a plea of trespass. Whereon he complains that Thomas illegally withholds a black horse and a basket filled with 10 shillings' worth of bread which Warenne bought on Friday in Easter

in villa de Berewyk et adhuc detinet ad grave dampnum ipsius comitis etc. Et predictus Thomas presens dicit quantum ad equum quod emit predictum equum de quodam Johanne cissore quem vocat ad warantum. Et quia non habuit predictum Johannem liberatum est prisone.

Et quoad panem nunc dicit quod in nullo est culpabilis. Petit quod inquiratur. Et predictus comes similiter. Postea per licenciam concordati sunt. Et predictus Thomas ponit se. Et fecit finem ii solidorum.

(misericordia ii solidorum soluta)

10. Radulphus de Midhurst de comitatu Wiltes' et Johannes de Lemyng quia perrexerunt de vexillo ad predandum. Ideo ad prisonam quousque etc. Et Radulphus fuit manucaptus per dominum Hugonem de Herci. Et Johannes de Lemyng fuit manucaptus per Alanum de Penynton. Et non fecerunt finem. Ideo reattachiati. Et postea condonatur.

(misericordia condonatur)

11. Robertus de Westowe queritur versus Willelmum de Schirburn. Et non est prosecutus. Ideo plegii in misericordia scilicet Elias de Schirburn Johannes de Westowe.　　　(misericordia xii denariorum)

12. Elias de Schirburn non est prosecutus versus Willelmum Malebranck et Adam Aldric. Et ideo ipse et plegii de prosequendo scilicet Robertus de Wistouwe et Johannes de Hodleston in misericordia.

(misericordia xii denariorum)

13. Richerus de Laverton Thomas de Galeweye Willelmus Robyn Nicholaus Welifed Johannes de Schelden Adam de Kirkeby in misericordia quia contempserunt Robertum de Hoperton centenarium eorum videlicet iii solidorum quos solverunt statim.

(misericordia iii solidorum soluta)

14. Walterus Scot attachiatus fuit ad respondendum Matillde de Blakeburneschire de placito transgressionis. Et unde queritur quod predictus Walterus cepit injuste ab eadem unum clamidem precii iiii solidorum et adhuc detinet ad grave dampnum ipsius Matillde etc. Et

Week [30 March] in Berwick, and that he still withholds [them] to the earl's great damage etc. Thomas, who is present, says with respect to the horse that he bought it from a certain John the tailor, whom he calls to warranty. And because he does not have John he is sent to prison.

Concerning the bread he now says that he is in no wise guilty. He asks for enquiry to be made, as does the earl. Later they are agreed by licence. Thomas puts himself [on the country] and makes a fine of 2 shillings. (amercement 2 shillings, paid)

10. Ralph de Midhurst of the county of Wiltshire and John de Lemyng [were attached] because they departed from under the banner in order to plunder. Therefore they are put in prison until etc. Ralph is mainprised by Sir Henry de Hercy and John de Lemyng is mainprised by Alan de Pennington. They have not made a fine, therefore they are attached once again. Later [the amercement is] pardoned.

(amercement pardoned)

11. Robert de Westowe brings a suit against William de Schirburn and has not prosecuted. Therefore he and his sureties, namely Elias de Schirburn [and] John de Westowe, [are] in mercy.

(amercement 12 pence)

12. Elias de Schirburn has not prosecuted against William de Malebranck and Adam Aldric. Therefore he and his sureties for prosecution, namely Robert de Westowe and John de Hodleston, [are] in mercy. (amercement 12 pence)

13. Richerus de Laverton, Thomas de Galloway, William Robyn, Nicholas Welifed, John de Schelden and Adam de Kirkby [are] in mercy because they refused to obey Robert de Hoperton their centenar, namely for 3 shillings, which they paid immediately.

(amercement 3 shillings, paid)

14. Walter Scot was attached to answer Maud de Blackburnshire on a plea of trespass. Whereon she complains that Walter illegally took from her a cloak, value 4 shillings, and still withholds it to her great damage etc. Walter comes and says that he did not take any cloak from Maud as

predictus Walterus venit et dicit quod nullum clamidem a predicta Matillda cepit ut dicit. Et hoc petit quod inquiratur. Et predicta Matillda similiter.

Et juratores dicunt super sacramentum suum quod predictus Walterus cepit predictum clamidem de predicta Matillda. Ideo consideratum est quod predicta Matillda recuperet predictum clamidem seu valorem ii solidi vi denarii et dampna sua vi denarii. Et predictus Walterus adjudicatur prisone quousque etc.

(misericordia xx denariorum)

15. Johannes de Hotham miles attachiatus fuit ad respondendum Thoma Plater de placito transgressionis. Et unde queritur etc. Postea predictus Thomas non est prosecutus. Et ipse et plegii sui de prosequendo in misericordia. Condonatur ad instanciam Johannis de Bitterlegh per marescallum. (misericordia condonatur)

16. Willelmus de Barbary attachiatus fuit ad respondendum Willelmo le Wild in placito transgressionis. Postea per licenciam concordati sunt. Et postea predictus Willelmus de Barbary ponit se. Finem xii denariorum.

(misericordia xii denariorum)

17. Ricardus le Taillur centenarius de millenario Henrici de Brailleford fecit finem pro se et pro centena sua pro transgressione facta quia non fecit vigilationem i marca. (i marca soluta W. Bacon)

18. Radulphus de Linne quia fecit attachiamentum super socium suum sine marescallo. Ideo in misericordia. Et fecit finem vi denariorum. Solvit. (misericordia vi denariorum soluta)

Membrane 1d

19. Johannes de Smetheton Willelmus de Schefeud et Johannes Tilly attachiati fuerunt ad respondendum Radulpho de Bleyou militi de placito transgressionis. Et unde queritur quod cum idem Radulphus acomodasset predicto Willelmo quoddam hospicium in Berewyk ad hospitandum in eodem per unam noctem solummodo idem Willelmus et alii predictum hospicium contra voluntatem suam injuste detinet. Et bona sua in eadem inventa ad valenciam xl solidorum ceperunt et

she says. He asks for enquiry to be made, as does Maud.

The jurors say on their oath that Walter took the cloak from Maud. Therefore it is considered that Maud should recover the cloak or its value, 2 shillings 6 pence, and damages of 6 pence. Walter is condemned to prison until etc. (amercement 20 pence)

15. John de Hotham knight was attached to answer Thomas Plater on a plea of trespass. Whereon he complains etc. Later Thomas has not prosecuted, therefore he and his sureties for prosecuting [are] in mercy. [The amercement is] pardoned by the marshal at the instance of John de Bitterlegh. (amercement pardoned)

16. William de Barbary was attached to answer William le Wild in a plea of trespass. Later they are agreed by licence, and later William puts himself [on the country and makes] a fine of 12 pence.
(amercement 12 pence)

17. Richard le Taillur centenar of the *millenarium* of Henry de Braylesford made a fine of 1 mark for himself and his hundred [men] for a trespass committed, because he failed to perform watch and ward.
(1 mark paid to W. Bacon)

18. Ralph de Lynne [was attached] because he attached his fellow without the [permission of the] marshal. Therefore [he is] in mercy. He has made a fine of 6 pence. [The amercement is] paid.
(amercement 6 pence, paid)

19. John de Smetheton, William de Schefeud and John Tilly were attached to answer Ralph de Bloyou knight on a plea of trespass. Whereon he complains that when he made a loan to William of certain lodgings in Berwick intending that William should stay in them for one night only, William and the others illegally withhold the lodgings from him. They also took and carried away goods to the value of 40 shillings which they found there, to Ralph's great damage etc.

asportaverunt ad grave dampnum ipsius etc.

Et predictus Willelmus et alii veniunt et dicunt quod predictus Radulphus concessit eis predictum hospicium sine aliqua accomodacione. Postea per licenciam concordati sunt. Et predicti Johannes et Willelmus et Johannes ponunt se. Et fecerunt finem iii solidorum.

(misericordia iii solidorum soluta)

20. Johannes de Rotheclyve attachiatus fuit ad respondendum Rogero de Beauchamp de placito quod reddat ei unum capellum vervenum. Et predictus Johannes venit et dicit quod recepit dictum capellum de Roberto Roulaund quem vocat ad warantum. Et idem Robertus venit ad [sic] \et/ warantizat predictum Johannem. Et vocat ulterius Radulphum Stedeman garcionem Roberti de Kirketon qui venit et warrantizat et dicit quod invenit dictum capellum et reddit nec erat aliquis amerciatus. Teste W. Bacon. (misericordia nulla)

21. Willelmus de Hathethorn ponit se versus Willelmum de Kellom in placito transgressionis. Postea concordati sunt. Et idem Willelmus de Hathethorn ponit se. Et fecit finem xx denariorum.

(misericordia xx denariorum soluta)

22. Johannes de London armerarius queritur de Thoma de Queneby quod injuste cepit de eo unum gorgerium ferreum. Postea predictus Thomas satisfecit predicto Johanne de predicto gorgero. Et idem Thomas in misericordia. Condonatur ad instanciam domini Thome de Nevyle. (misericordia condonatur)

23. Johannes de Averinthe detentatus per Johannem de Pothou constabularium suum pro eo quod noluit vigilare nec ire ad forarum sicut premunitus fuit. Ideo ad prisonam quousque etc. (prisone)

24. Adam le Flemeng et Johannes le Taverner de Notyngham quia non habuerunt Petrum de Ry quem manuceperunt. Ideo in misericordia. Solvit. (misericordia xl denariorum soluta)

25. Petrus de Ry attachiatus fuit ad respondendum Johanni de Pethau militi de placito transgressionis. Et unde queritur. Postea per licenciam

William and the others come and say that Ralph gave them the lodgings without any loan. Later they are agreed by licence. John, William and John put themselves [on the country] and made a fine of 3 shillings.   (amercement 3 shillings, paid)

20. John de Rockcliff was attached to answer Roger de Beauchamp on the plea that the former return to him a vervain cap. John comes and says that he received the cap from Robert Roland, whom he calls to warranty. Robert comes and vouches John to warranty. He further calls Ralph Stedeman the servant of Robert de Kirkton, who comes and vouches John to warranty. He [Ralph] says that he found the cap and returned it. He is not fined for anything else. Witness W. Bacon.
(no amercement)

21. William de Hathethorn appears against William de Kellom in a plea of trespass. Later they are agreed. William de Hathethorn puts himself [on the country] and makes a fine of 20 pence.
(amercement 20 pence, paid)

22. John de London armourer brings a suit against Thomas de Queneby for illegally taking from him an iron gorget. Later Thomas gave satisfaction to John for the gorget. Thomas [is] in mercy. [The amercement is] pardoned at the instance of Sir Thomas de Neville.
(amercement pardoned)

23. John de Averinthe [was] detained by John de Pothou his constable because he did not wish to perform watch and ward or to go on a foray as ordered. Therefore [he is sent] to prison until etc.   (to prison)

24. Adam le Flemeng and John le Taverner of Nottingham [were attached] because they do not have Peter de Rye whom they mainprised. Therefore [they are] in mercy. [The amercement is] paid.
(amercement 40 pence, paid)

25. Peter de Rye was attached to answer Sir John de Pethau knight on a plea of trespass. Whereon he complains. Later they are agreed by

concordati sunt. Et Petrus liberatur prisone quosque etc. Postea condonatur ad instanciam Petri de Donewych clerici senioris.

(misericordia condonatur)

26. De Roberto de Notyngham pro transgressione facta Thome de Stotevill in misericordia vi denariorum.

27. Johannes Bochard queritur de Thoma de Derby. Postea concordati sunt. Et predictus Thomas ponit se. Et fecit finem vi denariorum.

(misericordia vi denariorum soluta)

28. Nicholaus de Oxenford et Gillotus cissor attachiati fuerunt ad respondendum Radulpho de Bloyeu militi in placito transgressionis. Et unde queritur quod predicti Nicholaus et Gillotus injuste deforciaverunt eum unam seudam. Et predicti Nicholaus et Gillotus veniunt et dicunt quod intraverunt predictam seudam per Ingramum de Gynes quem vocant ad warantum. Et predictus Ingramus venit et warantizat. Postea per licenciam concordati sunt. Et predictus Radulphus ponit se. Et condonatur per J. de Segrave.

(misericordia condonatur)

Membrane 2r

Adhuc de placitis apud Berewyk.

29. Jermanus de Broxfeld ponit loco suo Johannem de Fayrwath versus Willelmum de Barsam de placito transgressionis.

30. Thomas Dautre miles attachiatus fuit ad respondendum Nicholao de Baliden et Simone de Baliden de placito transgressionis. Et unde queritur quod predictus Thomas venit ad domum illorum cum ignotis et bona sua ibidem inventa die veneris in septimana Pasche circa mediam noctem videlicet unam super tunicam de persio precii iiii solidorum et alia bona sua ad valenciam xx librarum asportaverunt ad grave dampnum predictorum Nicholai et Simonis etc. Et predictus Thomas venit et dicit quod in nullo est culpabilis. Et petit quod inquiratur. Et alii similiter.

Et juratores dicunt super sacramentum suum quod predictus Thomas in nullo est culpabilis. Ideo consideratum est quod predictus

licence. Peter is sent to prison until etc. Later [the amercement is] pardoned at the instance of Peter de Dunwich senior, clerk.

(amercement pardoned)

26. Concerning Robert de Nottingham, for a trespass done to Thomas de Stotville, [who is] in mercy for 6 pence.

27. John Bochard brings a suit against Thomas de Derby. Later they are agreed. Thomas puts himself [on the country] and has made a fine of 6 pence.   (amercement 6 pence, paid)

28. Nicholas de Oxford and Gillotus the tailor were attached to answer Ralph de Bloyou knight in a plea of trespass. Whereon he complains that Nicholas and Gilotus illegally ejected him from a shop. Nicholas and Gillotus come and say that they came into [possession of] the shop through Ingram de Gynes, whom they call to warranty. Ingram comes and vouches them to warranty. Later they are agreed by licence. Ralph puts himself [on the country]. [The amercement is] pardoned by J. de Segrave.   (amercement pardoned)

More of the pleas [heard] at Berwick.

29. Germanus de Broxfeld appoints John de Fayrwath his attorney against William de Barsam in a plea of trespass.

30. Thomas Dautre knight was attached to answer Nicholas de Baliden and Simon de Baliden on a plea of trespass. Whereon they complain that Thomas came to their house with unknown persons around the middle of the night on Friday of Easter Week [30 March], and took away goods that they found there, namely a surcoat of perse worth 4 shillings and other goods to the value of £20, to the grave damage of Nicholas and Simon. Thomas comes and says that he is in no wise guilty. He asks for enquiry to be made, as do the others.

The jurors come and say on their oath that Thomas is in no wise guilty. Therefore it is considered that Thomas is acquitted. Nicholas and Simon [are] in mercy. [The amercement is] pardoned at the instance

Thomas eat inde quietus. Et predicti Nicholaus et Simon in misericordia. Condonantur ad instanciam domini Rogeri de Brabazoun.   (misericordia condonatur)

31. Johannes de Benefeud queritur de Nicholao de Poterton quod injuste detinet unum equum nigrum. Et predictus Nicholaus reddidit predicto Johanni predictum equum per licenciam et dampna dimidia marca. Et ponit se. Condonatur ad instanciam Johannis de Bytterlegh.
                                  (misericordia condonatur)

32. Johannes du Boys attachiatus fuit ad respondendum Johanni de Fenton de placito transgressionis. Et predictus Johannes du Boys fuit manucaptus per Henricum de Grentford. Et non venit. Ideo ipse et manucaptor suus in misericordia. Et preceptum est Stephano Marescallo attachiet predictum Henricum et alium. Quia de hospicio regis unde nichil actum est.

33. Willelmus de Rateford centenarius in millenarium Thome Malet queritur de Roberto de Chastel. Plegium de prosequendo Hugo Thorold et Robertus optulerunt se. Et predictus Willelmus non est prosecutus. Ideo ipse et plegii sui de prosequendo in misericordia.
                         (misericordia xii denariorum soluta)

34. Willelmus Armerarius de London recognoscit se deberi Johanni le Fauconer militi in unam marcam solvendam citra dominicam proximam sequentem. Et predictus Willelmus in misericordia.
                         (misericordia xii denariorum soluta)

35. Rogerus de Stapelford queritur de Willelmo Prymerole. Postea concordati sunt per licenciam. Et predictus Willelmus ponit se.
                         (misericordia vi denariorum soluta)

36. Rogerus le Pertricur queritur de Symone Prymerole. Postea per licenciam concordati sunt. Et predictus Symon ponit se.
                         (misericordia vi denariorum soluta)

37. Alanus Carettarius attachiatus fuit ad respondendum Ricardo Bruet de placito transgressionis. Et unde queritur quod die dominica in

of Sir Roger de Brabazon. (amercement pardoned)

31. John de Benefeud brings a suit against Nicholas de Potterton that he illegally withholds a black horse. Nicholas returned the horse to John, with damages of one half mark. He puts himself [on the country]. [The amercement is] pardoned at the instance of John de Bitterlegh.
(amercement pardoned)

32. John du Boys was attached to answer John de Fenton on a plea of trespass. John was mainprised by Henry de Grentford, and does not come. Therefore he and his manucaptor [are] in mercy. Stephen the marshal is ordered to attach Henry and the other. Because they are from the king's household nothing more is done.

33. William de Rateford, centenar in the *millenarium* of Thomas Malet, brings a suit against Robert de Chastel. The surety for prosecuting, Hugh Thorold, and Robert presented themselves and William has not prosecuted. Therefore he and his sureties for prosecuting [are] in mercy. (amercement 12 pence, paid)

34. William the armourer of London acknowledges that he is indebted to John le Fauconer knight for one mark, to be paid before Sunday next. William [is] in mercy. (amercement 12 pence, paid)

35. Roger de Stapelford brings a suit against William Prymerole. Later they are agreed by licence. William puts himself [on the country].
(amercement 6 pence, paid)

36. Roger le Pertricur brings a suit against Simon Prymerole. Later they are agreed by licence. Simon puts himself [on the country].
(amercement 6 pence, paid)

37. Alan the carter was attached to answer Richard Bruet on a plea of trespass. Whereon he complains that on Sunday in the quindene of

quindena Pasche venit predictus Alanus ad hospicium suum et quendam equum bay extra domum suam abduxit etc. Juratores dicunt super sacramentum suum quod predictus Alanus nullum equum cepit nec abduxit prout queritur set quod illum equum in foro\emit/ etc. Ideo predictus Alanus inde quietus. Predictus Ricardus in misericordia pro falso clamore que condonatur quia pauper.

(misericordia condonatur quia pauper)

Membrane 2d

38. Matheus de Forneys attachiatus fuit ad respondendum Laurencio de Preston de placito transgressionis. Et unde queritur quod cum venisset die veneris in septimana Pasche apud Berewyk cum excercitu domini Regis et valettus eius decendisset de equo suo precii viii marcarum cooperto trappa ad portam juxta domum fratrorum minorum ille equus a dicto valetto evasit quem in custodia dicti Mathei \postea/ invenit et petit. Unde dicit quod predictus Matheus predictum equum una cum treppa injuste detinet ad dampnum ipsius Laurencii xl solidorum. Et producit sectam etc.

Et predictus Matheus venit et dicit quod plures habet equos unde petit certiorare de quo equo narrat versus ipsum. Et predictus Laurencius dicit quod est quidem equus grysens quem semel vendicavit sub dicto Matheo et alias sub armigero suo et dicit signum treppe. Et predictus Matheus dicit quod plures habet equos griseos unde nescit de quo loquitur. Et super hoc dies datum est partibus usque ad diem Pentecostes prece partium.

39. Thomas Michel attachiatus fuit ad respondendum Ricardo de Hocclyve de placito transgressionis. Et unde queritur. Postea per licenciam concordati sunt. Et predictus Thomas ponit se per [erasure in MS].

(misericordia ii solidorum soluta)

40. Walterus de Hedreslawe filius Willelmi de Crocumbe attachiatus fuit pro suspicione quia insidiator et inimicus domini regis Anglie. Et quia nullus sequitur nisi ad sectam domini regis ideo committitur domino Waltero de Huntercumbe per suam manucaptionem quousque etc. Et idem Walterus de Hedreslawe dicit quod bonus est et fidelis et de hoc ponit se. Et juratores dicunt super sacramentum suum quod non est insidiator set bonus est et fidelis. Ideo inde quietus.

(manucaptio quietus)

Easter [8 April] Alan came to his lodgings and led away from the house
a bay horse. The jurors say on their oath that Alan neither took nor led
away a horse as [Richard] complains, but rather that he bought the
horse in the market. Thereofre Alan [is] acquitted. Richard [is] in mercy
for a false claim. [The amercement is] pardoned because [he is] a pauper.

                 (amercement pardoned because [he is] a pauper)

38. Matthew de Forneys was attached to answer Lawrence de Preston
on a plea of trespass. Whereon he complains that when he came on
Friday in Easter Week [30 March] to Berwick with the king's army and
his groom dismounted from his barbed and harnessed horse, value 8
marks, at the gate next to the [house of the] Friars Minors, the horse ran
away from the groom. Later he found the horse in the custody of
Matthew and asked for it. He says that Matthew illegally withholds the
horse with its trappings, to Laurence's damage of 40 shillings, and he
brings suit etc.

Matthew comes and says that he has many horses and he wishes to be
informed about which horse is claimed against him. Lawrence says that
it is a grey horse that he once claimed under Matthew and at another
time under his squire, and he describes the symbol on the trappings.
Matthew says that he has many grey horses and he does not know why
he is impleaded. Therefore a day is given to the parties until Whitsun, at
the prayer of the parties.

39. Thomas Michel was attached to answer Richard de Hocclyve on a
plea of trespass. Whereon he complains. Later they are agreed by licence
and Thomas puts himself [on the country] by [ ].

                               (amercement 2 shillings, paid)

40. Walter de Hetherslaw son of William de Crookham was attached on
suspicion of [being] a spy and an enemy of the king of England. And
because no one sues him, leaving only the suit of the king, therefore he
is committed to [the custody of] Sir Walter de Huntercumbe on the
latter's mainprise until etc. Walter de Hetherslaw says that he is a good
and loyal man, and he puts himself [on the country]. The jurors say on
their oath that he is not a spy, but a good and loyal man. Therefore [he
is] acquitted.   (surety; acquitted)

41. Johannes Cocus de Middleton attachiatus fuit pro subrepcione unius pallii per Johannem Sampson et commissus prisone. Et quia predictus Johannes non est prosecutus ideo predictus Johannes Cocus inde quietus. Et predictus Johannes Sampson in misericordia.

(misericordia)

42. Thomas Michel recognoscit se teneri Ade de Mohaut in duabas marcas solvendas infra quindenam sequentem. Et ad hoc inveniunt plegios subscriptos videlicet Ricardum de Hocclyve et Petrum de Munz.   (recognicio)

43. Willelmus le Fraunceis Walterus de la More et Thomas de Upton queruntur versus Oweynum de Mungomerry. Retraxerunt se de querela sua. Ideo in misericordia et finem xii denariorum.

(misericordia xii denariorum soluta)

44. Gregorius de Twyselton attachiatus fuit ad respondendum Ade le Harpur domini regis de placito transgressionis. Et unde queritur quod injuste detinet unum gladium qui quidem maliciose fuit alienatus de Hugone garcione ipsius Ade die veneris in septimana Pasche.

Et predictus Gregorius venit et dicit quod emit predictum gladium in foro domini regis et non maliciose adquisivit. Ideo petit quod inquiratur. Ideo preceptum est etc. Et super hoc predictus Adam non est prosecutus. Ideo in misericordia.   (misericordia)

45. Matillda de Blakeburneschire attachiata fuit ad respondendum Waltero Scot de placito transgressionis. Et unde queritur quod cum idem Walterus tradisset [sic] predicte Matillde unam supertunicam rubeam mixtam ad vendendum precii iii solidorum predicta Matillda de predicta supertunica nec de precio in aliquo sibi satisfecit ad dampnum ipsius Walteri etc.

Et predicta Matillda dicit quod predictam supertunicam de predicto Waltero nunquam recepit sicut ei imponit. Et hoc petit quod inquiratur. Et predictus Walterus similiter. Ideo preceptum est etc. Et predicta Matillda non venit. Ideo consideratum est quod distringatur ad audiendum judicium suum. Et alias non venit. Ideo consideratum est quod predictus Walterus recuperet predictam supertunicam. Et

41. John the cook of Middleton was attached by John Sampson for the robbery of a cloak and committed to prison. And because John [Sampson] has not prosecuted therefore John the cook [is] acquitted. John Sampson [is] in mercy. (amercement)

42. Thomas Michel acknowledges that he owes to Adam de Mohaut 2 marks, to be paid within the next two weeks. For this he finds the following sureties, namely Richard de Hocclyve and Peter de Munz. (recognisance)

43. William le Fraunceis, Walter de la More and Thomas Upton bring a suit against Owen de Montgomery. They have withdrawn from their suit. Therefore [they are] in mercy [and make a] fine of 12 pence. (amercement 12 pence, paid)

44. Gregory de Twyselton was attached to answer Adam the king's harper on a plea of trespass. Whereon he complains that Gregory illegally withholds a sword which was maliciously alienated from Hugh, Adam's servant, on Friday of Easter Week [30 March].

Gregory comes and says that he bought the sword in the king's market and did not acquire it by malicious means. Therefore he asks for enquiry to be made. Therefore [the sheriff] is ordered etc. Adam has not prosecuted, therefore he [is] in mercy. [*CDS*, ii, no. 822, p. 189.]

(amercement)

45. Maud de Blackburnshire was attached to answer Walter Scot on a plea of trespass. Whereon he complains that when he delivered to Maud a red surcoat of mixed cloth to sell, value 3 shillings, Maud did not satisfy him either for the surcoat or for its price, to Walter's damage etc.

Maud says that she never received the surcoat from Walter as he charges. She asks for enquiry to be made, as does Walter. Therefore [the sheriff] is ordered etc. Maud does not come. Therefore it is considered that she be distrained to hear judgment on the case, and again she does not come. Therefore it is considered that Walter should recover the

predicta Matillda in misericordia.

(Stephanus Marescallus respondebit de valore supertunice ii solidorum vi denariorum et de misericordia vi denariorum)

Membrane 3r

Placita exercitus domini regis apud Rokesburgh die jovis proxima post festum assencionis domini anno regni sui xxiiii.

46. Hugo de Schalton queritur de Adam de Hamerton. Adam non venit et fuit attachiatus per marescallum. Ideo in misericordia. Et preceptum est quod capiatur.   (in primis)

47. Ricardus le Seler et Margeria uxor eius queruntur de Roberto le Whyte de Scotia. Et super hoc episcopus Dunelm' testificat per Brianum filium Alani quod predictum factum attachiatus fuit ante reformacionem pacis de Rokesburgh unde ei inde respondere de predicto facto nec debet. Ideo consideratum est quod predictus Ricardus et Margeria nichil inde recuperant. Et predictus Robertus eat inde quietus etc.   (de misericordia nihil)

48. Adam de Hamerton attachiatus fuit ad respondendum Hugoni de Scalton de placito transgressionis. Et unde queritur quod cum dictus Adam tradidisset dicto Hugoni l solidos de denariis receptis in Garderoba ad solvendos peditibus suis et predictus Hugo predictos l solidos dicto Ade retradidisset custodiendos predictus Adam predictos denarios injuste detinet ad grave dampnum ipsius Hugonis etc. Et inde producit sectam.

Et predictus Adam venit et dicit quod postquam dictos l solidos tradidisset dicto Hugone illos denarios de predicto Hugone nullo modo recepit. Et hoc petit quod inquiratur. Et predictus Hugo similiter.

Et juratores dicunt super sacramentum suum quod predictus Adam recepit de predicto Hugone denarios in una poucha sigillo dicti Hugonis signata set sive l solidos sive plus sive minus nesciunt set dicunt quod predictus Adam tradidit predictam poucham Johanni de Croxton militi custodienda. Ideo preceptum est predicto Johanni quod faciat venire etc. Postea predictus Johannes pertulit predictam poucham in plena

surcoat and Maud [is] in mercy.

> (Stephen the marshal will render 2 shillings 6 pence
> of the value of the surcoat and 6 pence amercement)

Pleas of the king's army at Roxburgh on Thursday next after the feast of the Ascension in the king's 24th year [10 May 1296].

46. Hugh de Scalton brings a suit against Adam de Hamerton. Adam has not come and is attached by the marshal. Therefore he [is] in mercy. It is ordered that he be taken.   (firstly)

47. Richard le Seler and Margery his wife bring a suit against Robert le White of Scotland. Whereupon the bishop of Durham testifies through Brian FitzAlan that the deed was done before the making of peace in Roxburgh, so that he [Robert] should not be required to answer for it. Therefore it is considered that Richard and Margery should recover nothing. Robert is acquitted.   (no amercement)

48. Adam de Hamerton was attached to answer Hugh de Scalton on a plea of trespass. Whereon he complains that while Adam surrendered to Hugh 50 shillings of money received in the Wardrobe to pay his foot soldiers and Hugh gave back the 50 shillings to Adam to safeguard for him, Adam now illegally withholds them, to Hugh's serious damage etc. Thereon he brings suit.

Adam comes and says that after he handed over the 50 shillings to Hugh he never received them back. He asks for enquiry to be made, as does Hugh.

The jurors come and say on their oath that Adam received the money from Hugh in a pouch marked with Hugh's seal, but they do not know whether there were more or less than 50 shillings contained therein. But they say that Adam gave the pouch to John de Croxton knight to safeguard for him. Later John produced the pouch in open court, marked with Hugh's seal, as the jurors said. Therefore it is considered that Hugh should recover the money. Adam is condemned to prison

curia signatam sigillo dicti Hugonis sicut juratores dicebant. Ideo consideratum est quod predictus Hugo recuperet predictos denarios. Et predictus Adam adjudicatur prisone quousque etc. Et finem iiii solidorum. (misericordia iiii solidorum)

49. Galfridus de Rocresheye attachiatus \fuit/ ad respondendum Elie le Ferur et Willelmo de Actone de placito transgressionis. Postea per licenciam concordati sunt in hac forma videlicet quod dictus\Galfridus/ solvet incontinenti predictis Elie et Willelomo lxx solidos. Et predictus Galfridus in misericordia. Plegius de misericordia dominus Johannes de Hothom. (misericordia xii denariorum)

50. Willelmus de Lodelawe attachiatus fuit ad respondendum Willelmo de Lucy Johanni de \le/ Rous et Henricus de Brecon de placito transgressionis. Et unde queruntur quod cum essent in una comitiva ad predandum in Scocia super inimicos domini regis Anglie et venissent \ad/ quoddam manerium invenerunt quendam equum rubeum precii x marcarum quem predictus Willelmus de Lodelawe cepit et pro voluntate sua abduxit nec de aliqua porcione eis contingente satisfecit ad dampnum predictorum Willelmi Johannis et Henrici etc. Et predictus Willelmus venit et defendit vim et injuriam quando etc. Et dicit quod predictus equus erat ita infirmus quod eum secum ducere non curavit. Et hoc petit quod inquiratur. Et predicti Willelmus Johannes et Henricus dicunt quod predictus Willelmus predictum equum abduxit et inde fecit voluntatem suam ut predictum est. Et hoc petit [sic] quod inquiratur. Ideo preceptum est etc. Postea predictus Willelmus et alii non sunt prosecuti. Ideo in misericordia. (misericordia ii solidorum)

51. Michael de Rokesburgh clericus attachiatus fuit ad respondendum Waltero de Stobton de placito transgressionis. Et unde queritur quod dictus Michael venit ad hospicium suum et hostium cuiusdam camere ibidem fregit ad dampnum ipsius Walteri etc. Et predictus Michael venit et recognoscit predictum factum. Ideo adjudicatur prisone. Misericordia condonatur ad instanciam domini Hugonis de Louther. (misericordia condonatur)

52. Germanus de Broxfeld attachiatus fuit \ad respondendum/ Willelmo de Barsam de placito transgressionis. Et unde queritur quod

until etc. [He makes a] fine of 4 shillings.   (amercement 4 shillings)

49. Geoffrey de Rocresheye was attached to answer Ely the smith and William de Acton on a plea of trespass. Later they are agreed by licence in the following manner, namely that Geoffrey is to pay 70 shillings immediately to Ely and William. Geoffrey [is] in mercy. His surety for mercy [is] Sir John de Hotham.   (amercement 12 pence)

50. William de Lodelawe was attached to answer William de Lucy, John de le Rous and Henry de Brecon on a plea of trespass. Whereon they complain that while they formed a company for plundering the king's enemies in Scotland and came to a manor where they found a red horse worth 10 marks, William de Lodelawe took the horse for himself and led it away on his own and did not satisfy William, John and Henry for any of the share [of the horse] pertaining to them, to their damage etc. William comes and denies force and injury when etc. He says that the horse was so weak that he did not bother to lead it away with him. He asks for enquiry to be made. William, John and Henry say that William led away the horse and thereby did as he wished, as they say above. They also ask for enquiry to be made. Therefore [the sheriff] is ordered etc. Later William and the others have not prosecuted. Therefore [they are] in mercy. [*CDS*, ii, no. 822, p. 189.]   (amercement 2 shillings)

51. Michael de Roxburgh clerk was attached to answer Walter de Stobton on a plea of trespass. Whereon he complains that Michael came to his lodgings and broke the door of his chamber, to Walter's damage etc. Michael comes and acknowledges the deed. Therefore he is condemned to prison. [The amercement is] pardoned at the instance of Sir Hugh de Lowther. [*CDS*, ii, no. 822, p. 189.]

(amercement pardoned)

52. Germanus de Broxfeld was attached to answer William de Barsam on a plea of trespass. Whereon he complains that while he bought from

cum ipse Willelmus emisset de predicto Germano ciiii oves precii
xxxiiii solidorum viii denariorum et illos denarios predicto Germano
solvisset predictus Germanus de predictis ovibus nullam liberacionem
fecit set eas et predictos denarios penes se retinet injuste ad grave
dampnum ipsius Willelmi etc.

Et predictus Germanus venit et defendit vim et injuriam etc. Et dicit
quod cum ipse et quidam alius emissent oves de quadam comitiva
ingnota supervenit predictus Willelmus et optulit eis lucrum super
empcione sua videlicet denarios de lucro super qualibet ove ita quod
exirent de comparacione sua. Et ipse intraret. Et dicit quod si predictus
Willelmus aliquam pecuniam solvit illam solvit principali venditori et
non sibi quia de principali venditore fuit assignatus recipere liberacionem predictarum ovium. Et dicit quod de predictis denariis nichil
recepit solummodo ii solidos vi denarios et hoc per manus principalis
venditoris pro porcione lucri sibi contingente. \Et hoc/ paratus est
verificare. Et petit quod inquiratur. Et predictus Willelmus dicit quod
predictas oves de predicto Germano emit et sibi denarios predictos
solvit et nulli alii. Et hoc petit quod inquiratur. Postea Willelmus venit
in plena curia et recessit in contemptu curie. Ideo consideratum est quod
predictus Germanus eat inde quietus. Et predictus Willelmus et plegii
sui de prosequendo in misericordia.

(inquisicio misericordia xii denariorum)

53. Galfridus Capellanus de Rokesburgh attachiatus fuit ad respondendum Johanni de Novo Castro Capellano de placito debiti. Et unde
queritur quod predictus Galfridus injuste detinet dimidiam marcam
quam ei debuit ad dampnum ipsius etc. Et predictus Galfridus non
potest hoc dedicere set recognoscit. Ideo consideratum est quod
predictus Johannes recuperet dimidiam marcam. Et predictus Galfridus
in misericordia.   (misericordia xii denariorum soluta)

54. Johannes de Cantelou attachiatus fuit ad respondendum Henrico de
Percy de placito transgressionis. Postea per licenciam concordati sunt.
Et predictus Henricus ponit se. Et condonatur per marescallum.

(misericordia condonatur)

55. Johannes le Warener attachiatus fuit ad respondendum Petro de
Kertham homini Willelmi de Ros de placito transgressionis. Et unde

Germanus 104 ewes, value 34 shillings 8 pence, and paid the money to Germanus, the latter did not make delivery of the ewes, and illegally withholds them and the money, to William's serious damage etc.

Germanus comes and denies force and injury etc. He says that when he and certain others bought the sheep from an unknown company of men, William approached them and offered them a profit on the sale, that is a money profit for each ewe that they in turn sold to him. He says that if William paid money to anyone he paid it to the principal vendor [the company] and not to him [Germanus], because he was originally assigned to take delivery of the ewes. He says that he never received any of the said money except 2 shillings 6 pence, and this by the hands of the principal vendor as his share of the profit. He is prepared to prove this and he asks for enquiry to be made. William says that he bought the ewes from Germanus and that he paid the money to him and no one else. He asks for enquiry to be made. Later William comes to open court and withdraws [his suit] in contempt of court. Therefore it is considered that Germanus is acquitted. William and his sureties for prosecuting [are] in mercy. (inquest; amercement 12 pence)

53. Geoffrey the chaplain of Roxburgh was attached to answer John de Newcastle, chaplain, on a plea of debt. Whereon he complains that Geoffrey illegally withholds one half mark which he owed him, to his damage etc. Geoffrey is unable to deny this, but rather acknowledges it. Therefore it is considered that John should recover the half mark. Geoffrey [is] in mercy. (amercement 12 pence, paid)

54. John de Cantelou was attached to answer Henry de Percy on a plea of trespass. Later they are agreed by licence. Henry puts himself [on the country]. [The amercement is] pardoned by the marshal. (amercement pardoned)

55. John the warrener was attached to answer Peter de Kertham the man of William de Ros on a plea of trespass. Whereon he complains that

queritur quod cum predictus Johannes comperasset de predicto Petro vi carcosios multonum die lune in septimana Pentecostes precii cuiuslibet xv denariorum et cum predictus Johannes debuit solvisse predictum argentum idem Johannes tria carcosios cepit et asportavit et nil pro predictis solvit ad dampnum ipsius Petri etc.

Et predictus Johannes venit et defendit vim et injuriam quando etc. Et bene defendit quod nuncquam predictis die et anno aliquos carcosios de predicto Petro cepit nec asportavit nec aliquod dampnum ei fecit sicut ei inponit. Et hoc petit quod inquiratur. Et predictus Petrus similiter. Ideo preceptum est \etc/. Postea predictus Petrus non est prosecutus. Ideo in misericordia.   (misericordia xii denariorum)

56. Johannes le Husser attachiatus fuit ad respondendum Ade de Haveriton de placito transgressionis. Et unde queritur quod cum garcio dicti Ade tradidisset dicto Johanni i supertunicam unum par pannorum lineorum unum par caligarum et unum par sotularum ad portandum ipsi Ade predictus Johannes sibi liberavit supertunicam et residuum injuste detinet ad dampnum ipsius Ade etc.

Et predictus Johannes venit et dicit quod de predicto garcione nil recepit nisi supertunicam quam ei liberavit sicut predictus Adam recognovit. Et hoc petit quod inquiratur. Et predictus Adam similiter. Postea per licenciam concordati sunt. Et predictus Johannes ponit se.
                                        (misericordia viii denariorum)

Membrane 3d

Adhuc de placitis apud Rokesburgh.

57. Hugo Torold attachiatus fuit ad respondendum Roberto de Baumburgh in placito transgressionis. Et unde queritur quod predictus Hugo die mercurii ante Pentecostem injuste cepit predictum Robertum et ipsum inprisonavit falso et cxix oves attachiavit de ipso quas pro voluntate sua fugavit ad dampnum [a further 'ad dampnum' erased] ipsius Roberti xl solidorum et amplius etc. Et inde producit sectam. Et predictus Hugo venit et defendit vim et injuriam quando etc. Et bene advocat predictum inprisonamentum ad sectam cuiusdam Nigelli de Gronlawe hominis comitis Patricii qui quidam Nigellus inposuit predicto Roberto quod ipse predictas oves in terra pacis cepit maliciose

when on Monday in Whitsun Week [14 May] John procured from him 6 sheeps' carcasses each worth 15 pence and was due to pay him the money, he took and carried off three of the carcasses and paid nothing for them, to Peter's damage etc.

John comes and denies force and injury when etc. He denies absolutely that on the said day and year he took from Peter or carried off any carcasses or that he did him any damage as the latter charges. He asks for enquiry to be made, as does Peter. Therefore [the sheriff] is ordered etc. Later Peter has not prosecuted. Therefore [he is] in mercy.

(amercement 12 pence)

56. John le Husser was attached to answer Adam de Haveriton on a plea of trespass. Whereon Adam complains that when his servant gave John a surcoat, a pair of linen garments, a pair of hose and a pair of shoes to bring to Adam, John gave him only the surcoat and illegally withholds the remaining things, to Adam's damage etc.

John comes and says that he received nothing from the servant except the surcoat, which he surrendered to Adam as the latter acknowledges. He asks for enquiry to be made, as does Adam. Later they are agreed by licence. John puts himself [on the country].   (amercement 8 pence)

More of the pleas [heard] at Roxburgh.

57. Hugh Thorold was attached to answer Robert de Bamburgh in a plea of trespass. Whereon he complains that on Wednesday before Whitsun [9 May] Hugh illegally seized him, falsely imprisoned him, attached 119 of his sheep and wilfully drove them off, to Robert's damage of 40 shillings and more. Thereon he brings suit. Hugh comes and denies force and injury when etc. He readily acknowledges the imprisonment and says that it was done at the suit of one Nigel de Greenlaw, the man of Earl Patrick. Nigel charged Robert with seizing the sheep maliciously from land that was at peace, whereon Hugh, acting as the marshal's bailiff, sought to attach him. When Robert

unde predictus Hugo tanquam ballivus marescalli ipsum attachiare voluit ad respondendum etc. Et quod predictus Robertus noluit se justificare nec plegios invenire predictus Hugo ipsum inprisonavit sicut ei bene licuit. Et quo ad oves respondet et bene congnoscit [sic] quod predictas oves attachiavit et ad custodiendum liberavit quibusdam ingnotis de societate ipsius Roberti etc.

Et predictus Robertus dicit quo ad inprisonamentum quod nuncquam predictus Hugo aliquos plegios ab eo exigebat sicut ei inponit. Et de hoc ponit se super patriam. Et predictus Hugo similiter. Ideo preceptum est etc quod venire etc ponitur in respectu usque adventum regis. Et quo ad oves predictas Robertus petit judicium *desicut* predictus Hugo bene cognovit quod ipse predictas oves cepit et pro voluntate sua fugavit petit quod qualitercumque *vel cuiuscumque* eas liberavit ei non prejudicit. Et de hoc petit judicium. Et predictus Hugo similiter. Et habent diem usque die *lune post* octabas Pentecostes quo die predictus Hugo non venit. Ideo consideratum est quod Hugo distringatur ad *audiendum iudicium suum*. Et alias non venit. Ideo consideratum est quod predictus Robertus recuperet predictas oves versus predictum Hugonem. *Et predictus Hugo* in misericordia. [MS stained: italicised words supplied from Adv. MS.]

(judicium misericordia nil)

58. Willelmus de Bockele attachiatus fuit ad respondendum Waltero le Poure de placito quare quod cum ipse tradidisset ei bestias suas custodiendum die jovis proxima ante Pentecostem predictus Willelmus nocte sequente septem vaccas precii xxx solidorum de predictis bestiis alienavit ad dampnum ipsius Walteri etc.

Et predictus Willelmus venit et defendit vim et injuriam quando etc. Et dicit quod de predictis bestiis nullam vaccam alienavit sicut ei inponit. Et hoc petit quod inquiratur. Et predictus Walterus similiter. Ideo preceptum est etc.

Et juratores dicunt super sacramentum suum quod predictus Willelmus predictas vaccas non alienavit sicut ei inponitur. Ideo inde quietus. Et predictus Walterus in misericordia.

(misericordia xii denariorum)

59. Nicholaus filius Willelmi de Rypon attachiatus fuit ad respondendum Ade de Thorthweyt de placito quare cum ipse ivisset apud

refused to justify himself or to find sureties Hugh imprisoned him, as was his duty. With respect to the sheep, he answers and readily acknowledges that he attached them, and that he delivered them for safekeeping to unknown men of Robert's company etc.

Robert says with respect to the imprisonment that Hugh never required sureties of him as he charges. He puts himself on the country, as does Hugh. [The sheriff] is ordered etc to summon etc. [The case is] adjourned until the arrival of the king. Robert prays judgment with respect to the sheep, inasmuch as Hugh readily acknowledges that he seized them and that he wilfully drove them off. He asks that [his claim to them] not be prejudiced by the means in which, or the person by whom, they were delivered to Hugh. He prays judgment, as does Hugh. They have a day until Monday after the octaves of Whitsun [21 May], on which day Hugh does not come. Therefore it is considered that Hugh be distrained to hear judgment against him, and once again he does not come. Therefore it is considered that Robert should recover the sheep against Hugh. Hugh [is] in mercy. [*CDS*, ii, no. 822, p. 189.]

(judgment; no amercement)

58. William de Bockele was attached to answer Walter le Poure on a plea that when on Thursday before Whitsun [10 May] Walter surrendered his animals to William for safekeeping, the following night William alienated seven cows, value 30 shillings, from the animals, to Walter's damage etc.

William comes and denies force and injury when etc. He says that he alienated no cows from the animals as Walter charges. He asks for enquiry to be made, as does Walter. Therefore [the sheriff] is ordered etc.

The jurors say on their oath that William did not alienate the cows as he is charged. Therefore [he is] acquitted. Walter [is] in mercy.

(amercement 12 pence)

59. Nicholas son of William de Ripon was attached to answer Adam de Thorthweyt on a plea that when on Sunday after the feast of the

C

Hadington ad foriendum dominica proxima post festum Assencionis
domini et venisset in quadam domo juxta parcam fratrum infra clausum
eorum invenit in eadem in quadam cuva triginta libras argenti in duabus
pouchis quam quidem pecuniam predictus Nicholaus ab eo vi abstulit et
asportavit ad grave dampnum ipsius Ade xl solidorum et contra pacem
etc. Et predictus \Nicholaus/ venit et defendit vim et injuriam quando
etc. Et dicit quod de predicto Ade nullam pecuniam cepit nec asportavit
sicut ei inponit. Et petit quod inquiratur. Et predictus Adam similiter.
Ideo preceptum est etc. Juratores dicunt super sacramentum suum quod
predictus Nicholaus nullam denarium a predicto Ade cepit. Ideo
consideratum \est/ quod predictus Nicholaus eat inde quietus. Et Adam
in misericordia. Condonatur per marescallum ad instanciam Johannis
Gichard.   (misericordia condonatur)

60. Rogerus Hirdman de Corbrigge attachiatus fuit ad respondendum
Willelmo le *Teylurer* de eadem et Willelmo de *Tyndal* de placito quare
cum conventum erat inter eosdem quod fideliter partirent lucrum suum
in isto exercitu et predicti Willelmus et Willelmus tradidissent predicto
Rogero braseum ad braciendum quod quidem braseum ipse braciavit et
per duas vices lucrabatur de claro sex marcas quas penes se detinuit et
cum predictis Willelmo et Willelmo noluit partire contra convencionem inter eos initam ad dampnum ipsorum etc.

Et predictus Rogerus venit et defendit vim et injuriam quando etc. Et
dicit quod nullum conventum tale eis fecit. Et petit quod inquiratur. Et
predicti Willelmus et Willelmus similiter. Et juratores dicunt super
sacramentum suum quod predicta convencio erat facta set dicunt quod
predictus Rogerus semel lucrabatur iii solidos et alias xl solidos. Ideo
consideratum \est/ quod predicti Willelmus et Willelmus recuperent
versus predictum Rogerum porcionem eis contingentem de predictis
xliii solidis. Et predictus Rogerus in misericordia. [MS stained:
italicised words supplied from Adv. MS.]
                                      (misericordia xl denariorum)

61. Willelmus de Brampton attachiatus fuit ad respondendum
marescallo excercitus domini regis qui venit. Et ponit se in misericordia
marescalli per plevinam Walteri le Poure et Willelmi de la Grene.
                                                          (media)

Ascension of the Lord [6 May] Adam came to Haddington on a foray and came to a house next to the friars' enclosure, he found inside their close, in a bowl, two pouches containing £30, which money Nicholas took by force from him and carried off, to Adam's grave damage of 40 shillings and against the peace etc. Nicholas comes and denies force and injury when etc. He says that he did not take or carry off any money from Adam, as the latter charges. He asks for enquiry to be made, as does Adam. Therefore [the sheriff] is ordered etc. The jurors say on their oath that Nicholas did not take any money from Adam. Therefore it is considered that Nicholas is acquitted. Adam [is] in mercy. [The amercement is] pardoned by the marshal at the instance of John Gichard. (amercement pardoned)

60. Roger Hirdman of Corbridge was attached to answer William the tailor of the same place and William de Tyndale on a plea that while there was an agreement among them that they would all faithfully share the booty they won in the army and William and William gave Roger malt to brew, Roger brewed the malt and twice sold it for a profit of 6 marks, which he kept for himself. He refused to share the money with William and William in violation of their agreement, and to their damage etc.

Roger comes and denies force and injury when etc, and says that he never made any such agreement. He asks for enquiry to be made, as do William and William. The jurors say on their oath that an agreement was made, but that Roger made a profit once of 3 shillings and at another time of 40 shillings. Therefore it is considered that William and William should recover against Roger the share pertaining to them of the aforesaid 43 shillings. Roger [is] in mercy.

(amercement 40 pence)

61. William de Brampton was attached to answer the marshal of the king's army. He comes and puts himself in the marshal's mercy by surety of Walter le Poure and William de la Grene. (one half)

62. Rogerus de Bribour attachiatus fuit ad respondendum Johanni le Flemeng de placito quare cum predictus Johannes dimisisset equum suum in quadam pastura juxta Rokesburgh die dominica in festo Pentecostes quem postea invenit in custodia predicti Rogeri et dictum equum petiit ab eo et predictus Rogerus dictum equum noluit sibi liberare set eum injuste detinet ad dampnum etc. Et predictus Rogerus venit et defendit vim et injuriam quando etc. Et dicit quod fideliter emit predictum equum de denariis suis in foro de Rokesburgh longe ante predictam dominicam fere per unam septimanam et hoc paratus est verificare per bonam patriam. Et predictus Johannes dicit quod de predicto equo habuit possesionem per annum integrum ante predictam dominicam. Postea venit predictus Rogerus et reddidit predictum equum in plena curia. Ideo consideratum est quod predictus\Johannes/ recuperet dampna sua que adjudicantur ii solidi. Et ipse \Rogerus/ in misericordia.   (misericordia xii denariorum)

63. Robertus de Sancto Paulo attachiatus fuit ad respondendum Alano filio Warini militi de placito injuste detencionis unius\equi/. Postea per licenciam posuerunt se in arbitrariis.

64. Willelmus filius Mynne attachiatus fuit ad respondendum Thome de Fisseburn et Ade de Rue de placito transgressionis. Et predicti Thomas et Adam non sunt prosecuti. Ideo in misericordia plegius Willelmus de Haukeswell.   (misericordia ii solidorum)

65. Willelmus de Ercelden attachiatus fuit ad respondendum Ade le Mouner. Postea per licenciam concordati sunt. Et predictus Willelmus ponit se.   (misericordia vi denariorum)

66. Walterus le Poure ponit loco suo Johannes [sic] de Stayntton versus Oweynum de Mungomery et Adam Carbonil in placito transgressionis etc.   (attornatus)

67. Willelmus de Nevill Walterus le Poure Johannes Martel optulerunt se versus Oweynum de Mongomery. Et predictus Owynus non venit. Ideo Radulphus de Grendon et Johannes de Grendon plegii sui in misericordia.   (misericordia iiii solidorum)

62. Roger de Bribour was attached to answer John le Fleming on a plea that when on Whit Sunday [13 May] John put his horse in a pasture near Roxburgh, he later found the horse in the custody of Roger. He requested its return but Roger refused to surrender the horse and illegally withholds it still, to John's damage etc. Roger comes and denies force and injury when etc. He says that he bought the horse in good faith with his own money in the market in Roxburgh a long time before that Sunday, nearly one week before, and he is ready to prove the fact by a jury of good men. John says that he owned the horse for an entire year before that Sunday. Later Roger came and returned the horse to John in open court. Therefore it is considered that John should recover his damages, assessed at 2 shillings. Roger [is] in mercy.

(amercement 12 pence)

63. Robert de St Paul was attached to answer Alan FitzWarin knight on a plea of illegally withholding a horse. Later they agree by licence to submit themselves to arbitration.

64. William son of Mynne was attached to answer Thomas de Fishburn and Adam de Rue on a plea of trespass. Thomas and Adam have not prosecuted, therefore [they are] in mercy. [Their] surety [is] William de Haukswell.

(amercement 2 shillings)

65. William de Ercelden was attached to answer Adam le Mouner. Later they are agreed by licence. William puts himself [on the country].

(amercement 6 pence)

66. Walter le Poure appoints John de Staynton as his attorney against Owen de Montgomery and Adam Carbonnel in a plea of trespass etc.

(attorney)

67. William de Neville, Walter le Poure [and] John Martel presented themselves against Owen de Montgomery. Owen does not come. Therefore his sureties Ralph de Grendon and John de Grendon [are] in mercy.

(amercement 4 shillings)

68. Cristiana de Totentham et Cristiana de Londr' attachiate fuerunt per Robertum Prisonarium ad respondendum Angneti Lotrici de placito transgressionis. Et unde queritur quod die martis proxima post festum Trinitatis venerunt predicte Cristiana et Cristiana in villa de Rokesburgh et ipsam Angnetam ceperunt wlneraverunt [sic] et bona sua ad valenciam xx solidorum asportaverunt ad dampnum ipsius Angnetis dimidie marce et contra pacem.

Et predicte Cristiana et Cristiana venerunt et defenderunt vim et injuriam quando etc. Et dicunt quod tale die non venerunt nec predictam Angnetem wlneraverunt [sic] nec \bona sua/ asportaverunt. Et hoc parate sunt verificare per patriam. Et predicta Angnes similiter. Postea per licenciam concordate sunt. Et predicta Agnes ponit se.

(misericordia vi denariorum)

69. Symon de Criketot attachiatus fuit ad respondendum Roberto de Escores de placito transgressionis de quo placito habuit licenciam concordandi salvo jure marescalli. Et posuerunt se in arbitrio Willelmi Talemasch et Thome de Hauvill.

Membrane 4r

70. Lambertus de Burgo attachiatus fuit ad respondendum Willelmo de Swylington de placito transgressionis. Et unde queritur quod idem Lambertus vendidit Thome Trussebut tanquam ballivo suo ad opus eiusdem Willelmi vj^c oves precii cuiuslibet iii denariorum et unde idem Thomas solvit predicto Lamberto xx solidos argenti nomine arreragii quousque de superplusagio pecunie predicto Lamberto satisfactum fuisset super quod idem Thomas tanquam ballivus predicti Willelmi liberacionem predictarum ovium petit quam predictus Lambertus sibi facere recusavit. Et predictos xx solidos adhuc ei injuste detinet ad dampnum ipsius Willelmi etc. Et predictus Lambertus venit et defendit vim et injuriam quando etc. Et dicit quod predictus Thomas nuncquam de eo predictas oves emit ad opus predicti Willelmi nec predictos xx solidos de predicto Thoma recepit ut predictus Willelmus dicit. Et hoc petit quod inquiratur. Et predictus W. similiter. Et interim predictus Lambertus mortuus est.   (misericordia nil)

71. Radulphus de Toggesden attachiatus fuit ad respondendum

68. Christine de Tottenham and Christine de London were attached by Robert the gaoler to answer Agnes the laundress on a plea of trespass. Whereon she complains that on Tuesday next after the feast of the Trinity [22 May] Christine and Christine came to the town of Roxburgh, seized her and wounded her and carried off goods of hers worth 20 shillings, to Agnes's damage of one half mark and against the peace.

Christine and Christine come and deny force and injury when etc. They say that they did not come there on that day, nor did they wound Agnes or carry off her goods. They are ready to prove this on the country, as is Agnes. Later they are agreed by licence. Agnes puts herself [on the country].   (amercement 6 pence)

69. Simon de Criketot was attached to answer Robert de Escores on a plea of trespass, regarding which plea he had licence to make an agreement, saving to the marshal his right. They have submitted themselves to the arbitration of William Talemasch and Thomas de Hauville.

70. Lambert de Burgh was attached to answer William de Swylington on a plea of trespass. Whereon he complains that Lambert sold to Thomas Trussebut his bailiff, for William's use, 600 ewes each worth 3 pence, for which Thomas paid Lambert 20 shillings in silver as a downpayment until he should be satisfied for the balance. Thomas then asked for the release of the ewes, which Lambert refused. He still withholds illegally the 20 shillings, to William's damage etc. Lambert comes and denies force and injury when etc. He says that Thomas never bought the ewes from him for William's use, nor did he receive 20 shillings from Thomas as William says. He asks for enquiry to be made, as does W[illiam]. In the meantime Lambert has died.

(no amercement)

71. Ralph de Toggesden was attached to answer Llewellyn ap Ythel on

Lewelino ab Ythel de placito transgressionis. Et unde queritur quod die martis proxima post festum sancte Trinitatis venit predictus Radulphus injuste cepit de eo unum gladium precii iiii solidorum et unum mantellum precii ii solidorum vi denariorum et predictum gladium et mantellum asportavit ad grave dampnum ipsius Lewelini et contra pacem etc. Et predictus Radulphus venit et defendit vim et injuriam quando etc. Et dicit quod emit predictum mantellum in foro domini regis de Rokesburgh et quod eum maliciose non adquisivit. Petit quod inquiratur.

Et quo ad gladium dicit quod nullum gladium de predicto Levelino cepit nec asportavit sicut ei inponit. Et hoc petit quod inquiratur. Et predictus Lewelinus similiter. Ideo preceptum est etc. Postea predictus Lewelinus optulit se. Et predictus Radulphus non venit. Ideo ipse et plegii sui videlicet Johannes filius Ricardi de Edentham et Johannes filius eius in misericordia.   (misericordia ii solidorum)

72. Owinus le Engleys et Thomas Stragan attachiati fuerunt ad respondendum Magistro Elye de Heton de placito transgressionis. Postea per licenciam concordati sunt. Et Magister Elyas ponit se per plevinam domini Roberti de Engles.

(misericordia xl denariorum soluta)

73. Willelmus de B\y/ rmor attachiatus fuit ad respondendum Johanni Gychard de placito quod idem Willelmus injuste detinet eidem Johanni v solidos ad dampnum ipsius Johannis etc.

Et predictus Willelmus venit et defendit vim et injuriam quando etc. Et dicit quod predictus Johannes fecit sibi quandam convencionem quod salvaret domos et bona sua in Rokesburgh in adventu domini regis quam quidem convencionem in nullo sibi tenuit. Et hoc petit quod inquiratur. Et predictus Johannes dicit quod predictam convencionem in omnibus tenuit. Et petit quod inquiratur. Et juratores dicunt super sacramentum suum quod predictus Johannes tenuit predictam convencionem. Ideo consideratum est quod predictus Johannes recuperet predictos quinque solidos versus predictum Willelmum et dampna sua que adjudicantur ii solidi. Et predictus Willelmus in misericordia.

(dampna c misericordia xii denariorum)

a plea of trespass. Whereon he complains that on Tuesday next after the feast of the holy Trinity [22 May] Ralph came [and] illegally took from him a sword worth 4 shillings and a cloak worth 2 shillings 6 pence and carried them off, to Llewellyn's grave damage and against the peace etc. Ralph comes and denies force and injury when etc. He says that he bought the cloak in the king's market in Roxburgh and that he did not acquire it by malicious means. He asks for enquiry to be made.

With respect to the sword, he says that he did not take it or carry it off from Llewellyn as the latter charges. He asks for inquiry to be made, as does Llewellyn. Therefore [the sheriff] is ordered etc. Later Llewellyn presented himself in court and Ralph did not come. Therefore he and his sureties, namely John son of Richard de Ednam and John his own son, [are] in mercy. (amercement 2 shillings)

72. Owen le Engleys and Thomas Stragan were attached to answer Master Elyas de Heton on a plea of trespass. Later they are agreed by licence. Master Elyas puts himself [on the country] by surety of Sir Robert de Engles. (amercement 40 pence, paid)

73. William de Beyrmor was attached to answer John Gichard on a plea that William illegally withholds from John 5 shillings, to his damage etc.

William comes and denies force and injury when etc. He says that John made an agreement with him that he would reserve his houses and goods in Roxburgh for William's use when the king arrived there. He says that John failed to hold to the agreement, and he asks for enquiry to be made. John says that he held to the agreement in all respects and also asks for enquiry to be made. The jurors say on their oath that John held to the agreement. Therefore it is considered that John should recover the 5 shillings against William and also his damages, which are assessed at 2 shillings. William [is] in mercy.

(damages 100; amercement 12 pence)

74. Oweynus de Mongomery attachiatus fuit ad respondendum Willelmo de Nevill Johanni Martel Waltero le Poure de placito quare cum predicti Willelmus et alii una cum predicto Oweyno amplexissent quamdam predam quam vendiderunt die veneris proxima ante Pentecostem tesaurario domini regis pro cx libris de quibus dictus O. recepit c marcas. Et cum predictus O. esset assignatus per totam comitivam una cum domino Theobaldo de Nevill et Ada Carbonnel distribuere cuiuslibet porcionem sibi contingentem predictus O. predictis Willelmo et aliis de predictis cx libris solummodo distribuit viii libras et residuum injuste detinet ad dampnum ipsorum etc. Et predictus Oweynus venit et defendit vim et injuriam quando etc. Et petit judicium si teneatur predictis Willelmo et aliis respondere desicut recognovit plures esse distributores et petierunt integrum de ipso sine aliis distributores. Ideo consideratum est quod predictus O. eat quietus. Et predictus Willelmus et alii in misericordia.

(misericordia iii solidorum)

75. Walterus Clerk de Rokesburgh attachiatus fuit ad respondendum Rogero de Lyndesey capellano de placito quare cum predictus Walterus teneatur dicto Rogero in ix marcis argenti iiii solidis minus quod quidem argentum dictus Walterus sibi solvisse debuit ad Pentecostem proximam preteritam et illud nondum solvit ut dicit unde deterioratus est et dampnum habet etc. Et predictus Walterus venit et defendit vim et injuriam quando etc. Et petit judicium si teneatur in ista curia respondere dicto Rogero de aliquo contractu ante adventum domini regis facto. *Postea predictus Walterus tulit breve senescalli. Et ita respectuatur loquela.* [Italicised words added in a different but still contemporary hand.] (retornatus per breve senescalli)

76. De Nicholao de Heyttlestham pro licencia concordandi cum Johanne garcione Rogeri de Somervill vi denarii.

(misericordia vi denariorum soluta)

77. Johannes garcio Walteri de Stirton attachiatus fuit ad respondendum Nicholao capellano de domo Dei de Rokesburgh de placito transgressionis. Et predictus Nicholaus non est prosecutus. Ideo in misericordia. Et condonatur per marescallum ad instanciam Hunfridi de Boun.

(misericordia condonatur)

74. Owen de Montgomery was attached to answer William de Neville, John Martel [and] Walter le Poure on a plea that when William and the others, together with Owen, pooled their spoils of war, then on the Friday next before Whitsun [11 May] sold the goods to the king's treasurer for £110, O[wen] received 100 marks from that sum. While O[wen], Sir Theobald de Neville and Adam Carbonnel were assigned by the company to distribute to each man the share pertaining to him, O[wen] distributed to William and the others only £8 of the said £110 and illegally withholds the residue, to their damage etc.

Owen comes and denies force and injury when etc. He prays judgment whether he is required to answer William and the others, inasmuch as the latter acknowledges that there were many men charged with distributing [the money], but they asked only him, and no others, to hand over the entire sum. It is considered that O[wen] is acquitted. William and the others [are] in mercy.   (amercement 3 shillings)

75. Walter Clerk of Roxburgh was attached to answer Roger de Lindsay chaplain on a plea that whereas Walter was indebted to Roger for 9 marks of silver less 4 shillings and was to pay him the money at Whitsun last [13 May], he has not done so. Whereby he says that he has been wronged and has suffered damage etc. Walter comes and denies force and injury when etc. He prays judgment whether he is required to answer Roger in this court for a contract made before the arrival of the king. Later Walter brought a writ of the steward. Thus the suit has been adjourned.   (returned by writ of the steward)

76. Concerning Nicholas de Heyttlestham, for licence to make an agreement with John the servant of Roger de Somerville, 6 pence.
     (amercement 6 pence, paid)

77. John the servant of Walter de Stirton was attached to answer Nicholas the chaplain of the Maisondieu of Roxburgh on a plea of trespass. Nicholas has not prosecuted, therefore [he is] in mercy. [The amercement is] pardoned by the marshal at the instance of Humphrey de Bohun.   (amercement pardoned)

Membrane 4d

Adhuc de placitis excercitus apud Rokesburgh.

78. Walterus de Trilleyk attachiatus fuit ad respondendum Willelmo de Faucumberge de placito transgressionis. Et unde queritur quod predictus Walterus injuste detinet eidem viii solidos quos ei accomodavit die sabbati proxima ante assencionem domini anno regni regis E. xxiiii quod quidem denarios solvisse debuit dominica sequentem. Et nondum solvit unde dampnum habet etc. Et predictus Walterus venit et defendit vim et injuriam etc. Et petit judicium si teneatur respondere desicut de predicto debito producit neque scriptum neque talliam. Et predictus Willelmus dicit quod habet bonam sectam quam produxit. Et desicut ad sectam suam nil respondet petit judicium. Et consideratum est quod predictus Willelmus recuperet viii solidos versus predictum Walterum. Et predictus Walterus in misericordia. Condonatur ad instanciam domini Roberti Peverel fratris tesaurarii pro constabulario.

(misericordia condonatur)

79. Adam Carbonnel attachiatus fuit ad respondendum Saero de Huntingfeld. Et idem Saerus non est prosecutus. Ideo ipse et plegii sui de prosequendo in misericordia.

(misericordia ii solidorum condonatur)

80. Oweynus de Mongomery attachiatus fuit ad respondendum Waltero le Poure et Johanni Martel de placita quare cum predicti Walterus et Johannes una cum predicto Oweyno et aliis amplexissent quandam predam et eam die veneris proxima ante Pentecostem vendidissent Thoma de Nevill attornato tesaurarii domini regis pro c et x libris argenti de quo argento predictus O. recepit c marcas ad opus eorundem de societate predicto. Et de dictis c marcis distribuit predictis Waltero et Johanni iiii libros pro porcione eosdem contingentem de lx marcis et porcionem eosdem contingentem de xl marcis predictis Oweynus eis injuste detinet ut dicunt ad dampnum etc.

Et predictus Oweynus venit et defendit vim et injuriam quando etc. Et dicit quod quidem Adam Carbonnel erat distributor pecunie cum eo et petit auxilium de ipso Ade. Et predictus Adam fuit premunitus. Et habent diem usque diem mercurii ad quem diem predictus Adam venit.

More of the pleas of the army [heard] at Roxburgh.

78. Walter de Trilleyk was attached to answer William de Fauconberge on a plea of trespass. Whereon he complains that Walter illegally withholds from him 8 shillings, which he loaned to Walter on Saturday next before the Ascension of the Lord in the king's 24th year [28 April 1296], and which Walter was to repay on the following Sunday. He has not yet done so, whereby William has suffered damage etc. Walter comes and denies force and injury etc. He prays judgment whether he is required to answer William, inasmuch as the latter has shown neither a written record nor a tally regarding the debt. William says that the suit he has brought is good. And inasmuch as no answer is given to his suit he too prays judgment. It is considered that William should recover 8 shillings against Walter, and Walter [is] in mercy. [The amercement is] pardoned at the instance of Sir Robert Peverel, brother of the treasurer, on behalf of the constable.   (amercement pardoned)

79. Adam Carbonnel was attached to answer Saer de Huntingfield. Saer has not prosecuted. Therefore he and his sureties for prosecuting [are] in mercy.   (amercement 2 shillings, pardoned)

80. Owen de Montgomery was attached to answer Walter le Poure and John Martel on a plea that when Walter and John, together with Owen and other persons, pooled their spoils of war and then on Friday next before Whitsun [11 May] sold the goods to Thomas de Neville the attorney of the king's treasurer for £110 of silver, O[wen] received 100 marks of the silver for the use of their fellowship. He distributed only £4 to Walter and John, their share of 60 of the marks, but their share of the [remaining] 40 marks he illegally withholds, to [their] damage etc.

Owen comes and denies force and injury when etc. He says that one Adam Carbonnel was a co-distributor of the money with him, and he requests the latter's help. Adam is advised and they have a day on the following Wednesday. On this day Adam came but Owen did not. Therefore he is to be distrained. They had another day on the following Friday, on which day the parties came. At the request of the parties

Et predictus Oweynus non venit. Ideo distringatur. Et habuerunt diem usque diem veneris quo die partes venerunt. Dies datus est partibus usque diem binum prece partium quo die predicti Walterus et Johannes optulerunt se. Et predictus Owynus non venit. Ideo preceptum est quod distringatur per corpus etc. (misericordia ii solidorum)

81. Johannes Gychard attachiatus fuit ad respondendum Willelmo de Beyrmor. Et predictus Johannes non venit. Ideo plegii sui in misericordia. Condonatur per W. de Haukeswelle. Postea per licenciam concordati sunt. Et predictus Willelmus ponit se.

(misericordia xii denariorum)

82. Johannes de Grendon attachiatus fuit ad respondendum Augustino Peverel de placito quare cum predictus Augustinus tradidisset ei bestias suas custodiendas predictus Johannes alienavit de predictis bestiis v boves et iiii vaccas et permisit alienari ad dampnum ipsius etc. Et predictus Johannes venit et defendit vim et injuriam quando etc. Et bene defendit quod predictas bestias non alienavit nec permisit alienari. Et hoc petit quod inquiratur. Et predictus Augustinus similiter.

Et juratores dicunt super sacramentum suum quod predictus Johannes predictos boves et vaccas non alienavit nec in custodia sua per ipsum erant alienati. Ideo consideratum est quod predictus Johannes eat inde quietus. Et predictus Augustinus in misericordia. Et condonatur ad\instanciam/ J. de la Huse. (misericordia condonatur)

83. Henricus de Donboyne attachiatus fuit ad respondendum Reginaldo Leance de placito quare die mercurii proxima post octabas Trinitatis venit predictus Henricus in villa de Rokesburgh et ipsum Reginaldum insultum ei dedit et cum quodam gladio in capite et in brachio wlneravit [sic] ad dampnum ipsius etc. Et predictus Henricus presens et predictum factum recognoscit. Ideo adjudicatur prisone quousque etc. Et finem xii denariorum.

(misericordia xii denariorum)

84. Robertus Scot attachiatus fuit ad respondendum Johanne Clerk attornato Ricardi de Wytacre de placito quare ... [A large space is left blank in the MS, probably for the subsequent recording of the details of this case.] (r')

another day was given two days hence. On this day Walter and John presented themselves but Owen did not come. Therefore it is ordered that he be distrained in his person etc.   (amercement 2 shillings)

81. John Gichard was attached to answer William de Beyrmor. John does not come. Therefore his sureties [are] in mercy. [The amercement is] pardoned by W. de Haukeswell. Later they are agreed by licence. William puts himself [on the country].   (amercement 12 pence)

82. John de Grendon was attached to answer Augustine Peverel on a plea that when Augustine surrendered some animals to him for safekeeping, John alienated 5 oxen and 4 cows from the animals and permitted them to be so alienated, to Augustine's damage etc. John comes and denies force and injury when etc, and strongly denies that he alienated the animals or permitted their alienation. He asks for enquiry to be made, as does Augustine.

The jurors say on their oath that John did not alienate the oxen and cows, nor were they alienated while in his safekeeping. Therefore it is considered that John is acquitted. Augustine [is] in mercy. [The amercement is] pardoned at the instance of J. de la Huse.

(amercement pardoned)

83. Henry de Donboyne was attached to answer Reginald Leance on a plea that on Wednesday next after the octaves of Trinity [30 May], Henry came to the town of Roxburgh and assaulted Reginald and wounded him in the head and the arm with a sword, to his damage etc. Henry is present and acknowledges the deed. Therefore he is condemned to prison until etc, and [makes] a fine of 12 pence.

(amercement 12 pence)

84. Robert Scot was attached to answer John Clerk the attorney of Richard de Whiteacre on a plea that ...   (r')

85. Augustinus le Mercer de Rokesburgh et Angnes uxor eius attachiati fuerunt ad respondendum Alano de Peniton de placito quare cum predicti Augustinus et Angnes supplicassent eidem Alano quod ipse manucaperet Ricardum filium eorum in prisona de Berwik detentum et fideliter promiserunt quod ipsi facerent eidem Alano similem securitatem quam ipse faceret domino regi pro predicta manucapcione predictus Alanus predictum Ricardum a predicta prisona per suam manucapcionem liberavit et securitatem quam sibi facere deberent pro manucapcione predicta secundum promissionem et convencionem inter eos factam facere non curant unde deterioratus est et dampnum habet etc. *Et inde producit sectam.* [Italicised words added in a different but still contemporary hand.]

Et predicti Augustinus et Angnes veniunt et defendunt vim et injuriam quando etc. Et dicunt quod nuncquam fecerunt talem convencionem cum predicto Alano. Et hoc petunt quod inquiratur. Et predictus Alanus similiter. Ideo preceptum est etc quod venire etc qui tam etc.

Postea predictus Alanus optulit se. Et predicti Augustinus et Angnes non venerunt. Ideo consideratum est quod plegii sui videlicet Johannes de Kellawe de Rokesburgh et Ricardus le Porter de eadem sunt in misericordia etc. Et preceptum est etc quod predicti Augustinus et Angnes attachiati per corpora. Postea per licenciam concordati sunt. Et predictus Augustinus finit pro se et plegiis suis dimidia marcae.

(misericordia dimidie marce)

Membrane 5r

Placita de deliberacione prisone apud Rokesburgh die jovis in septimana Pentecosti anno regni regis Edwardi xxiiii.

86. Thomas de Croft Robertus de Alverton Nicholaus de Greneweye Willelmus Spaner Henricus Stalgu et Robertus le Bole attachiati fuerunt pro eo quod ceperunt et vi abstulerunt de quadam muliere cervis et lac ad valenciam dimidie marce. Et super hoc per marescallum inculpati dicunt quod de predicto facto in nullo sunt culpabiles. Et de hoc ponunt se super patriam. Et juratores dicunt super sacramentum suum quod predicti Thomas et alii de predicto facto in nullo sunt culpabiles. Ideo inde quieti. (quieti)

85. Augustine the mercer of Roxburgh and Agnes his wife were attached to answer Alan de Peniton on a plea that when Augustine and Agnes beseeched Alan to stand surety for their son Richard, who was detained in prison in Berwick, and faithfully promised that they would in turn stand surety for Alan before the king in return for this mainprise, Alan duly stood surety for Richard and secured his release from prison. But the mainprise which they owed him in return according to their promise and to the agreement made between them they do not now wish to perform, so that he has been wronged and has suffered damage etc. Thereon he brings suit.

Augustine and Agnes come and deny force and injury when etc, and say that they never made any such agreement with Alan. They ask for enquiry to be made, as does Alan. Therefore [the sheriff] is ordered etc that he summon etc.

Later Alan presented himself and Augustine and Agnes have not come. Therefore it is considered that their sureties, namely John de Kellaw of Roxburgh and Richard the porter of the same place, [are] in mercy etc. [The sheriff] is ordered etc that Augustine and Agnes be attached in their persons. Later they are agreed by licence. Augustine makes a fine of one half mark for himself and his sureties. [*CDS*, ii, no. 822, p. 189.] (amercement one half mark)

Pleas of gaol delivery at Roxburgh on Thursday in Whitsun Week in the 24th year of the reign of King Edward [17 May 1296].

86. Thomas de Croft, Robert de Alverton, Nicholas de Greenway, William Spaner, Henry Stalgu and Robert le Bole were attached because they took and with force carried away from a woman beer and milk, value one half mark. Charged with this by the marshal they say that they are in no wise guilty of the deed, and put themselves on the country. The jurors say on their oath that Thomas and the others are in no wise guilty of the deed. Therefore [they are] acquitted. (acquitted)

87. Hugo de Overton Johannes Faber Hugo de Wylingdon attachiati fuerunt pro roberia unius tunice. Et super hoc inculpati dicunt quod sequebantur inimicos domini regis et quidam projecit unam tunicam precii i denarii et oboli et ita ceperunt illam tunicam et non aliter. Et de hoc posuerunt se super patriam. Et juratores dicunt super sacramentum suum quod predicti Hugo et alii ceperunt predictam tunicam in forma qua dicunt et non aliter. Ideo inde quieti.   (quieti)

88. Johannes de Fymer attachiatus fuit pro incendio cuiusdam grangie. Et super hoc inculpati dicit quod de predicto incendio non est culpabilis. Et de hoc ponit se super patriam. Et juratores dicunt super sacramentum suum quod predictus Johannes bonus est et fidelis et de predicto incendio non est culpabilis. Ideo inde quietus.   (quietus)

89. Johannes de Salton et Johannes le Porter Scotici attachiati fuerunt et per marescallum inculpati quod erant insidiatores regis Scocie et inimici domini regis. Et predicti Johannes et Johannes dicunt quod non sunt inde culpabiles. Et de hoc ponunt se super patriam. Et juratores dicunt super sacramentum suum quod non sunt inde culpabiles. Ideo inde quieti.   (quieti)

90. Thomas de Lovenne et Hugo filius Roberti attachiati fuerunt ad sectam Ade aurafabris de Rokesburgh. Et predicti Adam presens requisitus si aliquid vellet [sic] dicere versus predictos \Thomam/ et Hugonem dicit quod non. Et ideo predicti Thomas et Hugo inde quieti.   (quieti)

91. Johannes de Poclinton attachiatus ad sectam Johannis de Mintor optulit se versus Johannem de Minton centenarium. Et Johannes erat in servicio domini regis apud Geddewrth ut testificatum est. Ideo predictus Johannes inde quietus quousque Johannes de Minton venerit.   (quietus)

92. Willelmus allutarius de Novo Castro captus et in prisona detentus. Et nemo sequitur versus predictum Willelmum. Ideo quietus.   (quietus)

87. Hugh de Overton, John the smith [and] Hugh de Wylingdon were attached for the robbery of a tunic. Charged with this they say that they were pursuing the king's enemies when one of them threw away a tunic worth 1 penny halfpenny. They took the tunic in this way and did not acquire it by any other means. They put themselves on the country. The jurors say on their oath that Hugh and the others took the tunic in the manner they describe and not otherwise. Therefore [they are] acquitted.   (acquitted)

88. John de Fymer was attached for the firing of a grange. Charged with this he says that he is not guilty and he puts himself on the country. The jurors say on their oath that John is a good and loyal man and that he is not guilty of the firing. Therefore [he is] acquitted.   (acquitted)

89. John de Salton and John the porter, Scots, were attached and charged by the marshal with being spies of the Scottish king and enemies of the [English] king. John and John say that they are not guilty of the charge and they put themselves on the country. The jurors say on their oath that they are not guilty. Therefore [they are] acquitted.
                                                                 (acquitted)

90. Thomas de Lovenne [Lothian?] and Hugh son of Robert were attached at the suit of Adam the goldsmith of Roxburgh. Adam, who is present, is asked whether he wishes to say anything against Thomas and Hugh and he says not. Therefore Thomas and Hugh [are] acquitted.
                                                                 (acquitted)

91. John de Pocklington, attached at the suit of John de Minton, presented himself against the said John de Minton his centenar. It is attested that the latter is in the king's service at Jedburgh. Therefore John [is] acquitted until John de Minton shall come.   (acquitted)

92. William the leather-dresser of Newcastle [was] taken and detained in prison. No one sues William, therefore [he is] acquitted.
                                                                 (acquitted)

93. Aymerus de Rotherford sequitur versus marescallum pro ii equis attachiati per marescallum precii x solidorum. Et nullus ei vendicat nec sequitur pro ipsis. Ideo consideratum est quod predictus Aymerus recuperet predictos equos. Et eat inde quietus. (quietus)

94. Robertus de Shocton Thomas de Trickelawe Alanus de Meldon et Diota de Hexham attachiati et inculpati de pluribus latrociniis roberiis incendiis homicidiis et aliis malis. Et requisitur qualiter se velint acquietare dicunt quod sunt boni et fideles et de predictis in nullo culpabiles. Et de hoc ponunt se super patriam. Et juratores dicunt super sacramentum suum quod predicti Robertus Thomas Alanus et Diota sunt boni et fideles et in nullo super sibi inpositus culpabiles. Ideo inde quieti. (quieti)

95. Patricius de Wytingham Willelmus de Senton et Robertus de Maxton Scoti attachiati pro pluribus latrociniis roberiis homicidiis et aliis malis. Et super hiis inculpati dicunt quod boni et fideles et de nullo sibi inpositus culpabiles. Et de hoc ponunt se. Et juratores dicunt [last word written over an erasure] super sacramentum suum quod sunt boni et fideles. Ideo quieti. (quieti)

96. Robertus de Erceldon et Johannes Heremita attachiati ad sectam Henrici forestarii et Willelmi de Sutton et per eosdem inculpati quod die sabbati proxima ante festum sancti Trinitatis venerunt predicti Robertus et Johannes et ipsos spoliaverunt etc. Et juratores dicunt super sacramentum suum quod non erant culpabiles. Ideo quieti. (quieti)

97. Ricardus de Gatesheved attachiatus fuit ad respondendum Kenewyk Abdavid de placito transgressionis. Et unde queritur quod cum die jovis proxima post octabas Trinitatis venisset in via regis in villa de Rokesburgh venit predictus Ricardus et ipsum cum saltu precogitato insultavit et ipsum male vulneravit in capite cum quadam securi ad grave dampnum ipsius xx librarum et contra pacem etc. Et predictus Ricardus venit et defendit vim et injuriam quando etc. Et dicit quod ipse non venit nec predictum Kenewyk insultavit nec wlneravit [sic] sicut ei inposuit. Et hoc petit quod inquiratur. Et predictus Kenewyk similiter. Postea predictus Kenewyk non est prosecutus. Ideo in misericordia. (misericordia ii solidorum)

93. Aymer de Rotherford brings suit against the marshal for two horses, value 10 shillings, attached by the marshal. No one claims them or sues for them. Therefore it is considered that Aymer should recover the horses. He is acquitted. [*CDS*, ii, no. 822, p. 189.] (acquitted)

94. Robert de Shocton, Thomas de Trickelawe, Alan de Meldon and Diota de Hexham [were] attached and charged with numerous larcenies, robberies, arsons, homicides and other misdeeds. Asked how they wish to plead they say that they are good and loyal persons and are in no wise guilty, and they put themselves on the country. The jurors say on their oath that Robert, Thomas, Alan and Diota are good and loyal persons and that they are in no wise guilty of any of the charges laid against them. Therefore [they are] acquitted. (acquitted)

95. Patrick de Whittinghame, William de Senton and Robert de Maxton, Scots, [were] attached for numerous larcenies, robberies, homicides and other misdeeds. Charged with these they say that they are good and loyal men and are in no wise guilty of any of the charges laid against them. The jurors say on their oath that they are good and loyal men. Therefore [they are] acquitted. (acquitted)

96. Robert de Ercelden and John the hermit [were] attached at the suit of Henry the forester and William de Sutton, and charged by the latter with despoiling them on Saturday next before the feast of the holy Trinity [19 May]. The jurors say on their oath that they are are not guilty. Therefore [they are] acquitted. [*CDS*, ii, no. 822, pp. 189-90.] (acquitted)

97. Richard de Gateshead was attached to answer Cynwrig ap David on a plea of trespass. Whereon he complains that when on Thursday next after the octaves of Trinity [31 May] he came into the king's road in the town of Roxburgh, Richard came and with premeditated assault attacked him and wounded him in the head with an axe, to his grave damage of £20, and against the peace etc. Richard comes and denies force and injury when etc. He says that he did not come [there] nor did he assault or wound Cynwrig as the latter charged. He asks for enquiry to be made, as does Cynwrig. Later Cynwrig has not prosecuted, therefore [he is] in mercy. (amercement 2 shillings)

98. Willelmus Carpentarius de Cotingham attachiatus fuit ad respondendum Ricardo de Swyneburn de placito roberie. Et unde queritur quod die martis in septimana Pentecostes venit predictus Willelmus in curia Willelmi de Beyrmor juxta aquam in villa de Rokesburgh et ibidem quoddam jumentum precii xx solidorum et unam sellam precii iiii solidorum cepit et furtive abduxit ad dampnum ipsius Ricardi etc. Et predictus Ricardus [sic] venit et defendit vim et injuriam quando etc. Et quo ad sellam dicit quod eam emit in foro domini regis pro xii denarios. Et quo ad jumentum dicit quod predictum jumentum non cepit nec abduxit sicut ei inponit. Et hoc petit quod inquiratur. Et predictus Ricardus similiter. Et juratores dicunt super sacramentum suum quod predictus Willelmus emit predictam sellam in foro domini regis et eam maliciose non adquisivit. Et quo ad jumentum dicunt quod in nullo est culpabilis ideo quietus. Et predictus Ricardus in misericordia. Et condonatur per marescallum ad instanciam J. de Swyneburn.   (misericordia condonatur)

99. Elias Bercarius et Adam filius Thome Thomas filius Eustacii Robertus de Coppenhop Adam Russel Willelmus Wyly Willelmus filius Roberti attachiati et inprisonati. Et ad sectam domini regis inculpati super combustione ecclesiarum domorum in Anglia et super roberiis et latrociniis quamplurimis dicunt quod de combustione nec aliquo latrocinio sunt culpabiles. Et de hoc ponunt se. Et juratores dicunt super sacramentum suum quod predictus Elyas et omnes alii predicti de conbustione ecclesiarum et domorum et de pluribus latrociniis sibi inpositus sunt culpabiles. Ideo suspendantur.

(suspendantur)

100. Nigellus de Grillawe attachiatus fuit ad sectam domini regis per marescallum inculpatus de pluribus latrociniis et aliis maleficiis. Qui dicit quod est bonus et fidelis et super sibi inpositus in nullo culpabilis. Et de hoc ponit se. Et juratores dicunt super sacramentum suum quod est bonus et fidelis. Ideo quietus.   (quietus)

101. Walterus de Wylteshyr vintenarius Johannes de Berdeshey Robertus Cocus de Tyreswell et Galfridus de Wylindon vintenarii attachiati fuerunt pro regrateria et forstallia farine et aliorum

98. William the carpenter of Cotingham was attached to answer Richard de Swynburn on a plea of robbery. Whereon he complains that on Tuesday in Whitsun week [15 May] William came to the court of William de Beyrmor near the water in the town of Roxburgh and took and furtively led away from there a mare, value 20 shillings, and a saddle, value 4 shillings, to Richard's damage etc. Richard [sic] comes and denies force and injury when etc. With respect to the saddle he says that he bought it in the king's market for 12 pence. As to the mare, he did not take it or lead it away as the other charges. He asks for inquiry to be made, as does Richard. The jurors say on their oath that William bought the saddle in the king's market and did not acquire it by malicious means. With respect to the mare they say that he is in no wise guilty, therefore [he is] acquitted. Richard [is] in mercy. [The amercement is] pardoned by the marshal at the instance of J[ohn] de Swynburn.   (amercement pardoned)

99. Elias the shepherd, Adam son of Thomas, Thomas son of Eustace, Robert de Coppenhop, Adam Russel, William Wyly [and] William son of Robert [were] attached and imprisoned. Charged at the suit of the king with setting fire to churches [and] houses in England and with numerous robberies and larcenies, they say that they are not guilty of any burning or larceny and put themselves [on the country]. The jurors say on their oath that Elias and all the others are guilty of the burning of churches and houses, as well as of the numerous larcenies with which they are charged. Therefore [they are] to be hanged. [*CDS*, ii, no. 822, p. 190.]   (to be hanged)

100. Nigel de Grillawe was attached at the suit of the king by the marshal and charged with numerous larcenies and other misdeeds. He says that he is a good and loyal man and is in no wise guilty of any of the charges, and he puts himself [on the country]. The jurors say on their oath that he is a good and loyal man. Therefore [he is] acquitted.
                                                      (acquitted)

101. Walter de Wiltshire vintner, John de Berdeshey, Robert Cook of Tyrewell and Geoffrey de Wylindon vintners were attached for regrating and forestalling flour and other victuals. Charged with these

victuallium. Et super hoc inculpati non possunt hoc dedicere. Ideo ad prisonam quousque etc. Et finem xl denariorum.

(misericordia xl denariorum soluta)

102. Stephanus Erl et Simon de Thorn in vintenario Galfridi de Spitele in constabularia Johannis de Mens attachiati pro simili. Et non possunt hoc dedicere. Ideo ad prisonam quousque etc. Et finem xii denariorum.

(misericordia xii denariorum soluta)

103. Willelmus de Etringham attachiatus fuit pro simili non potest hoc dedicere. Ideo ad prisonam quousque etc. Finem vi denariorum.

(misericordia vi denariorum soluta)

Membrane 5d

Deliberacio gayole apud Edeneburgh et placita de excercitu domini regis ibidem die martis proxima post festum sancti Barnabe anno regni regis Edwardi xxiiii.

104. Robertus de Castello et Johannes de Morpath pro pugnacione attachiati fuerunt. Et concordati sunt extra curia ideo etc unde R. Clarel respondeat.

(finis ii solidorum)

105. Henricus serviens Ricardi Burnel attachiatus fuit pro pugnacione ad sectam Walteri de Stretton' fratris eius. Et concordati sunt ideo etc unde R. le Prisonarius respondeat.

(finis ii solidorum)

106. Robertus de Heleswith et Ricardus de Burford attachiati sunt pro pugnacione. Et concordati sunt ideo etc unde R. le Prisonarius respondeat.

(finis ii solidorum)

107. Henricus Bay attachiatus fuit ad sectam domini regis pro uno capicio a quodam homine ignoto capto et per ipsum occiso. Et predictus Henricus ponit se super juratores de bono et malo ideo etc. Et juratores dicunt quod non est culpabilis. Ideo quietus.

(quietus)

108. Dies datus est est [sic] inter Griffinum Crakeyl et socios suos homines comitis Heref' querelantes ex parte una et Warinum de

[offences] they are unable to deny them. Therefore [they are sent] to prison until etc and [make] a fine of 40 pence.

(amercement 40 pence, paid)

102. Stephen Erl and Simon de Thorn, in the *vintenarium* of Geoffrey le Spitele, in the constabulary of John de Mens, were attached for the same. They are unable to deny it. Therefore [they are] sent to prison until etc and [make] a fine of 12 pence. (amercement 12 pence, paid)

103. William de Etringham, attached for the same, is unable to deny it. Therefore [he is sent] to prison etc [and makes] a fine of 6 pence.

(amercement 6 pence, paid)

Gaol delivery at Edinburgh and pleas of the king's army in the same place on Tuesday next after the feast of St Barnabas in the 24th year of the reign of King Edward [12 June 1296].

104. Robert de Castello and John de Morpeth were attached for fighting. They are agreed outwith the court. Therefore [they make a fine] etc, for which R. Clarel answers. (fine 2 shillings)

105. Henry the servant of Richard Burnel was attached for fighting, at the suit of Walter de Stretton his brother. They are agreed, therefore [they make a fine] etc, for which R[obert] the gaoler answers.

(fine 2 shillings)

106. Robert de Heleswith and Richard de Burford are attached for fighting. They are agreed, therefore [they make a fine], for which R[obert] the gaoler answers. (fine 2 shillings)

107. Henry Bay was attached at the suit of the king for taking a cloak from an unknown man and for the slaughter of the man. Henry puts himself on the jurors for good and ill. Therefore etc. The jurors say that he is not guilty, therefore [he is] acquitted. (acquitted)

108. A day is given to Griffin Crakeyl and his fellows, the men of the earl of Hereford, plaintiffs on the one part, and Warin de Staundon and

Staundon et alios homines Nicholai de Audele defendentes ex altera usque ad proximum diem licet prece parcium. Postea per licenciam concordati sunt. Et Broyl de Turbervill ponit se. Plegii de misericordia Griffinus ap Res et Howel ap Eynon homines comitis Heref'. Condonatur ad instanciam domini Gilberti de Boun. (prece partium)

109. Kenewrek ap Madok Yhereward ap Oweyn inculpati sunt ad sectam domini regis pro quodam homicidium facto apud Geddwrth quod interfecerunt quendam Wallensem socium suum qui dicunt quod non sunt culpabiles. Et hoc ponunt se. Juratores dicunt super sacramentum suum quod \non/ sunt culpabiles. Ideo sunt quieti.

(quieti)

110. Willelmus de Halole queritur de Thoma de Werworth quod injuste cepit equum suum et abduxit.

111. Therenard Barth inculpatus fuit per dominum regem eo quod occidit Enyon Vathan Wallensem. Et ponit se. Juratores dicunt super sacramentum suum quod occidit predictum Enyon felonice. Et dicunt quod catalla nulla.   (suspendatur catalla nulla)

112. Thomas Brenel attachiatus fuit ad sectam Ricardi de Hereford. Et petierunt prece parcium ita quod concordati sunt. Et predictus Ricardus posuit se in misericordia. Robertus Prisonarius respondeat.

(misericordia xii denariorum)

113. David ap Kenewrek attachiatus fuit ad sectam Henrici de Lancastre. Et unde queritur quod idem David cepit equum predicti Henrici die veneris proxima ante festum sancti Barnabe apostoli in campo de Edeneburgh contra pacem domini regis ad grave dampnum predicti Henrici dimidie marce. Et predictus David venit et defendit vim et injuriam dampnum etc. Et dicit quod emit predictum equum apud Karlel eo tempore quam Wallenses venerunt in partibus Scocie. Et hoc petit quod inquiratur. Et predictus Henricus similiter. Ideo ad inquisicionem.   (inquisicio)

other men of Nicholas de Audley, defendants on the other part, on the following day at the request of the parties. Later they are agreed by licence. Broyl de Turberville puts himself [on the country]. The sureties for amercement [are] Griffin ap Rees and Howel ap Eynon, men of the earl of Hereford. [The amercement is] pardoned at the instance of Sir Gilbert de Bohun. (at the request of the parties)

109. Cynwrig ap Madog [and] Iorwerth ap Owen were charged at the suit of the king with a homicide done at Jedburgh, [namely] for killing one of their fellows, a Welshman. They say that they are not guilty and put themselves [on the country]. The jurors say on their oath that they are not guilty. Therefore they are acquitted. (acquitted)

110. William de Halole brings a suit against Thomas de Werworth that he illegally took and led away his horse.

111. Therenard Barth was charged by the king because he slew the Welshman Enyon Vathan. He puts himself [on the country]. The jurors say on their oath that he killed Enyon feloniously. They say that [he has] no chattels. (to be hanged; no chattels)

112. Thomas Brenel was attached at the suit of Richard de Hereford. [An adjournment] was sought at the request of the parties, and they were agreed. Richard put himself in mercy. Robert the gaoler answers [for it]. (amercement 12 pence)

113. David ap Cynwrig was attached at the suit of Henry de Lancaster. Whereon he complains that on Friday next before the feast of St Barnabas the apostle [8 June] David took a horse of his from the field in Edinburgh, against the king's peace, to Henry's grave damage of one half mark. David comes and denies force, injury and damage etc. He says that he bought the horse at Carlisle, at the time when the Welshmen came to Scotland. He asks for enquiry to be made, as does Henry. Therefore [the matter is put] to an inquest. [*CDS*, ii, no. 822, p. 190.] (inquest)

Deliberacio gaole apud Stryvelyn die martis proxima ante festum sancti Johannis Baptiste anno regni regis Edwardi xxiiii.

114. Willelmus de Lonesdale captus fuit quia fregit prisonam apud Ross'. Et requisitus fuit qualiter evasit a prisona predictus Willelmus respondit quod per ostium apertum exivit propter defectum cibi et fu[g]it in partibus Scocie. Requisitur si venit ad pacem domini regis Anglie in partibus Scocie dicit quod non. Ideo etc.   (suspendatur)

115. Thomas Capellanus de Edeneburgh attachiatus fuit quia excommunicavit dominum regem Anglie publice campana et candela. Et hoc concedit coram marescallo se fecisse in despectu domini regis. Ideo ad voluntatem domini regis. Et Ricardus Gulle eo modo quia pulsavit campanam in despectu regis. Postea deliberati sunt ad archidiaconum de Lones' per preceptum regis.   (liberantur)

116. Thomas de Wollor attachiatus fuit per tesaurarium quia fuit vyntenarius et noluit venire ad monstracionem domini regis. Et habuit penitenciam. Ideo deliberatus fuit quietus. Ideo etc.   (quietus)

117. Yereward Walt attachiatus est ad sectam Radulphi filii Radulphi pro morte cuiusdam hominis. Plegii de prosequendo Willelmus Athelston et Rogerus le Heyward.

Deliberacio gaole apud Cluny die jovis in vigilia apostolorum Petri et Pauli anno regni regis E. xxiiii.

118. Willelmus de Cestria attachiatus quia inventus erat noctanter warardem [?]. Et inculpatus erat quod erat insidiator domini regis dicit quod non est culpabilis. Et de hoc ponit se super patriam. Et juratores dicunt super sacramentum suum quod bonus est et fidelis et in nullo culpabilis. Ideo quietus.   (quietus)

119. Yereword Wallensis attachiatus pro morte cuiusdam Willelmi filii Johannis. Et ad sectam domini regis super hoc inculpatus dicit quod de

Gaol delivery at Stirling on Tuesday next before the feast of the Nativity of St John the Baptist in the 24th year of the reign of King Edward [19 June 1296].

114. William de Lonesdale was taken because he broke prison at Ross'. When asked how he escaped from prison William answers that he left by the open door because of lack of food and went to Scotland. Asked if in Scotland he came to the peace of the king of England, he says no. Therefore etc. [*CDS*, ii, no. 822, p. 190.] (to be hanged)

115. Thomas the chaplain of Edinburgh was attached because he excommunicated the lord king of England publicly with bell and candle. He confesses before the marshal that he did this in contempt of the king. Therefore [he is] at the king's will. The same for Richard Gulle, because he rang the bell in contempt of the king. Later they are delivered to the archdeacon of Lothian by command of the king. [*CDS*, ii, no. 822, p. 190.] (delivered)

116. Thomas de Wooler was attached by the treasurer because he was a vintenar and refused to come to the king's muster. He was put to *peine forte et dure*, then released as acquitted. Therefore etc. (acquitted)

117. Iorwerth Walt is attached at the suit of Ralph son of Ralph for the death of a man. His sureties for prosecuting [are] William Athelston and Roger le Hayward.

Gaol delivery at Clunie on Thursday the eve of [the feast of] the apostles Peter and Paul in the 24th year of the reign of King E[dward] [28 June 1296].

118. William de Chester [was] attached because he was found [keeping watch?] at night. Charged with being a spy he says that he is not guilty and puts himself on the country. The jurors say on their oath that he is a good and loyal man and is not guilty. Therefore [he is] acquitted. (acquitted)

119. Iorwerth the Welshman [was] attached at the suit of the king for the death of one William son of John. Charged with this he says that he

morte predicti Willelmi non est culpabilis. Et de hoc ponit se super patriam. Et juratores dicunt super sacramentum suum quod predictus Yereward de morte predicti Willelmi non est culpabilis. Ideo quietus.

(quietus)

120. Johannes de Chatton attachiatus fuit ad respondendum Willelmo de Dureme de placito transgressionis. Et unde queritur quod injuste detinet eiusdem Willelmo unum gladium quem in custodia sua invenit ad dampnum etc. Et predictus Johannes dicit quod emit predictum gladium in foro domini regis ad villam Sancti Johannis. Et hoc petit quod inquiratur. Et predictus Willelmus similiter. Et juratores dicunt super sacramentum suum quod predictus Johannes emit predictum gladium in foro domini regis ut predixit. Ideo consideratum \est/ quod predictus Willelmus recuperet gladium suum. Et predictus Johannes quia emit predictum gladium eat inde quietus.   (quietus)

121. Radulphus de Hibernia attachiatus fuit ad respondendum Johanni Lovel de placito quare cum predictus Johannes venisset apud Edneburgh ad pacificandum contencionem inter Wallenses et Anglicos venit predictus Radulphus et dextrarium ipsius Johannis sub ipso wlneravit [sic] ad dampnum ipsius etc. Et predictus Radulphus venit et defendit vim et injuriam quando etc. Et dicit quod dextrarium predicti Johannis non wlneravit [sic]. Et hoc petit quod inquiratur. Et predictus Johannes similiter. Et juratores dicunt super sacramentum suum predictus Radulphus dextrarium predicti Johannis vulneravit sicut eum inculpavit. Ideo predictus Radulphus adjudicatur prisone quousque etc.

(prisone)

122. Simon le Chapman et Adam de Kendale attachiati fuerunt ad respondendum Brydok de Scratburg de placito roberie. Et unde queritur quod predicti Simon et Adam venerunt ad ecclesiam Novem Puellarum et dictam ecclesiam fregerunt contra defensionem domini regis ac bona sua ibidem inventa videlicet lanam et ollas eneas ad valenciam xl solidorum furtive asportaverunt ad dampnum ipsius B. et contra pacem etc. Et predicti Simon et Adam veniunt et defendunt vim et injuriam quando etc. Et dicunt quod de fractione dicte ecclesie nec de asportacione bonorum predicte B. in nullo sunt culpabiles. Et de hoc ponunt se. Et predicta B. similiter. Et juratores dicunt super

is not guilty of the death of William and puts himself on the country. The jurors say on their oath that Iorwerth is not guilty of the death of William. Therefore [he is] acquitted. (acquitted)

120. John de Chatton was attached to answer William de Durham on a plea of trespass. Whereon he complains that John illegally withholds from him a sword which he found in John's keeping, to his damage etc. John says that he bought the sword in the king's market in Perth. He asks for enquiry to be made, as does William. The jurors say on their oath that John bought the sword in the king's market as he said. Therefore it is considered that William should recover the sword. John, because he [also] bought the sword, is acquitted. (acquitted)

121. Ralph de Ireland was attached to answer John Lovel on a plea that when John came to Edinburgh to settle the dispute between the Welsh and the English, Ralph came and wounded John's destrier under him, to his damage etc. Ralph comes and denies force and injury when etc, and says that he did not wound John's destrier. He asks for enquiry to be made, as does John. The jurors say on their oath that Ralph wounded John's destrier as the latter charged him. Therefore Ralph is condemned to prison until etc. [*CDS*, ii, no. 822, p. 190.] (to prison)

122. Simon the chapman and Adam de Kendale were attached to answer Brydok de Scratburg on a plea of robbery. Whereon she complains that Simon and Adam broke into the church of the Nine Maidens in defiance of the king's protection and furtively carried off goods which they found there, namely wool and brass pots worth 40 shillings, to B[rydok's] damage and against the peace etc. Simon and Adam come and deny force and injury when etc, and say that they are not guilty of the breaking of the church or of the carrying off of B[rydok's] goods. They put themselves [on the country], as does B[rydok]. The jurors say on their oath that S[imon] and A[dam] are not

sacramentum suum quod predicti Simon et Adam non sunt culpabiles.
Ideo consideratum est quod predicti S. et A. eant inde quieti. Et predicta
B. pro falso clamore in misericordia. Condonatur quia pauper.

(condonatur quia pauper)

Membrane 6r

**Deliberacio gaole apud Forfare die jovis proxima post festum
apostolorum Petri et Pauli anno regni regis E. xxiiii.**

**Deliberacio prisone apud Forfare die jovis proxima post festum
apostolorum Petri et Pauli anno regni regis E. xxiiii[to].**

123. Patricius de Hibernia attachiatus fuit ad sectam Roberti Benedicite
de placito roberie. Et unde queritur quod die mercurii proxima post
festum apostolorum Petri et Pauli venit predictus Patricius apud Forfare
et seudam suam fregit et flammeas iii duodecim precii xii solidorum
furtive cepit et asportavit ad dampnum etc. Et predictus Patricius venit
et defendit vim et injuriam quando etc. Et dicit quod quidam armiger
comitis de Hulestr' emit predictas flammeas et eas sibi tradidit
custodiendas et quod non furtive eas nec maliciose adquisivit. Petit
quod inquiratur. Et predictus Robertus similiter. Et juratores dicunt
super sacramentum suum quod predictus Patricius furtive cepit
predictas flammeas sicut ei impositum est. Ideo etc. Requisitur de
catalla dicunt quod catalla nulla.　　　(suspendatur catalla nulla)

124. Henricus Brodfot appellatus pro morte cuiusdam Johannis de
Kestevene ad sectam cuiusdam Willelmi filii predicti Johannis qui infra
etatem est. Et super hoc inculpatus dicit quod in nullo est culpabilis. Et
de hoc ponit se super patriam. Et juratores dicunt super sacramentum
suum quod predictus Henricus de morte predicti Johannis non est
culpabilis. Ideo inde quietus.　　　　　　　　　　　(quietus)

125. Thomas le Barber et Mychael le Schymere appellati de roberia ad
sectam Johannis Poleyn. Et unde queritur quod predicti Thomas et
Michael venerunt apud Forfare die mercurii proxima post festum

guilty. Therefore it is considered that S[imon] and A[dam] are acquitted. B[rydok] is in mercy for a false claim. [The amercement is] pardoned because [she is] a pauper. [*CDS*, ii, no. 822, p. 190.]

(pardoned because [she is] a pauper)

Gaol delivery at Forfar on Thursday next after the feast of the apostles Peter and Paul in the 24th year of the reign of King E[dward] [5 July 1296].

Gaol delivery at Forfar on Thursday next after the feast of the apostles Peter and Paul in the 24th year of the reign of King E[dward] [5 July 1296].

123. Patrick de Ireland was attached at the suit of Robert Benedicite on a plea of robbery. Whereon he complains that on Wednesday next after the feast of the apostles Peter and Paul [4 July] Patrick came to Forfar and broke into his shop and furtively took and carried off three dozen kerchiefs, value 12 shillings, to his damage etc. Patrick comes and denies force and injury when etc. He says that an esquire of the earl of Ulster bought the kerchiefs and gave them to him for safekeeping, and that he did not acquire them by furtive or malicious means. He asks for enquiry to be made, as does Robert. The jurors say on their oath that Patrick furtively took the kerchiefs as he is charged. Therefore etc. Asked about his chattels they say that [he has] none. [*CDS*, ii, no. 822, p. 190.]   (to be hanged; no chattels)

124. Henry Broadfoot [was] appealed of the death of one John de Kesteven at the suit of John's son William, who is under age. Charged with this he says that he is in no wise guilty and puts himself on the country. The jurors say on their oath that Henry is not guilty of the death of John. Therefore [he is] acquitted.   (acquitted)

125. Thomas the barber and Michael le Schymere [were] appealed of robbery at the suit of John Poleyn. Whereon he complains that on Wednesday next after the feast of the apostles Peter and Paul [4 July]

D

apostolorum Petri et Pauli et ab eodem furtive ceperunt iiii libras vii solidos et asportaverunt ad grave dampnum ipsius etc et contra pacem.

Et predicti Thomas et Michael venerunt [a second 'venerunt' crossed out] et defenderunt vim et injuriam quando etc. Et dicunt quod predictam pecuniam a predicto Johanne non ceperunt nec asportaverunt sicut inculpati. Et de hoc ponunt se. Et predictus Johannes similiter.

Et juratores dicunt super sacramentum suum quod predicti Thomas et Michael de predicto facto non sunt culpabiles. Ideo inde quieti. Et predictus Johannes adjudicatur prisone quousque etc. Et finivit ii solidos unde R. Prisonarius respondeat.

(prisone misericordia ii solidorum soluta W. Bacon)

126. Ricardus de Pulisdon attachiatus et inculpatus quod depredaverat in terra pacis post proclamacionem et contra defensionem domini regis. Qui dicit quod non post proclamacionem. Et de hoc ponit se. Et juratores dicunt super sacramentum suum quod super sibi inpositus non est culpabilis. Ideo quietus. (quietus)

127. Mauricius Brun attachiatus fuit ad respondendum Margerie de Ledes de placita felonie. Et unde queritur quod die lune proxima post festum sancti Johannis Baptiste anno regni regis E. xxiiii venit predictus Mauricius apud villam Sancti Johannis in domo predicte Margerie et quoddam jumentum album in eodem cepit et abduxit quod quidem jumentum Ricardus de Ledes maritus suus sequebatur. Et predictus Mauricius ipsum interfecit unde predicta Margeria predictum Mauricium appellat de morte predicti Ricardi viri sui etc. Et predictus Mauricius venit et defendit vim et injuriam quando etc. Et dicit quod de morte predicti Ricardi nec de roberia predicti jumenti est culpabilis. Et de hoc ponit se. Et predicta Margeria similiter. Et juratores dicunt super sacramentum suum quod predictus Mauricius in nullo est culpabilis. Ideo inde quietus. Et predicta Margeria adjudicatur prisone quousque etc. Postea condonatur quia pauper. (condonatur quia pauper)

Deliberacio prisone apud Aberden die mercurie proxima ante festum sancte Margarete virginis anno regni regis E. xxiiii.

128. Johannes Page captus et inprisonatus. Et quia nullus sequitur versus predictum Johannem ideo quietus.

Thomas and Michael came to Forfar and furtively took and carried off £4 7 shillings, to his grave damage etc and against the peace.

Thomas and Michael came and denied force and injury when etc, and say that they did not take or carry off the money from John as they are charged. They put themselves [on the country], as does John.

The jurors say on their oath that Thomas and Michael are not guilty of the deed and [are] therefore acquitted. John is condemned to prison until etc. He makes a fine of 2 shillings, for which R[obert] the gaoler answers.   (to prison; amercement 2 shillings, paid to W. Bacon)

126. Richard de Pulisdon [was] attached and charged for plundering within lands protected by [the king's] peace subsequent to the proclamation, and in violation of the protection of the king. He says that he did not [do so] after the proclamation [had been made], and puts himself [on the country]. The jurors say on their oath that he is not guilty of the charge. Therefore [he is] acquitted.   (acquitted)

127. Maurice Brown was attached to answer Margery de Leeds on a plea of felony. Whereon she complains that on Monday next after the feast of St John the Baptist in the 24th year of the reign of King E[dward] [25 June 1296] Maurice came to Margery's house in Perth and took and led away a white mare. Richard de Leeds, her husband, pursued the mare and Maurice killed him, whereon Margery appeals him of the death of her husband. Maurice comes and denies force and injury when etc, and says that he is not guilty of the death of Richard or of the robbery of the mare. He puts himself [on the country], as does Margery. The jurors say on their oath that Maurice is in no wise guilty and [is] therefore acquitted. Margery is condemned to prison until etc. Later [the amercement is] pardoned because [she is] a pauper.

(pardoned because [she is] a pauper)

Gaol delivery at Aberdeen on Wednesday next before the feast of St Margaret the virgin in the 24th year of the reign of King E[dward] [18 July 1296].

128. John Page [was] taken and imprisoned. And because no one sues John, therefore [he is] acquitted.

129. Henricus le Wodeward Willelmus le Charettarius Willelmus de Berneston Henricus le Tene et Johannes Organ attachiati fuerunt pro morte cuiusdam Wallensis interfecti apud Rokesburgh videlicet de comitiva comitis Hereford'. Et super hoc in presencia senescalli inculpati dicunt quod de morte predicti Wallensis non sunt culpabiles. Et de hoc ponunt se. Et juratores dicunt super sacramentum suum quod predicti Henricus et alii de morte predicti Wallensis non sunt culpabiles. Ideo inde quieti.   (quieti)

Deliberacio prisone apud Elgyn die sabbati proxima post festum sancti Jacobi apostoli anno regni regis E. xxiiii.

130. Petrus Mercator de Burgo et Willelmus Mercator de Castro Bernardi attachiati ad sectam domini regis pro roberia pannorum et lane. Et Robertus le Smyth et Johannes Ossor attachiati pro roberia farine. Et Johannes de la Neyland attachiatus pro roberia lane. Et omnes prenominati attachiati ad sectam domini regis super predictis roberiis inculpati dicunt quod emerunt predictos pannos lanam et farinam in foro domini regis et quod aliter non adquisierunt. Ponunt se. Et juratores dicunt super sacramentum suum quod predicti Petrus et alii de predictis roberiis non sunt culpabiles. Ideo inde quieti.   (quieti)

131. Urgane et Hugo de Suhtthorp attachiati ad sectam domini regis super roberiis et latrociniis in sancta ecclesia factis inculpati dicunt quod de predictis roberiis non sunt culpabiles. Et de hoc ponunt se super patriam. Et juratores dicunt super sacramentum suum quod de predictis roberiis non sunt culpabiles. Ideo inde quieti.   (quieti)

132. Yhuwan de Gelthygaer attachiatus fuit pro morte cuiusdam pueri nomine Johannis. Et ad sectam domini regis super hoc inculpatus dicit quod de morte predicti Johannis non est culpabilis. Et de hoc ponit se. Et juratores dicunt super sacramentum suum quod predictus Yhuwan de morte predicti Johannis non est culpabilis. Ideo inde quietus.

                                                              (quietus)

129. Henry the woodward, William the carter, William de Berneston, Henry le Tene and John Organ were attached for the death of a Welshman killed in Roxburgh, namely [one] of the company of the earl of Hereford. Charged with the offence in the presence of the steward they say that they are not guilty of the death of the Welshman and put themselves [on the country]. The jurors say on their oath that Henry and the others are not guilty of the death of the Welshman and [are] therefore acquitted. (acquitted)

Gaol delivery at Elgin on Saturday next after the feast of St James the apostle in the 24th year of the reign of King E[dward] [28 July 1296].

130. Peter merchant of Burgh and William merchant of Barnard Castle [were] attached at the suit of the king for the robbery of lengths of cloth and wool. Robert the smith and John Ossor [were] attached for the robbery of flour. John de la Neyland [was] attached for the robbery of wool. All the aforenamed, attached at the suit of the king and charged, say that they bought the lengths of cloth, the wool and the flour in the king's market, and that they did not acquire them by any other means. They put themselves [on the country]. The jurors say on their oath that Peter and the others are not guilty, therefore [they are] acquitted. (acquitted)

131. Urgane and Hugh de Souththorp, attached at the suit of the king [and] charged with robberies and larcenies done in holy church, say that they are not guilty of the robberies and put themselves on the country. The jurors say on their oath that they are not guilty of the robberies. Therefore [they are] acquitted. (acquitted)

132. Ieuan de Gelthygaer [was] attached for the death of a boy named John. Charged with this at the suit of the king he says that he is not guilty of the death of John and puts himself [on the country]. The jurors say on their oath that Ieuan is not guilty of the death of John. Therefore [he is] acquitted. (acquitted)

133. Thomas Dun attachiatus pro roberia librorum et vestimentorum. Et super hoc ad sectam domini regis inculpatus dicit quod invenit predictos libros absconditos in terra et quod eos non furavit. Ponit se. Et juratores dicunt super sacramentum suum quod predictus Thomas furavit predictos libros et vestimenta in sancta ecclesia. Ideo suspendatur. (suspendatur)

Membrane 6d

Deliberacio prisone apud Kyndromy die mercurie in festo beati Petri quod dicitur advincula anno regni regis E. xxiiii.

134. Willelmus de Novo Castro et Robertus de Wodestok attachiati fuerunt ad sectam Ade de Caldewell Scotico de placito felonie. Et unde predictus Adam queritur quod predicti Willelmus et Robertus venerunt et ab eodem vi ceperunt x solidos et furtive asportaverunt ad dampnum ipsius dimidie marce et contra pacem etc.

Et predicti W. et R. veniunt et defendunt vim et injuriam quando etc. Et dicunt quod de predicto Ade nullum denarium ceperunt. Et de hoc ponunt se. Et predictus Adam similiter. Et juratores dicunt super sacramentum suum quod predicti W. et R. de predicto facto non sunt culpabiles. Ideo inde quieti. Et predictus Adam in misericordia. Condonatur quia pauper. (misericordia condonatur quia pauper)

135. Willelmus de Rotheys attachiatus fuit ad sectam domini regis quia duxit Johannem de Morers ubi fuit occisus. Et super morte predicti Johannis inculpatus dicit quod de morte predicti Johannis non est culpabilis. Et de hoc ponit se. Et juratores dicunt super sacramentum suum quod erat culpabilis de morte predicti Johannis. Ideo suspendatur. (suspendatur catalla nulla)

Deliberacio prisone apud Sanctum Johannem de Perth die mercurii proxima ante festum sancti Laurencii anno regni regis E. xxiiii.

136. Matheus de Eboraco attachiatus fuit ad respondendum Cristiane de Sancto Johanne de placito roberie. Et unde queritur quod die jovis

133. Thomas Dun [was] attached for the robbery of books and vestments. Charged with this at the suit of the king he says that he found the books hidden in the ground and that he did not steal them. He puts himself [on the country]. The jurors say on their oath that Thomas stole the books and vestments in holy church. Therefore [he is] to be hanged. [*CDS*, ii, no. 822, p. 190.]   (to be hanged)

Gaol delivery at Kildrummy on Wednesday the feast of the blessed Peter's Chains in the 24th year of the reign of King E[dward] [1 August 1296].

134. William de Newcastle and Robert de Woodstock were attached at the suit of Adam de Caldwell, Scot, on a plea of felony. Whereon he complains that William and Robert came, forcibly took and furtively carried off 10 shillings, to his damage of one half mark and against the peace etc.

W[illiam] and R[obert] come and deny force and injury when etc, and say that they did not take any money from Adam. They put themselves [on the country], as does Adam. The jurors say on their oath that W[illiam] and R[obert] are not guilty of the deed. Therefore they [are] acquitted. Adam [is] in mercy. [The amercement is] pardoned because [he is] a pauper.   (amercement pardoned because [he is] a pauper)

135. William de Rothes was attached at the suit of the king because he led John de Morers to the place where the latter was slain. Charged with the death of John he says that he is not guilty and puts himself [on the country]. The jurors say on their oath that he is guilty of the death of John. Therefore [he is] to be hanged.   (to be hanged; no chattels)

Gaol delivery at Perth on Wednesday next before the feast of St Lawrence in the 24th year of the reign of King E[dward] [8 August 1296].

136. Matthew de York was attached to answer Christine de Perth on a plea of robbery. Whereon she complains that on Thursday next before

proxima ante festum sancti Botulphi anno predicto venit predictus Matheus ad villam Sancti Johannis predictam in societate cuiusdam furis Willelmi le Waleys et in domo sua in eadem villa bona et catalla sua ibidem inventa videlicet cervisiam precii iii solidorum cepit et furtive asportavit contra voluntatem suam ad dampnum ipsius Cristiane etc et contra pacem. Et inde producit sectam etc.

Et predictus Matheus dicit quod non tenetur predicte Cristiane respondere eo quod clericus est. Ideo capiatur inquisicio ex efficio. Et juratores dicunt super sacramentum suum quod predictus Matheus venit ad predictam \villam/ in societate predicti Willelmi et bona ipsius Cristiane asportavit sicut eum inculpavit. Ideo adjudicatur ad penitentiam.

Membrane 7r

Placita excercitus domini regis apud Edenburgh die veneris proxima ante festum sancti Barnabe apostoli anno regni regis E. xxiiii^{to}.

137. Eynonus Day attachiatus fuit ad respondendum Ricardo Sparhauk de placito transgressionis. Postea remittitur per W. de Haukwele ad instanciam domini Willelmi de la Pole.   (misericordia condonatur)

138. Ythel Abkaclyn de Albo Monasterio attachiatus fuit Rogero valetto Johannis de Swyneburn de placito transgressionis. Postea per licenciam concordati sunt. Et predictus Ythel ponit se. Et finem ii solidorum.   (misericordia ii solidorum soluta)

139. Johannes le Ferrur attachiatus fuit ad respondendum Nicholao de Cateby de placito injuste subrepcionis unius equi. Et ibidem Johannes optulit se. Et predictus Nicholaus non est prosecutus. Ideo ipse et plegium suum de prosequendo in misericordia videlicet Willelmus Fraunceis.   (misericordia xii denariorum soluta)

140. David Gam attachiatus fuit ad respondendum Ricardo de Hale de placito transgressionis. Et unde queritur quod injuste ei subripuit unam supertunicam stragulatam apud Le Whele ad dampnum ipsius etc.

Et predictus David venit et defendit vim etc. Et dicit quod fideliter

the feast of St Botulph in the said year [14 June 1296] Matthew came to Perth in the company of a thief named William le Waleys and took and furtively carried off against her wishes goods and chattels which he found in her house, namely beer, value 3 shillings, to Christine's damage etc and against the peace. Thereon she brings suit etc.

Matthew says that he is not bound to answer Christine because he is a clerk. Therefore an inquest is taken. The jurors say on their oath that Matthew came to the town in the company of William and that he carried off Christine's goods as she charged him. Therefore he is condemned to penance. [CDS, ii, no. 822, p. 191.]

Pleas of the king's army at Edinburgh on Friday next before the feast of St Barnabas the apostle in the 24th year of the reign of King E[dward] [8 June 1296].

137. Eynonus Day was attached to answer Richard Sparhauk on a plea of trespass. Later [the case] is adjourned by W. de Haukeswell at the instance of Sir William de la Pole.   (amercement pardoned)

138. Ythel ab Kaclyn of Whitchurch was attached [to answer] Roger the servant of John de Swynburn on a plea of trespass. Later they are agreed by licence. Ythel puts himself [on the country]. [He makes] a fine of 2 shillings.   (amercement 2 shillings, paid)

139. John the smith was attached to answer Nicholas de Cateby on a plea of illegal robbery of a horse. John presented himself but Nicholas has not prosecuted. Therefore he and his surety for prosecuting, namely William Fraunceis, [are] in mercy.
                         (amercement 12 pence, paid)

140. David Gam was attached to answer Richard de Hale on a plea of trespass. Whereon he complains that David illegally robbed him of a striped surcoat at Wheelkirk [the obsolete parish west of Southdean, Roxburghshire], to his damage etc.

emit predictam supertunicam in foro domini regis de Gedeworth pro xvi denarios et non maliciose adquisivit. Et hoc petit quod inquiratur. Et predictus Ricardus similiter.

Et jurati dicunt super sacramentum suum quod predictus David maliciose furavit predictam supertunicam ut fur. Requisiti de predicto dicunt quod valet ix denarii. Ideo ad prisonam quousque etc.

(prisone misericordia xii denariorum)

141. Petrus de Mompelers Robertus serviens Gilberti Alanus de Henton Eustachius Mowere Gilbertus Coliere et Walterus de Fernacles appellaverunt Meuricum Abeuan Walensem de morte cuiusdam Willelmi socii eorum de subrepcione unius tunice et unius ensis. Et predictus Petrus et alii non sunt de [sic] prosecuti et quilibet eorum fuit plegium alterius. Et non sunt prosecuti. Ideo capiantur.

Et quo ad sectam domini regis dicit quod est bonus et fidelis et in nullo culpabilis. Et de hoc ponit se. Et juratores dicunt super sacramentum suum quod bonus est et fidelis et in nullo culpabilis. Ideo inde quietus. (capti quietus)

142. Willelmus le Vielur et Matillda de Waketon attachiati fuerunt ad respondendum Meurico quid [sic] de placito transgressionis. Et unde queritur quod die sabbati proxima ante quindenam Trinitatis venit predictus Willelmus et sagittavit ad eum et ipse male vulneravit ad grave dampnum ipsius Meuricii et contra pacem etc.

Et predictus Willelmus dicit quod ad predictum Meuricum non sagittavit nec ipsum vulneravit sicut ei inculpavit. Et hoc petit quod inquiratur. Et predictus Meuricus similiter. Et juratores dicunt quod super sacramentum suum predictus Willelmus et Matillda non sunt culpabiles sed siquid fecerunt hoc fecerunt vim vi repellendo. Ideo consideratum est quod predicti Willelmus et Matillda eant inde quieti. Et predictus Mauricus in misericordia. Plegius dominus Johannes le Estraunge. (misericordia xii denariorum)

143. Thomas Davy attachiatus fuit ad respondendum Thome Etecal de placito quod idem Thomas Davy injuste cepit et detinet ei unum equum precii quinque solidorum etc. Et predictus Thomas Davy venit et

David comes and denies force etc. He says that he bought the surcoat in good faith in the king's market in Jedburgh for 16 pence, and that he did not acquire it by malicious means. He asks for enquiry to be made, as does Richard.

The jurors say on their oath that David maliciously stole the surcoat and that he is a thief. Asked about its value they say that it is worth 9 pence. Therefore [he is sent] to prison until etc. [*CDS*, ii, no. 822, p. 191.] (to prison; amercement 12 pence)

141. Peter de Mompelers, Robert the servant of Gilbert, Alan de Henton, Eustace Mowere, Gilbert the collier and Walter de Fernacles appealed Meuric ab Ewan Welshman of the death of their fellow William [and] of the robbery of a tunic and a sword. Peter and the others have not prosecuted, and as each stood surety for the other and none has prosecuted, therefore they are to be taken.

With respect to the suit of the king, he [Meuric] says that he is a good and loyal man and is in no wise guilty, and he puts himself [on the country]. The jurors say on their oath that he is a good and loyal man and is in no wise guilty. Therefore [he is] acquitted.

(taken; acquitted)

142. William le Vielur and Maud de Waketon were attached to answer Meuric on a plea of trespass. Whereon he complains that on Saturday before the quindene of Trinity [2 June] William came and shot at him with a bow and seriously injured him, to Meuric's damage and against the peace etc.

William says that he neither shot at Meuric with the bow nor injured him as the latter charged. He asks for enquiry to be made, as does Meuric. The jurors say on their oath that William and Maud are not guilty but that if they did do this, they did it in self-defence. Therefore it is considered that William and Maud are acquitted. Meuric [is] in mercy. His surety [is] Sir John le Strange. (amercement 12 pence)

143. Thomas Davy was attached to answer Thomas Etecal on a plea that Thomas Davy illegally took and withholds from him a horse worth 5 shillings etc. Thomas Davy comes and denies force and injury

defendit vim et injuriam quando etc. Dicit quod emit predictum equum in foro domini regis de Edenburgh pro denariis suis et non maliciose adquisivit. Et hoc petit quod inquiratur. Et predictus Thomas\Etecal/ dicit quod ipse erat verus possessor predicti equi ante adventum domini regis apud Edenburgh. Et hoc petit quod inquiratur. Et juratores dicunt super sacramentum suum quod predictus Thomas Etecal erat verus possessor predicti equi set dicunt quod predictus Thomas Davy emit predictum equum in foro domini regis ut predixit. Ideo consideratum est quod predictus Thomas Etecal recuperet suum equum. Et predictus Thomas Davi qui [sic] emit predictum equum quietus.   (quietus)

144. Robertus de Merilou attachiatus fuit ad respondendum Willelmo de Cressingham de placito quod idem Robertus injuste cepit et detinet ei unum equum precii iiii solidorum qui quidem equus a custodia sua erat alienatus fere per unam septimanam unde dampnum habet etc.

Et predictus Robertus venit et defendit vim et injuriam quando etc. Et dicit quod emit predictum equum fideliter pro suis denariis in foro domini regis de Edenburgh. Et hoc petit quod inquiratur. Et predictus Willelmus similiter.

Et juratores dicunt super sacramentum suum quod predictus Willelmus erat verus possessor predicti equi et quod predictus Robertus non emit in foro domini regis. Ideo consideratum est quod predictus Willelmus recuperet equum suum. Et predictus Robertus quia emit predictum equum eat inde quietus.   (quietus)

Placita excercitus domini regis apud villam Sancti Johannis in Pert anno regni regis E. xxiiii[to].

145. Cristiana Lotrix attachiata fuit ad respondendum Waltero Bucher de placito transgressionis. Postea per licenciam concordati sunt. Et predicta Cristiana ponit se.   (misericordia vi denariorum soluta)

146. Johannes Lovel attachiatus fuit ad respondendum Alebino de Whelton de placito transgressionis. Et unde queritur quod cum die veneris in septimana Pasche anno supradicto venisset cum excercitum domini regis apud Berewik et cepisset quoddam hospicium et in eodem pernoctavit et denarios in eodem invenisset. Ita quod die mercurii

when etc. He says that he bought the horse in the king's market in Edinburgh with his own money and that he did not acquire it by malicious means. He asks for enquiry to be made. Thomas Etecal says that he was the lawful owner of the horse before the king's arrival in Edinburgh, and he also asks for enquiry to be made. The jurors say on their oath that Thomas Etecal was the lawful owner of the horse, but they also say that Thomas Davy bought the horse in the king's market as he said. Therefore it is considered that Thomas Etecal should recover the horse. Thomas Davy, because he also bought the horse, is acquitted.   (acquitted)

144. Robert de Merilou was attached to answer William de Cressingham on a plea that Robert illegally took and withholds from him a horse worth 4 shillings which was alienated from his custody almost a week ago, whereby he has suffered damage etc.

Robert comes and denies force and injury when etc, and says that he bought the horse in good faith with his own money in the king's market in Edinburgh. He asks for enquiry to be made, as does William.

The jurors say on their oath that William is the lawful owner of the horse and that Robert did not buy [it] in the king's market. Therefore it is considered that William should recover his horse. Robert, because he also bought the horse, is acquitted.   (acquitted)

Pleas of the king's army at Perth in the 24th year of the reign of king E[dward] [1296].

145. Christine the laundress was attached to answer Walter Bucher on a plea of trespass. Later they are agreed by licence and Christine puts herself [on the country].   (amercement 6 pence, paid)

146. John Lovel was attached to answer Alebinus de Whelton on a plea of trespass. Whereon he complains that when on Friday in Easter Week [30 March] in the said year he came with the king's army to Berwick, took lodgings and spent the night there and found some money there, on the following Wednesday John came and took the money, namely

sequentem venit predictus Johannes et predictos denarios videlicet xxix libras xiii solidos iiii denarios cepit et per valettum suum Thomam de Breuse asportavit. Et postea predictum Alebinum cepit et inprisonavit quousque recognovisset se teneri coram justiciarios domini regis in xx marcas predicto Johanni certis terminis solvendum. Et ulterius predictus Johannes predictum Alebinum in eodem statu tenuit quousque fecisset Thome Lovel militi fratri predicti Johannis quoddam scripturam acquietancie de xxvi marcis in quibus predictus Thomas predicto Alebino tenebatur unde deterioratus est et dampnum habet.

(vacatus quia alibi)

Placita domini regis apud Clony die sabbati proxima post festum sancti Johannis Baptiste anno regni regis E. xxiiii^{to}.

147. Johannes de Biterlegh attachiatus fuit ad respondendum domino Willelmo de la Pole. Et predictus Johannes non venit. Ideo plegium suum videlicet Willelmus de Haukeswelle in misericordia. Et consideratum est attachiari predictum Johannem per corpus.

(misericordia condonatur)

148. Adam Chabbe attachiatus fuit ad respondendum Roberto de Ripun de placito transgressionis. Postea per licenciam concordati sunt. Et predictus Adam ponit se ad recognituram se teneri predicto Roberto in tribus solidis. (misericordia vi denariorum soluta W. Bacon)

149. Willelmus de Lucy attachiatus fuit ad respondendum Tebaldo de Neville de placito quare cum predictus Willelmus et socii sui promisissent eidem Thome [sic] duas marcas pro quadam preda ad opus eorum solvendum quas quidem duas marcas predictus W. de seipso et sociis suis recepisset predictus Willelmus predictas marcas sibi injuste detinet ad dampnum ipsius T. xx solidorum etc.

Et predictus Willelmus venit et dicit quod nullum denarium sibi promisit nec de sociis suis aliquem denarium ad opus predicti Teobaldi recepit. Et hoc paratus est verificare per consideracionem curie. Et predictus Teobaldus concessit ei sacramentum sola manu. Postea predictus Willelmus recessit in contemptu curie. Ideo consideratum est

£29 13s 4d, and carried it off by means of his groom Thomas de Breuse. Later he took Alebinus and imprisoned him until the latter should agree to appear before the king's justices to declare his indebtedness to John for 20 marks, and to repay the money within a certain term. Furthermore, John kept Alebinus in this state until he agreed to make out for Sir Thomas Lovel, the brother of John, a note of discharge for 26 marks in which Thomas was indebted to him, whereby Alebinus has been wronged and has suffered damage.

(cancelled because [it is] elsewhere)

Pleas of the king at Clunie on Saturday next after the feast of St John the Baptist in the 24th year of the reign of King E[dward] [30 June 1296].

147. John de Bitterlegh was attached to answer Sir William de la Pole. John does not come. Therefore his surety, namely William de Haukeswell, [is] in mercy. It is considered also that John should be attached in his person. (amercement pardoned)

148. Adam Chabbe was attached to answer Robert de Ripon on a plea of trespass. Later they are agreed by licence and Adam agrees to make a recognisance of debt to Robert for 3 shillings.

(amercement 6 pence, paid to W. Bacon)

149. William de Lucy was attached to answer Theobald de Neville on a plea that while William and his fellows promised to pay to Thomas [sic] two marks for some spoils of war for them, which two marks' worth [of plunder] William received from Theobald and his fellows, William now illegally withholds the marks, to T[heobald's] damage of 20 shillings etc.

William comes and says that he never promised [Theobald] any money, nor did he ever receive any of Theobald's money from his fellows. He is prepared to prove this by judgement of the court. Theobald grants him an oath by his own hand. Later William withdraws in contempt of court. Therefore it is considered that

quod predictus Teobaldus recuperet predictas duas marcas versus predictum Willelmum et dampna sua dimidia marca. Et predictus W. in misericordia.   (misericordia)

Membrane 7d

150. Johannes de Banet attachiatus fuit ad respondendum Johanne de la Reil constabulario Walensium domini Walteri de Bello Campo de placito transgressionis. Et predictus Johannes de la Reyl non est prosecutus. Ideo ipse et plegii sui de prosequendo in misericordia.

(misericordia xii denariorum)

151. Johannes Russel Maudok Gen Moraduc de Frodesham et Gronon Walensis attachiati fuerunt ad respondendum David Apthomas et Madok ab Crenewey de placito transgressionis. Et unde queruntur quod predictus Johannes et alii die veneris in festo beati Petri venerunt apud Clony et ipsos insultaverunt et male vulnerunt [sic] ad grave dampnum ipsius [sic] etc et contra pacem. Et inde producunt sectam.

Et predicti Johannes et alii veniunt et dicunt quod ibidem non venerunt nec ipsos vulneraverunt sicut inculpantur. Et hoc petunt quod inquiratur. Et predicti David et Maddok non sunt prosecuti. Ideo in misericordia.   (misericordia ii solidorum)

152. Adam le Taillur Symon de Blye et Sibilla uxor eius Johannes de Cherley et Johanna de Cardoil attachiati fuerunt ad respondendum Aspedoni de placito transgressionis. Et unde queritur quod predictus Adam et alii venerunt apud Kynclevyn et predictum Aspeden ceperunt et bona et catalla sua ad valenciam xl solidorum asportaverunt ad dampnum ipsius Aspeden xx solidorum et inde producit sectam.

Et predictus Adam et alii veniunt et defendunt vim et injuriam quando etc. Et dicunt quod nulla bona de predicto Aspeden ceperunt nec asportaverunt sed dicunt quod invenerunt predictum Aspeden cruces super feminas Scocie inponentem et quia ipsum attachiare voluerunt ipse non permisit attachiamentum sed fugit et pannos suos ibidem dimisit. Et ita pannos suos ceperunt et non aliter. Et hoc petunt quod inquiratur.

Et quia compertum est quod predictum attachiamentum facere voluerunt sine warranto ideo consideratum est quod restituant predicto Aspeden pannos et bona sua et quod sint in prisona quousque finem

Theobald should recover the two marks against William as well as damages of one half mark. W[illiam] [is] in mercy.　　(amercement)

150. John de Banet was attached to answer John de la Reil, constable of Sir Walter de Beauchamp's Welshmen, on a plea of trespass. John de la Reyl has not prosecuted, therefore he and his sureties for prosecuting [are] in mercy.　　(amercement 12 pence)

151. John Russel, Maudok Gen, Mordach de Frodesham and Gronon the Welshman were attached to answer David ap Thomas and Madog ap Goronwy on a plea of trespass. Whereon they complain that on Friday the feast of the blessed Peter [29 June] John and the others came to Clunie, assaulted them and seriously wounded them, to their grave damage etc and against the peace. Thereon they bring suit.

John and the others come and say that they did not come there, nor did they assault David and Madog as they are charged. They ask for an enquiry to be made. David and Madog have not prosecuted. Therefore [they are] in mercy.　　(amercement 2 shillings)

152. Adam the tailor, Simon de Blye and his wife Sybil, John Cherley and Joan de Carlisle were attached to answer Aspeden on a plea of trespass. Whereon he complains that Adam and the others came to Kinclaven and took and carried off goods and chattels of his worth 40 shillings, to Aspeden's damage of 20 shillings. Thereon he brings suit.

Adam and the others come and deny force and injury when etc. They say that they did not take or carry off any of Aspeden's goods. They say rather that they found Aspeden laying crosses on Scottish women and that they wished to attach him. He refused to allow this and fled, leaving behind him some lengths of cloth. They took them in this way and not otherwise, and they ask for enquiry to be made.

And because it is found that they wished to make an attachment without warrant, therefore it is considered that they restore to Aspeden the lengths of cloth and the other goods, and that they be sent to prison until they make a fine to the king for the trespass. The women are pardoned [the trespass]. Adam pays a fine of 2 shillings, Simon de Blye

fecerint domino rege pro transgressione. Et condonatur feminis. Et predictus Adam finit ii solidos. Et Simon de Blie vi denarios. Et predictus Johannes de Cherley condonatur per W. Bacun quia pauper. (misericordia ii solidorum vi denariorum soluta W. Bacon)

153. Robertus de Sancto Paulo attachiatus fuit ad respondendum Ricardo de Coquina de comitiva domini R. de Tateshale. Et predictus Robertus non venit. Ideo plegii sui videlicet Adam de Panetria de comitiva Comitis Warenn' et Willelmus de Walmesford in misericordia. Et consideratum est quod attachietur per corpus. Condonatur per marescallum in plena curia.   (misericordia condonatur)

154. Willelmus de Lou attachiatus fuit ad respondendum Gilberto le Mareschal. Et predictus Willelmus non venit. Ideo plegium in misericordia videlicet Philippus de la Botelerye. Et consideratum est quod attachietur per corpus. ['Condonatur per marescallum in plena curia' scored out.]   (misericordia)

Placita excercitus domini regis apud Forfare die jovis proxima post festum apostolorum Petri et Pauli.

155. Robertus de Ripun sequenti pro ii jumentis alienatis et in custodia marescalli inventis. Et quia nullus ea vendicat ideo deliberantur predicto Roberto per plevinam Hankyn de la Botelerye et Rogerus [sic] de Ripun.

156. Radulphus le Taillur attachiatus fuit ad respondendum Willelmo le Furbur de placito transgressionis. Postea per licenciam concordati sunt. Et predictus Radulphus reddit jumentum. Et ponit se.
(misericordia vi denariorum soluta)

157. Alanus de Blye attachiatus fuit ad respondendum Johanni ad portam de Forfare de placito transgressionis. Et unde queritur quod predictus Alanus venit et unam suem suam cepit et asportavit ad dampnum ipsius Johannis etc et contra pacem etc.
Et predictus Alanus venit et defendit vim et injuriam quando et dicit

6 pence. John de Cherley is pardoned [the amercement] by W. Bacon because [he is] a pauper. [*CDS*, ii, no. 822, p. 191.]

(amercement 2 shillings 6 pence, paid to W. Bacon)

153. Robert de St Paul was attached to answer Richard of the kitchen of Sir R[obert] de Tattershall's company. Robert does not come. Therefore he and his sureties for prosecuting, namely Adam of the pantry of the earl of Warenne's company and William de Walmesford, [are] in mercy. It is also considered that he should be attached in his person. [The amercement is] pardoned by the marshal in open court.

(amercement pardoned)

154. William de Lou was attached to answer Gilbert the marshal. William does not come. Therefore he and his surety, namely Philip de la Botelerye, [are] in mercy. It is considered that he should be attached in his person. (amercement)

Pleas of the king's army at Forfar on Thursday next after the feast of the apostles Peter and Paul [5 July].

155. Robert de Ripon sues for two alienated mares found in the custody of the marshal. And because no one claims them they are surrendered to Robert by surety of Hankyn de la Botelerye and Roger de Ripon.

156. Ralph the tailor was attached to answer William le Furber on a plea of trespass. Later they are agreed by licence. Ralph returns the mare and puts himself [on the country]. (amercement 6 pence, paid)

157. Alan de Blye was attached to answer John at the gate of Forfar on a plea of trespass. Whereon he complains that Alan came and took his sow and carried it off, to John's damage etc and against the peace etc.

Alan comes and denies force and injury when [etc]. He says that he bought the sow in the king's market in Forfar for 10 pence from a

quod emit predictam suem in foro domini regis de Forfare pro x denariis de quodam Walense qui predictam suem depredavit. Et hoc petit quod inquiratur. Et predictus Johannes dicit quod predicta sus erat in custodia sua usque ad diem jovis predictam quod evasit ab eo et quam in custodia predicti Alani invenit. Petit quod inquiratur. Et juratores dicunt super sacramentum suum quod predictus Alanus est culpabilis de predicta sua. Ideo etc. (misericordia xii denariorum)

158. Elya filius Nicholai attachiatus fuit ad respondendum Willelmo de Denton. Et quia predictus Willelmus non est prosecutus ideo in misericordia. (misericordia xii denariorum)

Membrane 8r

Placita excercitus domini regis apud Monros die martis proxima post festum sancti Thome martyris anno regni regis E. xxiiii[to].

159. Willelmus le Park attachiatus fuit ad respondendum David Whanwhan de placito cuiusdam jumenti. Plegii de prosequendo Cluelyn Veil et Galfridus le Messager. Et predictus\Willelmus/ optulit se. Et predictus Davyd non est prosecutus. Ideo predictus Willelmus quietus. Et predictus Davyd\et/ plegii suum [sic] in misericordia. (misericordia xii denariorum)

160. Fulco filio Warini et David valettus suus attachiati fuerunt ad respondendum Gilberto de Lyndeseye de placito transgressionis. Et unde queritur quod cum die veneris in festo apostolorum Petri et Pauli venisset apud Aberbrothok et tamquam marescallus domini sui comitis Hereford' hospicium in eadem villa pro comitiva predicti comitis cepisset invenit in quodam hospicio equos et bona ad valenciam xx librarum quod quidem hospicium liberavit predicto Davyd valetto predicti Fulconis ad opus domini sui ita quod predicta bona ad opus predicti comitis salvaret. Super hoc venerunt predicti Fulco et Davyd et quendam equum precii x marcarum alienaverunt et adhuc seisiti sunt ad dampnum ipsius Gilberti c solidorum etc. Et unde ducit sectam etc.

Et predicti Fulco et Davyd venerunt [sic] et defendunt vim et injuriam quando etc. Et dicunt quod nullum hospicium de predicto

Welshman who had stolen it, and he asks for enquiry to be made. John says that the sow was in his keeping until the said Thursday, that it ran away from him, and that he found it in Alan's keeping. He also asks for enquiry to be made. The jurors say on their oath that Alan is guilty of [stealing] the sow. Therefore etc. [*CDS*, ii, no. 822, p. 191.]

(amercement 12 pence)

158. Elya son of Nicholas was attached to answer William de Denton. And because William has not prosecuted therefore [he is] in mercy.

(amercement 12 pence)

Pleas of the king's army at Montrose on Tuesday next after the feast of St Thomas the martyr in the 24th year of the reign of King E[dward] [10 July 1296].

159. William le Park was attached to answer David Whanwhan on a plea respecting a mare. The sureties for prosecuting [are] Llewellyn Veil and Geoffrey the messenger. William presented himself but David has not prosecuted. Therefore William [is] acquitted. David and his sureties [are] in mercy.

(amercement 12 pence)

160. Fulk FitzWarin and David his yeoman were attached to answer Gilbert de Lindsay on a plea of trespass. Whereon he complains that when on Friday the feast of the apostles Peter and Paul [29 June] he came to Arbroath and, acting as marshal for his lord the earl of Hereford, took lodgings in the town for the earl's company, he found in a house horses and goods to the value of £20. He delivered these lodgings to Fulk's yeoman David for the use of his lord, intending that the goods therein be reserved to the earl. Thereafter Fulk and David came and alienated a horse worth 10 marks. They are still seised of it, to Gilbert's damage of 100 shillings etc. Thereon he brings suit.

Fulk and David come and deny force and injury when etc. They say they they never took lodgings from Gilbert on condition that their contents be reserved for the use of the earl. They ask for enquiry to be

Gilberto tali condicione ceperunt ut bona in eodem inventa ad opus predicti comitis salvarent. Petunt quod inquiratur. Et predictus Gilbertus similiter. Postea posuerunt se in arbitrio. Et concordati sunt. Et predictus Fulco ponit se. Et condonatur per marescallum et similiter in loquela sequente. (misericordia condonatur)

161. Gilbertus de Lindesey et Michael de Furneys attachiati fuerunt ad respondendum Fulconi filio Warini de placito transgressionis. Et unde queritur quod die lune proxima post festum apostolorum Petri et Pauli venerunt apud Aberbrothok et in hospicio suo tres equos injuste ceperunt et abduxerunt ad dampnum ipsius Fulconi etc. Et inde producit sectam.

Et predictus Gilbertus et Michael veniunt et defendunt vim et injuriam quando etc. Et dicunt quod nullum equum de equis predicti Fulconi de hospicio suo abduxerunt. Petunt quod inquiratur. Et predictus Fulco similiter. Postea concordati sunt ut patet superius. (misericordia condonatur)

162. Robertus de Perci attachiatus fuit ad respondendum marescallo de placito unius jumenti alienati. Et predictus Robertus non venit. Ideo in misericordia. (misericordia ii solidorum)

163. Thomas Brun attachiatus fuit ad respondendum Magistro Thome medico de placito transgressionis. Et unde queritur quod in crastino sancti Johannis Baptiste venit predictus Thomas Brun ad hospicium ipsius Thome medici in villa Sancti Johannis in Perth in eodem hospicio cepit et asportavit unam loricam precii xx solidorum et unum tabardum precii dimidie marce et unum sacculum cum pixidibus unguentis precii c solidorum ad dampnum ipsius magistri Thome medici c solidorum. Et inde producit sectam etc.

Et predictus Thomas Brun venit et defendit vim et injuriam quando etc. Et dicit quod tali die predictam loricam nec saculum cepit nec asportavit. Petit quod inquiratur. Et predictus Thomas similiter. Postea predictus Thomas medicus non est prosecutus. Ideo in misericordia. Et condonatur ad instanciam comitis Warenn'. (misericordia condonatur)

164. Hugo Bakeler attachiatus fuit ad respondendum Alano de Penyton

made, as does Gilbert. Later they put themselves to arbitration and are agreed. Fulk puts himself [on the country]. [The amercement is] pardoned by the marshal. A similar verdict [is returned] in the following plea.   (amercement pardoned)

161. Gilbert de Lindsay and Michael de Forneys were attached to answer Fulk FitzWarin on a plea of trespass. Whereon he complains that on Monday next after the feast of the apostles Peter and Paul [2 July] they came to Arbroath and illegally took from his lodgings and led away three horses, to Fulk's damage etc. Thereon he brings suit.

   Gilbert and Michael come and deny force and injury when etc, and say that they did not lead away any of Fulk's horses from his lodgings. They ask for enquiry to be made, as does Fulk. Later they are agreed as appears above.   (amercement pardoned)

162. Robert de Percy was attached to answer the marshal on a plea respecting an alienated mare. Robert does not come and [is] therefore in mercy.   (amercement 2 shillings)

163. Thomas Brown was attached to answer Master Thomas the physician on a plea of trespass. Whereon he complains that on the day following [the feast of] St John the Baptist [25 June] Thomas Brown came to his lodgings in Perth, took from his lodgings and carried off a coat of mail, value 20 shillings, a tabard, value one half mark, and a little sack with boxes of ointment, value 100 shillings, to Master Thomas the physician's damage of 100 shillings. Thereon he brings suit.

   Thomas Brown comes and denies force and injury when etc, and says that on that day he did not take or carry off the coat of mail, tabard and sack. He asks for enquiry to be made, as does Thomas. Later Thomas the physician has not prosecuted. Therefore [he is] in mercy. [The amercement is] pardoned at the instance of the earl of Warenne. [CDS, ii, no. 822, p. 191.]   (amercement pardoned)

164. Hugh Bakeler was attached to answer Alan de Peniton on a plea

de placito quare cum idem Alanus tradidisset [sic] predicto Hugoni quinquaginta boves et vaccas custodiendum ad opus predicti Alani quousque ad partes Anglie devenisset idem Hugo de predictis bestiis xxxvi boves et vaccas precii cuiuslibet v solidorum alienavit ad dampnum ipsius Alani c solidorum. Et inde producit sectam.

Et predictus Hugo presens non potest hoc dedicere. Ideo consideratum est quod predictus Alanus recuperet de predicto Hugone vii marcas pro predictis bestiis una cum dampnis ejus qui estimantur ad xl solidos. Et predictus H. committitur prisone quousque etc.   (prisone)

165. Alebinus de Whelton attachiatus fuit ad respondendum domino regi de placito transgressionis. Et unde Johannes Lovel tanquam marescallus domini regis predicti in excercitu suo Scocie queritur quod [sic] eodem domino predicto quod cum die lune proxima post festum sancti Johannis Baptiste anno predicto idem marescallus apud Kynclevyn nomine ipsius domini Regis proclamacionem fecisset ne quis sub forisfactura domini regis predicti ante vexillum constabularii et marescalli quoquo modo transiret ac idem Alebinus non obstante proclamacione predicta apud Clony ante vexilla predicta temere transire presumpsit. Et super hoc venit predictus marescallus et predictum Alebinum tanquam ipsum qui domini regis precepta contempsit per corpus suum et duos equos secum inventos attachiavit et predicta attachiamenta cuidam valetto suo custodiendum commisit. Et predictus Alebinus se justiciare non permittendo se et alios de comitiva sua predicta attachiamenta per rescussum transfregerunt in contemptu domini regis et ad dampnum ipsius marescalli centum marcarum. Et hoc petit pro domino rege quod inquiratur.

Et predictus Alebinus venit et defendit vim et injuriam quando etc. Et dicit quod predictam proclamacionem penitus ignoravit. Et quia predictus Alebinus non potest hoc dedicere predictus marescallus pro domino rege inde petit judicium.

Et quo ad rescussum predictum dicit quod in nullo est culpabilis sicut ei ex parte domini regis inponitur. Petit quod inquiratur. Et predictus marescallus pro domino rege similiter. Ideo preceptum est etc.

Et juratores dicunt quod super sacramentum suum predictus Alebinus predictum rescussum fecit ut predictus marescallus ipsum inculpavit et de predicto rescusso adhuc seisitus remansit. Ideo consideratum est quod predictus marescallus rehabeat predictum

that when Alan delivered to Hugh 50 oxen and cows to safeguard for him until he should return from England, Hugh alienated 35 oxen and cows, each worth 5 shillings, to Alan's damage of 100 shillings. Thereon he brings suit.

Hugh, who is present, is unable to deny this. Therefore it is considered that Alan should recover 7 marks against Hugh for the animals, together with his damages, which are estimated at 40 shillings. H[ugh] is sent to prison until etc. (to prison)

165. Alebinus de Whelton was attached to answer the king on a plea of trespass. Whereon John Lovel, acting as the king's marshal in his Scottish army, complains that while on Monday next after the feast of St John the Baptist [2 July] he made a proclamation in the king's name that no one under pain of forfeiture should in any way go before the banner of the constable and marshal, nevertheless Alebinus had the temerity to presume to do so at Clunie, notwithstanding that proclamation. Thereupon the marshal came and attached Alebinus as one who had shown contempt for the king's precept, together with two horses which were found with him. These he committed to the custody of one of his yeomen. When he refused to permit Alebinus to clear himself the latter and others of his company effected a rescue, in contempt of the king and to the marshal's damage of 100 marks. He asks on behalf of the king for enquiry to be made.

Alebinus comes and denies force and injury when etc, and says that he was not aware of the proclamation. But because Alebinus is unable to deny [the rest] the marshal, on behalf of the king, prays judgment.

With respect to the rescue Alebinus says that he is in no wise guilty as charged at the king's suit. He asks for enquiry to be made, as does the marshal for the king. Therefore [the sheriff] is ordered etc.

The jurors say on their oath that Alebinus effected the escape as the marshal charged and that he bears responsibility for it. Therefore it is considered that the marshal should retain the [profits of the] attachment as is his right by forfeiture. Alebinus [is sent] to prison at the king's will until etc. [*CDS*, ii, no. 822, pp. 191-2.] (to prison)

attachiamentum tanquam ei forisfactum. Et predictus Alebinus ad prisonam domini regis ad voluntatem suam quousque etc. (prisone)

Membrane 8d

Placita excercitus domini regis apud Aberden die lune proxima ante festum sancte Margarete virginis anno regni regis E. vicesimo quarto.

166. Olyverus del Ewe Henricus de Worsop et Willelmus de London queruntur de Thoma de Topgrave et Jordano de Hertilpol de placito transgressionis. Et predicti Thomas et Jordanus presenti non possunt hoc dedicere. Ideo committuntur prisone quousque etc. (prisone)

167. Walterus de Angerton attachiatus fuit ad respondendum Huna Abtuder de placito subrepcionis unius jumenti. Et unde queritur quod cum die dominica proxima ante festum sancte Margarete virginis anno supradicto apud Aberden predictum jumentum erat ab ipso alienatum et quod in custodia predicti Walteri invenit predictus Walterus predictum jumentum injuste ei detinet ad dampnum ipsius etc. Et hoc petit quod inquiratur.

Et predictus Walterus venit et dicit quod emit predictum jumentum in foro domini regis de Aberden. Et hoc petit quod inquiratur.

Et juratores dicunt super sacramentum suum quod predictum jumentum est proprium catallum predicti Huna Abtuder et quod predictus Walterus predictum jumentum non emit set male advenit. Ideo consideratum est quod predictus Huna habeat predictum jumentum. Et predictus Walterus adjudicatur prisone quousque etc qui manucaptus per Radulphum de Novo Castro et mortuus est.

(misericordia)

168. Johannes de Morleie marescallus Roberti de Tatessale attachiatus fuit ad respondendum Waltero de Flemeng qui sequitur pro abbate de Lundores de placito quare reddat ei xxx animalia precii cuiuslibet iiii solidorum que in seisina predicti Johannis inventa fuerunt. Et predictus Johannes venit et dicit quod emit predicta animalia de Johanne de Renham et de Johanne de Conan hominibus senescalli etc. Et super hoc vocat etc. Et predictus Johannes de Renham venit pro se et pro Johanne

Pleas of the king's army at Aberdeen on Monday next before the feast of St Margaret the virgin in the 24th year of the reign of King E[dward] [16 July 1296].

166. Oliver del Ewe, Henry de Worsop and William de London bring a suit of trespass against Thomas de Topgrave and Jordan de Hartlepool. Thomas and Jordan, who are present, are unable to deny the charge. Therefore they are sent to prison until etc. (to prison)

167. Walter de Angerton was attached to answer Huna ap Tudor on a plea of robbery of a mare. Whereon he complains that when on Sunday next before the feast of St Margaret the virgin in the said year [15 July 1296] the mare was alienated from him and he found it in Walter's keeping, Walter illegally withholds the mare, to his damage etc. He asks for enquiry to be made.

Walter comes and says that he bought the mare in the king's market in Aberdeen. He also asks for enquiry to be made.

The jurors say on their oath that the mare is the legal chattel of Huna ap Tudor and that Walter did not buy it, but rather acquired it by evil means. Therefore it is considered that Huna should have the mare. Walter is condemned to prison until etc. He is mainprised by Ralph de Newcastle and has died. (amercement)

168. John de Morley marshal of Robert de Tattershall was attached to answer Walter de Flemeng, who sues on behalf of the abbot of Lindores, on a plea that John return to the abbot 30 animals each worth 4 shillings which were found in his seisin. John comes and says that he bought the animals from John de Renham and John de Conan men of the steward. Thereupon he calls them to warranty etc. John de Renham comes on his own and John Conan's behalf and vouches John de Morley

Conan et predictum Johannem de Morle warantizat etc. Ideo etc. Et super hoc predictus Johannes de Renham vocat ulterius ad warantum Gilbertum le Rede de Coul super vendicione predictorum animalium. Et predictus Gilbertus venit et primo dedicit eum warantum. Et postea cognovit predictam vendicionem predictorum animalia. Ideo consideratum est quod predicti Johannes de Morleye Johannes de Renham et Johannes Conan eant inde quieti. Et quod predictus Walterus habeat suum recuperare versus predictum Gilbertum de predictis animaliis vel de precio. Et idem Gilbertus in misericordia. Et committitur prisone quousque etc. Et obiit in prisona.   (prisona obiit)

169. Alanus de Rokebi queritur de Nicholao medico de Hibernia quod cum quidam equus ab ipso esset alienatus per dictum Nicholaum qui vocat ad warrantum Johannem le Fraunceis qui est in servicio episcopi Dunelm'. Et petit auxilium curie ad habendum warrantum et sibi concessum est unde preceptum est etc.

Et dictus Alanus querens invenit plegium de prosequendo Henricum Maunsel. Et dictus Nicholaus possessor per warantiam invenit securitatem dominum Milonem de Rotherford. Et predictus Johannes venit et warrantizat predictum Nicholaum. Ideo predictus Nicholaus inde quietus. Et predictus Johannes reddit predictum equum per licenciam predicto Alano. Et dictus Johannes in misericordia videlicet xii denariorum.   (misericordia xii denariorum soluta)

170. Honorius de Staunford attachiatus fuit ad respondendum Robeto de Ros de placito quod reddat ei viginti et unam bestiam [sic] videlicet boves et vaccas quas quidem bestias predictus Honorius ei injuste detinet ad dampnum ipsius Roberti etc. Et inde producit sectam.

Et predictus Honorius venit et defendit vim et injuriam quando etc. Et dicit quod emit predictas bestias dominica proxima preterita de Henrico Bray et Ricardo de Hibernia quos inde vocat ad warantum. Et predictus Ricardus de Hibernia venit et warrantizat predictas bestias predicto Honorio. Et dicit quod adquisivit illas bestias cum aliis Hiberniis per predam. Et quia compertum est quod predictus Ricardus predictas bestias depredavit post protectionem de pace predicto Roberto concessam ideo consideratum est quod predictus Robertus recuperet predictas bestias versus prediutuam Honorium et quod predictus Honorius habeat recuperare de sua empcione versus

to warranty, therefore etc. Thereafter John de Renham further calls to warranty with respect to the sale of the animals one Gilbert 'the Red' de Coul. Gilbert comes and at first denies the vouch to warranty but later acknowledges the sale of the animals. Therefore it is considered that John de Morley, John de Renham and John Conan are acquitted. Walter is to recover against Gilbert the animals or their value. Gilbert [is] in mercy. He is condemned to prison until etc. He died in prison. [*CDS*, ii, no. 822, p. 192.] (died in prison)

169. Alan de Rokeby brings a suit against Nicholas the physician of Ireland that a horse was alienated from him by Nicholas. Alan calls to warranty John le Fraunceis, who is in the service of the bishop of Durham. He requests the assistance of the court to secure warranty and this is granted. Therefore [the sheriff] is ordered etc.

Alan the complainant finds Henry Maunsel as a surety for prosecuting, and Nicholas, as the owner by warranty, finds as surety Sir Miles de Rotherford. John comes and vouches Nicholas to warranty. Therefore Nicholas [is] acquitted. John restores the horse to Alan by licence. John [is] in mercy, namely for 12 pence.

(amercement 12 pence, paid)

170. Honorius de Staunford was attached to answer Robert de Ros on a plea that he return to Robert 21 animals, namely oxen and cows, which Honorius illegally withholds to Robert's damage. Thereon he brings suit.

Honorius comes and denies force and injury when etc. He says that he bought the animals on the preceding Sunday from Henry Bray and Richard de Ireland, whom he calls to warranty thereon. Richard de Ireland comes and vouches to warranty Honorius's claim to the animals, and says that he and other Irishmen came to acquire them as spoils of war. And because it is found that Richard stole the animals subsequent to a proclamation of peace granted to Robert, therefore it is considered that Robert should recover the animals against Honorius and that Honorius should be permitted to recover against Richard the value of his purchase. Richard is committed to prison until etc. [He

predictum Ricardum. Et predictus Ricardus committitur prisone quousque etc. Et finem xl denariorum.

(misericordia xl denariorum soluta)

171. Davyd de Twynham attachiatus fuit ad respondendum marescallo pro transgressione facta in excercitu domini regis qui venit et ponit se. Et finem ii solidorum.   (misericordia ii solidorum soluta)

172. Walterus Heved attachiatus fuit ad respondendum Galfrido homini conversi de placito transgressionis. Et unde queritur quod die veneris proxima preterita venit predictus Walterus apud Aberden et ipsum insultavit cum quodam baculo et male vulneravit in capite ad dampnum ipsius Galfridi xx solidorum. Et inde producit sectam etc. Et predictus Walterus venit et dicit quod predictum Galfridum non insultavit nec vulneravit sicut ipsum inculpavit. Et hoc petit quod inquiratur. Et predictus Galfridus similiter. Postea predictus Galfridus non est eum prosecuti. Ideo in misericordia.   (misericordia)

173. Gregorius Sutor attachiatus fuit ad respondendum Maddok Clok de placito transgressionis. Et unde queritur quod predictus Gregorius injuste venit apud Aberden et ipsum vulneravit in capite et male tractavit ad dampnum ipsius Gregorii [sic] xx solidorum. Et inde producit sectam. Et predictus Gregorius venit et dicit quod predictus Maddok ipsum insultavit et se defendendo predictum Maddok vulneravit. Et quia predictam transgressionem cognovit ideo consideratum est quod predictus Maddok recuperet dampna sua que taxantur ad ii solidos. Et quod remaneat in prisona quousque etc. Et finem vi denariorum.   (misericordia vi denariorum)

Membrane 9r

174. Willemus de la Pole attachiatus fuit ad respondendum Roberto Scot de Hardelawe de placito debiti. Et unde queritur quod cum predictus Robertus vendidisset predicto Willelmo lxvi lagenas servisie precii lagene viii denariorum unde summam xliiii solidorum predictus Willelmus apud Edinburgh predictos xliiii solidos ei injuste detinet ad dampnum ipsius Roberti xx solidorum. Et unde producit sectam.

Et predictus Willelmus venit et defendit vim et injuriam quando. Et

makes] a fine of 40 pence.   (amercement 40 pence, paid)

171. David de Twynham was attached to answer the marshal on a plea of a trespass done in the king's army. He comes and puts himself [on the country] and makes a fine of 2 shillings.

(amercement 2 shillings, paid)

172. Walter Head was attached to answer Geoffrey the lay brother on a plea of trespass. Whereon he complains that on the preceding Friday Walter came to Aberdeen and assaulted him with a stave and seriously wounded him in the head, to Geoffrey's damage of 20 shillings. Thereon he brings suit. Walter comes and says that he did not assault or wound Geoffrey as the latter charged. He asks for enquiry to be made, as does Geoffrey. Later Geoffrey has not prosecuted him and [is] therefore in mercy.   (amercement)

173. Gregory the cobbler was attached to answer Madog Clok on a plea of trespass. Whereon he complains that Gregory came illegally to Aberdeen and assaulted him about the head and mistreated him, to Gregory's [sic] damage of 20 shillings. Thereon he brings suit. Gregory comes and says that Madog assaulted him and, while defending himself, he injured Madog. And because he acknowledges the trespass therefore it is considered that Madog should recover his damages, which are assessed at 2 shillings, and that he should remain in prison until etc. [He makes] a fine of 6 pence.   (amercement 6 pence)

174. William de la Pole was attached to answer Robert Scot of Hardelawe on a plea of debt. Whereon he complains that while in Edinburgh he sold to William 66 measures of beer, each measure worth 8 pence, making a total of 44 shillings, William illegally witholds from him the 44 shillings, to Robert's damage of 20 shillings. Thereon he brings suit.

William comes and denies force and injury when [etc]. He says that

dicit quod de predicto Roberto nichil cepit sed dicit quod invenit predictam cerviciam in hospicio suo apud Aberden et eam cepit de hospite domus et non de predicto Roberto. Et hoc petit quod inquiratur. Et predictus Robertus similiter. Ideo preceptum est etc quod venire faciat etc.

Placita excercitus domini regis apud Elgyn die sabbati proxima post festum sancti Jacobi anno regni regis Edwardi xxiiii.

175. Willelmus le Fraunceys attachiatus fuit ad respondendum Thome clerico de Elgyn de placito transgressionis. Et unde queritur quod cum idem Thomas deposuisset in ecclesia beati Marie de Inch cccclxxvi pelliculas angnellorum pro latronibus salvandas que quidem pellicule asportate et alienate fuerunt et in seysina predicti Willelmi invente quas quidem pelliculas predictus Thomas petit. Et predictus Willelmus eas sibi liberare noluit sed eas injuste detinet ad dampnum ipsius Thome etc. Et inde producit sectam. Et predictus Willelmus venit et defendit vim et injuriam quando etc. Et dicit quod emit predictas pelliculas de quibusdam hominibus ingnotis in villa de Elgyn die jovis proxima preterita. Et hoc paratus est verificare. Postea per licenciam concordati sunt. Et predictus Willelmus ponit se.   (misericordia xii denariorum)

Placita excercitus domini regis apud Sanctum Johannem die mercurie proxima ante festum sancti Laurencii anno regni regis E. xxiiii^to.

176. Teobaldus le Botyler attachiatus fuit ad respondendum Teobaldo de Nevill de placito transgressionis. Et unde queritur quod die jovis proxima post festum sancti Thome martiris anno predicto venit predictus Teobaldus le Botyler vi et armis cum hominibus ingnotis ad villam Sancti Johannis et in eadem villa de eodem Teobaldo de Nevill lxvi animalia i jumentum et unum pullum cepit et capere fecit per predictos ingnotos et predicta animalia abduxit et ea injuste detinet ad dampnum ipsius T. xx librarum. Et inde producit sectam etc.
Et predictus Teobaldus le Boytiler venit et defendit vim et injuriam

he never took anything from Robert, but rather that he found the beer in his lodgings in Aberdeen. The beer he therefore took from the house and not from Robert. He asks for enquiry to be made, as does Robert. Therefore [the sheriff] is ordered etc to summon etc.

Pleas of the king's army at Elgin on Saturday next after the feast of St James in the 24th year of the reign of King Edward [28 July 1296].

175. William le Fraunceis was attached to answer Thomas the clerk of Elgin on a plea of trespass. Whereon he complains that when he deposited 476 lamb pelts in the church of the blessed Mary of Inch in order to safeguard them from thieves, the pelts were taken and carried off and later found in the seisin of William. Thomas requested their return, but William refused to surrender them and illegally withholds them still, to Thomas's damage etc. Thereon he brings suit. William comes and denies force and injury when etc. He says that he bought the pelts in Elgin from some unknown men on the preceding Thursday and he is ready to prove this. Later they are agreed by licence. William puts himself [on the country]. [*CDS*, ii, no. 822, p. 192.]

(amercement 12 pence)

Pleas of the king's army at Perth on Wednesday next before the feast of St Lawrence in the 24th year of the reign of King E[dward] [8 August 1296].

176. Theobald le Butler was attached to answer Theobald de Neville on a plea of trespass. Whereon he complains that on Thursday next after the feast of St Thomas the martyr [12 July] Theobald le Butler came with force and arms with some unknown men to Perth and from there took from Theobald de Neville, and caused to be taken by the unknown men, some 66 animals, a mare and a foal, then led these away. He illegally withholds the animals still, to T[heobald]'s damage of £20. Thereon he brings suit.

Theobald le Butler comes and denies force and injury when etc. He

E

quando etc. Et dicit quod ibidem non interfuit nec ullam transgressionem ei fecit nec predicta animalia ad commodum suum devenerunt sicut ei inponit. Et hoc petit quod inquiratur. Et alius similiter. Ideo fiat inde jurata incontinenti. Postea predictus Teobaldus le Boytiler recessit de curia non expectando inquisicionem unde predictus Teobaldus de Nevill petit judicium de ipso tanquam de indefenso.

Placita excercitus domini regis apud Berwik die martis proxima post festum sancti Bartholomey anno regni regis E. xxiiii^to.

177. Amorus Pistor attachiatus fuit ad respondendum Roberto de Arcy de placito transgressionis. Et unde queritur quod die dominica a die Pasche in in [sic] tres septimanas anno supradicto venit predictus Amorus cum aliis ignotis ad hospicium suum in villa de Berwik in vico de Briggate et predictum hospicium suum intravit ac bona sua ibidem inventa ad valenciam lx solidorum cepit et asportavit et asportare fecit per predictos ignotos ad dampnum ipsius Roberti xl solidorum. Et inde producit sectam etc.

Et predictus Amorus venit et defendit vim et injuriam quando etc. Et dicit quod domum predicti Roberti non intravit nec bona ipsius Roberti cepit nec capere fecit sicut ei inponit. Et hoc petit quod inquiratur. Et predictus Robertus similiter. Ideo fiat inde jurata tam de curia domini regis quam de excercitu.

Et juratores dicunt super sacramentum suum quod predictus Amorus domum predicti Roberti non intravit nec bona sua prout queritur per se nec per suos asportavit nec asportare fecit nec ad commodum suum devenerunt. Ideo consideratum est quod predictus Amorus eat inde quietus. Et dictus Robertus pro falso clamore in misericordia. (misericordia)

178. Idem Amorus attachiatus fuit ad respondendum Johanni de Arcy de eo quod predictus Amorus predictis die et anno predictum domum intravit et bona sua ad valenciam iiii marcarum de cista sua cepit et asportare fecit ad dampnum ipsius Johannis xl solidorum. Et inde producit sectam etc.

says that he was not involved in this, that he did not commit any trespass and that the animals did not come into his possession as the latter charges. He asks for enquiry to be made, as does the other. Therefore let there be a jury [summoned] thereon immediately. Later Theobald le Butler has withdrawn from court without awaiting the inquest, whereon Theobald de Neville prays judgment on the grounds that the case is undefended.

Pleas of the king's army at Berwick on Tuesday next after the feast of St Bartholomew in the 24th year of the reign of King E[dward] [28 August 1296].

177. Aymer the baker was attached to answer Robert Darcy on a plea of trespass. Whereon he complains that on Sunday three weeks after Easter in the said year [15 April 1296] Aymer and some unknown men came to his lodgings in the town of Berwick in the vicinity of Briggate, entered them and took and carried off, and caused to be carried off by the unknown men, goods worth 60 shillings which he found there, to Robert's damage of 40 shillings. Thereon he brings suit.

Aymer comes and denies force and injury when etc. He says that he did not enter Robert's house, nor did he take or cause to be taken Robert's goods as the latter charges him. He asks for enquiry to be made, as does Robert. Therefore let there be a jury [summoned] thereon, both of men of the king's court as well as of the army.

The jurors say on their oath that Aymer did not enter Robert's house nor, as the latter complains, did he carry off or cause to be carried off by his men Robert's goods, nor did these come into Aymer's possession. Therefore it is considered that Aymer is acquitted. Robert [is] in mercy for a false claim. (amercement)

178. The same Aymer was attached to answer John Darcy [on a plea] that on the said day and year Aymer entered his house and took and caused to be carried off from a chest goods worth 4 marks, to John's damage of 40 shillings. Thereon he brings suit.

Aymer comes and denies force and injury when etc. He says that he

Et predictus Amorus venit et defendit vim et injuriam quando etc. Et dicit quod predictum domum non intravit nec bona ipsius Johannis cepit nec asportavit sicut ei inponit. Et hoc petit quod inquiratur. Et alius similiter. Ideo fiat inde jurata ut prius. Et juratores dicunt ut prius.

(misericordia)

179. Johannes Sampson attachiatus fuit ad respondendum Johanni de Roddom de eo quod die dominica proxima ante festum Nativitatis sancti Johannis Baptiste anno predicto venit predicti [sic] Johannes Sampson in villa de Akyld et bona et catalla predicti Johannis de Roddom videlicet xiii averia de bobus et vaccas ii jumenta i pullum i ollam eream [sc. 'eneam'] et i cacobum et alia bona et catalla ad valenciam c solidorum arestavit\et/ arestare fecit unde adhuc seisitus est et ipsum inprisonavit ad dampnum ipsius xl librarum. Et inde producit sectam etc. Et predictus Johannes Sampson venit et defendit vim et injuriam quando etc. Et quo ad septem averia ii jumenta i pullum et alia catalla advocat predictum arestacionem bonam et justam eo quod quidem Eustachius Toup se attachiavit per plegios de prosequendo versus predictum Johannem de Roddom de placito transgressionis. Et quo ad sex averia advocat predictam arestacionem bonam et justam eo quod predictus Eustachius Toup emit predicta sex averia de denarios domini regis de preda in excercitu domini regis in Scocia per preceptum ipsius Johannis. Et quod ipsum non inprisonavit prout queritur nec alium dampnum nec injuriam sibi fecit. Petit quod inquiratur.

Et predictus Johannes de Roddom dicit quod predictus Johannes Sampson ipsum attachiavit per collusionem inter ipsum J. Sampson et predictum Eustachium Toup et non aliter. Et hoc petit quod inquiratur. Ideo preceptum est vicecomiti Norhumbr' quod venire *faciat die* veneris etc. [MS stained; italicised words supplied from Adv. MS.]

180. Eustachius Deyvill attachiatus fuit ad respondendum Roberto de Derby capellano. Et predictus Robertus non est prosecutus. Ideo plegii sui in misericordia. R. Clarel respondeat.   (misericordia)

181. Johannes de Byterley attachiatus fuit ad respondendum Egidio de Aunebyri de placito quod reddat ei ix^{xx} et ii bestias unde quadraginta sunt boves vi^{xx} vaccas et xxii bovetti et jumenta quas quidem bestias predictus Egidius emit de predicto Johanne apud Clony pro x marcis et

did not enter the house, nor did he take or carry off John's goods as the latter charges him. He asks for enquiry to be made, as does the other. Therefore let there be a jury summoned thereon, as before. The jurors say as before. (amercement)

179. John Sampson was attached to answer John de Roddom [on a plea] that on Sunday before the feast of the Nativity of St John the Baptist in the said year [17 June 1296] John Sampson came to the town of 'Akyld' and seized and caused to be seized goods and chattels belonging to John de Roddom, namely 13 oxen and cows, 2 mares, a foal, a brass pot, a cooking pot and other chattels, value 100 shillings. He still has seisin of these. He also imprisoned him, all of this to his damage of £40. Thereon he brings suit etc. John Sampson comes and denies force and injury when etc. With respect to seven of the animals, the two mares, the foal and the other chattels, he claims the seizure as valid and legal because one Eustace Toup brought a plea of trespass for them against John de Roddom by means of sureties for prosecuting. With respect to the six other animals he claims the seizure as valid and legal because Eustace Toup bought the six animals with the king's money out of spoils of war taken by the king's army in Scotland on his, John Sampson's, order. He says that he did not imprison John Roddom as the latter complains, nor did he do him any damage or injury. He asks for enquiry to be made.

John de Roddom says that John Sampson attached him as the result of a conspiracy between the said J[ohn] Sampson and Eustace Toup and not otherwise. He also asks for enquiry to be made. Therefore the sheriff of Northumberland is ordered to summon etc on Friday etc.

180. Eustace Deyville was attached to answer Robert de Derby chaplain. Robert has not prosecuted, therefore he and his sureties [are] in mercy. R. Clarel answers. (amercement)

181. John de Bitterlegh was attached to answer Giles de Aunebyri on a plea that the former return to him 182 animals, of which 40 are oxen, 120 cows and 22 calves and mares, which Giles bought from him at Clunie for 10 marks and 20 pence and for which he paid him. When he

x denariis quod quidem argentum ei solvit et cum predictas bestias recipere debuisset predictus Johannes predictas bestias sibi liberare negavit et eas ei injuste detinet ad dampnum ipsius Egidii x librarum. Et inde producit sectam.

Et predictus Johannes venit et defendit vim et injuriam quando etc. Et bene recognovit predictam vendicionem predictorum averiorum sed dicit quod\cum/ predictus Egidius predicta averia recipere debuisset et ea sibi liberare voluisset dictus Egidius ea refutavit eo quod minus sufficientes fuerunt quam esse debuerunt. Et super hoc convenit inter eosdem quod predictus Johannes solveret predicto Egidio predictas x marcas una cum duabus marcas ut de predictis averiis commodum suum facere potuisset. Et si dictus Egidius hoc velit dedicere predictus Johannes paratus hoc verificare.

Et predictus Egidius petit judicium desicut predictus Johannes dictum contractum inter eos confectum plenarie cognovit si per alium contractum unde nichil habet in manu nec in curia cognitum de primo contractu se possit devolvere vel ad talem verificacionem debeat admitti.

Et predictus Johannes desicut dictus Egidius dicta averia refutavit et predictum convencionem paratus est verificare quam quidem verificacionem penitus refutat petit judicium.

Membrane 9d

Adhuc de placitis apud Berewyk.

182. Thomas Malet attachiatus fuit ad respondendum Willelmo de Toddenham de placito transgressionis. Et unde queritur quod cum dictus Willelmus fuisset in excercitu domini regis in Scocia et hernesium suum simul cum armis et\aliis/ bonis suis in hospicio domini sui Willelmi Tochet in villa de Berewik in quadam cista sub serrura dimisisset venit predictus Thomas et in hospicio predicto homines ignotos hospitavit per quos predicta bona sua ad valenciam viii librarum xiii solidorum iiii denariorum fuerunt asportata ad dampnum ipsius c solidorum. Et inde producit sectam.

Et predictus Thomas venit et defendit vim et injuriam quando etc. Et dicit quod quidam homines erant hospitati in predicto hospicio per custodem ville de Berwik sed quod ipse Thomas a predicto hospicio

was due to receive the animals John refused to surrender them and illegally withholds them still, to Giles' damage of £10. Thereon he brings suit.

John comes and denies force and injury when etc. He openly acknowledges the sale of the animals but says that when Giles was due to receive the animals and John wished to surrender them, Giles refused them because there were fewer animals than there ought to have been. Thereafter the two agreed that John should pay Giles 10 marks, with an additional two marks, so that the animals should remain his. And if Giles wishes to deny this John [is] prepared to prove it.

Giles prays judgment whether John, who openly acknowledges that a contract was made between them, can set aside the first contract by means of another, of which he has no proof either in his hand or by the knowledge of the court. If not, the proof he offers should be allowed.

John also prays judgment inasmuch as Giles refused the animals and is prepared to prove a contract on grounds which he rejects.

More of the pleas [heard] at Berwick.

182. Thomas Malet was attached to answer William de Toddenham on a plea of trespass. Whereon he complains that when he was in the king's army in Scotland and left his harness with his weapons and other goods locked in a chest in the lodgings of his lord William Tochet in Berwick, Thomas came and quartered unknown men in those lodgings, by whom his goods, valued at £8 13s 4d, were carried off, to William's damage of 100 shillings. Thereon he brings suit.

Thomas comes and denies force and injury when etc. He says that the men were quartered in the lodgings by [order of] the warden of the town of Berwick, but that he, Thomas, did not take or cause to be carried off any of William's goods, as the latter charges. He asks for enquiry to be made, as does William. Therefore let there be a jury

nichil de bonis predicti Willelmi cepit nec asportare \fecit/ sicut ei inponit. Petit quod inquiratur. Et predictus Willelmus similiter. Ideo fiat inde jurata etc. Et juratores dicunt super sacramentum suum quod predictus Thomas bona predicti Willelmi non cepit nec asportare fecit. Ideo consideratum est quod predictus Thomas eat inde quietus. Et predictus Willelmus pro suo falso clamore in misericordia.

(misericordia)

183. Walterus de Huntercumbe attachiatus fuit ad respondendum Waltero de Ibernia de placito quod reddat ei viginti sex averia videlicet xvi boves et decem vaccas. Et unde queritur quod predictus Walterus die lune proxima ante festum sancte Margarete virginis anno regni regis Edwardi xxiiii^{to} venit cum hominibus ignotis in quadam mora juxta Aberden versus australem et predicta averia cepit et capere fecit et ea fugam fecit per predictos ignotos usque ad terram suam etc. Et predicta averia adhuc injuste detinet ad dampnum ipsius Walteri de Ibernia c solidorum. Et inde producit sectam etc.

Et predictus Walterus de Huntercumbe venit et defendit vim et injuriam quando etc. Et dicit quod predicta averia non cepit nec per predictos ignotos capere fecit nec ea fugavit sicut ei inponit. Et hoc petit quod inquiratur. Et alius similiter. Ideo fiat inde jurata ad diem sabbati.

(inquisicio)

184. Johannes Sampson et Robertus le Eyr de Presfen attachiati fuerunt ad respondendum Hugone Despenser de placito transgressionis. Et unde queritur quod cum predictus Hugo misisset averia sua de partibus Scocie versus Angliam videlicet ix^{c} lxvi boves et vaccas stircos bovectos et juvencas et ii dextrarios jumenta in custodia hominum suorum qui dicta averia fugant in salvo conductu et sub proteccione domini regis et per litteram domini W. de Bello Campo de conductu predicti Johannes et Robertus predicta averia apud Presfen die veneris proxima ante festum translacionis sancti Thome martiris ceperunt similiter cum predictis dextrariis et ea fugaverunt usque ad castrum de Werk. Et ibidem predicta averia dextrarios et homines suos detinuerunt usque in crastino sancti Jacobi apostoli ad quem diem viii^{c} predictorum averiorum dextrarios et homines suos per preceptum domini regis deliberaverunt. Et residuum predictorum averiorum detinuerunt et

[summoned] thereon. The jurors say on their oath that Thomas did not take William's goods or cause them to be carried off. Therefore it is considered that Thomas is acquitted. William [is] in mercy for his false claim. (amercement)

183. Walter de Huntercumbe was attached to answer Walter de Ireland on a plea that the former return to him 26 animals, namely 16 oxen and 10 cows. Whereon he complains that on Monday next before the feast of St Margaret the virgin in the 24th year of King Edward's reign [16 July 1296] Walter de Huntercumbe came with unknown men to a moor near Aberdeen on the south and took the animals and caused them to be taken, and had the unknown men drive them to his own land. He withholds the animals still, to Walter de Ireland's damage of 100 shillings. Thereon he brings suit etc.

Walter de Huntercumbe comes and denies force and injury when etc. He says that he did not take the animals, nor did he cause them to be taken by the unknown men or driven away, as the other charges. He asks for enquiry to be made, as does the other. Therefore let there be [summoned] a jury thereon on the following Saturday. [*CDS*, ii, no. 822, p. 192.] (inquest)

184. John Sampson and Robert le Eyr of Prestfen were attached to answer Hugh Despenser on a plea of trespass. Whereon he complains that when he sent his animals, namely 966 oxen, and cows, bullocks, steers and heifers and two destriers, from Scotland to England in the custody of his men, which animals were being driven under safe conduct and the king's protection by letters under the hand of Sir W[illiam] de Beauchamp, John and Robert seized the animals and the destriers at Presfen on Friday next before the feast of the translation of St Thomas the martyr [6 July]. They drove them to the castle of Wark and there detained the animals and the men until the day after [the feast of] St James the apostle [26 July], on which day 800 of the animals, together with the destriers and the men, were released by order of the king. But they kept the remaining animals, and still withhold them illegally. He lost one of the destriers, value £50, through the harshness

adhuc detinent minus injuste. Et unum de predictos dextrariis precii l librarum amisit per duriciam quam idem Johannes et Robertus dum predicti dextrarii in attachiamento suo \erant/ eidem fecerunt. Et servicium hominum suorum per tres septimanas amisit unde producit sectam etc. Et dampnum habet ad valenciam c librarum etc. Et predicti Johannes et Robertus veniunt et defendunt vim et injuriam quando etc. Et predictus Robertus dicit pro se quod in nullo est culpabilis. Petit quod inquiratur.

Et predictus Johannes dicit quod quoddam hutesium erat levatur super homines predicti Hugonis qua racione dicta averia simul cum hominibus et equis arrestavit sicut ei bene licuit quousque dictum hutesium racionabiliter deductum fuerit in curia regis. Et postea deliberacionem predictorum averiorum cum predictis dextrariis hominibus dicti H. optinuit quos plenarie receperunt exceptis duabus bestiis quas recipere voluerunt. Petit quod inquiratur.

Et predictus Hugo dicit quod advocacionem predicte detencionis facere non potest absque causa racionabili quia dicit quod litteram de salvo conductu sigillatam cum sigillo senescalli ei ostendit quam videre recusavit. Et predictas clxvi bestias adhuc detinet contra tenorem predicte littere et in contemptu domini regis et proteccionis et conduccionis predictarum. Et hoc petit quod inquiratur. Et predictus Johannes dicit quod predictam litteram non vidit nec ei ostensa fuit. Petit quod inquiratur. Ideo preceptum est vicecomiti Norhumbr' quod venire faciat hac instanti die lune xii etc qui non sint tenentes de castro nec de libertate Castri de Werk tam milites etc tot et tales etc quod inquisicio non remaneat capienda pro defectu juratoribus.

185. Petrus valettus Roberti Uhttrys Willelmus de Throp Hugo de Rydal Rogerus Pyperkyn Robertus de Musgrave et Robertus Bernard attachiati fuerunt ad respondendum Roberto filio Payn de placito transgressionis. Et unde queritur quod die jovis proxima ante festum sancti Barnabe apostoli anno supradicto venerunt predicti Petrus et alii vi et armis ad hospicium eiusdem Roberti in villa de Berwik quod quidem hospicium quondam fuit Patricii Scot. Et in eodem hospicio contra voluntatem eiusdem Roberti intraverunt et ingnem sub torale extinxerunt per quod brasium suum deterioraverunt et ibidem pro thesauro querendo foderunt. Et preterea cameram suam intraverunt et armaturas suas ad valenciam c solidorum ceperunt et asportaverunt ad

which was brought about in the attachment of the animals by John and Robert. He also lost the service of his men for three weeks. Thereon he brings suit etc. He has suffered damages of £100. John and Robert come and deny force and injury when etc. Robert says that he is in no wise guilty and asks for enquiry to be made.

John says that the hue and cry was raised upon Hugh's men, for which reason he seized the animals, destriers and men, as was his duty, until the hue and cry should be reasonably dealt with in the king's court. After the restoration of the animals and destriers to Hugh's men it so happened that he received all of them except two. He asks for enquiry to be made.

Hugh says that he has no reason to admit that the detention was validly made because he showed John the letter of safe conduct, sealed with the steward's seal, but the latter refused to look at it. John still withholds the 166 beasts in violation of the tenor of the letter and in contempt of the king, his protection and his safe conduct. He asks for enquiry to be made. John says that he never saw the letter nor was it shown to him, and again he asks for enquiry to be made. Therefore the sheriff of Northumberland is ordered to summon on this coming Monday 12 [jurors] etc, who do not hold of the castle or the liberty of Wark, knights as well as etc; let there be no delay in the holding of the inquest for lack of jurors etc. [CDS, ii, no. 822, pp. 192-3.]

185. Peter the yeoman of Robert Ughtred, William de Thorp, Hugh de Rydal, Roger Pyperkyn, Robert de Musgrave and Robert Bernard were attached to answer Robert FitzPayn on a plea of trespass. Whereon he complains that on Thursday next before the feast of St Barnabas the apostle in the said year [7 June 1296] Peter and the others came with force and arms to his lodgings in the town of Berwick, which house was lately the property of Patrick Scot. They entered the lodgings and extinguished the fire under the malt-kiln, thereby destroying his beer, and dug there for treasure. Afterwards they entered his chamber and took and carried off armour worth 100 shillings, to Robert's damage of 100 shillings. Thereon he brings suit. Peter and the others came and

dampnum ipsius Roberti c solidorum. Et unde producit sectam. Et predictus Petrus et alii venerunt et defenderunt vim et injuriam quando etc. Et bene recognoverunt quod ibidem venerunt cum Roberto Uttrys per preceptum custodis de Berwik set dicunt quod ibidem non foderunt nec bona sua asportaverunt sicut eis imponit. Petunt quod inquiratur. Et predictus Robertus similiter. Ideo preceptum est etc.

denied force and injury when etc. They admitted openly that they came there with Robert Ughtred by order of the warden of Berwick, but they say that they did not dig or carry off Robert's goods as the latter charges. They ask for enquiry to be made, as does Robert. Therefore [the sheriff] is ordered etc. [*CDS*, ii, no. 822, p. 193.]

LETTERS OF JOHN GRAHAM OF CLAVERHOUSE

edited by Andrew Murray Scott

INTRODUCTION

The enduring reputation of John Graham of Claverhouse, 1st Viscount Dundee, is rooted within both Whig and Jacobite traditions of Scottish history. He was 'Bluidy Clavers' to his Covenanter opponents and their political successors. They believed that he was unfeeling, dispassionately cruel, but this belief has been proved by his biographers to be at odds with the known facts. The contrary myth, invented by Sir Walter Scott in his song 'Bonnie Dundee', has also confused the true character and personality of its subject. Scott merely adapted the 'Bluidy Clavers' myth and created a schizophrenic composite, described by Claverhouse's first biographer as 'a plum pudding of virtue and vice'. The dashing cavalier of the song, the bloodthirsty persecutor of *Redgauntlet* (1824) and the more moderate hero of *Old Mortality* (1816) have, however, more humanity than the portraits of him presented in John Galt's *Ringan Gilhaize* (1823) or James Hogg's *The Brownie of Bodsbeck* (1818).

There are two brief contemporary accounts of Claverhouse's life and career. The first of these, by 'an officer of the army', published in 1711, is a Jacobite tract.[1] The second, within the *Memoirs of Captain John Creighton*, transcribed by Dean Swift, suffers from inaccuracies and distortion, its author wishing to inflate his own importance in the events he described almost half a century later.[2]

---

[1] *Memoirs of Lord Viscount Dundee, the Highland Clans and the Massacre of Glencoe, with an account of Dundee's officers, after they went to France, by an Officer of the Army* (London, 1714).
[2] *The Memoirs of Captain John Creighton from his own material, drawn up and digested by Dr J.S. Swift* (London, 1731): in vol. xiii of the Hawkesworth edition of Swift's works.

The most important witnesses to Claverhouse's character are his own letters. In 1826, when Scott's song first appeared, the *Letters of John Grahame of Claverhouse, Viscount of Dundee*, edited by George Smythe of Methven, was published by the Bannatyne Club. The character of Claverhouse was then still popularly regarded as demonic, and he was certainly an unlikely choice for a collection of 'belles-lettres'. Smythe's great-great-grandfather, on his mother's side, was the brother of Lady Dundee, Claverhouse's wife. Whether this was Smythe's primary motive, he performed a service to Scottish history. Even though the slim collection contained only 20 of Claverhouse's own letters, it could be seen that these exhibited considerable literary ability, wit, sarcasm, humour and a delightful sense of irony. Smythe effectively reclaimed Claverhouse from the world of demons and devils to the human sphere. He was a man, warm, witty, organised, effective and above all, humane.

Scott had seen only one letter by Claverhouse, his dispatch of 1 June 1679, which contains the news of his own defeat at Drumclog. The letter ends, 'I am so wearied, and so sleepy, that I have wryton this very confusedly.' It was not one of his most considered epistles. Nevertheless, it was on this flimsy evidence that Scott's casual comment that Claverhouse 'spelt like a chambermaid' led others to go further and assert that Clavers lacked imagination, education and even brains. Thus began new calumnies of his stubbornness, his stupidity, his inflexibility, which, mingled in equal measure with Scott's tales of reckless bravado and gross evilness, persist to this day.

Smythe's collection was compiled by his friend, Kirkpatrick Sharpe, from two main sources: a garret in Callendar House, the ancestral seat of the Linlithgows, and the Leven and Melville Papers. The single letter previously mentioned was in the possession of the duke of Buckingham, having become detached from the other Linlithgow letters. Smythe included the letter to Lord Strathnaver (15 July 1689), which had been printed in the Sutherland Papers in the Appendix to volume 1 of *Memoirs of Great Britain and Ireland* in 1790 by Sir John Dalrymple of Cranstoun, although he did not credit this source in his short preface. Smythe felt that it was 'unnecessary to specify ... the sources from which the contents of the rest of the volume have been derived'. Thus, some of these sources have become lost to posterity. But Claverhouse was writing letters nearly every day at times and, on occasion, several

letters each day. If his was a life in the saddle, then his pen was rather more often in his hand than his cutlass. He was a dashing man of action but the possessor also of considerable epistolary ability, and of necessity a constant correspondent. It was therefore not surprising that more letters would soon come to light.

The first major biography of Graham of Claverhouse was *Memorials and Letters of John Graham of Claverhouse, Viscount of Dundee* by Mark Napier, published in 1859-62. This three-volume work printed 64 letters by Claverhouse. The main additional source was the papers of the duke of Buccleuch and Queensberry from Drumlanrig Castle, from which Napier claimed to reprint 40 (and in another chapter claimed 39) although there are only 37 in the collection! Not only did he alter, or modernise, the orthography of the letters, he transposed the sequence in which they appear. Many of the letters were not fully dated and the true date of some has had to be deduced. The present editor has attempted to restore the sequence of the Queensberry letters by study of their contents; the sequence of these 37 letters differs from both Napier's and the Drumlanrig sequences. In addition, one of these letters is now discovered to have been addressed not to Queensberry but to the bishop of Galloway. The other sources overlooked by Sharpe and Smythe which Napier utilised were the *Red Book of Mentieth, Letters to the Earl of Aberdeen*, the Nairn Papers in the Bodleian Library and the *Chronicles of the Families of Atholl and Tullibardine*.

Napier's primary aim had been to reclaim the character of his hero and to destroy the half-truths and myths that surrounded his name. In this he was successful and later biographers have found his pioneering research invaluable. Later biographers have included Mowbray Morris (1887), Alison Southern (1889), Louis Barbé (1903), Charles Terry (1905), Michael Barrington (1911), Gordon Daviot (Josephine Tey) (1937), A. & H. Tayler (1939), and in 1989, the tercentenary year of Claverhouse's death, new biographies appeared by Magnus Linklater & Christian Hesketh and by myself.

Letters have been gleaned from other sources, listed below. The present collection contains 100 letters, although two are only brief notes and a third is a discharge to the town of Dundee for payment of malt tax. The appendix gives three further items that are doubtful, including the letter of 27 July 1689, supposedly written from the battlefield of Killiecrankie, and a transcript of his speech to the troops before the battle.

The letters in this collection are a fraction of those originally written. There are numerous hints, both within the existing letters themselves and in other primary historical sources, of letters written by Claverhouse which are no longer extant. Some of these, were they to be discovered, would be of considerable historical significance: for example, the letter supposedly written from the change-house at Dunblane to the duke of Hamilton on 18 or 19 March 1689, after his withdrawal from Edinburgh as described in the song 'Bonnie Dundee'. This letter is referred to in his letter of 27 March from Dudhope, and would surely shed light on the precise reasons for his withdrawal. Claverhouse was corresponding regularly with the chancellor, Aberdeen, in 1683, and at least two letters referred to (13 and 31 March) are missing. One of the most tantalising of the missing letters is that to the duke of Hamilton warning him not to touch 'an hair of the tail' of Captain Creighton, who had been captured, or he would 'cut the Laird of Blair, and the Laird of Pollock, joint by joint, and would send their limbs in hampers to the council'. The only reference to this letter (written in May or June of 1689, if it ever existed) is in the unreliable *Memoirs of Captain John Creighton* as transcribed by Swift.

In Claverhouse's meticulous reports of 1679 there is no reference to the major event of the year, the assassination of Archbishop Sharp, an event which would have profoundly shocked him. Since presumably he did write of this event, these letters too must have been lost. Then there is a missing court deposition of 1685, apparently of several pages in length, referring to the trial of Lauderdale and his own mission to the royal court in London on behalf of Queensberry and Aberdeen. His letter to his cousin, the laird of Mackintosh, on 24 April 1689 refers to a previous letter of 22 April now missing. And what of the year 1686—of which not a single shred of evidence of Claverhouse's activities, including any letters, has survived? It is tantalising too, that the text of only a single letter to his brother remains in existence. Apart from the letter to his brother-in-law, Lord Cochrane (see the appendix), no other family correspondence is extant. An exhaustive search of private collections of autograph letters in the UK and the USA has not been possible, and it is quite likely that further letters will be unearthed. Many seventeenth-century documents were dispersed into private hands in Victorian times before rigorous archival study had noted their existence. Many of the original copies of the letters printed here have

long since been lost. Collections can never be assumed to be entirely complete.

The letters (apart from those for which the only source is a printed one with modernised spelling) are given in their original spelling, except for the modernisation of the letters u/v. Some punctuation and capitalisation has been modernised where this clarifies the sense, and paragraphing has been modernised. Dates, places and names of addressees have been standardised. The signature is omitted: Claverhouse signed 'J. Grahame' up to 27 March 1689 (with an intertwined 'J' and 'G'), and 'Dundie' thereafter.

While Claverhouse's orthography may seem erratic, with sometimes three different spellings of the same word on each page, this is by no means unusual. His letters were spelled almost phonetically and thus provide clues to the accent he used in speaking. His was the 'posh' Scots of the classically-educated St Andrews University graduate. He had sophistication and poise, the gravitas of command. His knowledge of languages had been widened by extensive travel in Europe. His letters are full of clues to his Scots dialect: the 'tays' (ties) of gratitude—a man 'days' (dies)—'lait him stur' (let him stir). He had an endearing habit of inserting 'couthy' phrases or homilies into his letters: 'one man may cast in the myr as we say what ten will not take out'—'I always laid the saddle on the right horse'—'we will be all merry about the hall fyr'.

Claverhouse is best able to tell his own story. From these entertaining and perceptive letters the reader can judge the character and personality of one of Scottish history's most romantic figures, and learn, at first hand, of the important historical events in which he played a leading, and ultimately tragic, role. A.M.S.

Sources

The source of each letter, whether printed source or library manuscript reference number, is indicated in the text by abbreviations; the full list of these sources is given below. Numbers immediately following the short titles in the case of printed sources relate to volume and page numbers.

Aberdeen Letters   *Letters … to George, Earl of Aberdeen,* ed.
                            J. Dunn (Spalding Club, 1851)

Atholl, *Chronicles*	*Chronicles of the Families of Atholl and Tullibardine*, ed. J. Murray, duke of Atholl (Edinburgh, 1908)
BL, Add. MS 12,068	British Library, Additional MS 12,068 fo. 137
Bodleian, Nairn Papers	Bodleian Library, Oxford, Carte's Collection vol. 'AL' in Nairn Papers
Dundee, *Charters*	*Charters, Writs and Public Documents of the Royal Burgh of Dundee, 1292-1880*, ed. W. Hay (Dundee, 1880)
Dundee, *Letters*	*Letters of John Grahame of Claverhouse, Viscount of Dundee, with illustrative documents*, ed. G. Smythe (Bannatyne Club, 1826)
Dundee, *Memorials*	M. Napier, *Memorials and Letters of Dundee* (3 vols., Edinburgh and London, 1859-62)
Fraser, *Grandtully*	W. Fraser (ed.), *The Red Book of Grandtully* (2 vols., Edinburgh, 1868)
Fraser, *Melvilles*	W. Fraser (ed.), *The Melvilles, Earls of Melville, and the Leslies, Earls of Leven* (3 vols., Edinburgh, 1890)
Fraser, *Menteith*	W. Fraser (ed.), *The Red Book of Menteith* (2 vols., Edinburgh, 1880)
'Gleanings', *TGSI*, xx	Provost MacPherson (ed.), 'Gleanings from the charter chest at Cluny Castle', *Transactions of the Gaelic Society of Inverness*, xx (1889)
Grierson Papers	Ewart Library, Dumfries, Grierson Papers

Leven Papers	*The Leven and Melville Papers*, ed. W.L. Melville (Bannatyne Club, 1843)
HMC, *Laing*	Hist. Manuscripts Comm., *Report on the Laing Manuscripts*, 72nd Report, vol. i, ed. H. Paton (London, 1914)
HMC, *Queensberry*	Hist. Manuscripts Comm., *Manuscripts of the Duke of Buccleuch and Queensberry*, 15th Report, Appendix, part viii (London, 1897)
MacKenzie, *Galloway*	W. MacKenzie, *History of Galloway from the Earliest Times* (Kirkcudbright, 1841)
Mackintosh, *Letters*	C.F. Mackintosh (ed.), *Letters of Two Centuries* (Inverness, 1890)
More Culloden Papers	*More Culloden Papers*, i, ed. D. Warrand (Inverness, 1923)
NLS	National Library of Scotland
RPC	*Register of the Privy Council of Scotland*
SHS Misc. III	'The bishop of Galloway's correspondence, 1679–1685', ed. W. Douglas, *Miscellany of the Scottish History Society*, vol. iii (1919)
SRO	Scottish Record Office
Warden, *Angus*	A.J. Warden, *Angus or Forfarshire* (5 vols., Dundee, 1880-85)

To Sir Thomas Stewart of Grantully   Fraser, *Grandtully*, ii, 229

Edinburgh, 7 March 1676

Sir, I think no wonder that a poor lad lyk yow should prig thus for five pound with your good friend, who will maybe never have the occasion to ask another favour of yow. Send but your horse here, and if he be wholl and sound, it shall not be so litell a business shall keep us from a bargon.

Give orders to Jhon Steuart, or Colin, to receive my obligation. If ther be anything wher in I can serve you, ether here or els wher, you know hou friely you may command me. I have always been, and shall still be, as much as I really am, Dear Sir, your most humble servant. [P.S.] I have got four of the best grou hounds of Scotland now, and you be a good fellow you will send me a setting dogue, and then I would be a prince.

To Sir Thomas Stewart   Fraser, *Grandtully*, ii, 230

[March 1676]

Sir, I have been upon your horse today, and am extreamly pleased with him. I shall give the tiket to Coline for the mony, and orders to James Grahame[1] to pay it as soon as he can. I have also received your setting bik,[2] for which I give you many thanks, and doe, indeed, tak it for a great complement. I begin nou to think sheim, and think my self myghtily in your debt, and knous not hou to acquyt my self of the obligation I have to you. The only favour I can desyr of you nou is to give me the occasion to shoe that I deserve those I have alraidy received. Adieu, dear Sir, Contineu your friendship for me, as I shall doe to be, Sir, your most humble servant.

To the earl of Linlithgow[3]   Dundee, *Letters*, 1-2

Moffat, 28 December 1678

My Lord, I came here last night with the troupe, and am just going to mairch for Dumfriche, wher I resolve to quarter the whole troup. I have

---

[1] Chamberlain to the Claverhouse family.
[2] Bitch.
[3] George Livingstone (d. 1690), 3rd earl of Linlithgow, commander in chief from 1677 to 1679.

not heard any thing off the dragoons, thogh it be now about nyn a clock, and they should have been here last night, according to your Lordship's order. I supose they must have taken some other rout. I am informed since I came, that this contry has been very loose; on Tusday was aight days, and Sondy, ther were grate field conventikles just by here, with great contempt of the reguler clergy, who complain extreamly, when I tell them I have no orders to aprehend any body for past misdemainers. And besyds that, all the particular orders I have beeng contined in that order of quartering, every place wher we quarter must see them, which maks them fear the less.

I am informed that the most convenient post for quartering the dragoons, will be Moffet, Lochmeben, and Anan, wherby the wholl contry may be keep in awe. Beseids that, my Lord, they tell me that the one end of the bridge of Dumbfrich is in Galaua, and that they may hold conventicles at our nose, we not dare[ing] to disspat them, seing our orders confines us to Dumfriche and Anandell. Such ane insult as that would not please me; and on the other hand, I am unwilling to exceed orders, so that I expect from your Lordship orders how to cary in such cases.

I send this letter with on of my troup, who is to attend orders till he be relleved. I will send on every Monday, and the dragoons every Thursday, so that I will have the hapiness to give your Lordship acompt of our affaires tuise a week, and your Lordship ocasion to send your comands for us as often; in the mean tym, my Lord, I shall be doing, according to the instructions I have, what shall be found most advantagious for the King's service, and most agreable to your Lordship. I am, my Lord, your Lordship's most humble and most obedient servant.

[P.S.] My Lord, if your Lordship give me any new order, I will bigue they may be keep as secret as possible, and send for me so sudenly, as the information som of the favorers of the fanatiks are to send, may be previned,[4] which will extreamly facilittat the executing of them.

To Linlithgow   Dundee, *Letters*, 3

Dumfries, 6 January 1679

My Lord, in the letter your Lordship has been pleased to honor me

---

[4] Forestalled.

with, you tell me that Captain Inglish[5] has given your Lord[shi]p notice that I had apointed him to quarter at Lochmeben and Anan; which must be a mistake in him, for the order I sent him was to quarter on half of his compagnie at Moffet, and the other at Anan, wher they ar, and have been since they came in to this contry. Lochmeben I left out, because I was informed that ther was no conveniency for lodging any body ther, which I fynd to be trew, having been upon the place since myself. Nor does all this disagree from what I wrot to your Lord[shi]p about there keeping gairde here in the castle, I having, in the order for quartering, apointed ten men to be sent hither out of each of those quarters, who wer to stay within the castle, ten of them to lay in beds which I have caused prepair in a chamber of the castle, and the other ten keep gaird in the great hall, and relieve on an other, for aight days, when ther should com as many in there place; and this is no hard deuty every tent night. I have six of my troop every night on gaird, which comes to the same proportion.

My Lord, since I have seen the act of counsel,[6] the scrupal I had about undertaking any thing without the bounds of ther two shairs, is indeed frivolous, but was not so befor; for if there had been no such act, it had not been save for me to have done any thing but what my order warranted, and since I knew it not, it was to me the same thing as if it had not been. And for my ignorance of it, I must acknowledge that till now in any service I have been in, I never inquyred further in the Lawes then the orders of my superiour officers.

After I had sent the counsels order to the Stewart deput,[7] he apointed Frydy last, the thrid of January, for the demolishing the meeting-house,[8] and that I should bring with me only on quaid of my troop. He broght with him fourscor of contry men, all fanatiks, for they would not lay to ther hands till we forced them; every body gave out that house for a bayr, but when they saw that ther was no quarter for it, and that we was com on the place, no body had the impodence to deny it to have been built a purpose for meeting, and that upon the expence of the comon purse of the disaffected. It was a good large house, of above

---

[5] John Inglis, a captain of dragoons under Claverhouse's command.
[6] The Committee of Public Affairs had drafted a set of wide new powers (approved by the king on 18 January) for the new sheriff deputes and bailie deputes.
[7] James Carruthers, stewart depute of Annandale.
[8] In the vicinity of Castlemilk which had been ordered to be destroyed by privy council.

sixty foot of lenth, and betuixt twenty and thretty broad; it had only on door, tuo windows in evry syd, an on in evry end; they had to put up staiks alongs evry syd, and a hek[9] and menger in on of the ends, to mak it pass for a bayr; but that was but don latly, after they had heard that it was taken notice of for a meeting house. The stewart deput performed his pairt punctually anogh; the walls wer throwen down, and timber burnt. So perished the charity of many ladys.

On Saturdays night when I came bak here, the sergeant who commands the dragoons in the castle came to see me, and whyll he was here, they cam and told me ther was a horse killed just by, upon the street, by a shot from the castle. I went imediately and examined the gaird, who denayed point blank that there had been any shot from thence. I went and heard the bayly tak depositions of men that wer looking on, who declaired upon oath that they sawe the shot from the gaird hall, and the horse imediately fall. I caused also searche for the bullet in the horse head, which was found to be of ther calibre. After that I found it so clear, I caused sease upon him who was ordered by the sergent in his absence to comand the gaird, and to keep him prisoner till he fynd out the man, which I supose will be found himself. His name is James Ramsey, an Angus-man, who has formerly been a lieuetenent of hors, as I am informed. It is an ogly business; for beseids the wrong the poor man has got in loosing his horse, it is extreamly against military disciplin to fyr out of a gaird. I have apointed the poor man to be here tomorow, and bring with him som neigboors to declare the worth of the horse, and have assewred him to satisfy him, if the captain, who is to be here also to-morow, refuse to doe it.

I am sory to hear of an other accident [that] has befallen the dragons, which I believe your Lordship knows better then I, seeing they say that there is a complent maid of it to your Lordship, or the Counsel, which is, that they have shot a man in the arm with small shot, and disinabled him of it, who had com this lenth with a horse to carry bagadge for som of my officers; but this being befor they cam to Moffet, does not concern me.

The stewart deput, befor good compagnie, told me that severall people about Moffet wer resolved to mak a complent to the Counsel against the dragoons for taking frie quarter; that if they would but pay

[9] A rack for fodder in a stable.

ther horse corn and ther ell, they should have all the rest frie; they ther
wer som of the officers that had at ther owen hand apointed themselfs
locality[10] above three myl from there quarter. I byged them to forbear
till the captain and I should com there, when they should be redressed in
every thing. Your Lordship will be pleased not to tak any notice of this,
till I have informed myself upon the place. This toun is full of people
that have recaited and lodged constantly in their houses intercomed
persons and fild preachers. There ar som that absent themselfes for fear;
and Captain Inglish tell me ther ar balays have absented themselfs there
at Anan, and desyred from me order to aprehend them, which I refused,
for they ar not included in all the Act of Counsell. Mr Cuper, who is
here baily and stewart for my Lord Stormont,[11] offered to aprehend
Bel,[12] that built the meeting house, if I would concur; I sayd to him that
it would be acceptable, but that the order from the Counsell did only
bear the takeñ up the names of persones accessory to the building of it. I
am, my Lord, your Lordship's most humble servant.

To the earl of Menteith[13]   Fraser, *Menteith*, ii, 170

[c. January 1679]
My Dear Lord, Since I pairted with you, I waited on my Lord
Montrose[14] at Sterling, and from thence to Comernad,[15] and so to his
owen house. I told him all that had passed betuixt your Lordship and
me; he seemes to be very well satisfyed, and assurs me that he will com
to Edinbourg when ever I shall advertise him. I would apoint no daye
till I akquainted your Lordship with it. So, my Lord, if you contineu
your resolution in it, I shall wait for your comands with this bearer.

My Lord, as your friend and servant, I doe tak the liberty to give you
on advise, which is that ther can be nothing so advantagious for you as
to setle your affaires, and to establish your successor in tyme, for it can
doe you no prejudice if you com to have any childring of your owen

---

[10] A levy for the maintenance of troops.
[11] David Murray (d. 1731), 5th Viscount Stormont.
[12] Possibly John Bell of Whiteside, shot in February 1685 by Sir Robert Grierson of Lag.
[13] William Graham (c.1634-1694), 2nd earl of Airth and Menteith.
[14] James Graham (1657-1684), 3rd marquis of Montrose.
[15] Cumbernauld.

body, and will be much for your quyet and confort if yoe have non; for who ever you mak choyse of will be in place of a sonne. You knou that Julius Caesar had no need to regrait the want of isseu, having adopted Augustus, for he kneu certenly that he had secured to himself a thankfull and usefull friend, as well as a wyse successor, neither of which he could have promised himself by having childring; for nobody knous whether they begit wyse men or fooles, beseids that the tays of gratitud and friendship ar stronger in generous mynds than those of natur.

My Lord, I may, without being suspected of self interest, offer some raisons to reneu to you the advantage of that resolution you have taken in my faveurs. First, that there is nobody of my estat out of your nam would confound there family in yours, and nobody in the nam is able to give you those conditions, nor bring in to you so considerable an interest, besids that I will easier obtine your cusin german[16] then any other, which brings in a great interest, and contineus your family in the right lyne. And then, my Lord, I may say without vanity that I will doe your family no dishonor, seeing there is nobody you could mak choyse of has toyld so much for honor as I have don, thogh it has been my misfortun to atteen but a small shear. And then, my Lord, for my respect and gratitud to your Lordship, you will have no raison to dout of it, if you consider with what a francness and easiness I lieve with all my friends.

But, my Lord, after all this, if thes raisons cannot perswad you that it is your interest to pitch on me, and if you can think on any body that can be mor proper to restor your family, and contribut mor to your confort and satisfaction, mak frankly choyse of him, for without that you can never think of geating any thing don for your famly: it will be for your honor that the world see you never had thoghts of alienating your family, then they will look no mor upon you as the last of so noble a race, but will consider you raither as the restorer then the ruiner, and your family raither as rysing than falling; which, as it will be the joy of our friends and relations, so it will be the confusion of our enimys. I am, my dearest Lord, your most humble and faithfull servant.

---

[16] Helen Graham, whose hand in marriage Claverhouse sought as part of his project to become Menteith's heir.

To Linlithgow   Dundee, *Letters*, 9

Dumfries, 7 February 1679
My Lord, The nixt day after I sent the rolls to your Lordship, I went to
Anan, and communicat the business to Captain Inglish, that he might
be in radyness again advertisement; and from thence I went to Moffet to
meet your Lordship's ordor, which was half a day longer a coming then
I expected. I gave Lieuetenent Cleland orders to cease on three, and sent
ane express to Captain Inglish that he might cease on other three, and
apointed them Wednesday at six a cloak at night to march. I cam hither,
and found twenty dragoons going to relieve, whom I made stay, and
sent them to cease on Howmens, Dormont, and Denby.[17] We got only
Dormont; the other two, as they say, ar gone to Edinbourg to give
satisfaction to the Counsel. If they stay in this country, I shall indever to
fynd them. I sent on of my corporalls for the two Welchs,[18] and he
found them both. I sent an other for to sease on Dalskarf,[19] but he found
him not at his own house. We made shearch for him here in town, but
did not fynd him, thogh he was here. The third brigadier I sent to seek
the wobster; he broght in his brother for him. Thogh he may be can not
preach as his brother, I dout not but he is as well principiled as he;
wherfor, I thoght it would be no great falt to give him the troble to goe
with the rest.

I send Captain Inglish letter and his lieuetenents to your Lordship,
which will give you acompt of there diligence. I have sent the prisoners
away this day with a gaird of twenty, ten troup horse, and ten dragons,
comanded by Mr Craford, on of my corporalls. I hop your Lordship
will send out to him when he comes neer the toun, to late him know to
what place he shall bring them. I expect orders from your Lordship
about the fyning of the others in the rolls. I am, my Lord, your most
humble and obedient servant.

To Linlithgow   Dundee, *Letters*, 11

Dumfries, 8 February 1679
My Lord, I was the day befor yesterday at Thornhille, which my Lord

---

[17] John Carruthers of Holmain, John Carruthers of Dormont, and George Carruthers of Denby.
[18] William and James Welch, both tried and convicted for treason in December 1682.
[19] Robert Grierson of Dalskarth.

Quensbury[20] had apointed for the place wher the comissioners[21] should meet with us about the furnishing hay and straw for the troupes quartered in the shyr and stewartry; but found no body there but my Lord himself and Craigdalloch,[22] who seemed very fordward in evry thing that might be for the King's service, and very rady to doe me particular kyndnesess, but not being a coram they could not proceed. They thoght strange that we, who have the honor to serve the King, should be ordered by the counsell to pay mor for hay and straw then will be asked from any strenger; that if it had been recomended to them, they would have given us a better bargain.

My Lord, I hope your Lordship will not suffer those under your comand to be thus used, nor the counsell suffer such a peremptor order of thers, as that was, to be thus neglected. I am forced to lait the dragoons quarter at lairge in the contry. I have visited ther quarter, and found it impossible they can subsist any longer ther without a locality; what prejudice the King's service may recaive by this, I know not, but I am seur that it is extreamly improper to be thus quartered, in a tyme that the counsell seems resolved to proceed vigourusly against the disorders of this contry. In the stewartry of Galowa we have got nothing don ether; there has not been al this whyl in the contry but two of the comissioners; the rest ar all at Edinbourg. What to doe in this case your Lordship can best tell; for my pairt, if my troup com to want hay and straw, I will goe to any of the comissioners lands that ar adjacent, and taik it, offering the rat[e]s, and think I doe nothing but what I may answer for, thogh I be very unwilling to disoblidge any gentlemen.

My Lord, good intelligence is the thing we want most here. Mr Welch[23] and others preach securly with in twenty or thretty myles of us, but we can doe nothing for want of spays;[24] if the counsell and your Lordship thoght fit, there should be so many intertined for every quarter, which would be of great use. I am, My Lord, your Lordship's most faithfull and most obedient servant.

---

[20] William Douglas (1637-1695), 3rd earl, marquis (1682) and 1st duke (1684) of Queensberry.

[21] Commissioners of supply.

[22] Robert Ferguson of Craigdarroch.

[23] John Welsh, minister of Irongray, a grandson of John Knox. A reward of 9,000 merks had been posted two days before for his arrest.

[24] Spies.

To Menteith   Fraser, *Menteith*, ii, 172

Dumfries, 14 February 1679

My Dear Lord, I have delayed so long to give a return to your kynd letter, expecting that my man should return from Yrland, that I myght have given your Lordship ane acompt of the state of my affaires, but nou that I begin to despair of his coming, as I doe of the succes of that voyage, I would not loose this occasion of asseuring your Lordship of my respects. I have recaived letters from my Lord Montros, who gives me ill neus, that ane Yrish gentleman has caryed away the Lady, but it is not certain, thogh it be too probable.[25] However, my Lord, it shall never alter the course of our friendship, for if, my Lord, either in history or romance, either in natur or the fancy man ther be any stronger names or rairer exemples of friendship then these your Lordship does me the honor to name in your kynd and generous letter, I am resolved not onlly to equall them, but surpass them, in the sinserite and firmnes of the friendship I have resolved for your Lordship. But, my Lord, seing it will, I hop, be mor easy for me to prove it by good dieds in tyme to com, then by fyne words to express it at present, I shall referr myself to tyme and occasion, by which your Lordship will be fully informed to what hight I am, my dear Lord, your Lordship's most faithfull and most obedient servant.

[P.S.] My Lord, I hope to hear from you, and knou if you hear any thing of what my Lord Montros wryts to me.

To Linlithgow   Dundee, *Letters*, 13

Dumfries, 24 February 1679

My Lord, I obeyed the order about seasing persons in Galowa that very night I receaved it, as far as it was possible, that is to say, all that was within fourty myles, which is the most can be riden in on night: and of six mad search for, I found only two, which are John Liviston, bayly of Kilkoubry, and John Blak, tresurer there. The other two balys wher flaid, and there wyfes laying above the clothes in the bed, and great candles lighted, waiting for the coming of the party, and told them they knew of there coming, and had as good intelligence as they themselfs,

---

[25] Helen Graham had numerous Irish suitors. She eventually married Captain Arthur Rawdon, heir to the earl of Conway, in 1682.

and that if the other two was seased on, it was ther owen falts, that would not contribut for intelligence. And the truth is, they had tyme anogh to be advertised, for the order was deated the 15, and came not to my hands till the twenty. I layd the fellow in the gaird that broght it, so soon as I considered the date, where he has layen ever since, and had it not been for respect to Mr Maitland,[26] who recomened him to me, I would have put him out of the troup with infamy. The names of the other two I made search for, were Cassenkary[27] and the lady Lauriston,[28] but found them not. Ther is almost no body lays in ther bed, that knowes themselfs any ways guilty, with in fourty milles of us, and with in a few days I shall be upon them three scor of mylles of, at on bout for seasing on the others contined in the order.

My Lord, I hop your Lordship will consider how hard it is to keep so vast a contry as this is with so few forces; betwixt Portpatrik, and som of the Duke of Monmouth[29] bounds laying with in the stewartry of Anandelle, wher I hear Mr Williamson[30] is at this present, there is above a hondred myles. However, my Lord, I shall doe my best indevors in every thing I am comanded, but it will be absolutly necessary to have garison here. I resolve to take up my quarter at Kilkoubrie, becaus it is in the center of the other quarters. There is on thing your Lordship would be pleased to give orders about, that thos of the quarter of Air send befor to secur the sea ports on that coast, as I shall doe at Portpatrik and Balantyr,[31] for all those rogues run over to Yrland, and no body should have lieve to pass with out a sufficient pass, nor anebody sheltered in any place, or recaved, that fley from any of there disafected places, wher the forces ar quartered. I wait for orders about our march. I am, my Lord, your Lordship's most humble and obedient servant.

[P.S.] Your Lordship will receave here inclosed a bond of cautionery for the apearance of the two we siezed on, which I am informed to be sufficient.

---

[26] Either Charles Maitland (c.1620-1691), Lord Halton, later (1682) 3rd earl of Lauderdale, or his son Richard (1653-1695), later 4th earl.
[27] John Muir of Cassincarry.
[28] Wife of Robert Elliott of Larriston; daughter of Thomas Scott of Todrig.
[29] James Scott (1649-1685), duke of Monmouth and Buccleuch, illegitimate son of Charles II.
[30] Possibly David Williamson, the covenanting minister whose escape from soldiers was the subject of the folk song 'Dainty Davie'.
[31] Ballantrae.

To Linlithgow   Dundee, *Letters*, 15

[Dumfries, c. February 1679]
My Lord, I take the liberty to wryt yet this lyn to your Lordship,
because in my other letter I forgot to give your Lordship an acompt of
an disorder that befelle som of the garison of Stranraer, when they
pairted from thence. William Graham,[32] who comanded there, was
marchd, and had comanded so many foot to wait on a prissoner whom
they wer to bring along with them, on of which offered to sease on the
old provist's horses, thogh without orders, which he indevared to
hinder, and layd hands on the soger, upon which he took out a durk and
gave the provist a mortall wound, of which he is not yet dead, but is
very ill. The soger was seased on by the toun's people, and his comrad
by the dragoons at Wigton; and since, when William Graham went
back to clear of his quarters, he demanded the soger of them, which
they refused. I desyr to know of your Lordship what is to be don in it. I
think it not fit a soger should be in there hands, but Philiphaugh[33] will
speak to you himself. I am, my Lord, your Lordship's most humble
servant.

To Linlithgow   Dundee, *Letters*, 18

Dumfries, 21 April 1679
My Lord, I have sette at liberty Major Johnston, according to your
Lordship's order. I was going to have sent in the other prisoners, but
amongst them there is on Mr Francis Irwin,[34] an old and infirm man,
who is extreamly troubled with the gravelle, so that I will be forced to
delay for five or six days. I fynd Mr Welch is acustoming both ends of
the contry to face the Kings forces, and certenly intends to brak out in
ane open rebellion. I expect him here nixt.

I am informed that there either was, or was designed yesterday, at
Bigner,[35] the teriblest convencle that has been yet heard of, but I have
no certenty of it, but it is generally beleved here. I expect opposition
when we com to pund upon our decrits, but I am not feared we be
forced. We lay all now at Kilkoubright and this place. There is here in

---

[32] Cornet of troop of dragoons.
[33] Sir James Murray of Philiphaugh.
[34] Minister of Kirkmahoe, who was later jailed in the Bass.
[35] Biggar.

prison a minister was taken above a year agoe by my Lord Nidsdelle,[36] and by the well affected magistrats of this has had the liberty of an open prison, and mor conventicles has been keept by him there, than has been in any on house of the kingdom. This is a great abuse, and if the magistrats be not punished, at least the man oght not to be suffered any longer here, for that prison is more frequented than the kirk. If your Lordship think fit, he may be sent in with the rest.

My Lord, I think it my deuty to put your Lordship in mynd that the armes of militia in this shyr, as well as in that of Wigton, and Annandelle, ar in the hands of the contry people, thogh very disaffected. This may prove in a sudain dangerous; and beseids this, the armes wer taken from the Stewartry ar in the custody of the toun of Kilkoubright, the most irregular place of the kingdom. It wer fit we had the gaird of them, and lieve in case of necessity to provyd our infantry with sourds, and to change som of our pistolles for the horse. All those I gote out of the castelle ar worth nothing. I am, my Lord, Your Lord[shi]p's most humble and obedient servant.

[P.S.] My Lord, I know not how to doe for hay, now when we lay so strong: we have not yet had any locality, nor ar we lyk to gate mony; for my pairt I'l never solist it mor, but if the Kings service suffer, lat the blame lay wher it should.

To Linlithgow   Dundee, Letters, 24

Dumfries, 6 May 1679

My Lord, On Saturday's night last, I ordered Captain Inglish, with the garison at Kilkoubright, to be here on the Sonday morning, which he did. I mounted the foot, and marched with all towards those places where the conventicles had been the Sonday befor, first, to the head of Glenlea, wher Vernor[37] had preached, and then to the Queensbery hille, wher Arnot[38] and Archibald[39] had preached, and then to the borders of Craford moor, wher Cameron[40] had preached the Sonday

---

[36] Robert Maxwell (c.1627-c.1683), 4th earl of Nithsdale.
[37] Either Patrick Warner or Thomas Warner, both covenanting ministers associated with John Welsh.
[38] Samuel Arnot, minister of Tongland. A reward of 3,000 merks was posted for his capture, and he was hanged on 14 December 1682.
[39] Hugh Archibald, minister of Strathaven.
[40] Richard Cameron, founder of the Cameronian sect. Killed at Airds Moss on 2 July 1680.

F

befor, and did actually preach that very day, the mater of three myles from the place we was at, thogh we could see no apearance of them in any place we had been, because of the thikness of the fogue. We lost two partys we sent af; they [did] not fynd us till next morning: they took three tenent men coming from that meeting: I have not had the tyme to examin them strikly, but I hear it was really Cameron preached, and yet it is thoght he would not have waited for us if we had found him out.

I must say, that amongst officers and sogers I found a great desyr to be at those rogues; and I have declared to them that, if ever we meet, they must aither fight in good earnest, or be judged as cowards by a counsell of warre. The dragoons marched that day, without a bait, above fyfty myles, of which there was about fiveteen of horid hilles.

My Lord, I have received ane order yesterday from your Lordship, which I doe not know how to goe about in a sodain, as your Lordship seems to expect, for I know not what hand to turn too to find those partys that ar in armes. I shall sent out to all quarters and establish spays, and shall endevor to ingadge them Sonday nixt, if it be possible; and if I gate them not here, I shall goe and visit them in Tiviotdalle or Carak, wher, they say, they dar look honest men in the face. But, my Lord, it had been necessary that the counsell had not only waranted us to give out mony for spays, but also had apointed where we should fynd it; for, I declare, I had to doe to pay that nights quarter we wer out. In the toun we gate some credit, but, if we march, I must tak free quarters, for I can not pay mony, if I gate non. Sir William Sharp[41] is short of paying us neer six hondred pounds sterling, and has now send billes upon the excyse of the Steuartry for a small pairt of it, yet mor then is dew in either Steuartry or shyr.

My Lord, we have now got a locality here with a great deall of difficulty. My Lord Queensbery has been very unkynd to us, and has a mynd to aply himself to the Councel to gate the shyr eased of a pairt of the locality, and for bygons intends no reparation for the poor troopers. My Lord, I bigue that there be nothing done in that without we be heard.

My Lord, I hope your Lordship will pardon me that I have not sent in the prisoners that I have here; there is on of them that has been so tortered with the gravell, it was impossible to transport him. Beseides,

---

[41] The king's cash-keeper, brother of Archbishop James Sharp.

expecting considerable orders, I had no mynd to pairt with 30 or 40 horses; and then Sondays jorny has a little gaded our horses. No apearance here of any steer. I am, my Lord, your Lordships most humble servant.

To Linlithgow   Dundee, *Letters*, 27

Falkirk, 29 May 1679

My Lord, I came here last night with the horse and dragoons and munition in good pass. This morning a shoomaker fyred, out at his wyndow, in at the present baylys (where three of my men where siting at meat and bread,) two bullets with in a foot of them. The rogue flaid imediatly out of toun. Two contry men, after we had brok up his doors and missed him, came and declared they had seen him runing a quarter of a mylle of toune. I send a party after him, who found him lurking in a house. He is otherways a great rogue, and frequents field conventicles, and, they say, taks upon him to exercise.

I am certenly informed there is resolution taken amongst the whigues, that aighteen parishes shall meet Sonday nixt in Kilbryd moor with in four myles of Glascow. I resolve, thogh I doe not believe it, to advertise my Lord Rosse,[42] so that with our joint force we may attaque them. They say the ar to pairt no mor but keep in a body. I am, my Lord, your Lordship's most humble servant.

To Linlithgow   Dundee, *Letters*, 28

Glasgow, 1 June 1679

My Lord, Upon Saturday's night, when my Lord Rosse came in to this place, I marched out, and because of the insolency that had been done tue nights befor at Ruglen,[43] I went thither, and inquyred for the names. As soon as I got them, I sent out partys to sease on them, and found not only three of those rogues, but also ane intercomend minister called King.[44] We had them at Streven about six in the morning

---

[42] George, 11th Lord Ross (d. 1682), captain of dragoons.

[43] The covenanters, led by some of the murderers of Archbishop Sharp, had issued the Rutherglen Declaration (29 May) against all violations of the covenants.

[44] John King, chaplain to Lord Cardross. He was eventually convicted of treason and hanged at Edinburgh Cross on 14 August 1679.

yesterday, and resolving to convey them to this, I thought that we
might mak a little tour to see if we could fall upon a conventicle; which
we did, litle to our advantage; for, when we came in sight of them, we
found them drawen up in batell, upon a most advantagious ground,[45]
to which there was no coming, but throgh moses and lakes. They wer
not preaching, and had gat away all there women and shildring.

    They consisted of four bataillons of foot, and all well armed with
fusils and pitch forks, and three squadrons of horse. We sent both,
partys to skirmish, they of foot, and we of dragoons; they run for it, and
sent down a bataillon of foot against them; we sent threescor of
dragoons, who mad them run again shamfully; but in end, they
percaiving that we had the better of them in skirmish, they resolved a
generall ingadgment, and imediatly advanced with there foot, the horse
folouing; they came throght the lotche, and the greatest body of all
made up against my troupe; we keeped our fyr till they wer with in ten
pace of us; they recaived our fyr, and advanced to shok; the first they
gave us broght doun the coronet,[46] Mr Crafford, and Captain Bleith,
besides that, with a pitch fork they mad such an opening in my sorre[l]
horses belly, that his guts hung out half an elle, and yet he caryed me af
an myl; which so discoroged our men, that they sustined not the shok,
but fell into disorder.

    There horse took the occasion of this, and perseud us so hotly, that
we got no tym to rayly. I saved the standarts, but lost on the place about
aught or ten men, besides wounded; but the dragoons lost many mor.
They ar not com esily af on the other side, for I sawe several of them fall
befor we cam to the shok. I mad the best retraite the confusion of our
people would suffer, and am now laying with my Lord Ross. The toun
of Streven drou up, as we was making our retrait, and thoght of a pass
to cut us of; but we took couradge and fell to them, making them run,
leaving a dousain on the place. What these rogues will dou yet I know
not, but the contry was floking to them from all hands. This may be
counted the beginning of the rebellion in my opinion. I am, my Lord,
your Lordships most humble servant.

[P.S.] My Lord, I am so wearied, and so sleapy, that I have wryton this
very confusedly.

---

[45] Loudon Hill, also known as Drumclog.
[46] Cornet Robert Graham, commissioned 27 September 1678.

To Menteith   Fraser, *Menteith*, ii, 183

London, 3 July [1680]
My Lord, Whatever wher the motives obliged your Lordship to
cheange your resolutiones to me, yet I shall never forgate the
obligations that I have to you for the good desseins you once had for
me, both before my Lord Montrose cam in the play and after, in your
endewering to mak me nixt in the tayly,[47] especially in so generous a
way as to doe it without so much as latting me knou it.[48] All the return I
am able to mak is to offer you, in that franc and sincere way that I am
known to deal with all the world, all the service that I am capable of,
wer it with the hazard or even loss of my lyfe and fortun. Nor can I doe
less without ingratitud, considering what a generous and disinterested
friendship I have found in your Lordship. And your Lordship will doe
me, I hop, the justice to acknouledge that I have shouen all the respect to
your Lordship and my Lord Montrose in your second resolutions that
can be imagined.

I never enquyred at your Lordship nor him the reason of the cheange;
nor did I complain of hard usadge. Thogh really, my Lord, I must
bygue your Lordship's pardon, to say that it was extreamly grievous to
me to be turned out of that business, after your Lordship and my Lord
Montrose had ingadged me in it, and had wryten to Yrland in my
faveurs, and the thing that troubled me most was that I feared your
Lordship had mor estim for my Lord Montrose then me, for you could
have no other motive, for I am seur you had mor sense then to think the
offers he made you mor advantagious for the standing of your family
then those we wer on, for he would certenly mad up his owen, and I
would have brought in all myn to yours, and been perfaitly yours. Sir
James[49] and I togither would have boght in all the lands ever belonged
to your predecessors, of which you would have been as much maister as
of those you ar nou in possession; and I am sorry to see so much trust in
your Lordship to my Lord Montrose so ill rewarded.

If you had contineued your resolutions to me, your Lordship would

---

[47] Entail.

[48] In February 1680, Menteith granted the conveyance of his heavily-indebted lands and titles to
Montrose, retaining the liferent. The king, however, insisted on severe modifications to the grant. In
the event, Montrose did not live to inherit.

[49] Sir James Graham, father of Helen Graham.

not [have] been thus in denger to have your estate rent from your family; my Lord Montrose would not have loosed his reputation, as I am sorry to see he has don; Sir James would not have had so sensible an afront put upon them, if they had not refused me, and I would have been by your Lordship's faveur this day as hapy as I could wish. But, my Lord, we must all submit to the pleaseur of God Almighty without murmuring, knouing that evry body will have there lote.

My Lord, fearing I may be misrepresented to your Lordship, I think it my deuty to acquaint your Lordship with my cariadge since I cam hither in relation to those affaires. So soon as I cam, I told Sir James hou much he was obliged to you, and hou sincer your desseins wer for the standing of your family; withall I told him that my Lord Montros was certenly ingadged to you to mary his dochter, but that from good hands I had raison to suspect he had no dessein to perform it; and indeed my Lord Montrose seemed to mak no adress there at all in the begining, but hearing that I went somtymes there, he feared that I might gate ane interest with the father, for the dochter never apeared, so observent they wer to my Lord Montrose, and he thoght that if I should com to mak any friendship there, that when he cam to be discovered I might com to be acceptable, and that your Lordship might turn the cheass upon him. Wherfor he went there, and entred in terms to amuse them till I should be gon, for then I was thinking evry day of going away, and had been gon, had I not fallen seek. He contineued thus, making them formall wisits, and talking of the terms, till the tyme that your signature should pass, but when it cam to the King's hand it was stoped, upon the acount of the title, conform to the preperative of my Lord Caithness.[50]

My Lord Montrose, who, during all this tyme had never told me any thing of these affaires, nor almost had never spok to me, by Drumeller[51] and others, leat me knou that our differences proceeded from mistakes, and that if we mate we might com to understand on another, upon which I went to him. After I had satisfyed him of som things he complained of, he told me that the title was stoped, and asked

---

[50] John Campbell of Glenorchy (c.1635-1716) had a patent as earl of Caithness in 1677, as principal creditor of the late George Sinclair, 6th earl of Caithness. The king regretted agreeing to the transaction, which led to fighting in Caithness between the new earl and the legitimate heir. The earldom was restored to the latter in 1681, Campbell being granted a new patent as earl of Breadalbane.

[51] William Hay of Drumelzier.

me if I had no hand in it; for he thoght it could be no other way, seing Sir James concured. I asseured him I had not medled in it, as befor God I had not. So he told me he would setle the title on me, if I would assist him in the passing of it. I told him that I had never any mynd for the title out of the blood. He answered me, I might have Sir James' dochter and all. So I asked him hou that could be. He told me he had no dessein there, and that to secur me the mor, he had given comission to speak to my Lady Rothes about her dochter,[52] and she had recaived it kyndly. I asked hou he would com of,—he said upon ther not performing the terms, and offered to serve me in it, which I refused, and would not concur. He thoght to mak me serve him in his desseins, and brak me with Sir James and his Laidy; for he waint and insinuated to them as if I had a dessein upon their dochter, and was carying it on under hand.

So soon as I heared this, I went and told my Lady Graham all. My Lord Montrose came there nixt day and denyed it. Houever, they went to Windsor and secured the signature, but it was alrady don. They have not used me as I deserved at ther hands, but my dessein is not to complain of them, and they had raison to trust intierly on whom your Lordship had so strongly recomended. After all cam to all that Sir James offered to perform all the conditions my Lord Montros requyred, he knew not what to say, and so, being asheamed of his cariadge, went away without taking lieve of them, which was to finish his triks with contemp.

This is, my Lord, in as feu words as I can, the most substantiall part of that story. My Lord Montrose and som of his friends indevored to ruin that yong laidy's reputation to gate an excuse for his cariadge, and broght in my name. But I mad them quikly quyt those desseins, for there was no shadew of ground for it. And I must say that she has suffered a great deall for to complay with your Lordship's desseins, but could not doe less considering the good things you had desseined for her, and treuly, my Lord, if you ken her, you would think she deserved all, and would think strange my Lord Montrose should have neglected her.

My Lord, I know you want not the best advise of the nation, yet I think it not amiss to tell you that it is the opinion of evry body that you may recouer your estate, and that you oght to com and make your case

---

[52] Margaret Leslie (d. 1700), countess of Rothes. Her daughter, Anna, was born in 1676.

knouen to the King and Deuk.[53] Your family is as considerable as Caitnes or Maklen,[54] in whose standing they concern themselves highly. My Lord, you would by this means recover your affaires; you would see your cusing; and you and Sir James would understand on another, and tak right mesures for the standing of your family. If you lat your title stand in the airs male, your family must of necessity perish, seing in all apearance you will outlieve Sir James, and then it would com to the nixt brother, who has nether airs nor estate, so that your only way will be to transfer the title to that young laidy, and gate the father and mother to give you the disposing of her. The Deuk asseurs me that if my Lord Montrose would have maryed her, the title should have passed, as being in the blood, and that it may be don for any body who shall mary her with your consent. My Lord, if I thoght your Lordship wer to com up, I would wait to doe you service; for your oncle is old and infirm.

My Lord, I hop you will pardon this long letter, seing it is concerning a business touches you so neer, and that of a long tym I have not had the hapiness to intertain your Lordship. Tyme will shoe your Lordship who deserves best your friendship.

My Lord, things fly very high here; the indytments apear frequently against the honest Deuk, and I am feared things must brake out.[55] I am sorry for it; but I knou you, impatient of the desyr of doing great things, will rejoyse at this. Asseur yourself, if ever ther be baricades in Glascou again, you shall not want a call; and, my Lord, I bespeak ane imployment under you, which is to be your lieutenent generall, and I will asseur you we will mak the world talk of us. And therfor provyd me treues, as you promised, and a good bleu bonet, and I will asseur you there shall be no treuse trustier then myn. My Lord, dispond not for this disapointment, but shou resolution in all you doe. When my affaires goe wrong, I remember that saying of Loucan, *Tam mala Pompeii quam prospera mundus adoret.*[56] On has ocasion to shou there vigeur after a wrong stape to make a nimble recovery. You have don nothing amiss, but trusted too much to honor, and thoght all the world held it as sacred as you doe.

---

[53] James, duke of York, Claverhouse's patron.

[54] See p. 158, n. 50, and p. 161, n. 57.

[55] A reference to the Exclusion Crisis.

[56] 'The world should reverence Pompey as much in his misfortune as in his triumphs.' Lucan, *De Bello Civili* (*Pharsalia*), vii, l. 708.

My dear Lord, I hop you will doe me the honor to late me hear from you, for if there be nothing for your service here I will be in Scotland imediatly, for nou I am pretty well recovered. I knou my Lord Montrose will indevor to misrepresent me to your Lordship, but I hop he has forfited his credit with you, and anything he says to you nou is certently to abuse you.

My Lord, I have both at hom and abroad sustained the caracter of an honest and franc man, and defys the world to reproach me of anything. So, my Lord, as I have never fealed in my respect to your Lordship, I hop you will contineu that friendship for me which I have so much ambitioned. When I have the honor to see you, I will say mor of my inclination to serve you. I will bygue the favour of a lyn with the first post. I am, my Lord, Your Lordship's most faithfull and humble servant.

[P.S.] Excuse this scribling, for I am in heast, going to Windsor, thogh I wryt tuo sheets.

To Menteith   Fraser, *Menteith*, ii, 188

London, 8 July 1680

My Lord, I knou not if myn came to your Lordship's hands, wherin I gave you a full account of all that has passed here concerning your Lordship's affairs, and I hop you will give faith too it. All I dessein is to inform your Lordship, so that you may not be abused by those who desseins ill betuixt you and your oncle, apurpose to ruin your family. I will bear them that testimony, that they have gone so great a lenth to complay with your Lordship's desseins, that they have don things far belou there quality for to oblidge my Lord Montrose, and the yong lady cannot be but sensible of the affront that is don her by this neglect, after your Lordship had procured her consent, and her father and mother made so great advances. But they regrait nothing, as they say, seing they have had ocasion to testify there respects to your Lordship, and to shoe the world hou great a desyr they had to preserve your ancient family.

Speaking with the Deuk the other day concerning the Maclen's business, which is nou setled,[57] I took ocasion to tell the Deuk that your

[57] Sir John Maclean of Duart had reached an agreement with the earl of Argyll, who promised to pay him £500 sterling per year.

Lordship's case was very hard, and mad him understand a litle the business, as far as could be don without wronging my Lord Montrose' reputation too much, which I should be unwilling to doe, whatever he doe by me. The Deuk sheuk his head, and said it was not tyght. I said nothing, seing I had no comission, and that it was only by way of discours.

My Lord, I owe you all the good offices ar in my pouer, and if you will imploy your friends, I doute not to see you again maister of your owen affaires, which is the thing the world I wish most. I am going, for oght I knou, to Dunkerk with the envoyes to see the Court of France. I am only to be away aight days, so your Lordship may lay your comands on me. I am, my Lord, Your Lordship's most humble servant.

To Menteith   Fraser, *Menteith*, ii, 189

London, 24 August 1680

My Lord, I wes very glaid at the recait of yours to hear that you wer in good health, and am very sensible of the kynd expressiones of your Lordship's friendship, which I shall by all meens indevor to deserve. I was surprysed at the reading of your Lordship's letter to hear that my affaires went ill in Scotland, and had been mor alarumed had I not by the same post had a lyn from on who has the direction of all my affaires,[58] who asseured me they wer never in better order, both the affaires of my estate and troup, only ther was a stop in the passing my signatur of the forfitur,[59] and I stayed here a purpos for to secur it, which nou, I think, I have don, tho' I never had raison to fear it, notwithstanding all oposition I had, and the King and Deuk, my friends.

My Lord, I hop your Lordship did not mistak the dessein of my letter to you, which was only to inform you of my cariadge, least I might be misrepresented to you, and to offer you my service in the recoverie of your affaires, being informed that you was resolved to put yourself in your owen place. This I owed to your friendship, and to the good wishes I have for the standing of your ancient family. But, as I have always been, I shall be still far from pressing you anything in faveurs of myself. I think you will not tak in ill pairt that I wish you not to suffer so

[58] Possibly his brother David Graham.

[59] Patrick Macdowall of Freugh was forfeited in February 1680 for his part in the Bothwell Bridge rising of the previous year. His estate was granted to Claverhouse in February 1681.

noble a family to fall, in the standing of which I know you have so much concearn, as that I believe you mak it your only care, your honor and memory being inseparably attached to it, but the way to doe it I leave to yourself, as the only propre judge; whatever way you doe it, I shall asseur you of my weak indevors.

They say they have never don any thing to disoblidge you, and really, my Lord, they have got a great slight put upon them by complaying with your desseins, nether is it fit to loose them, for I have heard my Lady say that if her dochter dayed, she had resolved to leave to recover your family the best pairt of her estate. I am, with all the sincerity imaginable, my Lord, Your Lordship's most humble servant. [P.S.] My Lord, your cousin has been seek these ten days of the small poks, but in all apearance will recover, tho' she has tham mighty ill. I will have the honor to see your Lordship shortly.

To Menteith   Fraser, *Menteith*, ii, 198

London, 1 October 1681

My Dear Lord, In enswer to what your Lordship was pleased to wryt me, concerning the information a certain person[60] gave you, that I should have given ill caracters and said things of your Lordship to my Lord Duk of Lauderdelle[61] that I am ashamed to repeat, I shall vindicat myself in feu words. My Lord, I swear befor God Almighty, and renonces all right to His blissings, if ever directly or indirectly I ever gave good or bad caracters of your Lordship to my Lord Lauderdell, or ever cam upon your person or affaires with him. And to shou you hou clear I am of it, I give upon my salvation, which I believe you doe me the justice to think I would not doe for the world if I wer no absolutly inocent. You shall have both on soull and body, for I am ready to spend my blood in revenge of so base and couerdly an injury as that was to forge upon dessein of interest so untreu and improbable storys; and heir I declair that certain person ane infamous layer, and humbly bigues your Lordship to shou him this letter, wherin I tell him, if he dars owen it, he will late me knou his name. But no man that is capable of the baseness to invent such lays can have the couradge to sustain them.

---

[60] Either Sir John Dalrymple (1648-1707), later 2nd Viscount and 1st earl of Stair, or an anonymous correspondent on his behalf.
[61] John Maitland (1616-1682), 2nd earl and (1672) duke of Lauderdale, secretary of state from 1660 to 1680.

My Lord, this story is dessein'd to wrong your reputation. They mak me say the storys which they would gladly make you believe the world thinks. But believe no such thing, for your reputation is as intyr here as ever, and the world is perswaded of your ability in affairs, and knous you not to be chan[ge]able, that you ar fixt to the interest and standing of your family as you ar to honor and honesty. I should have had raison to think you as they say, if such storys as those could have made any impressiones upon you. I hop you doe not pairt so easily with your friends, nor alters upon so slight grounds your measures, and I rejoyce to see how generously you have used me in it. You will be pleased that you have don so when you see my inocency deserves it.

My Lord, the world does you justice here. Every body says you did nothing but upon very just and honorable grounds, and that if people has delt unhandsomly with you they ar seur you ar sensible of it, and will in your owen tyme and way resent it, and your friends oght to confyd and refer all to your owen conduct, since by experience they see that from nothing you have recovered your esteat by your industry and activity, which shall hender me from having the least thoght that you can tak wrong meseurs. When I have the honor to see you at Mentieth, I hop to intertain you of other things than that certain person did. I will reather study to gain you friends then rob you of the frankest you have, for without vanity I pretend to that title, and doutes not to deserve it.

I rejoice to hear by the letter you wryt to my Laidy Grahame you have nou taken my trade of my hand, that you ar becom the terror of the godly. I begin to think it tyme for me set a work again, for I am amoulous[62] of your reputation, not by what I have heard by any relationes cam from the Counsell, but what I had from people came from Scotland, who gave me particular acount of all, which maks me think that there is no such care taken to inform the King, or to perswad him to recompense your services as certain person maks you believe. But, my Lord, comfort yourself with the satisfaction you have to doe well, and that if you be not rewarded it is nether your falt nor the King's, since you doe good things, and he is ready to reward them wer he acquainted with them.

My dear Lord, Labe has made me in love with the Yles of Mentieth. He says the greatest things in the world of it. There is nothing in the

---

[62] Emulous: desirous of rivalling.

world I long so much for as to see you there. It shall be the first place I goe to when I com to Scotland. Labe tells me of all your kyndness to him, for which I return your Lordship a thousand thanks. I had forgot to justify myself as to all other persons of quality here, and I swear frely upon my salvation I never spok to any of you but as I oght to doe, with all the respect and estim imaginable.

I always laid the sadle on the right horse, and if you dout, which I think you will not, after what I have said, I will gate your uncle Sir James to justify me, who will bear me witness how often he has heared me doe you justice, confirming him in the good opinion he has of you, both as to your capacity in affaires and sincer desseins for the good of your family. Far from being reproached for speaking ill of you, I expected thanks for the good things I said of you and your family. Tyme will mak you knou whou are treu friends and who ar not. You shall be seur to fynd me, as I say I am, my dearest Lord, Your Lordship's most obedient and most humble servant.

To Menteith   Fraser, *Menteith*, ii, 201

London, 1 October 1681

My Dear Lord, I thoght fit to wryt this apairt, and not to put it in the other letter, dessein your Lordship should sho it to evry body for my vindication. My Lord, I am infinitly sensible of your Lordship's kyndness to me in wryting so kyndly to my Lady Graham and her dochter, especially when people had been representing me so foolly to you. I have not dared to present them, because that in my Laidy's letter you wished us much joy, and that we might live happy togither, which looked as if you thoght it a thing as good as don. I am seur my Laidy, of the heumeur I knou her to be, would have gon mad that you should think a business that concerned her so neerly concluded before it was ever proposed to her; and in the dochter's you was pleased to tell her of my affections to her, and what I have suffered for her; this is very galant and oblidging, but I am afeared they would have misconstructed it, and it might doe me prejudice; and then in both, my Lord, you wer pleased to take pains to shoe them almost clearly they had nothing to expect of you, and teuk from them all hopes which they had, by desyring them to requyr no mor but your consent.

Indeed I think it not propre your Lordship should ingadge yourself at

all. They would be glade to knou that you only had a resolution to recover your business, they would leave the reast to your owen goodness; and for my [part] I declair I shall never press your Lordship in any thing but what you have a mynd to, and I will asseur you I need nothing to perswad me to take that yong laidy. I would take her in her smoak.

My dear Lord, be yet so good as to wryt neu letters to the same purpose, holding out those things which it wer to anybody els might be very well said, and, if you please, when you say you give them your advyse to the match, tell them that they will not repent it, and that doing it at your desyr you will doe us any kyndness you can, and look on us as persons under your protection, and indevor to see us thrive, which oblidges you to nothing, and yet incouradges them.

Sir James and his Laidy say when they goe to Conelton, their neu purchase, that they will com to Scotland, or if they be not able to goe so far, they wil meet you about Carlil, or any other place you would doe them the honor to com toe, raither then goe bak to Yrland without having had the hapiness to see you, since you have the goodness to say you would have seen them or nou had they stayed in Yrland. I really believe if you would invyt them they would com and see you a purpose. I will be in impatiance till I have those letters.

I bygue your Lordship not to grudge at the truble I give you to wryt tuyse. I hope you shall not have occasion to regrait any thing you doe for me, and in doing this you doe me the greatest favour I can recaive of any mortall, so I hop, my Lord, you will think it worth the whyll to oblidge a friend of yours at so high a rait, for tho' you never doe mor for me, I will be eternelly yours, and by geating me that yong laidy you mak me happy, and without you I can never doe it, so I am in your reverence, and yet looks not on my fate as mor desperat for that. For the love of God wryt kyndly of me to them, and promise them kyndness, but I never shall suffer them to think of any engagements from you.

Long may you lieve to enjoy your esteat, whill I have the occasion to acquyt myself of so many and so considerable obligations I owe you. I am, my dearest Lord, Your Lordship's most faithfull, most oblidged, and most humble servant.

[P.S.] My Lord, Sir James, his Laidy, Madam Coxdeall, and your fair cusing kisses most kyndly your hands, and desyrs me to present to you there humble service.

To Menteith   Fraser, *Menteith*, ii, 203

Edinburgh, 11 December 1681

My Dear Lord, I was longing extreamly to hear from you, impatient for to know the good newes of your perfait recovery, and am exceedingly overjoyed with it now. I have been looking for an occasion to wryt to you these five or six days bypast to give you acount how my Lord Montrose is using you. He has boght an infeftment from Mr Riven upon the barony of Drumond, and has given for it a thousand pounds sterling; but I am informed that it is not good for much, because my Lord Readfoord has the right in his person; this you oght to know better then I.

My Lord, you see by this and many other things, hou prejudiciall it is for you not to com to som settlement in your affairs, ether on way or other, and in the mean tyme my aidge slips away, and I loose other occasions, as I supose the young laidy also does. And now I am very glaid to see your Lordship pressing it. For my pairt, I shall be wanting in nothing that can contribut to your Lordship's satisfaction or the standing of your noble family. Your Lordship's letter I shall send fordward, and perswad them by all the motives I can to undertake this jorny your Lordship proposes. But I fear they ar alraidy gon out of Ingland, and will be unwilling to cross the seas so soon again. However if they be in Yrland, I shall propose that they com to my house in Galoua, and there they shall need no protection, for I am in good hope not only to comand the forces there, but be Scherif of Galoua.

My Laidy Graham is a very cuning weoman, and certenly will wryt bak that she will be unwilling to com so far upon uncertentys; yet she did propose, a mater of four moneths agoe, to meet your Lordship in sum pairt of Ingland. I shall send ane express for Yrland so soon as I goe in to Galoua, which will be within ten days or a fourtnight. If your Lordship would wryt to this purpose directly to my Laidy, they would take it much more kyndly, and be far the readier to comply with your deseirs. The raison why I know so litle of them is that I was ashamed to wryt, not knowing what to say, seing your Lordship was not resolved after all I had promised to them on your behalf. I am perswaded that we may bring it yet to a hapie close, if your Lordship doe your pairt, of which I shall not doubt. I am, my dearest Lord, Your Lordship's most humble and most obliged servant.

[P.S.] My Lord, It is no mater whither the Yle be prepaired or not, I am seur they raither be in it as it is, and welcom to your Lordship then in any palace in Christandoom, and I hop we will be all merry about the hall fyr. My humble service to Mr Archibald and James and his laidy, and most particularly to the verteus gentlewemen, yo...

To Queensberry   HMC, *Queensberry*, 264

New Galloway, 16 February 1682

My Lord, I hope you will pardon me that you have not heared from me till nou. I send your Lordship here inclosed a copy of what I have wryten to the generall,[63] which is the first acount I have given to any body of my concern in this contry. I shall not need say any thing of the general of affairs here, having, may be, given but too long ane acount alraidy; houever, I thoght better say mor then anogh then omit any thing [that] should be sayd. As I came from Stranrau about Glenluse, I maite with Castlesteuart and his brother,[64] to whom I gave all the asseurance imaginable of my caire of their concerns, as I did to my Lord Galoua,[65] whom I had the honor to see at his owen house; and loot them knou that it was particularly recomended to me by your Lordship; they seemed very sensible of your faveur and satisfyed with it. I had the good fortun to see Bruchten, Baldun and Ylle,[66] who offer their assistance in all [that] may concern the King's service.

When I was at Dumfries severall of your Lordship's friends did me the faveur to see me and asseur me upon your Lordship's acount of their friendship. I waited on my Lord Nidsdell and wee have established a corespondence. Stenes[67] did me the faveur to call here yesterday as he went to see som of his relations. He told me Craigdaloch and Maxwelltoun[68] and severall others waited at Maxiltoun for me, thinking I would pass that way, so that I am here resolved to lieve in

---

[63] General Thomas Dalyell (c.1599-1685), who replaced Linlithgow as commander in chief after the battle of Bothwell Bridge.

[64] William Stewart of Castlestewart and Robert Stewart of Robeinston were suspected of covenanting sympathies but were cleared of all charges.

[65] Alexander Stewart (d. c.1690), 3rd earl of Galloway.

[66] Richard Murray of Broughton, Sir David Dunbar of Baldoon, and Thomas Lidderdale of St Mary's Isle, stewart-depute of Kirkcudbright.

[67] John Douglas of Stenhouse.

[68] Robert Ferguson of Craigdarroch and Robert Lawrie of Maxwelltown.

perfait friendship will all that ar your friends; and I must acknouledge I fynd them extreamly disposed to it; which I atribut to your Lordship's influence. I was last night to wait on my Laidy Kenmur, my Lord being from hom, who she said kneu nothing of my coming. I told her what peins your Lordship had been at to keep her house from being a garison, and she seemed very sensible of it. I am sorry that I must acquaint you, but I shall doe it to no body els, that I am certenly informed my Lord Kenmure[69] has conversed frequently with rebeles, particularly Barskob.[70]

As to the Treasury Comission,[71] I fear I shall not be able to doe what I could wish because of the season, for of their corn and straw their is not much left, and their beasts this tyme of the year ar not worth the dryving. The rebelles have lieved, I fynd, peacably here till nou and their wyfes ar still in their houses, and takes it worse nou then they would have don at first to be ruined; for then they expected it, and nou after so long forbearance they wer becom secur.

The contry here abouts is in great dreed. Upon our marche yesterday most men wer flaid not knouing against whom we desseined; but the act of counsell about the saif conduct[72] amuses many, and will be of use to make them mor unexcusable in the eyes of the people, if they make not use of it, which I am feared feu will doe. My humble opinion is, that it should be unlawful for the donators[73] to compound with any body for the behoof of the rebell, till once he have made his peace; for I would have all footing in this contry taken from them that will stand out. And for the securing the rents to the donators and the King, it is absolutly necessary their be a fixt garison in Kenmur instead of Dumfries; for without it I am nou fully convinced wee can never secur the peace of this contry, nor hunt those rogues from their hants. It is a mighty strong pleace and propre above all ever I sau for this use. I shall give this advise to no body but your self, and I doe it the mor friely that my Laidy told

[69] Alexander Gordon (d. 1698), 5th Viscount Kenmure.

[70] Robert McLellan of Barscobe.

[71] A commission of 27 October 1681 empowered sheriffs to fix prices of corn, hay and straw requisitioned for military use: RPC, 3rd ser., vii, 235-7. See also the proclamation on the subject: RPC, 3rd ser., vii, 327-9.

[72] A reference to the privy council's warrant of 27 January 1682, empowering Claverhouse to quarter his troops in Galloway, and to summon suspected covenanters before him, granting them a safe-conduct for up to 14 days: RPC, 3rd ser., vii, 323.

[73] Those to whom forfeited estates were granted.

me, if the King would bestou two or three hondred pounds to repair the house, she would be very well pleased his souldiers came to lieve in it. Doe in it as you think best; but if it could be don with their satisfaction, it would be great service to the King; for having that post seur I might with the pairty I have answer for the rest.

I have taken out the half of Captain Strachans pairty from Dumfries, not seing what they ar good for their, unless it be to lay secur and doe nothing. I sent yesterday tuo pairtys in search of those men your Lordship gave me a list of; on of them to a buriall in the Glencairn, the other to the fair at Thornhill; neither of them are yet returned; but Stenes tells me that the pairty at the buriall miscaried; that he pointed to them on of the men, and they took another for him, tho I had choysed a man to comand the pairty that was born their about. They shall not stay in this contry but I shall have them.

The first thing I mynd to doe is to fall to work with all that have been in the rebellion, or accessory their too by giving men, mony or armes; and nixt recetts, and after, field conventicles; for what remains of the lawes against the fanatiks, I will threaten much, but forbear sever excicution for a whyll, for fear people should grou desperat and increase too much the number of our enimys.

My Lord, their is on faveur I must deseir of you and I believe when I have got it I will not by land with it; which is, that your Lordship would be pleased to consider, that having business in so many places and with so many people, I will be put to great expence; and there is no doing business without being open handed; so would desyr your Lordship would speak to the Deuk and represent the thing to the Lords of the Treasury, that I may have the gift of any that ar not yet forfited that I can fynd probation against. I mean only of ther movables; and shall with it suport all the expence of the government, as mantinence of prisoners, witness, speys, and all other expence necessary in this contry; for your Lordship would lait them knou that I have many things to doe extrinsik to the office of an officer.

Your Lordship will doe me ane other faveur, which is, that the Lords of the Treasury lait me not suffer in my absence, that I be payed the three moneths pay we ar in areer. I would not, my Lord, take this friedom if you had not aloued me to doe it. If there by any thing you would have me to doe, or any thing I doe amiss, you will doe me great

kyndness to tell me. I shall wryt often and much. I am, my Lord, your most faithfull servant.

To Menteith   Fraser, *Menteith*, ii, 204

New Galloway, 17 February 1682

My Dear Lord, Tho' I have nothing to say that is worthy your noticing, yet I would [not] neglect any opportunity of asseuring you of my respects. Befor it be long, I will may be have som thing to say that you will not be displeased with. So fair you well. I am in great heast; their is a water rysing betwixt me and the other half of my pairty, so I must decamp. I am, my Lord, Your most faithfull servant.

To Queensberry   HMC, *Queensberry*, 266

Dumfries, 22 February 1682

My Lord, There is no body has mor raison then I to rejoyse in evry thing that contributs to your Lordships honor and greatness; and I can not forbear to congratulat this leat marke of faveur the King has put upon you, and perswade my self he will not stop there.[74] I wish he may always confer his honors on such persons as your Lordship, whose merit and fortun will adde lustre to that dignity.

My Lord, I had a lettre from Lague[75] by your Lordships comand, wherein he told me the Deuk compleaned I had been so long a wryting. I sent ane express on Friedy morning with lettres to your Lordship; nor could I wryt sooner, for it would have been to no purpose to doe it befor I cam to Stranawe, and from thence I could not have given any acount of the contry; beseids, I marched hither almost as fast as any body I could have sent; so I hop he will [not] atribut it to neglect in me. The other pairt of Lagues lettre was for remouving the garison from this; which I should imediatly doe, wer it not that I perswad my self that your Lordship will think better, what I am to propose; and in the mean tyme the contry suffers no prejudice; for I have discharged calling for any mor locality till I knou your Lordships pleaseur, there being anogh till then.

---

[74] Queensberry had just been raised to a marquis.
[75] Sir Robert Grierson of Lag, the real-life model for Sir Walter Scott's Redgauntlet.

My Lord, your Lordship would see by my letter to the generall hou I have provyded for my pairty, 2 weeks provisions at Stranrau, 3 at Wiguetoun, 3 at Kilkoubrie, 3 at Dumfries, from the ten parishes in the Steuartrie, and 2 at the Neutoun, which will serve us till the grass. There remained Captain Strahans troup to provyd for, and befor I cam hither there was a meeting apointed of the Comissioners, but they mait since. I was not present nor kneu I what they wer to doe but I am informed they continueued the former raits, which wer very saisonable; and apointed a locality for three scor of horses or mor, as the comanding officer should requyre, to be layd on upon Nidsdeall and Anandell, and that imediatly ther should be a moneths provision broght in, which was done by some parishens befor I came bak or kneu any thing of all this; which I see proceeded all from their not knouing my dessein, which I supose has been the raison why they have addressed themselfs to your Lordship, thinking it would fall heavy.

My Lord, you would see by my last that I remouved the half of the garison then. I purpose not to keep any here but tuenty, and that provision, which was layd on for on month for thriescor of horse will serve tuenty horse for three moneths; so that wee need no mor from this contry but that on moneth for threescor of hors; and they have not furnished any befor. I am informed it will be hardly worth the noticing. If you doe not aprove of this, lait me knou, and I shall imediatly remove them, but I will have difficulty to reach with partys this contry from Kilkoubrie; beseids the generall will be mad.

My Lord, I caused sease on in your Lordships list at the Thornhill hill fair called Williamson of Overcaitloch. He is a tenent of Craiguedall-ochs, who has wryten to sett him at liberty upon his promise to produce him which I bygued his pardon for, till I should hear from your Lordship.

My Lord, you desyr by your memorandum that I should send to Edinbourg any of those persons I take. I can doe any thing with them your Lordship pleases here, by vertue of my Comission; but lait me knou if you dessein to have them there it shall be don. I have spok with most pairt of the forfited heritors wyfes at their owen houses, but see litle inclination in them to compound with the donators, or mak their peace with the King, save only Machremors brother. I have so far prefered the publik concern to my owen, that I have not so much as

called at Freuch,[76] tho I passed in sight of it. I can catch no body, they are all so alarumed.

My Lord Deuk Hamilton[77] was pleased to tell me befor I pairted, that I would doe well to lay closs in houses, for he would make it so uneasy for the Whighs to lieve in the West, that, he would send them all in to me; but by what I see yet, I send mor in on him then he does on me. My Lord, I have a proposition to make which would secur the peace both of the West and this contry, and I am perswaded will seem raisonable to your Lordship, and I wonder no body has thoght on it yet; but I will say nothing till I have put things to som order here, and I will bigue lieve for three or four days to com to Edinbourg and give you ane acount of it.

My Lord, be pleased to lait me knou if your Lordship desseined by your deseiring I should doe nothing here till you com, that I should not medle with rebells and recetts, or only the lawes against fanatiques. I hop your Lordship has mynded me for the movobilles of any [that] ar not yet forfited. If I give you the trouble of long letters, remember your comands at pairting to your Lordships most humble and faithfull servant.

[P.S.] Since the writing of my letter the provist of Wiguetoun cam to me and compleaned of my Lord Kenmores deforcing a messenger first; and then the second tym his factor robed the messenger, and would force him to swear he should not reveal that he had taken the letters from him. This is a hygh misdemaineur, and it is fit your Lordship make him sensible; for this and other things might hailp to ruin a man [who] had no friends. Your Lordship may see by this hou necessary a constant force is here for the excicution of the lawes in ordinary cases betuixt man and man, lait be in the concerns of the government.

To Queensberry   HMC, *Queensberry*, 267

New Galloway, 1 March 1682
My Lord, I received your Lordships of the 21 at Kilkoubrie on the 26, and the other of the 25 I recaived just nou, and am very sensible of your Lordships care of the publik concern, and goodness to me in giving me

[76] The forfeited estate granted to Claverhouse in 1681.
[77] William Douglas (1634–1694), 3rd duke of Hamilton.

so particular and exact returns,[78] which others neglect to doe, and especially my good friend, the Advocat,[79] who wreats to me very kyndly; but very litle in return of any thing I desyr of him; but I knou he ordinarly loses the letter, and forgats the business befor he have the tyme to make any return.

My Lord, I am very happy the Deuk is pleased with my procedeurs. I knou much will depend upon your Lordships testimony. I shall be carfull of all your Lordship recomends to me in your letters. For my Lord Kenmur, I have taken information of his business, and he will not be as yet onworthy of your protection, as my brother will tell you, and as you will see by my letter to the generall; so I need not trouble your Lordship with any particulars. I wish the Gordons here wer transplanted to the north, and excheanged with ane other branch of that family, who ar so very loyall there and so disaffected here.

Mr Alexander[80] is here and I shall follou his advyse: that gentleman in the Glencairn shall have the honor of frequent visits, and all other faveur I can shou him. Craigdallochs man upon his letter, which I have receaved, I shall lait ut upon caution, and all other things in either of your letters I shall faithfully observe. The proposal I wrot to your Lordship of, for securing the peace, I am seur will please in all things, but on, that it will be som what out of the Kings pokett.

The way that I see taken in other places is to put lawes severly against great and small in excicution; which is very just: but what effects does that produce, but mor to exasperat and alienat the hearts of the wholl body of the people; for it renders three desperat wher it gains on; and your Lordship knous that in the greatest crymes it is thoght wyse[s]t to pardon the multitud and punish the ringleaders, wher the number of the guilty is great, as in this case of wholl contrys.

Wherfor I have taken ane other cours here. I have called two or three parishes togither at on church, and after intimating to them the pouer I have, I raid them a libell narating all the acts of parlement against the fanatiks, wherby I made them sensible hou much they wer in the Kings reverence, and asseured them he was relenting nothing of his former severity against dissenters, nor care of mantening the esteblished

---

[78] Unfortunately, none of Queensberry's letters to Claverhouse have survived.

[79] Sir George Mackenzie of Rosehaugh (1636–1691), Lord Advocate.

[80] Alexander Cairncross (d. 1701), minister of St Michael's, Dumfries; in 1684 he became successively bishop of Brechin and archbishop of Glasgow.

goverment, as they might see by his doubling the fynes in the late Act of Parlement; and, in end, told them that the King had no dessein to ruin any of his subjects he could recleam, nor I to inrich my self by their crymes, and therfor any who would resolve to conform and lieve regularly might expect faveur, excepting only recetters and ring-leaders.

Upon this on Sunday last their was about three hondred people at Kilkoubrie church: som that for seven year befor had never been there. So that I doe expect, that with in a short tyme, I could bring tuo pairts of three to the church. But, when I have don that, it is all to no purpose; for we will be no sooner gon but in coms there ministers, and all repents and fall bak to ther old ways; so that it is in vain to think of any setlement here, without a constant force pleased in garison; and this is the opinion of all the honest men here, and their deseir; for there ar som of them, doe what they lyk, they cannot keep the preachers from their houses in their absence: so made ar som of their wyfes.

So the thing I would propose for remedie for all this, is, that their be a hondred dragoons reased for this contry. The King may give maintenence to the men and the contry to the horses; which I shall answer for they shall doe, because they or all in our reverence; and is it raisonable that this contry should be at less expence then other well affected pairts of the kingdom? Doe not we pay the suply for there follys? Have we not mor then they the expense of the militia? Their disaffection is a good raison why they should have less trust, but their trouble and expense should be equall to ours; so when the steuartry and shyr of Galoua give maintenance to a hondred horses, which is the on half of the wholl expence of the troup, they ar but equall with others, considering their want of militia and their disorders; and if the King will doe his pairt, I shall undertake for the contry as a Galoua Laird.

The ways I will propose will lessen the expence extreamly; first, if the Deuk pleases, I will offer myself to take the surintendence of them with out any pay; and for the nixt officer who is to be the drudge, he may have six pounds a day by taking tuo men of evry on of our troups of horse. We wer sixty and there is on taken of for the artilleri, so there nou remains 59 which does not well: but if these 2 were taken of, we would be just the establishment of Holland which is 57, and with the corporalls in rank as they oght to be maks just 20 in each rank, which is right.

For the cornet, I must be excused if I propose to destroy a goverment

was made for the governors cause.[81] I think the pay would be as well bestoued this way, seing he has no body to gaird but solen geese and ministers; the first will not flee away, and the others would be as well in Blakness or Dumbarton. Nou for the hondred men at sixpence a day, I would first mak use of the four and tuenty ar in the Bass, remains 76 which would amount to about seven hondred pounds a year; and for that your Lordships of the Treasury might fynd a way to cut of som ydle pension, and I hear my Lord Neuwark[82] is dead, which is four of it; and if it could be got no where els, it were better sell that rok, and the money of it would serve both here and in the West, for I could undertake the same thing might be don there.

I will asseur you there has been no mor faisable project, tho I say it myself; for, first, it would secur this contry, then if those of the West wer frustrat of this retreat, they would be easilyer found. Then this might in all occasions be a brave troup of fuseliers or granadiers, when iff euer the King had occasion; for I should bread them to either or both, as the Deuk had a mynd; and I would desyr lieve to drawe out of the tuo regiments a hondred of the best musketiers had served abroad, and I should take horses here amongst the suffering siners; and I will take the liberty to say, that what ever way be taken to doe it, we need mor horse and dragoons. If this doe not, I may brake my head to no purpose; for I knou after that no other way but to doe as others, and gate as much mony as I can, which I have not thoght on as yet, by puting the lawes in exeicution. I desyr, if your Lordship lyk it, you may late the Deuk hear it, as I propose it, and speak the Generall, and the Advocat, and my Lord President,[83] and the Register[84] about it. I am, my Lord, your Lordships most humble and faithfull servant.

To Menteith   Fraser, *Menteith*, ii, 205

New Galloway, 1 March 1682
My Dear Lord, If you be gon from Edinbourg befor this com to your hands, I knou not what to say; but if you be stil their, I must tell you it is

---

[81] The governor of the Bass Rock, which was garrisoned and used as a prison.

[82] David Leslie, Lord Newark (d. 1682), the covenanting general.

[83] Sir George Gordon of Haddo (1637-1720), lord president of the court of session, 1681-1682, later chancellor, 1682-1684. Created earl of Aberdeen, November 1682.

[84] Sir George Mackenzie of Tarbat (1630-1714), clerk register, 1681-1689. Created Viscount Tarbat, 1685; earl of Cromartie, 1703.

most necessary ẏee meet. If you could com to the Bille,[85] which is aighteen mylle from Edinbourg, I should be seur to meet you there. My brother will see you, and lait him know your measeurs, that he may advertise me. I have had on in Yrland whom I shall bring alongs [with] me, and you shall knou all. Send no body to Yrland, but take no newe measeurs till I see you, for I have thought s[uch wi]ll [be be]st for ... family to doe in the circumstances you ar in. So fair you well, my dearest Lord. Your humble servant.

To Queensberry   HMC, *Queensberry*, 269

Wigtown, 5 March 1682

My Lord, you needs not expect great things from me on heast as to the seasing any considerable rebelles; for I never mak so much as the least search for them, knouing hou much they ar upon their gaird, if they be not out of the contry; and by this I desein not to harass the troupes, till I have made them secur. Old Craichley[86] cam yesterday and got a saif conduct for his son and an other heritor called Makgie[87] that has not yet been heard of. Here in the shyr I fynd the lairds all folluing the exemple of a leat great man, and still a considerable heritor here amongst them,[88] which is, to lieve regularly themselfs, but have their houses constant hants of rebelles and intercomed persons, and have their childring baptysed by the saim, and then lay all the cleam on their wyfes, condeming them and swearing they can not help what is don in their absence.

But I am resolved this gest shall pass no longer here, for it [is] laghing and fooling the goverment; and it will be mor of consequence to punish on considerable laird then a hondred litle bodys. Beseids, it is juster, because these only sin by exemple of those. I have not fallen yet to work in good earnest in any pairt, because I thoght best to understand the steat of the contry befor I layed doun my measeurs; but am now ready to make it in a feu days to goe all of a piece over all this contry.

---

85 Bellspool, near Drumelzier on the upper Tweed.
86 James Gordon of Craichlaw.
87 Alexander MacGee of Drumbuy.
88 Sir James Dalrymple (1619-1695), later 1st Viscount Stair: exiled in 1681 for refusing to take the Test.

My Lord, there will [be] a necessity befor I can setle,this contry, that I have lieve yet to give the bond to litle people, for there ar a great numbre guilty especially of the second rysing[89] and mustering; for which your Lordship remembers I was sent hither; and all people that went not out of the contry, I think there should be som test of loyalty put to them, and so many years rent taken af them; and then secured of their lyfe and fortune: and if the Counsell thoght fit, with som instructions I might doe this.

I forgot to give your Lordship acount last tyme about the rents of the rebelles. I fynd it the hardest thing in the world to make a rentell of those lands wer never sett; hou ever I am taking all the peins I can, and in a feu days will be able to give your Lordship acount, but I am informed by all the gentry that it will be as good a way as any to take the valeued rent, and ad som what mor, as a fourt pairt, as for exempell a man of three thousand pounds of valued rent is worth neer seven. In heast, I am, my Lord, your Lordships most humble servant.

[P.S.] I have again waited on my Lord Galouay, and seen his brothers here; and Mr Alexander and I have confered and fynd him very frank.

My Lord, I hear you have taken on Mr Patrik Verner at Edinbourg, and fearing that he might be represented as no dangerous man, I have thoght fit to send your Lordship this information, which may be all proven, I have it from a very worthy man who desyrs not his hand be seen. I have not the tyme to copy it over. I shall say nothing but desyr your Lordship to remember that from such men flous all our evills.

To be shoune to the Duke.

To Queensberry   HMC, *Queensberry*, 270

Stranraer, 13 March [1682]
My Lord, I am sorry that their comes such alarums from the West. I can hardly believe that things ar com that lenth yet. I am seur there is not the least apearances here as yet, and if any thing give them couradge it will be the retyring of the forces. I think it is very just we should be on our gaird; and I am resolved to keep closer, tho I should loss the movibles and take feu prisoners. I was just begining to send out many pairtys, fynding the rebells becom secur and the contry so quyet in all apearance.

[89] The rising led by Richard Cameron and Donald Cargill, defeated at Airds Moss, 22 July 1680.

I sent out a pairty with my tutor, Labe, three nights agoe. The first night he teuk Drumbui, and on Mkelellen and that great villain MkClorg,[90] the smith at Menegaff, that made all the clikys,[91] and after whom the forces has troted so often; it cost me both paines and mony to knou hou to fynd him. I am resolved to hang him, for it is necessary I make som exemple of severity least rebellion be thoght cheap here. There can not be alyve a mor wiked fellou. The pairty is not yet com bak, which maks me in hopes there is mor taken.

I am to meet to morou with all the heritors of this shyr, to see how they ar inclyned as to bringing their people to church and securing the peace of the contry, that I may be favorable to them. I fynd it no hard work to confirm this shyr, had I but tyme anogh; but I bygue your Lordship to believe there is no fear of this pairty, for tho all Galoua would ryse I would fynd a way to gett by them.

Nou when your Lordship is to see the King and that the state of this contry is to be considered, it wer necessary to lait him knou that we have not forces anogh for all the work we have. It wer no great business for the King to send as much mony as would mantain fvye or six hondred mor dragoons; and in tuo or three years this contry I am seur would be broght to forgett all there follys. I knou I need not recomend to your Lordship to doe me good offices about the King and Deuk; only remember it is inabling to doe you service on, who is so sincerly, my Lord, your Lordships most humble and faithfull servant.

To Queensberry   HMC, *Queensberry*, 271

Edinburgh, 25 March 1682

My Lord, I have taken the occasion to com hither with Barscob and other prisoners, that I might give acount to the general and those of the goverment of my proceedings; for I begood to aprehend that in your Lordships absence som people might take the occasion to misrepresent me. I have informed them fully of all my measurs; and I am so happy as that they all seem satisfyed, and particularly the generall; hou long it will be so, God knous.

I was very sorry at my aryvall here to fynd your Lordships brother, the Collonell, ingaidged in an unluky business; but am extreamly

90 John McClurg.
91 Cleeks: crooked blades fixed on pikestaffs.

pleased that he is nou com af so much to his honor.[92] I shall not give your Lordship the trouble of particulars, but I must say that I was asheamed to see hou unkynd people wer to him. I have broght in your man, Wilson, who is a great villan, and shall be keeped till your Lordships return.

My Lord, believe nothing of any alarums you may gate of rysing, for I dar swear there is no dessein, and the Whigues wer never louer. I must bygue of your Lordship the faveur to doe me what good offices you think propre about the King and Deuk; in doing of which your Lordship will inable for your service on who is intirly yours, my Lord, your Lordships most humble and faithfull servant.

To Queensberry   HMC, *Queensberry*, 271

Kirkcudbright, 1 April 1682
My Lord, I am very happy in this business of this contry, and I hop the Deuk will have no raison to bleame your Lordship for advysing him to send the forces hither; for this contry nou is in parfait peace. All who wer in the rebellion ar ether seased, gon out of the contry, or treating their peace; and they have alraidy so conformed as to going to the church that it is beyond my expectation. In Dumfries not only almost all the men ar com, but the woemen have given obedience; and Earngray, Welshes owen parish, have for the most pairt conformed; and so it is over all the contry; so that, if I be suffered to stay any tyme here I doe expect to see this the best setled pairt of the kingdom on this seyd Tay; and if those dragoons wer fixt, which I wrot your Lordship about, I might promise for the continuance of it.

Your Lordships friends here ar very asisting to me in all this work; and it does not contribute a litle to the progress of it that the world knous I have your Lordships countenance in what I doe. All this is don without having received a farthing mony, ether in Nidsdell, Anandell or Kilkoubrie, or impresoned any body; but in end there will be need to make examples of the stuborn that will not complay; nor will there be any denger in this after we have gained the great body of the people, to whom I am becom acceptable anogh having passed all bygons upon bonds of regular cariadge hereafter. Your deputs wer lyk to have taken

---

[92] Colonel James Douglas (d. 1691) had run up large debts, which the duke of York arranged to have paid.

measurs that wer not so secur nor exceptable; but I have diverted them, and they ar to take the course I doe, and I have prevented all other jurisdictions by attaching first.[93]

My Lord, we hear noyse here of any Indulgence. I hop no body is so mad as to advyse it; but Lord Tuedell[94] could not goe up but it would be thought ane Indulgence would com doun with him. The mor I consider the business of this contry the mor [I] see hou ill the King has been served.

My Lord, you have nou the occation to put things in the right chanell, and I am perswaded you will make use of it. Barscob is very penitent, and offers if he could gate a remission he would be active and usfull to me in the business of the Glenkens. A word to the King or Deuk would doe the business, but in this doe what your Lordship thinks fit. I have Stenes with me, and we ar about your brother the Colonell business. I can fynd nothing almost of the movibles,[95] for I am unwilling to devyd in small pairtys, and, beseids, I prefer the setling of the country. I shall not trouble your Lordship with particulars, because I knou you ar taken up nou with other things. So I am, my Lord, your Lordships most humble and faithfull servant.

[P.S.] Since the wryting of this I have been at church, where there was not ten men and not above thretty woemen wanting of all the toun; where there used to be ten, I sawe six or seven hundred; and amongst others there was on Gordon of Barharou,[96] to whom being a rebell heritor I had given save conduct to com and treat his peace apeared in testimony of his sincer conversion.

To Queensberry   HMC, *Queensberry*, 272

Moffat, 17 April 1682

My Lord, All things ar here as I could wish in parfait peace and very regular. Barharu has asseurance of his peace from the Counsell. Bar[97]

---

[93] Claverhouse had a commission (31 January 1682) as sheriff of Wigtown, and sheriff depute of Kirkcudbright, Annandale and Dumfries. So as to preserve the semblance of authority of the stewarts of Kirkcudbright and Annandale and the sheriff of Dumfries, his commission there was limited to those cases 'when he is the first attacher', i.e. first to make the arrest: *RPC*, 3rd ser., vii, 326-7.
[94] John Hay (1626-1697), 2nd earl and 1st marquis (1694) of Tweeddale.
[95] Moveable property belonging to rebels.
[96] John Gordon younger of Barharrow.
[97] John Lockhart of Barr.

has given me a declaration under his hand, as full as I could desyr it. I have spok with a brother of Sir Robert Maxwells,[98] who was out, and Litle Park and Glenkaird[99] ar in terms with me, and severall others of less not[e].

I must say I never sawe people goe from on extremity to another mor cavalierly then this people does. We ar nou com to read lists evry Sonday after sermon of men and woemen, and we fynd feu absent. Mr Allexander does very well at Dumfries, but I have heard that the shyr does not conform so well, and I have heared the menisters complean of the baylys of your Lordships regality; what ground there is for it I cannot tell. I told Stenes and offered troups to bring the people in awe.

I have examined every man in the shyr, and almost all the Steuartry of Galouy, and fixt such a guilt upon them, that they ar absolutly in the Kings reverence, and I shall give them no discharge, would they give me millions, till I have bond from them for their regular cariadge, and maintenance for those dragoons, if the King think fit to rease them; and if I doe this, I think it is not ill use of that comission.

Did the King and the Deuk knou what those rebellious villans, which they call minesters, put in the heads of the people, they would think it necessary to keep them out. The poor people about Menegaff confess upon oath that they wer made [to] reneu the Covenant, and belieue the King was a Papist, and that he desseined to force it on them. But I shall tell your Lordship mor of this when the Deuk comes doun. I am, my Lord, your Lordships most humble and most faithfull servant.

To Queensberry   HMC, *Queensberry*, 272

Dumfries, 17 June 1682

My Lord, I thoght to have waited on your Lordship befor this, but I was stayed at Edinboug tuo days beyond what I had desseined, which has proved favorable for me. Yesterday when I came at the Bille, I was certenly informed that severall pairtys of Whigues in armes to the number of six or seven scor wer gon from thence but six hours befor. They came from Clidsdelle upon Mondays night and passed Tueed at the Bille going towards Teviotdelle, but went not above three mylles further that way. They stayed there about devyded in small pairtys,

---

[98] Hugh Maxwell of Cuil, brother of Sir Robert Maxwell of Orchardton.
[99] James Heron of Littlepark and Anthony McKie of Clonkaird.

most all on foot, Teusday, Wednesday, and Thursday, till Frayday morning, when they passed the hilles towards Clidsdell. Som say they hade a meeting with the Teviotdelle folks; others would make me believe they had a mynd for me.

They did ask in severall places what they heard of me, and told they wer seur my troup was far in Galaway; others say they wer flaying the West for fear of the diligen[c]e the gentry is deseined to use for their discovery. I could believe this, wer they not returned. I spok with the minister and severall other people in whose houses they wer, but he keeped himself out of the way. They did not prejudice in his house further then meatt and drink: they gave no where that I could learen any acount of there dessein there; only I heared they said they wer seeking the enimys of God, and inquyred rooghly if any body there keeped the church. The contry keeps up this business. I heared nothing of it till I was with in tuo mylles of the Bille; and that was from a gentleman on the road who had heared it at a buriall the day befor. Ther was a dragoon all Teusdays night, at the change house at the Bille, and the mester of the house confessed to me he loot him knou nothing of it. They pretend it is for fear of bringing trouble to the contry.

I sent from the Bille ane express to acquaint my Lord Chancelour with it; for I thoght it fit the quarters should be advertised not [to] be too secur, when those rogues had the impudency to goe about so. If your Lordship be at hom on Monday, or lait me knou where you will be, I will have the honor to wait on you. I am, my Lord, your Lordships faithfull and humble servant.

To General Thomas Dalyell   SRO, Hamilton muniments, GD406/1/9383

Dumfries, 18 June 1682

May it please your Excelence, I would have informed yow befor this lyne of what I learned passing at the Bile on frayday, that thair hav com thairabout (as the Maister and wyvs told me) about six or seven scoir of Armed men but I have wasted all this day to gett further intelligence of them but can learn nothing more nor I heared then which was that they caime from Clydsdaill and crossed Tweed at the Bile but went not above three mylles beyond it and returned nixt day and stayed about that watter in severall pairties from Mundays night till fraydayes Morning when they returnd west from whence they came. What was thair

dessigne I could not learn. We are hear in great peace and all in obedience. I am Sir your Excelence most faithfull and humble servant.[100]

To the bishop of Galloway[101]   *SHS, Misc. III*, 85-6[102]

Dumfries, 28 July 1682

My lord, The goodnes th[a]t the Clergy believes your lordshippe hes for me is the reason that they adresse themselves often to me and force me to importune you with recomendation; houever I alwayes hertily imbrace the occasion of assuring your lordshipe of my respeckts.

My Lord the bearer hereof Mr Chrystie, brother to the minister of Wigton,[103] as I am informed a very discreit and deserving young man, hes got a presentation to the kirk of KirkCouan from Barnbaroch who pretends right of patronag & is indubtedly in possession. But Mr Hamilton the subde[a]n of Ed[inbu]r[gh] I hear pretends also right.[104] I have writen to him in favors of this gentleman wherfor I beg your lordshipe will countenance him and persuad Mr Hamilton to approve what is doen or give him a neu presentation. I recomend wholly this busines to your lordshipes goodnes.

My Lord you was plesed to promise th[a]t you wold wreit to me befor yow cam into this cuntrei which I beg yow not to faill because I intend to cause some attend you on the rod, their ar a duson or sextein of our men that will be in on tuysday to whom I shall give order to wait on your Lordshipe and either who will be readie to pairt wednesday or wait tuo or thre dayes upon your lordshipe but houeve[r] I pray yow let me hear from you by them. I am, my lord your lordshipes most faithfull and humble servant.

[100] This letter was enclosed in a packet sent by Dalyell to the duke of Hamilton on 20 June (GD406/1/9382).

[101] James Aitken (d. 1687), bishop of Galloway from 1680.

[102] See also the original, NLS, MS 8886, fos. 1-4.

[103] Mr James Christie was presented to the parish of Kirkcowan on 12 October 1682. Mr Thomas Christie was minister of Wigtown.

[104] John Vaus of Barnbarroch disputed the patronage of the parishes of Kirkcowan and Kirkinner with John Hamilton, sub-dean of the Chapel Royal. It was Hamilton who finally presented Christie.

To Kenmure   Mackenzie, *Galloway*, ii, 244

New Galloway, 21 October 1682

My Lord, It is a good tyme since the last Chancelor[105] wrot to your Lordship by order of Councell to make raid[y] and void your house of Kenmure for to receave a garison, and when I cam into this contry som moneths agoe it was then in debeat wither or not the garison should enter, but it was put of at my Lord treasurers[106] deseir and my undertaking to secur the contry from rebelles without it, but this sumer the Councell thoght fit to give me new orders about it, wherfor my Lord I expect your Lords[hip] will remove what you think not fit to leave there, for the garison must be in by the first of November. I expect your Lord[shi]p answer and am my Lord, your most humble servant.

To Aberdeen   *Aberdeen Letters*, 101

1 March 1683

My Lord, I have don all I had to doe here, as my Lord Treasurer may inform your Lordship, and will be to morou at Carlyll, and I hop at Neumarket on Monday or Tuesday.

I found Clidsdeall full of lays: such as my Lord Huntly's[107] gitting a regiment, but that my Lord Deuk Hamilton and Atholl[108] oposed it strongly in Councell; and that the King was either dead or daying at least quyt deaf; and many other lays. On treuth I heard confirmed that Lie[109] had don wonders for bringing the peopell to conformity, and had certenly, whatever som people say, cast a good pairt of his land waist by it. This I had from the minister of Seimington.[110] I am, My Lord, Your Lordship's most faithfull and humble Servant.

To Queensberry   HMC, *Queensberry*, 275

Newmarket, 9 March 1683

My Lord, I shall not trouble your Lordship with any thing of business,

---

[105] John Leslie (c.1630-1681), 7th earl of Rothes.
[106] The marquis of Queensberry.
[107] George Gordon (c.1649-1716), 4th marquis of Huntly; created duke of Gordon, 1684.
[108] John Murray (1631-1703), 2nd earl and 1st marquis (1676) of Atholl.
[109] Cromwell Lockhart of Lee.
[110] Angus Mackintosh, minister of Symington from 1682 to 1685.

G

seing I knou my Lord Chancelor[111] will shoe you what I have wryten to him, which I think will please, for I fynd all in a very good temper here. I spok to the Deuk concerning what your Lordship gave me in comission, and he desyred me to asseur you that he had all the estime imaginable for you, and that no body had offered to doe you ill offices with him, and, if they had, they would not have succeeded; and expressed him self very kyndly and francly of you.

It is hard to gate any business don here. I walked but nyn mylles this morning with the King, beseids cock faighting and courses. I have not spok as yet concerning the muster maister but I shall. I am, my Lord, your Lordships most faithfull and humble servant.

To Queensberry   HMC, *Queensberry*, 276

Newmarket, 13 March 1683

My Lord, Last night, so soon as I recaived your Lordships, I went to the Deuk and acquainted him hou much you wer concerned to knou his thoghts of you; upon which he very kyndly and francly told me so well he was satisfyed with you, that he had that very afternoon been making his vant to the King of having made choyse of so good a man; and that the King was very sensible hou good service it was; and I may asseur your Lordship upon all occasions you will fynd the effects of it.

The Deuk is so proud of the success of our affairs, that he very justly atributs to himself the ryse and bigining of all to his sending me, contrair to the opinion of most except your Lordship and a feu others, with those comissions in to Galloway; and the King is very resolved that it shall be folloued; and all here magnify what you doe, and says it is a good copie [for] them, and the noyse of it helps to keep there affairs right. Lie[utenant] Gen[eral] Drumond[112] has pressed his affairs here, but the Secretarys[113] ar not pleased with his usadge of them; he treats them cavallierly.

My Lord, I have asseured my Lord Muray here and my Lord Midletoun of your Lordships friendship and the Chancelors, and they ar both mightily inclyned to lieve in ane entier corespondence with you. If they have anything to doe, I hop your Lordship and my Lord

---

[111] The earl of Aberdeen.

[112] Lieutenant-General William Drummond of Cromlix.

[113] The joint secretaries of state for Scotland were Charles Middleton (1650-1719), 2nd earl of Middleton, and Alexander Stewart (1634-1700), 5th earl of Moray.

Chancelor will assist them, and I am seur they will doe the lyk to you both; and I bygue your Lordship to tell my Lord Chancelor that it will be both your advantadge and theirs you lieve well togither, and I see it is the King and Deuks inclination. I hear the rest of the people of the goverment ar alarumed and think I will represent them as usless. I can not imagin hou they com to think so. It is very hard to doe any thing here either with King or Deuk, for the Deuk hunts, beseids going where ever the King goes.

I bygue your Lordship will speak to the Advocat,[114] or any [who] uses to wryt here, not to disconcert our affairs by writing things I knou not of; but nothing as from me. My Lord Chancelor, I know, will comunicat all I wryt to him to you. Tho there be no need of doing you good offices here, I doe as I oght your Lordship all justice where ever I com. I am, my Lord, your Lordships most humble and faithfull servant.

[P.S.] My service to My Lord Kinnaird.[115] My lord Tumont is ill; he cannot be here. My Lord, I forgot to tell you how sincerely Sir Andrew Forrester[116] is your lordship's servant.

To Queensberry   HMC, *Queensberry*, 275

London, 20 March 1683

My Lord, We have all raison to complean that you did us not the favor to comunicat to us your dessein to have the campagnie of dragoons for Kelhead,[117] for it had almost gon wrong. The Deuk thinks the army his owen province, and that he understands both the men and business of it better then any body, and he has his owen maximes that it is hard to put him af; and I am seur had the Councell desyred him to put that troup by the Captain Lieutenent, he would hardly have don it; he told me it was his deu, and having received wounds in the service he could not put it by him, and the mor he would doe it that he was recomended by no body.

My Lord Deuk Hamilton wrot for ane other, and was certenly

---

[114] Sir George Mackenzie of Rosehaugh.
[115] George, 1st Lord Kinnaird (d. 1689).
[116] Under-secretary of state for Scotland.
[117] Sir James Douglas of Kelhead, grandson of the 1st earl of Queensberry and married to the marquis of Queensberry's sister.

seconded by his friends here, but to no purpos. Houever after both secretarys had been refused and I toe, we made a second stake, wherin they both sheu themselfs mightily concerned, and we prevailed with him that Kelhead should either gate that campagnie, or Inglish imediatly turned out, and he gat that. The Deuk, I believe, was not pleased that Kelhead refused the cornets place, after he had soght it; and I am informed that the Deuk asked my Lord Dumbarton[118] if Readhouse had served in his regiment, and he said not, which wronged his business, and had not the Deuk been aprehensive that you might have thoght this refusall had been the effects of the ill offices you suspected, I dout if it would have don. But I shall tell both your Lordship and the Chancelour what the Deuks method is as to the disposing offices in the army at my return. There was a litle debate about Stenhouse business; why he needed a presentation from the King, if the Chancery could not have given him a brief for it; but it is ordered.

My Lord, I am mighty glaid to fynd the Secretarys so much your servants. They have no less kyndness for you both then you have for on ane another, and taking them along facilitats mightily affairs here. My Lord Midletoun particularly thinks himself oblidged to serve you, and has assured me of ane intyr friendship and corespondence with you; so lait there be franc dealing on both seids. He tells me your Lordship has generously offereed your assistance to him, and given him lieve to talk to me about his business. I fynd he has run himself in debt by this mariadge and furnishing himself of necessarys for a family, to about tuo thousan pounds; and I think less nor three thousand cannot be offered him; and seing the fynes ar coming in, tho he got fyve, it wer well bestoued. This would be generous in you; all honest men would comend you for it, and it would secur you a friend here for ever, that has great interest and is a firm and reall friend, where he professes it. My Lord Ch[ancellor] I am seur, will aprove it upon many acounts, and particularly seing he is so concerned for his business here. I dare swear nothing in my Lord Midletouns pouer here, but he would doe for your Lordship as for himself, and it is wyse to oblidge airly. Lait me hear from you with the first in this particular, because my Lord Midletoun is impatient.

My Lord Ch[ancellor] will sheu your Lordship myn to him by which

---

[118] George Douglas (c.1636–1692), 1st earl of Dumbarton.

you will see all is don, saive only my Lord Chancelours business; which is resolved, and only is delayed, till the state of the mint com up.[119] It is not saif I pairt, till it be secured: so, my Lord, I expect to have the acount of my Lord Lauderdells business shortly and your pleaseur in it.

My Lord, I have written to my Lord Ch[ancellor] about a business concerns my self, of which he and I talked befor I pairted, as my Lady Aroll[120] will tell you. I must bygue your Lordships assistance in that business of the lands of Didop. My Lord Ch[ancellor] deseins nothing but to sell it, and bay land in the north, seing he is to gat Stirling Castle to duell in. Wherfor I desyr lieve to ask the house of Didop and the Constablerie and other jurisdictions of Dondie belonging to my Lord Lauderdelle; and I offer to bay fourty chalders of victuall from my Lord Ch[ancellor] laying about it, tho I should sell other lands to doe it. I have no house and it lays within half a myl of my land; and all that business would be extreamly convenient for me, and signify not much to my Lord Chancelour, especially seing I am willing to bay the land. I would take this for the greatest faveur in the world, for I cannot have the patiance to build and plant.

But, my Lord, I should raither make use of this occasion to thank your Lordship for what you haue so generously proposed for me to the Deuk than ask neu favears. I hardly could have thoght you could have remembred that of the tuo years purchass. The Deuk asseured me he should have that, and what your Lordship recomended about my being on the councell don befor I pairt.[121]

My Lord I am sensible, as I oght to be, of so much goodness, and losses no occasions here to doe you any litle service you alloued me. I am sorry that you honored me with no greater things, for I think nothing could nor should be denayed you. I am, my Lord, your faithfull and most humble servant.

To Breadalbane   SRO, Breadalbane Muniments, GD112/39/135

London, 23 March 1683
My Lord, I recaived yours and delyvered the inclosed to the deuk. He

---

[119] Charles Maitland, Lord Halton, was treasurer depute and general of the mint. He was being investigated for defrauding the revenue.
[120] Anne Drummond (b. 1656), countess of Errol, daughter of the 3rd earl of Perth.
[121] Claverhouse became a privy councillor on 11 May 1683.

gave me answer that he did not knou upon what grounds that proces[122] was reased against your lordship and therefor could give no answer till he had acount of it from those who ar intrusted with the direction of affairs there. Nor is it propre for me, nor will your Lordsh[i]p expect of me, that I press too much any thing here, especially things the goverment hes concerned them selfs in, with out warand, if your lordship knou that I am here upon a publik acount and so oght not to say nor doe any thing but what I have comission. Houever, my lord, in a fair way and as far as I can with out betraying my trust, you may asseur your self of all the service is in the pouer of my lord, your lordships most faithfull and humble servant.

To Queensberry   HMC, *Queensberry*, 277

London, 29 March 1683

My Lord, I was at my Lord Mideltons dining, when your last came to my hands. Imediatly after diner, notwithstanding of all the orders of secrecie you have so stricly given me, I ventured, talking of the state of things, to tell him hou necessary it was that som persons, whom I named,[123] should have equalls; and fynding he intered in to the same sense, I poussed it further, and told him that I had alraidy sounded the Deuk and had not found him averse. But, with all, I told him that my lord treasurer,[124] when I pairted, had not given me the least order to that purpos; but, on the contrary, when I told him that it was propre for him and offered him my service, he positively desyred me, if I tendered his interest not to maidle with it; but that my Lord Chancelor had laift me Cristian liberty.

After having raisoned the business, and prepaired against all difficultys [that] might be objected, we went to St James, when we desyred of the Deuk to speak with leaseur with him; upon which he teuk us in to his closet, and having for introduction begun with the

---

[122] Breadalbane was being prosecuted for treason in connection with the Caithness affair, at the instigation of Chancellor Aberdeen. After he submitted to the duke of York in July, the proceedings were dropped.
[123] The duke of Hamilton, perhaps even Monmouth. Queensberry sought to succeed the late duke of Lauderdale.
[124] The marquis of Queensberry.

Mint business and my Lord Maitland, [125] we fell imediatly on your affair. The Deuk proposed difficultys. We discussed all, and convinced him and made him acknouledge it, and after having given many arguments from different heads; and then we tossed the business from hand to hand, that we broght him quyt about. Then it was concluded my Lord Huntlie must also be. Then my Lord Midletoun spok of the Register. [126] It was not my pairt to opose any thing that was proposed for a man [who] hade often don me kyndness; but on the other hand I will take on my salvation that I never heared of it till that afternoon, nor believe I the Register expects it at this tyme; but it seems there has been sumthing betwixt them when the Register was here. The Deuk seemed very inclyned and said 'Is it ane Earle?' and would have late it pass, as I thought, but my Lord Midletoun said, No, but a Vyscount; upon which the Deuk underteuk to indevor it all with the King.

We had the francest conference that I believe ever was, and his Hyghness expressed a great deall of kyndness to you all. My Lord Register is to be made friends with your Lordship, and I am to bring orders about it. You will have no raison to complain of the way; and that business of Maitland is to lay over till then.

My Lord Midletoun and I wroght all we could at the muster maisters business, but never neamed the desseined successor, but it would not doe. He told us laghing that we would all be as great tyrants as my Lord Lauderdelle was, and lait you alon. He has his owen maximes and politiques, but all was very friendly. He said Inglish business will doe but with all he would not hear but Clieland should be the first captain. We shall not give over till we have brought it to a cloase, or it will feall at the King, which I hop not.

My Lord, I hop you will pardon me for puting my Lord Midleton on the secret. It does not concern you, seing he thinks it is with out your knouledge what we doe; and that it is mainly on the publict acount we doe it. My Lord, it hade been better for me to have had all the honor of doing it alon, as by my last to my Lord Ch[ancellor] you will see in all apearance I might have don; but if your business be don, I shall be content with out considering who gate the thanks. My Lord Midletoun

---

[125] Maitland had become earl of Lauderdale in August 1682. On 20 March 1683 the Court of Session had ordered him to repay £72,000 sterling that he had embezzled. The king later reduced this sum to £20,000, of which £4,000 was assigned to Claverhouse.
[126] Sir George Mackenzie of Tarbat was to be raised to a viscountcy.

is most sincer both to your Lordship and to the Ch[ancellor]; wherfor, I think, you have thoght of to litle for him and on ane ill fonds, seing my Lord Ch[ancellor] is befor him. The fynes and forfiteurs, if your Lordship pleases, will doe better.

My Lord, I promise to my self that you will perswad my Lord Ch[ancellor] to consent to my gating Didop and the jurisdiction, which can not wrong him, seing I am willing to buay a pairt of the land. My Lord, I have wryten this in great heast. I dout if you will be able to read it. I am, my Lord, your Lordships most humble and faithfull servant.

To Queensberry   HMC, *Queensberry*, 278

London, 10 April 1683
My Lord, I delayed giving any answer to yours of the 29 of March, wating for ane oportunity to speak with the Deuk, or raither to see if he would say any thing to me concerning your Lordship. But having yesterday recaived yours of the thrid of Apryl, I thoght not fit to delay it any longer. I went imediatly to the Deuk, who gave me ocasion to speak too him at full lenth.

First, I shoued him that peaper about the feu deutys, whch he raid all over. I told him that if there was any persons concerned therein, to which there needed be any regaird had, it was for so inconsiderable sums that it would be no ground of complaint; beseids, that it was all the Kings right, tho neglected heretofor by those intrusted in the Treasury affairs.

I raid som pairts of your letters I thoght propre for seuerall subjects to the Deuk. He aproved of what was don; desyrs your Lordship to goe on, and looks on it as good service. After that I told him that I had given your Lordship acount of what had passed betuixt his Hyghness, my Lord Midletoun and me, concerning your affair, and that I had recaived a return full of gratitud, and the sense of so great ane oblgation to his Hyghness. I hoped he had not forgot to press the King to it. He told me he had used all the arguments he could to perswad the King; but that he could not move him to it. I did aledge that I feared the King or he must have been diverted from it by Inglish councell, and there upon took the liberty to tell him in a respectfull way hou unsaive it wer to take measeurs from people that could not knou our business nor the circumstances of our affairs. The Deuk very fairly denayed all, but told

me the King had been so vexed with the nobilitating people here (for when the door was once opened all would be in) that he could not willingly hear any thing upon that subject.

I will say without vanity that nothing was unsaid that could make for the purpose; but the Deuk in end told me it was impossible. I told him then, that in all this I hade only raison to complean; for I was very seur that both the King and he would be at last convinced hou much it was there interest, and would certenly doe it; only I would be so unhapy as not to be the bearer; upon which the Deuk told me that he thoght some tyme after the King might be broght to it. I desyred he would be so good as to wryt to you or the Chancelour to that purpose. He told me there was no need nou, but that he would doe it when I went doun.

I think I need not tell your Lordship hou concerned I was; if it had been for my lyfe, I could doe no mor. But, my Lord, I hop you will bear patiantly a litle delay; for I understand any thing it will certenly doe; and at meeting I will tell you mor fully my owen thoghts, which will fully convince you. I shall doe my best ... [letter torn] Deuk to wryt as clear and plain as y... not this litle stop in ill pairt for the gr[eat]est men in Ingland ar glaid to gate it after many pulls. Therfor, contineu cheerfully your indevors in the Kings service, and it can not faill. The Deuk told me that he found my Lord Chancelour mightily inclyned it should be. He may reneu the attaque when he pleases; my Lord Midletoun will be always ready, who is of the same opinion with me in all this affair.

I have not spok to the Deuk concerning the blank comission, but I fear he will be unwilling to give a comission without he be seur to whom. If you desein any body els that he declynes it, we will gate it in any bodys name you please. The comission anent the excyse is gon severall days agoe. The Deuk had ane acount by my Lord Advocat of what passed in exchaiquer concerning the touns business,[127] which he raid all over to me. It was fair anogh, raither desseined for to magnify his oun pairt then wrong or lessen others. I sawe nothing that the Deuk suspected the least difference betuixt the Chancelour and your Lordship. Somthing he understood concerning my Lord Tuedaill, and I said what I thoght propre to hold him at that. It was only from the Deuk himself that I kneu of your Lordships recomending Kelhead.

---

[127] In March 1683, the tacksmen who farmed the excise were dismissed and its collection was taken into crown hands, along with the collection of an additional imposition on ale and beer in Edinburgh. This was a serious financial loss to the burgh council, who lobbied unsuccessfully against it.

The Deuk told me yesterday that you hade recomended my Lord Ross[128] for to be Lieutenent Coll[onel] to my regiment, and that he had given you answer that there oght be non in horse, which I told my Lord Chancelor befor I came away. I fynd the Deuk will be content he be Major, and I did not at all opose it, because recomended by your Lordship; tho I have a some raison to take a litle unkyndly in my friend, my Lord Ross, that he should indevor any alteration in the regiment without lating me knou it.

My Lord, I think I gave your Lordship acount hou that the King had comanded me in his name to wryt to your Lordship and my Lord Chancelour, that he might have from you a particular acount of my Lord Mars[129] right to the Castle and Lordship of Stirling; for he is resolved not to suffer any heritable comand there, if there be any way in lawe to hinder it. There is nothing I see the King so concerned in as in that place. Wherfor, my Lord, I bygue you will heasten up the acount of it, seing it is the only thing the King himself has desyred of a long tyme. The peaper you sent up I shall take cair to keep till meeting. I am, my Lord, your most faithfull and most obedient servant.

[P.S.] There will be wars imediatly betuixt Swaid and Danmark, which will draw in all the rest. Conte de Roy goes generall for Denemaak.

To Queensberry   HMC, *Queensberry*, 280

London, 12 April 1683

My Lord, I hear nothing mor of the toun of Edinbourg business, nor nothing that folloued on it. So I say nothing aither; but if I doe, I'l knou hou to give things a right turn. Nor is there need that you take so easily alarums; the Deuk will not so easily alter the opinion he has of you. I told him what diligence you wer using concerning the excyse comission. I cannot yet give answer as to Kelheads business. I supose there will be nothing don in it till Captain Inglish either demit or be trayed.[130] I fynd the Deuk thinks Meldrum[131] most propre to be Major; but will not condeshend to put him over ane older Captains head, that is a man of quality: tho I indevored to perswad him to it. In these things it

---

[128] William, 12th Lord Ross (c.1656-1738).
[129] Charles Erskine (1650-1689), 5th earl of Mar.
[130] Captain Inglis had become less efficient, either through illness or disaffection, and others wanted his cornet's position.
[131] Captain Adam Urquhart of Meldrum.

is hard to impose upon him. Wherfor, I told him it would be best to lait it alon all togither, that we may see if tyme can bring it about. I knou not well what he will doe in it, but I supose he may take advyce.

I spok to him also about Gilcryst, and told him that befor I recaived your Lordships I had persons in search of him. I was this morning by the Deuks order at Sir Leonard Jenkins about that affair. When I learn anything of it, I shall give you notice. Sir John Cochraine[132] treated both Secretary's, my lord Aran,[133] and Lord Charles Muray,[134] yesterday at the George and Volter, but I fynd neither of the first have any kyndness for him. I have recaived from my lord Chancelor the State of Stirling and have given him acount of our opinion here, which I supose he will acquaint your Lordship with. That will be a mighty augmentation of the customs you speak of. I shall lait the Deuk knou of it. All other things in your Lordships letters I take cair of according to directions. I am, my lord, your Lordship's most faithfull and most humble servant.

[P.S.] My Lord, the inclosed papere[135] I desseined to have keeped till meeting conform to your first letter, but nou I send it doun as you desyr by your last.

To Queensberry   HMC, *Queensberry*, 280

London, 26 April 1683

My Lord, The Provist of Edinbourg[136] has wrytent to the Deuk and sent up a memoriall, ane information, and petition to the Councell anent the Mint, recomended by the Bishop of Edinbourg.[137] I supose, my Lord Midletoun will send your Lordship all those peapers. I told the Deuk that it was not propre, without better recomandation then what he had, to take any resolution in the thing; and that there will be nothing don here, till the Deuk hears from your Lordship and the Chancelor; nor doe I see that the Deuk blames as yet your Lordship in the least. We

132 Sir John Cochrane of Ochiltree, uncle of Claverhouse's future wife Jean Cochrane.
133 James Douglas (1658-1712), earl of Arran, son of the 3rd duke of Hamilton.
134 Charles Murray (1661-1710), later (1686) 1st earl of Dunmore, younger son of the 1st marquis of Atholl.
135 Not extant.
136 Sir James Fleming.
137 John Paterson (d. 1708), bishop of Galloway, 1674; bishop of Edinburgh, 1679; archbishop of Glasgow, 1687.

all here will take speciall cair that he understand the business aright, nor
can I see hou it is possible to suspect any other dessein then peurly the
King's interest in what you doe.

There will be a letter to your Lordship in a feu days for securing the
Lordship of Stirling for the Kings use, and ane other waranding you to
treat with him[138] for the heritable right of the Castle and lands anexed
there too. As to the Mint, there is a letter ordered for your Lordship
telling that the King Pleaseur is that my Lord Lauderdeall dispon to the
Chancelour the lands about Dondie, and to me the house and
jurisdiction, for which I render your Lordship most hairty thanks.

Sir John Falconer[139] is to pay four years and one half purchase of all
his esteat and the rest six years purchase of their, but the King has
ordered nothing be said of this till the letter com to your Lordships
hands. My Lord Maitland knous nothing what is don.

I will have the honor to see your Lordship before you goe from toun.
I am to pairt next week. I am, my Lord, your Lordships most faithfull
and humble servant.

[P.S.] The seasing the Lord Mair will doe mor ill then good to the
disafected pairty. All is very well here and the King firm.

To Queensberry   HMC, *Queensberry*, 281

London, 28 April 1683
My Lord, I have not seen the King and the Deuk since my last. So I have
no neu thing to wryt. My Lord Midleton and I goe on Monday for
Windsor, when we will be seur to doe what we oght. As to the toun of
Edinbourgs business, I am sorry to see that the world is not wyser, and I
must say that I think your Lordship gats hard measeur; houever, I am
glaid to hear from the honest Advocat that both the pairty and the
Advocat ar ordered to cray *pecavi*.

Who ever does not give your Lordship all incouradgement in the
work, you goe so francly about, does you not justice, nor serves the
King aright. We are all here extreamly convinced hou well you deserve
of the King; and non can knou it better then, my Lord, your Lordships
most faithfull and most humble servant.

---

[138] The earl of Mar.

[139] Sir John Falconer, master of the mint under Halton, gave evidence against him to no avail for
himself.

To Queensberry   HMC, *Queensberry*, 281

Windsor, 3 May 1683

My Lord, you need not be in pein about that business of the toun of Edinbourg, and the Bishop had better laiten that affair alon; for the Deuk has been better informed of him then I believe he was ever befor. The peaper concerning my Lord Lauderdaill is sent down by this post as I informed by my last. My Lord Muray and Midletoun will be provyded for out of the rest. The *quo quaranto* will succeed. I pairt the nixt week. I am, my Lord, your Lordships most humble and faithfull servant.

To Aberdeen   *Aberdeen Letters*, 107

[c. May-June 1683]

Claverhouse being called befor the Comitty of Counsell, gave this account of the affaires of Galouay:[140]

That there was no need to tell them what was the state of it befor he went thither, seing the Government had looked on it for many moneths befor as almost in a state of war; and it was thoght unsaife for any thing less then an army to ventur in to it. And at his aryvall there he kneu not what to say of it, fynding above three or four hundred people actually guilty of the late rebellion, who, notwithstanding, had lieved these three years by past almost in parfait friedom, and posessed in, dispyt of authority, betuixt thretty and fourty thousand marks a year; and that, beseids those, there wer many hondred mor guilty of recett and comuning with rebelles who were all on wing: The churches were quyte desert; no honest man, no minister in saifty.

The first work he did was to provyd magasins of corn and strawe in evry pairt of the contry, that he might with conveniency goe with the wholl pairty wherever the King's service requyred; and runing from on place to ane other, nobody could knou wher to surpyse him: And in the mean tyme quartered on the rebelles, and indevoured to distroy them by eating up their provisions; but that they quikly perceived the dessein, and soued their corns on untilled ground. After which, he fell in search of the rebelles, played them hotly with pairtys, so that there

---

[140] The original, in Claverhouse's own handwriting, was transcribed by a clerk for the earl of Aberdeen.

wer severall taken, many fleid the contry, and all wer dung from their hants; and then rifled so their houses, ruined their goods, and imprisoned their servants, that their wyfes and schildring were broght to sterving; which forced them to have recours to the saif conduct, and made them glaid to renounce their principles, declair Bothwell Bridge ane unlawfull rebellion, swear never to ryse in armes against the King, his airs or successors, or any having comission or authority from him, upon any pretext whatsomever, and promise to lieve orderly hereafter: And that all the heritors almost, except Earlestoun,[141] and tuo or three mor that wer not in the contry, had actually seigned a bond much to the purpose: and that it was his opinion that the most pairt of them might be broght to take the Test, seeing they and their family goe in the mean tyme to church without any further assurance from him, but that he should plead for them.

Then he gave acount that all most all the litle people had made aplication to him; but that he had refused them saif conduct; but promised he should represent their cease to his Hyghness at his return, and douted not but their would be som way aloued to secur them of their lyfes and libertys: And declaired to the Comitty it was absolutely necessary for setling the country; and douted they could be broght to take the Test by cuase of their ignorance, but easily to some thing equivalent. For amongst all the prisoners he made, he found non that was ambitious of the honor of martirdom; but all renounced their principles befor they would give testimony, saif only on, upon whom was found Grey's[142] letter, and is nou coming hither by order of Counsell; and that even he acknowledged the King's authority in civilles: so that even he had no occasion to make use of the Comission of Justiciary, but sett them aluays at liberty upon sufficient caution to apear when called; and that by advyse from my Lord Advocat.

Then he gave Comitty acount hou that he had asisted the donators to take posession of their esteats, and forced the tenants to [take] taks of the King or his donators in all the forfited esteats. With all it uas his opinion, that it uas not fit any of those esteats should be sould to the rebelles' friends, or least for their use, till they make their peace, or be dead.

---

[141] Sir Alexander Gordon of Earlston, arrested after the Rye House Plot, having lived for two years under the assumed name of Alexander Pringle. He was tried for treason, imprisoned in the Bass and released at the Revolution.
[142] Thomas, 2nd Earl Grey (1654–1720), one of the Rye House plotters.

After he had broght the rebelles to this pass, he concluded there could be no sudain dessein of reising. And seing people uho had loosed there fortunes and ventured their lyfes for that quarell, had not only given obedience, but uer broght to conformity, he judged there could be no danger to indevor, by discreet measeurs, to bring the uholl body of the people to the church; which was the second pairt of his comission.

And, in order to this, the first thing he did, least the people should take too hotly the alarum, was to goe along all the contry, and calling them, by three or four parishes togither, to read his Comission and lybell against them; and after assour them that, notwithstanding of all they might knou themselfs guilty of by the breache of those lawes, they needed not be aprehensive if they had a mynd to give obedience; that the King had no dessein to ruin them, nor yet to inrich himself, but only was positively resolved to bring them to conformity; and, if there were sever things don, they might bleam themselfs. After which for their incouradgement, he caused publish a peaper at all the parish churches to this purpose: that all, under heritors, that uer not guilty of recett or comuning with rebells or intercommuned persons, or of field conventicles, or insulting the regular clergy, should be free of all bygons if they would goe to church. And fynding that the most pairt wer guilty of field conventicles, he thoght fit to give a second intimation that even those might expect favour; and in end fynding hou good effects this had produced, he asseured them that, whatever there guilt was, if they gave obedience they needed fear no great severity.

And in the mean tyme he sett up deputs in evry pairt of the contry with puer to examin upon oath; uhich they did, man by man, and marque their deposition; and orders to acquaint them that if, uithin so many days, they gave not obedience, they uould be used with the utmost severity of lawe; and uho remained obstinat, especiall[y] heritors, be punished severly, by laying them in prison till they should fynd sufficient caution for the payment of their fyne; But, upon offer of obedience, he excepted alluays of a bond for a blank sum, and filled up may be the tuentieth pairt to shou them it might all be mony; and then discharged them for so much, leaving the rest over their head for sourty for their good cariadge; and making som examples of this of the first gentry of the contry, the rest did not put him to the trouble, giving tymous obedience.

Those measours brought things to that pass that it could not be

knouen in most pairts uho uere absent: uherupon he ordered the colecttors of every parish to bring in exact rolls, upon oath, and atested by the minister; and caused read them evry Sonday after the first sermon, and marque the absents; who wer severly punished if obstinat. And wherever he heard of a parish that was considerably behynd, he went thither on Saturday, having aquainted them to meet, and asseured them he would be present at sermon; and whoever uas absent on Sonday was punished on Monday; and who would not apear either at church or court, he caused arest there goods, and then offer them saif conduct: which broght in many and will bring in all, and actually broght in tuo outed disorderly ministers; the on was glaid for to gate the arestment loosed to fynd caution never to set his foot within that jurisdiction whyll he had any interest, and was fynd in somthing to the poor; and the other goes to church, and promised never to preache or baptyse mor in the contry.

And it may be nou saifly said that Galouay is not only as peacable, but as regular as any pairt of the contry on this seyd Tey. And the rebelles ar reduced without blood, and the contry broght to obedience and conformity to the church government without severity or extortion; feu heritors being fyned, and that but gently; and under that non is or are to be fyned, but tuo or three in a parish; and the authority of the church is restored in that contry, and the ministers in saifty. If there wer bonds once taken of them for regularity hereafter, and some feu men put in garison uhich may all be don in a few moneths, that contry may be secur for a long tyme both to King and Church.

To Aberdeen   *Aberdeen Letters*, 121

Stirling, 9 June 1683

My Lord, The Lords having thoght fit to delay the exicuition of this man[143] till they should knou your Lordship's opinion, because of the neuness of the thing and consequence, I would feall in my deuty if, being on place, I did not give your Lordship my thoghts of it. Tho I need not repeat this man's story intyrly, because you have received particular acounts from the Justices, yet I myst mynd you of the heads of his caise. He was actually in the rebellion, continued in that state for

---

[143] The covenanter William Bogue.

four years, and nou comes in with a false sham certificat[144] to fooll the Judges: for being desyred to give his oath that he had taken the bond, he postively refused; being asked if Bothwell Bridge was a rebellion, refused to declair it so; or the Bishop's murder an murder; and positively refused, in face of the Court, the benefit of the King's Indemnity by taking the Test.

Upon which the Judges, moved by the outcry of all the bystanders, as by their conviction of the wikidness of the man, refered the mater to the knouledge of an inquest, who broght him in guilty; after which, he begged to acknouledge his folly, and offered to take the Test with the old gloss, as far as it consisted with the Protestant religion, and the glorie of God; and after that was refused him, offered in end to take it any way. By all which, it clearly apears that he would doe any thing to saive his lyf; but nothing to be reconciled to the government.

Nor can it be thoght any sourty for the government the taking of the Test by men after they ar condemned; seing all casuists agree that ane oath imposed where the alternative is hanging can [not] any ways be binding; and it is to be suposed, who refused it when they had the freedom of choyse, and taks it after condemned, does it only because they think themselfs not bound to keep it.

And the Proclamation seems to dessein favour only to those who offer volenterly, by these words: all uho aplay themselfs; and that meetings be appointed for giving the Test by those intrusted, that all concerned may knou when and where: all which shoes cleerly it was desseined for people at liberty.

Then, my Lord, in point of prudence, if this be the method, no man will com in to the Justice Air for to take the Test, but may contineu all his triks till the first of August, and speak traison in face of the Court and the people, if he be taken and condemned and after nik them with taking the Test: which turns all in ridicull. For great clemency has and oght to be shoen to people that ar sincerly resolved to be reclaimed; but the King's Indemnity should not be forced on villains.

All that I can hear of inconvenience is, that it may terify those in his circumstances to com in. I say there is not such ane other in all the Kingdom, that is, a comon man condemned: so that they can not be terifyed.

---

[144] Certificates were issued to those who had taken the Test oath in the approved manner.

It may be said that his caise may be mistaken, and it may deter all from coming in. Experience of this day answers that. Above tuenty have taken the Test since he was condemned; and the teror of his usadge, as I am informed, is lyk to cause most com in that ar to-day declared fugitives, of which the number, in four shyres, will not be much above a hondred. If this man should not be hanged, they would take advantadge that they have disapointed us by resceuing the other, and given us such aprehensions that we durst not venter on this.

I am as sorry to see a man day, even a qhigue, as any of them selfs; but when on days justly for his owen faults, and may save a hondred to fall in the lyk, I have no scrupull.

I understand not that any of the forces and on the Liuet[enant] Gen[eral] should, for hunting people for only stealing koues, leave the atending this service, where the King's interest and the peace of the contrey is so neerly concerned; for the tuo compagnies of foot laift this place to-day.

All the Justices doe their deuty francly and cheerfully. My Lord Castilhill[145] and I have not yet differed in any point, and my Lord Advocat sustined this business vigourusly. I am impatient to be at Glascou, when we will have neu mater. I am, my Lord, Your Lordship's most faithfull and humble servant.

To Queensberry   HMC, *Queensberry*, 281

Stirling, 9 June 1683

My Lord, Tho I can not dout but severall others give your Lordships particular acounts of all that passes at this court, yet I would faill in my deuty, if nou at the closs of it here, I did not give you som acount of it. There has been three letters wryten to the Chancelour, giving acount to him of all and asking advyse in som particulars. Of the first, I cannot have the scroll, but I send your Lordship a copie of the answer. The second was sent last night, and the scroll is also lost, but it was only giving notice that there was a fellou being called in the Porteous Roll[146] apeared, and pretended he had taken the bond; and for proving it produced a false and sham certificat; but being suspected and asked

---

[145] Sir John Lockhart of Castlehill, one of the justices in the current circuit court.

[146] The list of those accused in the circuit court.

upon oath if he had seigned it, refused to swear it, and refused to say, that Bothellbridge was a rebellion, or the Bishops murder a murder; upon which the Lords, after he had refused to take the test, put him to the knouledge of ane inquest, who broght him in guilty.

Then he thoght fit to recant, and offered to take the test, but the lords refused it upon good grounds, and condemned him to dey on Wednesday at Glasgow, as your Lordship will see by this scroll of the thrid letter to the Chancelor, which pairts tonight, and this bearer going just a way I have not the tyme to transcryve it. I have wreaten to the Chancelor my opinion upon many reasons that the man should be hanged.

This Justice Air has suceeded mervilusly. Many gentlemen of good quality, that wer in the Porteous Roll upon mistake, after they wer assolyed teuk the test. Above a hondred and fivety rebelles comoners have here taken the test, and I believe almost all will; so that the nomber of fugitives will be feu. The judges goe on very unanimusly, and my Lord Advocat does wonders. This murder they have comitted gives us all neu vigeur.[147]

From Glasgoe your Lordship will hear from me, for there will be the scene of the most considerable things. I am, my Lord, your Lordships most faithfull and humble servant.

To Grierson of Lag   Grierson Papers, 26

Johnstone, 13 June [1683]

Sir, I dout not myn has come to your hands giving you acount that my lord Home's[148] regiment was ordered to lay at Minegaffe and the heritors of the shyr wer to be assisting to them. Corespond with that quarter frequently and give them acount of all that occurs; they ar ordered to doo the lyk to you so that on all occasions you may be ciffill to on ane other.

You ar as I wrot befor to be in a particular maner assisting to S[i]r William Douglas at the Newtoun with the Teviotdalle regiment, my Lord Kenmuir is to doo the lyk ane all things relating to the Kings service in these must be conjuctly caryed on by you three. So far Gods

---

[147] On 8 June, a rescue party had released a prisoner on the way to Glasgow, killing two soldiers.
[148] James Home (d. 1687), 5th earl of Home.

cause lay asyd all Kenmuirs and animositys if there be any amongst you and unit your selfs francly in the Kings Service and your contreys defence; it is all our doutys and it will certenly be our honer and interest so to doo. I am Sir your most humble servant.

[P.S.] There is no newes here: som straglers over the border: look to your self.

To Aberdeen   *Aberdeen Letters*, 138

Jedburgh, 5 June [sc. July] 1683

My Lord, In obedience to the order I received from your Lordship, I have commanded fourty dragoons to the Langom, which is the hairt of the Deuk of Monmouth's interest; and tuenty there ar at Anan. My troup lays at Moffet, and a pairt of Captain Strachan's troup at Dumfries, to cape what may eskeap the tuo advanced posts. They have orders conform to the proclimation.[149] On this hand we have sent out three partys of ten horses a piece, who have orders to bate along the Borders, and corespond with the pairtys of Langom and Coll[onel] Struthers on the other seyd. So soon as the Lords ar gon, all the troupes here shall march to different posts closs on the border.

All the comons here have given obedience, and most of the gentry, save Hardens, Idington, Ridell,[150] who will stand out, with some feu small heritors. Hume of Basington[151] is flaid. My Lord Yester,[152] for to give good example to others, took the Test befor the Court yesterday, and so did Sir Francis Scot,[153] and severall other gentlemen. I think it will doe no great prejudice tho tuo or three of the rich lairds stand out.

I am glad to hear that the conspiracy is lyk to be so well dicovered, and that the King resolves so sudenly and vigourusly to bring to punishment the wicked authors of it. We hear from people comes from the other seyd, that great dilligence is doing there for search of those traitors. I am, My Lord, Your most humble and faithfull Servant.

[149] A proclamation issued on 4 July for the arrest of the duke of Monmouth and other Rye House plotters: *RPC*, 3rd ser., viii, 187-9.
[150] Sir William Scott of Harden, Sir William Scott younger of Harden, George Ramsay of Edington, and Sir John Riddell of that Ilk.
[151] George Home of Bassendean.
[152] John, Lord Hay of Yester (1645-1713), son of the 1st marquis of Tweeddale.
[153] Sir Francis Scott of Thirlestane.

[P.S.] Since the writing of this, I am told young Harden will take the Test.

To Queensberry   HMC, *Queensberry*, 282

Edinburgh, 28 August 1683

My Lord, Heu Wallace[154] comunicat to me what your Lordship gave him comission, and since I have had the honor of your letter to the same purpose. I have spok to my Lord Chancelor severall tymes about those garisons; but he refuses to doe any thing till the councell day. I told him that if I could gate the consent of those to whom the houses belong, I would venter to garison them with out any other warand but what I have to quarter these troupes where I please in that contry. But since, I am informed the generals troup is ordered by himself to march to Kilmarnock; so that there can be no mor don as to garisons except what I have already ordered about the Kaitloch; only if your lordship can have the consent of the maister of that house neer Drumlainrik mentioned in your letter to Heu Wallace, Captain Strachan may alou ten or fyveteen men, which will be anogh in that pairt of the contrie. I have given him advice about it.

I have spok to the Chancelor that the generall might be called for against the councell day, and all things concerning the disposing the quarters for the troupes might be adjousted. He seemed to inclyn that I should give a s[c]heam of it in wryting, which I am unwilling to doe in the terms we ar in, not knouing what use might be made of it. Houever, befor the Kings service suffer I will ventur on it. It is not possible for me to leave this place nou that I have writen for lieve to goe up, till I knou the Deuks pleaseur; beseids the necessity I have to atend the poursuit about the decreet of the mint, which makes slou progress. If your Lordship have once to wryt to Heu Wallace, he would needs be put in mynd, for as yet he has don nothing.

I shall not feall to give my Lord Midleton and our other friends there franc acount of the state of things here, particularly those your Lordship wryts of. For that Highland project,[155] the Register and I both have

---

154 Hugh Wallace of Ingliston, receiver-general and king's cash-keeper.
155 A circuit court held at Inverlochy in August, with military backing provided by Lieutenant-General Drummond.

refused to maidle mor, and we haue signifyed that it braid not in our breast.

As to the bringing bak the Advocat, the councell understood no such thing, and I have asked the Chancelor about it. He says so, but that he knous not hou the clerks may have drawen the letter; he seigned it on the comon faith. I shall wryt to the generall about Streven. I had alraidy heared how extravagant the expense was desseined. Houever suspects me of having given advice to the Deuk to lait things be governed by the chief minister alon, wrong me mightily. I can apeall to the Deuk and my Lord Midleton, if I did not always say that things by cause of secrecy oght to be manadged by you tuo; and if you could not agree, by a Juncto; and I think I was right. When I hear from London, your Lordship shall knou. I am, my Lord, your most faithful and most humble servant.

To Queensberry   HMC, *Queensberry*, 274

[c. August 1683]

My Lord, The Generall is satisfyed with the reparations of Streven as they ar intended in the paper he recaived from your Lordship, and desyrs your Lordship will be pleased to order it be gon about as soon as can be. The compagnie of foot is marched with the enseign. The Lieutenent has been with my Lord Perth, [156] and is nou going after it. He has comanded them to recaive orders from your Lordship, hou they shall dispose of them self. I spok to him that Captain Strachan might be waranded to quarter them by your Lordships advice, but he would not. He will give no orders concerning my troup till the first of November, that every body be com to toun, but that they contineu at Dumfries.

I hear the comitty at Edinbourg has called a councell and have found difficultys in Earlston business. This letter about Bayly Drumond and Rochead opens the eyes of people mightily, and gives good hopes of success of all other things. [157] I hop your Lordship will not neglect to give advyce hou you would have all things goe, especially as to the

---

[156] James Drummond (1648-1716), 4th earl of Perth.

[157] The dispute of James Rocheid of Inverleith, burgh clerk of Edinburgh, with the trustees of Heriot's Hospital, was a protracted legal affair which attracted widespread interest. He was also involved in a faction of the burgh council which attempted to prevent the crown-sponsored election of George Drummond as provost in September 1683.

Juncto, for that is the great point. I dout not but they ar able to doe all that can reasonably be desyred. If I goe I shall acquaint your Lordship that I may recaive the honor of your comands. I am with all respect, my Lord, your most faithfull and obedient servant.

To Queensberry   HMC, *Queensberry*, 286

[c. August 1683]

My Lord, I called at the Generalls this fornoon, and he was gon out to diner. Som time after he sent the order to councell to me without any order from himself, and sent me word by his servant that that was all he hade to say. I told his man I would wait on him immediatly after diner, and, when I cam to his lodging, his man told me he was layen doun, and that he had not been well for som days. I offered to stay till he was awak, but his man told me I needed not, for he would give me no other orders. I can doe nothing without his orders, for act of councell says the Generall is to comand my Lord Balcares[158] troup and mine and Cap[tain] Clielands to Clidsdelle; and that he should give orders to Coll[onel] Bouchan[159] and me to comand there.

Houever, least the Kings Service suffer in the time, I will goe and join my Lord Ross troup till the half of the Gairds and the other troops com. I hop your Lordship will cause dispatch them. If the Generall will not, the councell may give the orders immediatly to the respective troupes. I am, my Lord, your most faithfull and most humble servant.

To Queensberry   HMC, *Queensberry*, 283

Edinburgh, 13 September 1683

My Lord, I thoght I had prepared that affair of the garisons so well that there could not have been the least difficulty in it; for my Lord Chancelor seemed satisfyed and made me wryt about it to the Generall, but when it came in councell the Ch[ancellor] refered all to the Generall. I sustined with all the might I could; but was not able to bring about the Generall nor perswad the councell to doe it of themselfs.

The Ch[ancellor] is nou resolved to please the Genrall by all means; but he seems not to cair for it. The Ch[ancellor] will never give him all

---

[158] Colin Lindsay (1652-1723), 3rd earl of Balcarres.
[159] Lieutenant-Colonel Thomas Buchan.

he deseirs. Houever, the thing being so raisonable, and a proposell of your Lordships and sustined by me, who they had raison to believe understood that contry, your Lordship may easily guess I was not well satisfyed; and I took the liberty to tell my Lord Ch[ancellor], that if the Deuk had been at that boord, as he was when I was first sent to Galloway, I would have been believed in maters of that contry, especially when I was but seconding my Lord Treasuror.

The Ch[ancellor] then desyred the Gen[eral], my Lord Linlithgou and Livingston[160] and I to confer about it nixt morning, which would have turned to nothing, had not your Lordships leter com to my Lord Chancelor; which pleased him so well that there was not the least difficulty thereafter. He made speaches both in councell and to me in pryvat of your Lordships great cair and vigilence for the peace of that contry, and the Kings interest, and comended mightily your giving your owen houses and provyding them with out any expense to the King for to be garisons; and fynding him in that temper, I told him that your Lordship had a mynd to have Capt[ain] Dallayells compagnie if any was sent, which he also undertook cheerfully. The generall said nothing.

I then asked whither or not I should contineu my former cair of that contry or not. The Ch[ancellor] shuned to make answer; but being pressed, all he answered was that they took nothing from me. After I asked hou they would dispose of my troup. The Ch[ancellor] had a myn[d] it should lay here for a tyme; the generall was for sending it to Fyfe. I told it was usless to the King service here, and would be so in Fyfe. I desyred it might be sent in Comlok, Maybolle or som place neer Galloway; that in caise there be need I may mak inrods nou and then. It was refered to the Generall. So I knou not hou it will be, but I am seur I am very indifferent; for I told in Councell that wherever it went I thoght may self no ways obldiged to march with it, because that was the Cap[tain] Lieutenents business.

I shall indevor to be with your Lordship again that compagnie com in. I spok to my Lord Ch[ancellor] abour my Lord Kenmors business, and he seemed resolved, but nothing was don anent it yesterday in Councell: I shall put him in mynd of it; he can always call a corum. My Lady Aroll and I aprove mightily of your Lordships way with the

[160] George, Lord Livingstone (d. 1695), son of the 3rd earl of Linlithgow.

Ch[ancellor], not to stand upon the cerimony of writing first, when the Kings service requyrs it, and I am glaid to see hou pleased he is with it. It seems he would be better pleased with mor corespondence which I should be glaid to see in such terms as would be acceptable to your Lordship. I have received a very kynd letter from my Lord Treasuror deput,[161] wherin he gives me good hopes of my affairs and great asseurance of his assistance; and with all laits me knou that beseids his owen inclination he has your Lordships comands to sustin all my concerns.[162]

If it wer not that I dessein raither returns of services then speeches, I would imbrace this occasion to say somthing to your Lordship on the head of obligation and gratitud. I hop your Lordship will believe me sensible of both, and that I will not forgait my deuty. I shall never forgait hou generous it was in your Lordship to alou me your friendship in a tyme that you was offered concurrence of persons who oght to have been my friends. There ar people who think I have lost by the change, but I am far from it, for they knou not so well as I what I had or what any man can have there to loss. But whatever there had been in it, I would not have regraited it, and I think my self very happy whyll I am asseured of your Lordship protection and friendship.

On Fryday last I was told by the Bishop of Galloway that by a letter from my Lord St Andreus[163] he understood that the Bishop of Edinbourg was asking his lieve to goe up, and that he desyred no comission and would goe on his owen expence; but that my L[ord] St Andreus had asseured him that he would by no means consent to it. I soght for him to give him my opinion, but could not fynd him as yet. The Archbishop of Glasgou[164] has asseured me he will imploy his interest against it, and if the primat should com to be abused in it he will protest against that jorney. The Bishop of Edinbourg seems a little out of heumeur, and he told me yesterday he would com and see me and talk of many things, which is no sign things goes to his mynd.

Whyll I am wryting I just nou received a letter from my Lord Advocat telling me my business is don, and on from my Lord Midelton

[161] John Drummond of Lundin (c.1649-1714); created earl of Melfort, 1686.
[162] The pending lawsuit with Lauderdale over the purchase of Dudhope.
[163] Alexander Burnet (d. 1684), archbishop of St Andrews.
[164] Arthur Rose (d. 1704), archbishop of Glasgow, 1679; archbishop of St Andrews, October 1684.

giving me acount of his diligence, that the Deuk had promised no remission should pass till I was satisfyed. Colin[165] wryts that ane explanatory letter is to com doun that will leave no ground of debeat. The Advocat says he has been recaived to admiration.

Your Lordship may remember I got licence to import read cloath for my troup, and so much gray cloath for the trompeters and ketledrumers.[166] The cloath being imported I presented to my Lord Ch[ancellor] in councell a declaration under the colectors hand that it had been visited and the deus payed, and therefor desyred up my bond of 500 p[ounds] st[erling]. My Lord was pleased to refer all to your Lordship. I also informed him that the gray cloath was not of the right color, and therefor desyr I might have lieve to cary it bak to Ingland and bring other in the place of it, or els that those of the manifactory[167] might have it, and I aloued to bring in as much, which was also refered to your Lordship. I was content thinking myself in good hands; so must expect your Lordships faveur in both; for I desyred the Clerk to mark it was refered to your Lordship; the thing is mightily raisonable. My Lord Glasgou was very earnest that I should asseur your Lordship of his service, and he swears he will be most firm to your interest.

My Lady Aroll is still where you laift her. I see not that the Court grous much here. I fynd myself worse there evry day but I take no notice of it. I goe thither as I used to doe, but only when I have business of publik concern; and houever things goe am resolved to doe as a good subject oght and a man of honor. I will by no means prejudge the Kings service for my interest, nor will I doe mean things to insinuat myself.

If I have forgot any thing here, I shall mend it by the nixt. Heu Wallace will give you acount of the toun of Edinbourg business and that Air befor the Councell. I did all I could in both. Your Lordship may consider both and doe what you think proper, for I should be sorry it went so. I am, my Lord, as I oght to be most francly, your Lordships most faithfull humble servant.

To Queensberry   HMC, *Queensberry*, 285

                                    Ayr, 27 September 1683

My Lord, Before I came to this toun things wer past recovery, so I

[165] Colin Mackenzie, brother of the Advocate.
[166] For the licence, dated 31 May 1683, see *RPC*, 3rd ser., viii, 172-3.
[167] The Newmills cloth manufactory near Haddington, founded 1681.

thoght it not fit to make use of your Lordships name at all. I only, fynding Brisben[168] would cary it, advysed him to take on the councell and make magistrats as many as his interest could alou, that the heats and animositys among them might in som measeur be alayed; and he promises so to doe. I fynd they perswad them selfs they will be suported in all they doe.

I am glaid to hear of the defeat of the Turks.[169] I am informed my Lord Montrose is to goe up, and is to wait on your Lordship; but I begg I be not neamed in this. This contry believes a certain man caryes all, and that every body els will be distroyed. I shall wryt to your Lordship from Edinbourg. I am as I oght to be, my Lord, your most faithfull and obedient servant.

To Queensberry   HMC, *Queensberry*, 274

Edinburgh, 2 October [1683]
My Lord, I came here on Saturday's morning in tyme to the Councell, when Earlston was delayed till the King should see the answers he had given to the interogatorys; nor was there any shuning of it, most persons being of opinion that he had no mor to say, tho' he said almost nothing neu. Ther was nothin els of consequence brought in save a remission for Moncland[170] which I got stoped and he contineus in prison, because he refused to give up upon oath all his wryts and peapers.

On Sunday morning Mr Rocheads wyf sent to me to knou where she might see me. I told I should see her at her owen house wither after sermons or on Monday morning; never the less Mr Rochead waited my out coming from the Tron Church and invyted me to super, which I refused; but Mrs Rochead sending again this morning I went to her, when she told me the history of the family and that of the goverment of the good toun, and after asked my advice if her husband should goe up, and begood to propose that I would doe them kyndness if I went up.

From the first, I told her that I might safly tell her my opinion in it, that they who had the interest to procur that letter would be able anogh to gate him sent hom with out a hearing; and for my owen pairt, in all

---

[168] James Brisbane of Bishopton.
[169] They had recently been forced to retreat from Vienna.
[170] Robert Hamilton of Monkland.

apearance I was not to goe, but if I did, I would not undertake for no man to maidle in any of my Lord Treasurers concerns without his lieve and that I thoght they had taken wrong measeurs from the begining in not puting themselfs in your Lordships reverence, but that at present I could give them no advice, till your Lordship was com to toun and these returned that kneu the Kings mind in that mater.

I fynd they think Colin Makenzy is at London for to procur that place. I send your Lordship here inclosed the treasurer deputs letter, by which I see the Deuk will not lait me up. I supose he has no mind the thing should be heared by the King, because it would load a certain person.[171] They seem satisfyed that the Deuk promises he will see it don, and that my Lord Maitland shall not have lieve to speak of it. But I am of a quyt contrary opi[ni]on, for I knou hou much ons presence prevails with the good natur of the King and Deuk. Beseids, if the explanotary letter be not signed, I see by this suspension I will have a very evill game. But I have wryten positivly either that I have lieve to come, or that the explanatory letter, which I have sent up be seigned; otherways, I have raison to believe that evill offices have been don me from this to the Deuk.

It is thoght very strange that the Lords should have suspended fourty thousand pounds with out a cautioner, beseids other things; but I never can complean of the King's judges. I expect to knou mor by the nixt post, if I goe up or not, I shall not faill to acquaint your Lordship in tyme. I am, my Lord, your most faithfull and obedient servant.

To Queensberry   HMC, *Queensberry*, 285

Edinburgh, 12 October 1683
My Lord, There has nothing occurred here worthy your Lordships noticing since my last. I fynd by letters from my Lord Treasurer deput, my Lord Advocat and Colin that the Deuk has no mynd I should com up; but gives all asseurances that he will have the thing performed without fraud or trik.

The Bishop of Edinbourg did me the faveur to com and see me yesterday, being under fisik, when he took occasion to tell me all had passed betuixt your Lordship and him as to the business of the toun of

171 The chancellor, Aberdeen.

Edinbourg; and made shou of great grief that he had had the misfortun to incur your Lordships displeaseur, but desyred nothing of me neither to represent it to your Lordship nor any body els. I told him I had never been on the subject with your Lordship; but that, seing the tuo Archbishops had concerned themselfs in the mater, as he told me they had don, I believed your Lordship would not be implacable; for I had always found you ready to alou people to vindicat them selfs, or to accept of raisonable satisfaction upon aknouledgement of their fault.

I spok this day with the Bishop of Galloway to knou if ther wer any hopes of his translatione, but he told me by what he could learn from the primat, Dumblean was fixed in Ross.[172] I am glaid to see that the Kintyr project is blouen up, but it is to be feared that tho that esteat be anexed to the croun it may be easily disolved.[173] I fynd the Advocat is not satisfyed; he has got nothing, tho he says he had no desein but to saive this contry from slavery, and honest men from ruin. He comes af the 15.

The Treasurer deput has thoght it worth his whyll to gate the Kings orders to stop Munglands remission. Great pakets in great heast com from my Lord Maitland to my Lord Chancelor. Things seem to goe very right; but if the Juncto be not fixed again winter, all will yet goe wrong. I am goin for Angus where I will be till the Advocats return. Som folks here ar in great aprehension. I wish it may be well grounded. I am, my Lord, your Lordships most humble and faithfull servant. [P.S.] I am glaid to hear your Lordships sonns ar com to London and so much esteemed there.

To Queensberry   HMC, *Queensberry*, 286

Edinburgh, 30 October 1683
My Lord, I had not been so long without asseuring your Lordship of my respects, had I not been always since my last in Angus, where I could neither fynd occasion nor business to wryt. Since my coming here I have had severall letters from London, wherby I learn my Lord Advocat came af the 24 and pretty well satisfyed; of which I am extreamly glade for my raisons; for he is very usfull in many things and

---

[172] James Ramsay (d. 1696), bishop of Dunblane, was translated to Ross in April 1684.
[173] The background to this was the forfeiture of Argyll: see P. Hopkins, *Glencoe and the End of the Highland War* (Edinburgh, 1986), 85-6.

his friends must resolve to bear with his litle infirmitys as long as he holds right on the main.

My Lord Maitland[174] is to be sent imediatly doun to atend the Justice Court, and has don nothing. I have here from good hands that his great masterpiece was to perswad on of those two above to cheange with a certain man here; which indeed would have don a deall of mischieff, but I supose it is above his reach; and L[ord] M[iddleton] is advertised of it by a good friend of his, to look to it as a thing that concerns him as much as any other.

I have still neu asseurances that the Deuk will not see me wronged. I hear the B[ishop] of Edinbourg has changed his ton since he thinks the storm is over. The affaire of the Juncto[175] is no secret here, and evry body thinks it was the only thing could have keeped people with in bounds; but by what I can learn, if it be at all it will turn to the old Juncto, or to the officers of state only. I hear D[uke] H[amilton] has been trying to be of the nombre, but was refused as being officer of state.

I fynd my Lord Register[176] as your Lordship left him. I am glaid to her by Heu Wallace that you desseine to be hear on the sixt, which will be about the tyme of the Advocats arryvall; when, after hearing all has passed at London with circumstances, your Lordship may mor saifly take your measeurs. I have a great deall to say to your Lordship in faveurs of Colin Makenzy but shall delay it till I have the honor to see your Lordship here. I fynd M[y] L[ord] Mid[dleton] is greatly his friend, but all is expected from your Lordships goodness.

I shall wait on your Lordship som mylles from the toun and give you acount of all I can learn again that tyme, and shall nou only begge your Lordship to believe me still as much as I realy am, my Lord, your Lordships most faithfull and most humble servant.

To Queensberry   HMC, *Queensberry*, 291

Edinburgh, 4 November [1683?]

My Lord, Last night I had the honor of your Lordships, and this day,

---

[174] Charles Maitland, earl of Lauderdale, was still Lord Justice-Clerk, but was removed from office in 1684.

[175] A scheme to appoint a powerful inner committee of the privy council, excluding such as the duke of Hamilton.

[176] Sir George Mackenzie of Tarbat.

after sermons, Heu Wallace told me he was just going to dispatch your servant. I begged him to delay so long as I could see my Lady Arroll, because the Ch[ancellor] had been there. She bids me tell your Lordship that there passed a great deal betuixt them; but because he compleaned that things he had only told to your Lordship and her wer com abraad, she thoght best to forbear giving you acount of it till meeting. I hear he is mad against me, tho I have mor raison to be so against him. He and all his people seem very confident, and they say talks briskly. Houever, by all I have yet heared, they have no very solid fundation.

Sir George Locart[177] is com home, who, it is thoght, has been a considerable agent, and has got a neu light, for, as I hear, he stood to Glory to the Father with the Chancellor to-day. My Lord Lauderdell came up in the coatch from Lieth with the Ch[ancellor], and was above an hour closs with him imediatly after he came up, and Sir John Dalrimple is assidous there as he used to be. It is said here the Treasurer-Deput[178] is coming doun, but my Lady Aroll bids me tell you not to lait him stur till my Lord Pr[esident][179] be com aff. For it is thoght things will be as hot as ever, and that this man has wryten up having nou heared all that they alleadge has been said against him, and will be vindicat. He and I fell fooll in councel yesterday about the fanatiks bakslyding, and the causes of it. I told that we wer interupted by his telling that those who had taken the Test could not be fyned; and that there wer abondance had taken it, as I was informed, and yet would not lieve orderly. Litle or nothing of moment was done.

Deuk Hamiltone is to be in on Wednesday, and that business of his will turn to nothing, for Meldrums will not be heard of; he being gon north. And for the other about the conventicles, he will say he did all diligence so soon as he was advertised, and it will be taken of his hand. Mr Johnston,[180] my Lord Deuks writer, was this day wait[ing] on the Ch[ancellor] from his Grace, and the Ch[ancellor] bid him assure the Deuk that he should not be wronged where he sat. It is said here that your Lordship stays out of the way a-purpose, because of that business.[181]

---

[177] Sir George Lockhart, later (1686) Lord President of the Court of Session and Lord Advocate.
[178] The earl of Melfort.
[179] Sir David Falconer of Newton.
[180] James Johnstone, writer to the signet.
[181] Queensberry was married to Hamilton's sister.

I am to goe out and meet the Advocat at Musselbrogh, that I may prepair him befor he com in. I am mighty glaid to hear he has got [sic]; it will be a great mortification to som, for they deseign his ruin by all imaginable means. I long to see your Lordship; and am, my Lord, your most faithful and most humble servant.

To Queensberry   HMC, *Queensberry*, 287

Edinburgh, 19 May 1684

My Lord, Tho I got all the asseurances imaginable from the Generall that day I pairted with you, that his orders for me should be as soon at Glasgou as I: yet I waited at the Haket and there about for fyve or six days and heard nothing from him. So I was forced to wryt to him, as I did to the L[ieutenant] G[eneral] Drumond and the President of the Session, that if the Kings service was retarded the blame should not lay on me; upon which he sent me orders; but he is in a terible huff.

I marched to Air with Coll[onel] Bouchan and the fyve compagnies of foot, and the half of the Gairds with my Lord Ross troup. After which I went in to Galloway, and visited the houses apointed for garisons, and I fynd them very propre; so soon as beds and other necessarys ar provyded the troupes will enter into them, which will be imediatly. I was at Dumfries and gave all necessary orders for those that lay there, and I sett the commission to work; after which I went into Clidsdelle, and considered the houses apointed for garisons there. They ar propre anough for the use, but by what I can perceive they will not be provyded on a sudain with necessarys.

I am nou com in to give the Comitty acount of this, and to knou if there be any thing further to be don in thos contrys for the Kings service. I fynd the want of the garisons in Galloway, and the withdrawing the forces from the shyr of Air has occasioned all the insolency that appeared in those rogues this last winter, and nou that the troups ar so posted I shall answer for the peace and good order of all those contreys which in a maner is all the fanatik pairt of the kingdom, and I must say that the neu alleya that I am lyk to mak is not unusfull to me in the shyr of Air and Ranfrou.[182] They have the guyding of those shyrs and they doe strenthen my hands in the Kings service, particularly

---

[182] His prospective bride, Jean Cochrane, was from that area.

my Lord Montgomrie,[183] whom I recomend to your Lordships faveur. I will answer for him that he will be very fordward in the Kings service, and very sincer in his friendship and deuty to your Lordship. I have wryten to his Royall Highness anent that match, hearing that Deuk Hamilton had scrupulled to allaya with that family without the King and Deuks lieve. I feared that this might have been advysed by som persons to load me that had not been so circumspect.

For my owen pairt I look on myself as a cleanger. I may cur people guilty of that plaigue of presbitry be conversing with them, but can not be infected, and I see very litle of that amongst those persons but may be easily rubed of. And for the yong ladie herself, I shall answer for her. Had she [not?] been right principled she would never in dispyt of her mother and relations made choyse of a persicutor, as they call me. So who ever thinks to misrepresent me on that head will fynd them selfs mistaken; for both in the King and churches interest, dryve as fast as they think fit, they will never see me behynd. Houever, my Lord, malice som times carys things far; so I must begg your Lordship will defend me if you fynd any thing of this natur sturing.

The Bishop of Glasgou, when I waited on him at his house desyred me to asseur your Lordship of his respects and put you in mind of what he spok to you concerning Mr Ross being principill of the Coledge of Glasgou. I had a letter from Sir John Falconer, wherin he tells me he waits your Lordships up coming, and that he expects you will be generous when you have him at mercey; and I hop your Lordship will shou him faveur after my Lord Midletoun is satisfyed for his concern in that affair. We ar all very impatient to hear such newes from your Lordship as we wish, and your cair and zeall in the Kings service deserves;[184] and there is non has so good raison to wish you succes as, my Lord, your most humble and faithfull servant.

[P.S.] Mr Colin MacKenzie desyrs to assure your lordship of his respects, and begs your assistance in the Clerk's place. For Menzies will die. Sir John Gordon is gon up for it. Sir William Paterson designs the wholl office, and many pretenders there are.[185]

---

[183] Alexander, Lord Montgomery (c.1660–1729), son of the 8th earl of Eglinton.
[184] Queensberry expected a dukedom.
[185] Patrick Menzies and Sir William Paterson were joint clerks of council. After the former's death, Colin Mackenzie was appointed in his place (29 July 1684). Sir John Gordon was justiciary clerk.

H

To Queensberry   HMC, *Queensberry*, 288

Edinburgh, 19 May 1684

My Lord, I have been in the West and posted the fyve compagnies of foot at Air, and the half of the Gairds with my Lord Ross troup there about. I have visited the garisons both in Galloway, Dumfries, and Clidsdelle, and every thing is ordered conform to instructions; and nou you will fynd by the sucsess the raisonableness of this advice. The contry is much disposed to peace and order; and I will answer for both in all those contreys as long as the forces contineu thus posted, and Ingland keeps quyet.

My Lord Deuk Hamilton has refused to treat of giving his dochter to my Lord Cochrane,[186] till he should have the King and the Deuks lieve. This I understand to have been advysed him to load me, wherfor I have wryten to the Deuk and told him that I would have don it sooner had I not judged it presumtion in me to trouble his Hyghness with my litle concerns; and that I looked upon myself as a cleanger that may cur others by coming amongst them, but can not be infected by any plaigue of presbitery.

Beseids that, I sawe nothing singular in my lord Dundonalds[187] caice, saive that he has but on rebel on his land for ten that the rest of the lords and lairds of the south and west have on theirs; and that he is willing to depon he kneu not of their being such. The Deuk is juster then to charge my Lord Dindonald with Sir Johns crymes.[188] He is a mad man and lait him parish. They deserve to be damned [who] would owen him. The Deuk knous what it is to have sons and nepheus that follou not advice.

I have taken peins to knou the state of the contreys guilt as to recett, and if I make it not apear that my Lord Dindoriald is on of the clearest of all that contrey, and can hardly be reached in lawe, I am content to pay his fyne. I never pleaded for any, nor shall I here after; but I must say I think it hard that no regaird is had to a man in so favorable circumstances—I mean considering others, upon my acount, and that nobody offered to medle with him till they heared I was lyk to be concerned in him. They have flaiged him; so that he has not given me so

---

[186] John Cochrane (d. 1690), later 2nd earl of Dundonald, brother of Claverhouse's future wife Jean Cochrane.

[187] William Cochrane (1605-1685), 1st earl of Dundonald, grandfather of Jean Cochrane.

[188] Sir John Cochrane of Ochiltree, Jean Cochrane's uncle, was a fugitive in the Netherlands after the Rye House Plot.

much as he would have given to any body that could have don him no service. And since faveur might have been shouen him without prejudging the Kings service, considering his aidge and the imployments he has had, it was not friendly to fall upon him to my prejudice; but mor shall goe with him, or manifest partiality shall apear.

I hop Sir George Locart will be used acording to lawe. Tuo or three days agoe, there was on Scot, a declaired rebelle, seised on his lands, who has deponed that he has lived there ever since Bothwell, but did not pay the rent out of his owen hand, but caused a brother in lawe of his to doe it. I have raire caises prepared, if it be the Kings interest the rigeur of the lawe be used against all. On man may cast in the myr, as we say, what ten will not take out.

After all, I am very indifferent whether my Lord Dindonald be fyned or not; it will concern my Lord Cochran, not me. I will gate no mor nor I have got, unless it should be signifyed from above that he has got faveur on my acount, which I would not dispair of if I wer at London; and my friends, if they lyked might doe; which would put D[uke] H[amilton] made; for he thinks to doe all for them or not maidle with them. I will make ane other use of those people then is expected. They offer me all asistance in those shyres, and my Lord Montgomrie is very fordward in the Kings service; he will wryt to you when I return to the West, and Bouchan will give you acount of all at the same time.

If there be a necessity of having mony, I can give lists, and prove them, of persons ten times guiltier then Dindonald and able to pay. What ever com of this, lait not my enimys misrepresent me; they may abuse the Deuk for a time, and hardly; but or long I will in dispyt of them lait the world see that it is not in the pouer of love, nor any other folly, to alter my loyalty. My Lorde, pardon this idle letter, and believe me your faithfull servant.

[P.S.] Be kynd to Sir John Falconer. I spok to Dindonald about giving sumthing and gating his grand chylds forfitur and sons echeat: but he will not maidle with them, and will stand his own tryall.

To Queensberry   HMC, *Queensberry*, 289

                                   Edinburgh, 29 May 1684
My Lord, I would have been gon to the West or nou; but that I was desyred by the Comitty to stay till the Councell day, and I was desyrous

to hear what newes came from London. It is no small joy to all honest men, who ar your Lordships friends, that the King and Deuk ar lyk to understand so well there interest. I knou certenly that the Ch[ancellor's] friends wryt that he will demit, and thinks he does not his business right at Court. It is very wysly don in your friends, not to bragg too much of your affairs, hou ever successfull, for they wryt very modestly, yet so as they ar understood. I hop when your great concerns ar over, you will mind your friends.

The tuo years purchase lays still over my head,[189] tho I have the Kings promise that I should pay nothing, and the bond for the superplus of the fynes of Galloway, tho' the King ordered a letter implouring your Lordship to give acount of what we should have, both for expence and reward; and this I may saifly say was spent. I can doe nothing but recomend all to your goodness, for I need not wryt to the Deuk; a word from your Lordship will doe it.

I hop my lord Midleton will doe me that justice as to give you acount how sincer I was for your service when I was there, tho I was not able to doe any thing, and that your Lordship did not need me. I flatter myself with the hopes that you will doe me such good ofices with his R[oyal] H[ighness] as you have often done heretofore to so good purpose; so that I will not need to fer any misrepresentations can be made against me. I am, my Lord, your most humble and most faithfull servant.
[P.S.] Mr Menzys can not lieve many days, and honest Colin and his friends relays mightily upon your Lordship.

To Sir David Falconer of Newton   Dundee, *Memorials*, ii, 397

Paisley, 13 June 1684
My Lord, Upon the news of the conventicle near Blackloch, and that one hundred of them had passed Clyde, towards the moors in our quarter, I marched with the half of the Guards—which, by the way, are but twenty-two, when they ought to be fifty—and my Lord Ross's troop, and some dragoons, and thirty foot, and scoured all the mosses but one part towards Lesmahago, which I left Colonel Buchan to seek in his back-going. And he having ordered the foot to march on his right hand a mile or two, they fell on an ambuscade of two hundred rebels,

---

[189] Since the earl of Lauderdale had been forced by the king to sell Dudhope to Claverhouse, he spitefully insisted on payment over only two years.

seven of which, being off their body, fired on four of ours, and wounded one of them. They followed the rogues, and advertised Colonel Buchan; but before he could come up, our party had lost sight of them.

Colonel Buchan is yet in pursuit, and I am just taking horse. I shall be revenged some time or other of this unseasonable trouble these dogs give me. They might have let Tuesday[190] pass. I am, my Lord, your Lordship's most faithful servant.

To General Thomas Dalyell   Dundee, *Memorials*, ii, 400

Kilbride, 15 June 1684

May it please your Excellency: I parted on Friday (13th) at twelve o'clock from Paisley, went by Kilmarnock and Mauchlin, but could hear nothing of these rebels. So, hearing Colonel Buchan was at the old castle of Cumnock, I took by Ochiltree, who sent an express to a tenant's house of his, near Airdmoss, and he brought certain notice that they had been at a meadow near his house the night before, to the number of fifty-nine, all armed.

Upon which I sent immediately to the Glenkens, to Captain Strachan, to march to Dalmellington, and to the Sorn, and to leave Mauchlin on the left hand, and Newmilns and Loudon-hill on the right, and so to this place, scouring all the suspected places as he came along. I sent to Dumfries, to Earlshall,[191] to march by the Sanquhar, by the Muirkirk, the Whitrick, and the Ploughlands, and so to Streven.

Colonel Buchan, with twenty dragoons, and thirty foot mounted on horseback, marched round Cairntable, and by Lieburn and Greenock-head, and so down. My Lord Ross and I, with the horse, came through the hills more easterly, leaving Douglas and Lesmahago a mile or two on our right. We have left no den, no knowe, no moss, no hill, unsearched. There is a great drought, so [we] could go almost through all.

We traced them from the boghead near Airdmoss to the Hakhill, within two miles of Cumnock town, and from that to Gap, towards Cairntable, but could never hear more of them. They are separated, as

---

[190] His wedding day.
[191] Lieutenant Andrew Bruce of Earlshall.

most believe, and gone towards the hills of Moffat. I am sure there is
not one man of them within these bounds.

Earlshall is not yet come this length, nor Captain Strachan. But they
are, I am sure, near; for the last was at Cumnock all night. The troops
complain mightily of this march; and I know not what further can be
done. So I have sent Colonel Buchan with the troops to Dalmellington,
and the troops of Galloway to their quarters. I am your Excellency's
most humble servant.

To the archbishop of Glasgow   Dundee, *Memorials*, ii, 401[192]

Paisley, 16 June 1684

May it please your Grace, I had not needed any order to have written to
your Grace, if I had been sure my letters would have found you at
Edinburgh. I have given account of what has passed here, every post, to
those of the King's servants that are at London; and have given the
General particular accounts of everything, from time to time; whose
business it was to acquaint the Council with it. However, since your
Grace desires me to do it, I shall.

It will not be necessary to repeat what I have already written to my
Lord President. However, to follow the thread of that affair, there was a
Conventicle at Blackloch, on Sunday was eight-days. It seems the
General got notice of it that day, about twelve o'clock, and sent out a
party of foot and dragoons, who, being led straight to the place, missed
the rebels, who were marching some way on the right hand toward
Clyde; and when they got notice and made after them it was too late.
The foot wearied, and the rebels were got over Clyde, and no further
intelligence could be found of them. So they returned to Glasgow.

I passed at the Kirk-of-Shotts, which is not far from the place, on the
Saturday before, about six o'clock at night; and about eight, as I passed
at Glasgow, I sent to acquaint the General that I would be at Paisley, if
he had any orders for me. Yet I heard nothing of this till Tuesday
morning, that my Lord Ross told me he had a letter from the General
about it.

Upon which, I sent immediately and ordered Colonel Buchan to
meet me at Newmills, with the half of the troop of Guards, my Lord

---

[192] This and the previous two letters were claimed by Napier to have been found in the Queensberry
Papers; none are in the HMC edition of the *Buccleuch and Queensberry Papers*.

Ross's troop, and the thirty Fusiliers he had with him at Dalmellington; and I call[ed] out Captain Inglis's dragoons; and, on Tuesday night, and Wednesday all day, we came through the moors and over the hills that lay betwixt Clydesdale and the shire of Air; and made exact search and enquiry for those rebels, but could not hear the least of them. But only at Ploughlands, in the head of Strathaven, we saw two men running to the hills; we followed them, but because of the mosses could not reach them.

We examined all the people about upon oath, and learned that the one was a fellow called William Young, born in the same parish, and the other was one Leith, born about Newmills, both rebels, and was in arms at that time. The people also deponed, that, about a fortnight before, they had seen twelve men in arms, and that several times they had seen lesser numbers since, but could give no account of any that had been seen for three or four days before. Upon which we concluded that they had not taken that way, or were dissipated.

So, when we came to Streven, I left the command to Colonel Buchan, and desired him to return the troops to their quarters; but, in his march to search the skirts of the hills and moors on the Clydesdale side; which he did, and gave me an account that, going in by the Greenock-head, he met a man that lives down on Clydeside, that was up buying wool, who told him that on Lidburn, which is in the heart of the hills on the Clydesdale side, he had seen a great number of rebels in arms, and told how he had considered the commanders of them. One of them, he said, was a lusty black man with one eye, and the other was a good-like man, and wore a grey hat. The first had on a velvet cap.

But before he [Colonel Buchan] could come near the place, a party of foot, that he had sent to march on his right, fell accidentally on them. Four of our soldiers going before to discover, were fired on by seven that started up out of a glen, and one of ours was wounded. They fired at the rebels, who, seeing our party of foot making up, and the horse in sight, took the alarm, and gained the hills, which was all moss. The foot seeing them so numerous, and the ground such as they could not come to their relief, thought not fit to engage wholely, but advertised Colonel Buchan, who, though he made all imaginable diligence, could never come in sight of them after the first view. However, they having taken up towards Cumloch, he made haste thither to stop their pass at Galloway.

This passed on Thursday; and on Friday morning, Colonel Buchan acquainted me with it. I went immediately to Mauchlin, and from this to Cumlock, where we learned that on Thursday night they had passed at the bog-head, near Airdsmoss, and were then only fifty-nine in arms. They were running in great haste, barefooted many of them and taking horses in some places to help them forward. We heard they went from that to a place called the Hakhill, within two miles of Cumlock, and from that to the Gap, which goes to the hills lying betwixt the Sanquhar and Moffat. But we could never hear more of them.

I sent on Friday night for my troop from Dumfries, and ordered them to march by the Sanquhar to the Muirkirk, to the Ploughlands, and so to Streven. I sent for Captain Strachan's troop from the Glenkens, and ordered him to march to the old castle of Cumlock, down to the Sorne, and through the country to Kilbryde, leaving Mauchlin and Newmills on his left, and Loudon-hill on his right. By this means they scoured this country, and secured the passages that way. Colonel Buchan marched with the foot and dragoons some miles on the right of my troop, and I, with the Guards, and my Lord Ross and his troop up by the [Shaire?]. We were at the head of Douglas. We were round and over Cairntable. We were at Greenock-head, Cummer-head, and through all the moors, mosses, hills, glens, woods; and spread in small parties, and ranged as if we had been at hunting, and down to Blackwood, but could learn nothing of those rogues.

So the troops being extremely harassed with marching so much in grounds never trod on before, I have sent them with Colonel Buchan to rest at Dalmellington, till we see where these rogues will start up. We examined all on oath, and offered money, and threatened terribly, for intelligence, but we could learn no more. I am, my Lord, your Grace's most faithful and most humble servant.

To Queensberry   HMC, *Queensberry*, 289

Strathaven, 5 August 1684

My Lord, I came by Douglas and Ocheltrie, and by Machline and Neumilles, which is the muir contrey, and from this I am going throu Ranfrou and through the high pairts of the shyr of Air up to Drumelington. The foot is marched this night from Air to the Foggy Road, and from that they goe east al the way throgh the hilles to Moffet.

I have writen to the garisons of Galloway to drawe out and march al along on the right, and I with the troups I have here will march on their left on this seid the hilles. I caused make a search throu there muirs a purpose to chease them from this to the hilles, and make them think themselfs secur there, but they have such inteligence that there is no surprising them.

When we cam here, they told they heared of my coming; and last night I was asking if there wer any troupes at Neumilles as I came from Machline, and tho it was undernight and no body but my owen servants, they told me my Lord Ross troup was there and that I was expected. I fear we doe nothing, for so soon as I com I fynd they acquaint all the contrey expecting a search. I shall be with your Lordship on Monday, and give you my opinion of the state of things here. I am, my Lord, your most faithfull and most humble servant.

To Queensberry HMC, *Queensberry*, 290

Dudhope, 25 August 1684

My Lord, By a letter from Mr Colin Makenzy I hear your Lordship will advertise me when you have any service for me. Houever, I thoght it my deuty to lait your Lordship knou that whyll I injoy here the fruits of your faveur, I am not unmindfull what I awe you; and tho your Lordship have nothing to comand me, I will wait on you at Edinbourg before you goe hom. Tho I stay a few days here, I hop no body will reproach me of eating the bread of ydleness, seing no body has and will goe mor cheerfully about any thing that concerns the Kings or your Lordships service, then, my Lord, your Lordships most humble and obedient servant.

To Cornet David Graham[193] *RPC*, 3rd ser., ix, 351-2

Edinburgh, 9 September 1684

Dear Brother, my Lord Treasurer hes bene pleased to take me in with himself and his sone[194] in a commissione which the Council hes given us of Justiciary and Councill, and he, being desyrous all should be

---

[193] Claverhouse's younger brother.

[194] James Douglas (1662-1711), Lord Drumlanrig; later (1695) 2nd duke of Queensberry.

exactlie done that relates to the Kings service in these partes, hes allowed me to write to yow to prepare some things for us. I doubt not but, seing yow have bene busie these severall weeks bypast in the shyre, yow can give ane exact acount of it. My Lord Treasurer will expect to know from yow quhat heritors have bene slak in attending divin ordinance, for, I supose, ther are non withdrauers altogether, and particularlie concerning the ladies of which I know some are yet obstinat. Besides this, we will expect that yow can give us account of all resetters or conversers with rebells, especiallie since the circuit in that shyre.

As to the Steuartrie, wher, I supose, yow now are and wher most disorders have bene, yow most take the paroch of Minigaff, the four paroches of the Glenkens, Partoun, Kirkpatrick and Irongray, and examine everie man concerning all maner of church disordors. The commons yow may judge according to your ordinary method, but heritors, onlie take there depositions, and make report therof to my Lord Treasurer quhen he coms as to resett. Examine all the commons on oath except some against quhom yow have any informatione, and in that caice examine there servants and neighbours, becaus, if they be found guiltie since the circuit, they must hang, which cannot be done if it be once referred to ther oath.

Any yow find guiltie since the circuit of comons of this cryme, whither it be by probation of wittnesses or oath of partie, secure in prison and doe all dilligence to aprehend all who refuse to apear befor yow or are in the fugitive rolls. Examine not onlie who hes reset in there houses but all who hes resett on there lands since the circuit, and, if anie heritors be found guiltie, yow may give informatione att our incomming; but if yow suspect they will flee, secure them. If yow find heritors have resett declared rebells in ther housses or conversed with them, secure them quhatever they be, but examin noe heritor concerning his oun guilt in that cryme, becaus we will doe it, but examin all the comons against them and there oun servants.

Acquaint the moderators of all presbiteries to intimat to there respective ministers that they make readie lists of all persons duelling within there parochins, heritor, tennent, cottar, sons or daughters above tuelv years of age or other persons reciding with them, alse welle women as men, and that they make readie ane account who of them withdraues as yet or keeps not the church ordinarlie or are guiltie of

any fanatik disordors and all this upon oath to the best of there knouledge.

Everie heritor most be acquainted by the shereff to doe the like within there oun lands, soe they most bring lists of all and account who of them are disorderlie or resettars upon oath according to there knouledge, and they most depon befor us, both ministers and heritors, that they have done there endevor to discover and inform themselves all they could efter this intimation was givene. The minister will onlie need to swear as to there lists and church disordor.

Inquire alsoe upon oath of the comons if the souldiers have [been] payed ther locallitie, particularlie those two years bypast. Be exact in this and precipitat not, for, though our dyett be the tuentie fifte of this moneth, yet my Lord Treasurer will may be allow yow to the thirtie, quhill he is going on in uther jurisdictions, Lag will doe the rest in the Steuartrie. Adieu.

To Queensberry   HMC, *Queensberry*, 290

Burntisland, 30 October [1684]
My Lord, That day I pairted from Sir Robert Dayells[195] I came to Edinbourg with clear day light, and your letters were delyvered to Heu Wallaces wife in good time. I souped at Blairs with my Lord Balcares, Drumeller, the Advocat and several others. Nixt morning I sawe our friends saive the Register, who was not com to toun. I spok about Fyfe and the Lauthians joining in this suplie. Many thinks it raisonable; but Balcares told me friely that he durst not undertake it; and when I spok to him that others would, that pretended to mor interest in that contrey, he laughed at it.

Yesterday I dined at Blairs with the Chancelor, Secretary, and all the good compagnie in toun; and it was said that Nidsdelle had given nothing, because it was left to the Councell to impose, which they in all apearence would not doe. I doe not knou if it was heared by all, but I said out, that I believed those of the secret comitty would not refuse to tell their privat opinion, and without any act of Councell my Lord Treasurer would cause these shyrs make offer acordingly. I told that the raison why the offer was in generall terms was, that they thoght the

195 Sir Robert Dalyell of Glenae, justice of the peace for Nithsdale.

government would not think it raisonable to take so much of them as af Galloway, and yet they thoght it might seem not loyall anogh to offer less.[196]

I am informed that it is said that we ar far short of Clidsdelle in the Bond of Peace, and that Clidsdelle could have been broght to tuenty moenths suplie, if the Bond had been in the terms Galloway or Nidsdelle took. As to that, I said that befor we sawe that draught, we had proposed all we thoght raisonable or practicable; but we could have easily broght them to seign the other, if we had thoght it good for any thing, but to insnair people. Houever, I fynd it is the opinion of your Lordships friends, and the President tells me he desyred Heu Wallace to wryt so to you, that it wer good to cause the Bond be seigned acording to their draught of Clidsdelle, and after it might be explained and restricted here.

If your Lordship think fit to send it to my brother with order to see it seigned, I dout not but it will be don, and Lagg may doe so in Kilkoubright, in Nidddelle and Anandelle. Your Lordship may doe it being on the place; after which they will have nothing to say, and when it is don, I think it should be altered, for it is unjust to desyr of others what we would not doe our selfs. For I declair I think it a thing not to be desyred, that I should be forfaited and hanged, if my tenents wife, tuenty mille from me, in the midest of hilles and woods give m[e]ate or shelter [to] a fugitive.

The Register I could not see, but I have writen from this my mind to hime. All your Lordships friends ar very desyrous to see you soon at Edinbourg, for things will take no setlement till then. I dessein to be over again the end of the nixt week.

My Lord Lauderdaille is com doun, and desseins, as I hear, to goe briskly on and lait lay the submission in my affair. But in this and all other things, I relay upon your Lordship intyrly; and, tho I can not make so many compliments as others doe, yet I am with all sincerity and respect, my Lord, your most humble and faithfull servant.

[P.S.] My Lord, excuse this way of wryting for peaper is as ill to be hade here as at Kilkoubrigh.

---

[196] The heritors of the south-western counties were being pressured to offer an extra 'voluntary' payment of cess to pay the troops quartered there.

To [Moray?]   HMC, *Laing*, 430

22 January [1685]

My Lord, I am sorry that I have occasion to tell you that my Lord
Treasurors displeaseur lasts still against me. I think my self very happy
that your Lordship was present when it first begood from nothing, and
I wish you had seen to what hight it was com nixt morning when I went
to pay my respects to his Grace at his owen lodgings. I am seur you
would have thoght I was not used lyk a gentlemen; and yet, my Lord,
by what I hear he thinks it not anogh that I should have been so used.
Nothing will satisfy but that I be put out of the Kings service. If that be a
raisonable thing I leave to your Lordship to judge; but I hop I serve a
juster maister and I flatter my self with the thoghts that his Royal
Highness has mor goodness for me then to sacrifice me to the heumeur
of any body. The preparative wer not good; for who asks to have me
distroyed the day would ask ane other to morou.

It is said that my Lord Treasurer wryts up a great deall against me,
but I satisfy myself with that, that seing the Deuk has not aloued me to
com up to vindicat myself, he will not believe anything to my prejudice
till he com doun that I have lieve to speak for myself. I need not say
anything of particulars. I had the good fortun to inform you of all that
affair befor you pairted from this. I hear my Lord Treasurer wryts to
you often on this subject, but I declair I have not the least suspition that
you will give any evill advice against me; for I remarked whyll you wer
with us here you understood very well to pay deu respect to persons of
character, but you still used that freedom and liberty in Councell and
elswhere that becomes a gentleman.

As to the state of affaires here, they ar much about on as they wer
when your lordship left them. Lieut[enant] General Drumond and I did
all wes recomended to us in that party was ordered befor you went of,
but as long as there is on of these fellous alive, they will never give it
over. The secret comitty did not think fit to imploy us again but have
sent Col[onel] Douglas out with tuo hundred foot and the comand of all
the troops in these garisons, who, I dout not, will setle the contrey, tho
he never was there befor.

I regrait the condition of the shyr of Wigtoun of whiche I have the
honor to be sherif. They have all taken the Test tuo year agoe, heritor,
tenent, cotar and servant, and lieved as orderly as the shyr of Angus

during that time without the asistance of any of the Kings forces; and in our last circuit we disbanded their militia and disarmed them all; and yet the government refuses them a small garison to defend them against the incursions of the rebelles that are beaten in upon them by the garisons in the nyghbouring shyres.

There ar as many troops now in garison in Nidsdell as ever I had for Anandelle, Nidsdell, the Steuarty of Kilkoubright and Wigton. I can not denay but there is som raison to have garisons thik there, for there ar parisheus there that have tuelve or sixteen men in armes constantly in the hilles. We had acount from Dumfries yesterday that when the troops went in to make a search in Galloway the wigs would not loose such ane oportunity but gathered togither and came to the house of Dalswinton, ordered to be on of the Nidsdell garisons, and caryed away the yron gate and brok all the yron bars that mad the house strong. They bate and wounded severall persons in Nidsdelle at the same time.

When the Deuk comes doun I shall tell your lordship what methods I think would prove effectuall for securing the peace of the west, but nothing that comes from me now is relished here, because of my Lord Treasurer. However, if I see the Kings service be done I shall easily be satisfyed. I will expect your lordships favour and am most sincerly, my lord, your most faithfull and most humble servant.

[P.S.] My Lord Balcares and I have got all don in Fyfe with great ease that was recomended to us by the Government, but I am of opinion that bonds of peace is of mor consequence then mony.

To Queensberry   HMC, *Queensberry*, 292

Galston, 3 May 1685

May it please your Grace, On Frayday last amongst the hilles betuixt Douglas and the Plellands, we perseued tuo fellous a great way throu the mosses, and in end seised them. They had no armes about them and denayed they had any, but being asked if they would take the abjuration the eldest of tuo called John Broun refused it, nor would he swear not to ryse in armes against the King, but said he kneu no King; upon which, and there being found bullets and match in his house and treasonable peapers, I caused shoot him dead, which he suffered very unconcernedly. The other, a yong fellou, and his nepheu, called John Brounen,

offered to take the oath; but he would not swear that he had not been at Neumilles in armes at the rescuing the prisoners.

So I did not knou what to doe with him. I was convinced that he was guilty, but sawe not hou to proceed against him; wherfor after he had said his prayers and carabins presented to shoot him, I offered to him that if he would make ane ingeneous confession and make a discoverie that might be of any importance for the Kings service, I should delay puting him to death, and plead for him; upon which he confessed that he was at that attake of Neumilles, and that he had com straight to this house of his uncles on Sunday morning.

In the time he was making this confession the souldiers found out a house in the hille under ground, that could hold a dusen of men and there wer swords and pistolles in it; and this fellou declaired that they belonged to his uncle, and that he had lurked in that place ever since Bothwell where he was in armes. He confessed that he had a halbart and told who gave it him about a month agoe, and we have the feleou prisoner. He gave acount of the names of the most pairt of those that wer there. They wer not above sixty and they wer all Gaston and Neumilles men, saive a feu out of Streven parish. He gave also acount of a conventicle keeped by Renek[197] at the bak of Carantable, where there wer threttin scor of men in armes mustered and exersised, of which number he was with his hallard.

He tells of ane other conventicle about three moneths agoe keeped near Louden Hille, and gives acount of the persons wer at both and what childring wer baptised, particularly that at Carntable which was about the time that Lieu[tenant] Muray and Crichton[198] should have laiten them eskeap. He also gives acount of those who gave any assistance to his uncle, and we have seised there upon the good man of the upmost Plellands and ane other tenent about a myll belou that is flaid upon it.

I dout not but if we had time to stay, good use might be made of his confession. I have acquyted my self when I have told your Grace the caise. He has been but a moneth or tuo with his halbart; and if your Grace thinks he deserves no marcy, justice will pass on him, for I having no comission of justiciary myself have delyvered him up to the

---

[197] James Renwick, one of the Cameronian ministers.
[198] Lieutenant George Murray (in command of a troop of guards) and Lieutenant Francis Crichton.

Lieuetenent Generall to be disposed of as he pleases. I am, my Lord, your Graces most humble servant.

To Queensberry   HMC, *Queensberry*, 293

Johnstone, 16 June 1685

May it please your Grace, I am very sorry that any thing I have don should have given your Grace occassion to be dissatisfyed with me, and to make complaints against me to the Earle of Dumbarton. I am convinced your Grace is ill informed, for after you have raid what I wrot to you tuo days agoe on that subject, I dar say I may refer myself to your owen senseur. That I had no dessein to make great search there, any body may judge. I came not from Air till after eleven in the fornoon, and went to Bellagen with fourty heritors again night.

The Sanquair is just in the road, and I used these men I mett accidentily on the road better then ever I used any in these circumstances, and I may saively say that as I shall answer to God if they had been lieving on my ground I could not have forborn drawing my sword and knoking them doun. Houever, I am glaid I have recaiued my Lord Dumbartons orders anent your Graces tenents which I shall most punctually obey, tho I may say they wer saif as any in Scotland befor.

Your Grace may remember you signifyed your opinion to me that the heritors of Nidsdelle would be better in the centricall pairts of the shyr then at Dumfries, and the generall persones have given orders they should be assisting to the Highlanders at the Leadhilles, which I have signifyed to the Earle of Anandelle.[199] Nevertheless he wryts to me, that he is to march to morou by four a cloak in the morning to Anan, and tells me that he expects that there-upon I will stop the march of the troopes that I had ordered to Anan or Canapie parisheus for the gaird of the Border.

I have writen to my Lord my opinion, and with all told him that if he be very positive in the thing, I am not to hinder him. I an unwilling to shok any body that serves the King in such a time, tho I think it not just that my lord or any other should think to exclud the rest of the forces from doing their deuty in any pairt they ar comanded too. If he come to

---

[199] William Johnstone (1668-1721), 2nd earl of Annandale and Hartfell.

Anan, Drumeller to Canopie, and Kilseith[200] at Ewes, they will be too thik. I am, my Lord, your Graces most humble servant.

[P.S.] My Lord Anandelle wrytes to me, that he had got of late instructiones from the secret comitty to act with his heritors for the security of that contrey; by which I perceive he concluds he is to take his measeur by himself, and therupon has taken that resolution to goe to Anan contrary to what I had wryten to him was the Generalls mind.

To Queensberry   HMC, *Queensberry*, 293

Thorlesthorpe, 3 July 1685

May it please your Grace, Some time agoe I hade ane order seigned by your Grace and some other of the lords of the secret comitty, to apley the movables of rebelles for the maintenence of the forces; and accordingly I gave to them all the sheep and couse [that] wer eatable; these [t]hat wer not I caused carry in to Ingland, and make mony of them, of which I have recovered fourty pounds sterling, which I desseined for the Highlanders of Leadhilles; but seeing they ar gon home I have sent it to the Earle of Homes regiment; for Sir William Douglas has got for his a'bove a hondred pound sterling of the mony of the D[uke] of Monmouthes regiment as they call it here. There is a hondred pound sterling owing by bond for mor of the rebelles goods by persones in Ingland, but is not payable till Lambas.

So your Grace will be pleased to lait me knou if you aprove of what is don, and what way you will have me to dispose of that mony when it falls deu. I am, my Lord, your Graces most humble servant.

To Mr Blathwayt, Secretary of War[201]   NLS, MS 591, no. 1836

Dudhope, 10 October 1688

Sir, I have received the ordor for marching those troops under my comand to London which I shall doe with all convenient dilligence. I am sir, your most humble servant.

---

[200] Lieutenant-Colonel William Livingstone (1650–1733), later (1706) 3rd viscount of Kilsyth.
[201] William Blathwayt, secretary at war from 1683 to 1704. Formally secretary to the English commander in chief, but in practice almost a minister of state.

To the burgh of Dundee   Dundee, *Charters*, 114

Dudhope, 11 March 1689

I, John, Viscount of Dundee, Grants me to have receaved ane thousand merkes, which Alexander Cathcart receaved upon the fourth day of October last by past from John Grahame, Colector of the towne's gift of two merkes upon each boll of malt broun and sold within the town of Dundie,—the qu[hi]lk sowme is payable to me termlie out of the first end of the said gift, and discharges the said town of the terme of Martimes, i^m vi^c eightie-eight, as Witnesse my hand, at Dudhope the 11 of March 1689.

To Hamilton[202]   Dundee, *Letters*, 32

Dudhope, 27 March 1689

May it please your Grace, The coming of an herauld and trumpeter to summon a man to lay down arms, that is living in peace at home, seems to me a very extraordinary thing, and, I suppose, will do so to all that hears of it. While I attended the Convention at Edinburgh, I complained often of many people's being in arms without authority, which was notoriously known to be true, even the wild hill men; and, no summons to lay down arms under the pain of treason being given them, I thought it unsafe for me to remain longer among them.

And because some few of my friends did me the favour to convey me out of the reach of these murderers, and that my Lord Levingston and several other officers took occasion to come away at the same time, this must be called being in arms. We did not exceed the number allowed by the Meeting of Estates: my Lord Levingstone and I might have had each of us ten; and four or five officers that were in company might have had a certain number allowed them; which being, it will be found we exceeded not. I am sure it is far short of the number my Lord Lorne[203] was seen to march with. And, tho I had gone away with some more than ordinary, who can blame me, when designs of murdering me was made appear?

---

[202] The duke of Hamilton had been elected president of the Convention of Estates on its first day, 14 March.

[203] Archibald Campbell (c.1658-1703), 10th earl and (1701) 1st duke of Argyll: referred to as Lord Lorne because his late father's forfeiture had not yet been reversed.

Besides, it is known to every body, that, before we came within sixteen miles of this, my Lord Levingston went off to his brother, my Lord Strathmoir's[204] house; and most of the officers, and several of the company, went to their respective homes or relations; and, if any of them did me the favour to come along with me, must that be called being in arms? Sure, when your Grace represents this to the Meeting of the States, they will discharge such a groundless pursuit, and think my appearance before them unnecessary.

Besides, tho' it were necessary for me to go and attend the Meeting, I cannot come with freedom and safety, because I am informed there are men of war, and foreign troops in the passage; and, till I know what they are, and what are their orders, the Meeting cannot blame me for not coming. Then, my Lord, seeing the summons has proceeded on a groundless story, I hope the Meeting of States will think it unreasonable, I should leave my wife in the condition she is in.

If there be any body that, notwithstanding of all that is said, think I ought to appear, I beg the favour of a delay till my wife is brought to bed; and, in the meantime, I will either give security or paroll not to disturb the peace. Seeing this pursuit is so groundless, and so reasonable things offered, and the Meeting composed of prudent men and men of honour, and your Grace presiding in it, I have no reason to fear farther trouble. I am, may it please your Grace, your most humble servant.

[P.S.] I beg your Grace will cause to read this to the Meeting, because it is all the defence I have made. I sent another to your Grace from Dumblein, with the reasons of my leaving Edinburgh: I know not if it comes to your hands.[205]

To the earl of Dunfermline[206]   Fraser, *Melvilles*, ii, 103

Collithie, 21 April 1689

My Lord, So soon as I cam to Clait I wrot a letter giving your lordship acount of my being in this contrey, and desyring to know what way I could wait on your lordship, which Tarpersey undertook to delyver; but befor he was the lenth of the Kirktoun of Inch he mett a servant of your lordships coming to him, by whom he understood that you wer

---

[204] Patrick Lyon (1643-1695), 1st earl of Strathmore and Kinghorne.
[205] One of the missing letters—if actually written.
[206] James Seton (d. 1694), 4th earl of Dunfermline.

gon to Castle Gordon, so he returned bak and then went towards Castle Gorden, and befor he came this lenth he found on the way a gentleman with your lordships letter to me, which I was extreamly glaid to see; not that I could dout your lordships forwardness for the Kings service; but was extreamly pleased that I should have the hapiness to concert with you these affaires, that concerns us all so much. There is no body in this contrey, both on your oun acount and the Duke of Gordons,[207] so proper to influence it.

I will send Major Graham[208] from Kieth to know where I may wait on you, or what comands you have for me. I am, my lord, your most humble faithfull servant.

To Dunfermline   *Leven Papers*, 13

Keith, 21 April 1689

My Lord, I would certenly have sent Major Grahame to wait on your Lordship this night, as I wrote to you, but that he was stayed on the road with compagnie, without my knowledge, till it was too leat. He shall be with your Lordship to-morrow at the hour appointed. I am, my Lord, your most humble and faithful servant.

To Sir Lachlan Mackintosh[209]   Mackintosh, *Letters*, 119

Coxton, 24 April 1689

Sir, I wrote to you the day before yesterday, concerning the present state of affairs, yet having the occasion of this bearer, I am so concerned that you make no wrong step to the prejudice of your family, or to your own dishonour, I would forbear to mind you of the just cause the King has, or the objections you have to him, and the happy occasion you have now by declaring for the King to oblige him and all honest men in such manner. As you will be sure to be established in all your ancient rights,[210] and rewarded according to your deservings, you may assure yourself ever of all the good offices and services lays in the power of, sir, your affectionate cousin and most humble servant.

---

[207] The duke of Gordon held Edinburgh Castle for King James.
[208] Major William Graham.
[209] Chief of the Mackintoshes, and Claverhouse's cousin.
[210] A reference to Mackintosh's disputes with the Camerons of Lochiel and MacDonalds of Keppoch.

To Cluny Macpherson   'Gleanings', *TGSI*, xx, 202

[Strone?,] 19 May 1689

Sir, I hear M[ajor] G[eneral] McKay[211] has been by threats and promises indevoring to engadge you in his rebellion against our Laufull Suverain King James, but I knou your constant Loyalty your honor and your conscience will secur you against such proposals. I have nou received Letters from Yrland by which I am seur nothing but want of fair wynd can hinder the landing of a considerable force in this contrey from thence, and that the King will be with us very soon. In the meantime he is pleased to apoint me to be L[ieutenan]t Gen[eral] and comand the forces whereupon I am to requyr all honest men to attend the Kings Standart.

I perswad my self you will not be wanting in so good ane occasion as this is of indevoring under God to restor our gracious monarch. I will not desyr you to apear in armes untill such time as you see us in body able to preserve you which I hop in God you shall in a feu days see.

There is on thing I forwarn you of not to be alarumed with: the danger they would make the world believe the protestant religion is in. They must make the religion the pretext as it has been in all times of rebellion. I am as much concerned in the protestant religion as any man, and will doe my indevors to see it secured. I am, Sir, your most humble servant.

To Malcolm Fraser of Culduthie   *More Culloden Papers*, i, 206

11 June 1689

Sir, I fynd that the Earle of Dumfermling has warand which I have seen for making up of all the Duk Gordons rents and things belonging to him for the use of the Kings servants and I see he has ordered you as the Dukes chamberlain in these pairts to send up to the head of Loch Ness ane hundred bolles of meale. I thoght fit to signify to you that I second my lords order and seing it is so necessary for our troops I have ordered to secur som house of yours till obedience be given to E[arl] Dumfermlings order, if the meale be not at the Loch head with in four and tuenty hours after E[arl] Dumfermlings orders is delyvered at your house the house will be fallen on, this is from Sir your humble servant.

---

[211] Major-General Hugh Mackay (c.1640–1692), commander in chief.

To [Unknown]   Warden, *Angus*, iv, 217

                                                    14 June 1689[212]

Sir, Thes day I recue a leter of yours writ the last of May. I admier it was
so long of coming to yre, I hop mie men hes bin with you to recive the
oxen what mony thay ar mor let me knou and you shall have it. For
gave thes truball from sir, your asured frind and servant.

To John Macleod of Macleod   Dundee, *Letters*, 38

                                                Moy, 23 June 1689

Sir, Glengaire[213] gave me ane account of the substance of a letter he
receaved from yow: I shall only tell yow, that if yow heasten not to land
your men, I am of opinion yow will have litle occasion to do the King
great service; for if he land in the wesst of Scotland, yow will come too
late, as I believe yow will thienk yourself by the news I have to tell yow.

The Prince of Orange hath wreaten to the Scots Councell not to fatig
his troops any more by following us in the hills, but to draw them
together in a body to the west; and, accordingly, severall of the forces,
that were in Pearthshire and Angus, are drawn to Edin[bu]r[gh]; and
some of McKay's regments are marcht that way from him: he further
informs them that, besids the fifty-two sail alraidy in Irland of French
men of warr, there are eighty more from Brest, who have fivteen
thousand land souldiers aboord, and that he knows not whither they
design for England, or Irland. He orders the whole kingdome to be put
in ane posture of defence, so that all persons must drawe to armes, and
take pairty one way or other.

There came ane express, some weekes ago, from Londondairy to
Duke Hamiltone, telling, if they got not imediat releif, they could hold
out no longer. We hear also from Edin[bu]r[gh] that they offered to
render, if the King wold give any capitulation, which the King refuses,
being advised that its necessar to make exemple of them for the terrour
of others. Mr Hay,[214] who came hither yesterday from Irland, gives

---

[212] The date of this letter was altered by Claverhouse from 12 to 14 June, a period during which he was
in retreat from Keppoch to Strone. It was found among the papers of Alexander Graham of Balmuir,
Kincaldrum and Meathie.
[213] Alasdair MacDonald of Glengarry, known as 'Black Alasdair'.
[214] The brothers John and George Hay were both King James's messengers.

account that, above three weeks ago, he was at the seige, and then hors flesh was sold for sixpence a pound, and for cannon bullets they were shooting lumps of brick wrapped in peuter plates. It is now certainly rendert. Mr Hay saw relief offer to land, but was beat back with great loss. Some of the Freinch fleet hath been seen amongst the islands, and hath taken the two Glasgow frigots.

The King, being thus master by sea and land, hath nothing to do but bring over his army, which many people fancy is landed alraidy in the west. He will have litle to oppose him there, and probably will march towards England; so that we who are in the graitest readiness will have ado to join him. I have receaved by Mr Hay a commission of Lieutennent Genral, which miscarried by Breidy.[215] I have also received a double of a letter miscairied by Breidy to me, and a new letter, dated the 18 of May; both which are so kind, that I am asham'd to tell.

He counts for great services, which I am conscious to myself that I have hardly done my deutie. He promises not only to me, but to all that will join, such marks of favour, as affer ages shall see what honour and advantage there is, in being loyall. He sayes, in express terms, that his favours shall vy with our loyalty. He hath, by the same letters, given full power of Councell to such councellers here, as shall be joined in the King's service, and given us power, with the rest of his freends, to meet in a Convention, by his authority, to counteract the mock Convention at Edin[bu]r[gh], whom he hath declaired traitours, and comanded all his loyall subjects to make warr against them; in obedience to which, I have called all the clannes.

Captain of Glenrannald[216] is near us these severall dayes; the Laird of Baro[217] is there with his men. I am persuaded Sir Donald[218] is there by this. McClean[219] lands in Morven to-morrow certainly. Apen, Glenco, Lochell, Glengaire, Keppock,[220] are all raidy. Sir Alex[ander] and Largo[221] have been here with there men all this while with me, so that I

[215] Quartermaster David Brady was an officer in the duke of St Albans' regiment, and one of the few who did not defect to William of Orange at Salisbury.

[216] Alan MacDonald of Clanranald.

[217] Alasdair Macneill of Barra.

[218] Sir Donald MacDonald of Sleat.

[219] Sir John Maclean of Duart.

[220] Robert Stewart of Appin, Alasdair MacDonald of Glencoe, Sir Ewen Cameron of Lochiel, Alasdair MacDonald of Glengarry, and Coll MacDonald of Keppoch.

[221] Sir Alexander Maclean of Otter and Alexander MacDonald of Largie.

hop we will go out of Lochaber abour thre thousand. Yow may judge what we will gett in Strathharig, Badenock, Athol, Marr, and the Duke of Gordon's lands, besides the loyall shires of Bamf, Aberdeen, Merns, Angus, Pearth, and Stirling. I hope we will be masters of the north, as the King's army will be of the south.

I had almost forgot to tell yow of my Lord Broad Alban,[222] who I suppose now will come to the feelds. Dumbeth,[223] with two hundred hors and eight hundred foot, and said to be endevouring to join us. My L[ord] Seaforth[224] will be in a few dayes from Irland to rais his men for the King's service.

Now, I have layd the whole business befor yow, yow will easily know what is fitt for yow to do. All I shall say further is, to repeat and renew the desyre of my former letter, and assure yow that I am, Sir, your most humble servant.

[P.S.] Yow will receave the King's letter to yow.

To Melfort   Dundee, *Letters*, 44

                                           Moy, 27 June 1689

My Lord, I was not a little surprised to find by yours that my name has been made use of for carrying on designs against you. Mr Carleton[225] is extremely in the wrong, if he says I gave him any commission to the King, or warrant to say any thing to him in my name. Earl Bredalbin sent him to me with a credential, which he desired me to burn as soon as I had read it. I had never seen the man in the face before, nor heard of him. He was not two hours in my company; and when he gave me an account of his pretended business to Ireland, I disliked most of it, as I signified to you by McSwyne;[226] nor did I give him so much as a line with him that I remember.

I leave you to judge if it be probable, that I would intrust myself so far to any, in such circumstances, as to emply him in so nice and dangerous a point as that is, of accusing so great a man, and so much my friend, as you are, to the King. If I had any such design, I would rather have

---

[222] The earl of Breadalbane.   .
[223] William Sinclair of Dunbeath.
[224] Kenneth Mackenzie (1661-1701), 4th earl of Seaforth.
[225] Thomas Carleton, apparently a messenger from the Jacobite headquarters in Dublin.
[226] Dennis McSwyne, Dundee's messenger to Dublin, where Melfort then was.

trusted myself to the King, and written frankly to himself. I will assure you, all my endeavours to lay you aside were only to yourself. I thought myself bound in duty to the King, and friendship to you, not to dissemble to you the circumstances you stand in with the generality of this country, and many in the neighbouring.

Your merit and rising fortune has raised envy; your favour with the King is crime enough with his enemies, and I am feared even with his ambitious friends, which I am sure can never be imagined to be one with me, for I can never have any pretensions in your way. Besides, you have contributed to all the considerable steps of my fortune. But I must tell you that, besides these generals, there are many pretend to have received disobligations from you, and others, no doubt, with design on your employment; yet the most universal pretext is the great hand you had in carrying on matters of religion, as they say, to the ruin of king and country.

I must tell you I heard a great resentment against you for advising the giving the bulls for the bishops, and I am feared they themselves believe it. You know what the Church of England is in England; and both there and here, they generally say, that the king of himself is not disposed to push matters of religion, or force people to do things they scrupled in conscience; but that you, to gain favour with these of that religion, had proved and prevailed with him, contrary to his inclination, to do what he did, which has given his enemies occasion to destroy him and the monarchy.

This being, as I assure you it is, however unjust, the general opinion of these nations, I thought, in prudence, for your own sake as well as the King's, you would have thought it best to seem to be out of business for a time, that the King's business might go on the smoother, and all pretext be taken away for rebellion; and this only in case the King find difficulty in his affairs: for I am obliged to tell you, that, if the people take umbrage as to their religion, it will be, notwithstanding of all the foreign aid, a long war. But I think you may come over; and when you have seen the state of affairs on the place, and spoke with everybody, you may think what will be best for you to do.

You desire me to recommend a proper man to be secretary. You know it is hard to do. But, if you really resolve not to seem to meddle, I would, were I you, advise the King to employ one, to be turned out when things altered would not much disoblige, or could have

no consequence. But, I think, I have said enough, if not too much of this.

My Lord, I have given the King in general, account of things here; but to you I will be more particular. As to myself, I have sent you it at large. You may by it understand a little of the state of the country. You will see there, when I had a seen advantage, I endeavoured to profit on it, but, on the other hand, shunned to hazard anything, for fear of a ruffle; for the least of that would have discouraged all. I thought if I could gain time, and keep up a figure of a party without loss, it was my best, till we got assistance, which the enemy got from England every day. I have told the King I had neither commission, money, nor ammunition. My brother-in-law, Albar,[227] and my wife found ways to get credit. For my own, nobody durst pay to a traitor. I was extremely surprised when I saw Mr Drummond, the advocate, in Highland habit,[228] come up to Lochaber to me, and gave account that the Queen[229] had sent L. 2,000 sterling to London, to be paid to me for the King's service, and that two more was a-coming.

I did not think the Queen had known anything of our affairs. I received a very obliging letter from her with Mr Crain;[230] but I know no way to make a return. However, when the money comes, I shall keep count of it and employ it right. But I am feared it will be hard to bring it from Edinburgh.

When we came first out, I had but fifty pounds of powder; more I could not get; all the great towns and sea-ports were in rebellion, and had seized the powder, and would sell none. But I had one advantage, the Highlanders will not fire above once, and then take to the broad-sword. But I wonder above all things that in three months I never heard from you, seeing by Mr Hay, I had so earnestly recommended it to you, and told of this way by Inverlochie; as sure, if you would not have sent expresses, we thought you would at least have hastened the dispatch of these we sent.

McSwyne has now been away near two months, and we know not if

---

[227] Robert Young of Auldbar.
[228] David Drummond, afterwards treasurer of the Bank of Scotland, after a period of imprisonment in Edinburgh Tolbooth beginning in December 1689.
[229] Mary of Modena, queen of James VII.
[230] The messenger who had brought King James's letter to the Convention.

the coast be clear or not. However, I have adventured to advise Mr Hay to return straight, and not go farther into the country. It would have been impossible for him to get through to Edinburgh; but there was no need. He came not here until the 22d, and they surrendered on the 13th.[231] It was not Mr Hay's fault he was so long a coming; for there has been two English men-of-war and the Glasgow frigates among the islands till of late.

For the rest of the letters, I undertook to get them delivered. Most of the persons to whom they are directed are either put under bond, or in prison, or gone out of the kingdom. The Advocate[232] is gone to England, a very honest man, firm beyond belief; and Athol is gone too, who did not know what to do.[233] Earl Hume,[234] who is very frank, is taken prisoner to Edinburgh, but will be let out on security. Earl Bredalbin keeps close in a strong house he has, and pretends the gout. Earl Errol[235] stays at home; so does Aberdeen. Earl Marshal[236] is at Edinburgh, but does not meddle. Earl Lauderdale is right, and at home. The bishops, I know not where they are. They are now the kirk invisible. I will be foreced to open the letter, and send copies attested to them, and keep the original, till I can find out our primate.

The poor ministers are sorely oppressed over all. They generally stand right. Duke Queensberry was present at the Cross, when their new mock King was proclaimed, and, I hear, voted for him, though not for the throne vacant. His brother the Lieutenant General, some say, is made an earl. He has come down to Edinburgh, and is gone up again. He is the old man, and has abused me strangely, for he swore to me to make amends.

Tarbat is a great villain. Besides what he has done at Edinburgh, he has endeavoured to seduce Lochiel by offers of money, which is under his hand. He is now gone up to secure his faction, which is melting, the two Dalrymples[237] and others, against Skelmurly, Polwart, Cardross,

---

[231] The duke of Gordon surrendered Edinburgh Castle on 13 June.
[232] Sir George Mackenzie of Rosehaugh.
[233] The marquis of Atholl retired to Bath to avoid taking sides.
[234] Charles Home (d. 1706), 6th earl of Home.
[235] John Hay (d. 1704), 12th earl of Errol.
[236] William Keith (c.1664-1712), 8th Earl Marischal.
[237] Sir James Dalrymple of Stair, and his son Sir John Dalrymple of Stair.

Ross,[238] and others, now joined with that worthy prince, Duke Hamilton. M. Douglas[239] is now a great knave, as well as beast; as is Glencairne; Morton; and Eglinton:[240] and even Cassills[241] is gone astray, misled by Gibby.[242] Panmure[243] keeps right, and at home; so does Strathmore, Southesk,[244] and Kinnaird. Old Airly[245] is at Edinburgh, under caution; so is Balcarras and Dunmore. Stormont[246] is declared fugitive for not appearing. All these will break out, and many more, when the King lands, or any from him. Most of the gentry on this side the Forth, and many on the other, will do so too. But they suffer mightily in the meantime; and will be forced to submit, if there be not relief sent very soon.

The Duke of Gordon, they say, wanted nothing for holding out, but hopes of relief. Earl of Dunfermling stays constantly with me, and so does Lord Dunkell,[247] Pitcur,[248] and many other gentlemen, who really deserve well, for they suffer great hardships. When the troops land, there must be blank commissions sent for horse and foot, for them, and others that will join. There must be a Commission of Justiciary, to judge all but landed men: for there should be examples made of some that cannot be judged of by a council of war. They take our people and hang them up, by their new sheriffs, when they find them straggling.

My Lord, I have given my opinion to the King concerning the landing. I would first have a good party sent over to Inverlochy, about 5000 or 6000, as you have conveniency of boats; of which as many horse as conveniently can. About 600 or 800 would do well; but rather more; for had I had horse, for all that yet appeared, I would not have feared

[238] Sir James Montgomery of Skelmorlie; Sir Patrick Home of Polwarth (1641-1724); Henry Erskine (d. 1693), 3rd Lord Cardross; and William, 12th Lord Ross. All were members of the 'Club' which co-ordinated radical opposition to the employment of supporters of the previous regime, such as Sir John Dalrymple.

[239] James Douglas (c. 1646-1700), 2nd marquis of Douglas, who was granted Dundee's forfeiture in 1690.

[240] John Cunningham (d. 1703), 11th earl of Glencairn; James Douglas (c.1652-1715), 12th earl of Morton; Alexander Montgomery (c.1660-1729), 9th earl of Eglinton.

[241] John Kennedy (d. 1701), 7th earl of Cassillis.

[242] Gilbert Burnet of Leys (1643-1715), created bishop of Salisbury in 1688.

[243] James Maule (c.1658-1723), 4th earl of Panmure.

[244] Charles Carnegie (1661-1699), 4th earl of Southesk.

[245] James Ogilvy (d. 1703), 2nd earl of Airlie.

[246] David Murray (d. 1731), 5th Viscount Stormont.

[247] James Galloway (d. 1705), 3rd Lord Dunkeld.

[248] David Haliburton of Pitcur.

them. Inverlochie is safe landing, far from the enemy, and one may chuse from thence, to go to Murray by Inverness, or to Angus by Athol, or to Perth by Glencoe, and all tolerable ways. The only ill is, the passage is long by sea and inconvenient, because of the island; but in this season that is not to be feared. So soon as the boats return, let them ferry over as many more foot as they think fit to the Point of Kintyre, which will soon be done; and then the King has all the boats for his own landing. I should march towards Kintyre, and meet at the neck of Tarbitt the foot, and so march to raise the country, and then towards the passes of Forth to meet the King, where I doubt not but we would be numerous.

I have done all I can to make them believe the King will land altogether in the west, on purpose to draw their troops from the north, that we may the easier raise the country, if the landing be here. I have said so, and written it to every body; and particularly I sent some proclamations to my Lady Errol, and wrote to her to that purpose, which was intercepted and carried to Edinburgh, and my lady taken prisoner. I believe it has taken the effect I designed; for the forces are marched out of Kintyre, and I am just now informed M[ajor] G[eneral] McKay is gone from Inverness by Murray towards Edinburgh. I know not what troops he has taken with him as yet; but it is thought he will take the horse and dragoons except a few; and most of the standing forces, which, if he do, it will be a rare occasion for landing here, and for raising the country. Then, when they hear of that, they will draw this way, which will again favour the King's landing.

Some think Ely[249] a convenient place for landing, because you have choice of what side, and the enemy cannot be on both; others think the nearer Galloway the better, because the rebels will have far to march before they can trouble you; others think Kirkcudbright, or thereabouts, because of that sea for ships, and that it is near England. Nobody expects any landing here now, because it is thought you will alter the design, it having been discovered; and to friends and all I give out I do not expect any. So I am extremely of opinion, this would be an extreme proper place, unless you be so strong that you need not care where to land. The truth is, I do not admire their mettle. The landing of troops will confound them terribly.

[249] Islay.

I had almost forgot to tell you that P... O...,[250] as they say, has written to his Scotch council, telling them he will not have his troops any more harassed following me through the hills; but orders them to draw to the west, where he says, a great army is to land; and, at the same time, gives them accounts, that eight sail of men-of-war is coming from Brest, with 15,000 men on board. He knows not whether they are designed for England or Ireland.

I beg you will send an express before, whatever you do, that I may know how to take my measures; and, if the express that comes knows nothing, I am sure it shall not be discovered for me. I have told Mr Hay nothing of this proposal, nor no man. If there come any party this way, I beg you send us ammunition, and three or four thousand arms of different sorts, some horse, some foot.

I have just now received a confirmation of McKay's going south, and that he takes with him all the horse and dragoons, and all the standing foot; by which I conclude, certainly they are preparing against the landing in the west. I entreat to hear from you as soon as possible, and am, in the old manner, most sincerely, for all Carleton can say, my Lord, your most humble and faithful servant.

To Iain Macnachtan of Dunderawe   BL, Add. MS 12,068

Lochiel, 28 June 1689
Sir, I dout not but you have received the kings commission; it will be hard for you to raise your regiments, however do your best; a man that has goo[d] will will fynd ways. So I desyr you will gate ready as soon as you can all your name follouers and kyndly men whosoever they ar and march them this way. Concert with MakDougall[251] that you may come togither and then Apen may come with you. Lait me knou when you hear any newes.

I have receaved letters by tuo different expresses from Yrland; all goes there to our wish. Only Darie[252] has been obstinat; but it is over befor nou, which is the only reason we have not had news from thence. My Lord Melfort says that befor his come to my hands tho dated the 1

---

[250] The Prince of Orange (William II).
[251] Alan Macdougall of Dunollie (d. 1695).
[252] Derry;

of June relief will come to us. So if you be ... by your nighboors it is on confort it will not be long. I am sir, your most humble servant.

To Melfort   Dundee, *Letters*, 64

28 June 1689

My Lord, After Mr Hay was dispatched, I was informed that Achtera[253] and Major Farcharson[254] were landed, so sent and stopt Mr Hay, and came down here to know what news they brought. I am very glad to hear by your Lordship's that the King's affairs prosper so well, and that Derry will be soon ours. But I hear it was not on Monday last. I know not what the matter is, but I would think Mackay's going south, and the troops drawing back from Kintyre towards Edinburgh, would import some alarm they have got.

I have so often written over all that Derry was ours, that now, say what I like, they hardly believe, and when I talk of relief out of Ireland they laugh at it, though, I believe, ere long, they will find it earnest, and then our enemy's confusion will be great.

As to the places of landing, I am still of the same mind. For the number, I must leave to the conveniency you have. The only inconveniency of the delay is, that the honest suffer extremely in the low countries in the time, and I dare not go down for want of horse, and in part for fear of plundering all, and so making enemys, having no pay. I wonder you send no ammunition, were it but four or five barrels. For we have not 20 pound.

As to yourself, I have told you freely my opinion, and am still of the same mind. You desire I may tell you your faults. I use to see none in my friends; and for to tell you what others find, when I do not believe them, were to lose time. But I must tell you, many of them who complained of you have carried themselves so, that what they say deserves not much to be noticed. However, they have poisoned the generality with prejudice against you; and England will, I am afraid, be uneasier to you than Scotland. It is the unjustest thing in the world, that not being popular must be an argument to be laid aside by the King. I do really think it were hard for the King to do it; but glorious for you, if once you be convinced that the necessity of the King's affairs requires it,

[253] Ranald MacDonald of Achtera.
[254] John Farquharson of Inverey.

to do it of yourself, and beg it of him; but this only, as I said in my last, in case of great difficulties, and in the way I advised, which I think the King will not refuse you; I mean as to filling up of the place; for the King may have enemies, some by your continuing; but he may put in one who may ruin all, which, I am sure, if he gave it some that pretends, it would, I am afraid, certainly fall out.

I wonder you could have the least thought that I would concert with anybody against you, having parted so good friends. I spoke not to Dunmore since he came from London. I mind not I spoke of you to Bredalbine. I remember, when I was endeavouring to make friends for the King in the country, and in the Convention, many did tell me that there would be no living if you returned; so, when no arguments for you could prevail, I have, may be, to smooth them, said that, if all were well, you would be prevailed with not to meddle any more.

I would have written letters of encouragement to all the King has written to, from yourself, and assured them of your friendship, and satisfied them of your real designs of living, and letting live, every one in their own way in matters of religion, which would mightily allay, I think, as to Scotland; and let them see you do favours to Cavaliers and to Protestants, for by some steps that, may be, you was forced to make in favours of these ungrate beasts the Presbyterians,[255] you gave unhappy umbrage to both the other; but they were fools, for never will they get one whose family, education, and inclination is so cavalier. They long at the King's restoration to have a Lauderdale to destroy Middleton, and poor suffering cavaliers. Let not this be their plague.

I am sure you shall be sure of all my endeavours for to bring the minds of people to reason. If you will allow, I will say, that, though you come to see the King once landed, you design not to stay, unless you think that you may embolden your enemys. I give my humble service to my lady,[256] and am, my Lord, your most humble and faithful servant.

---

[255] A reference to the Indulgence of June 1687, granting toleration to presbyterians.
[256] Euphemia Wallace, Melfort's second wife.

To the heritors of Atholl[257]   Atholl, *Chronicles*, i, 284

Strone, 10 July 1689

Sir, By certain accounts from Irland I am sure the king is just at the landing. The enemie knows this and are now designing, I hear, to make a last endeavor, being in despair to prosper if the king land. They strugle to ruine all honest men. I hope, seing you have caryed yourself so well hitherto, and that so litell tym will releive us and yow from your trobel intirly, that yow will not loose your honour, nor wrong your consiences, by joyning with the rebells or looking on till honest men be ruind, which is wors.

Therfor I require you in the Kings name and authoritie, and intreats you as your friend, to rise in armes and come to Blair of Atholl or any other place, in that contrey, that shall be thought most convenient by Pitcur and the rest of the loyall gentrie of your countrey who will joyn him. You need not have the least aprehension; I will bring such a body of men to your imediat assistance as will confound all the enemies dares apear. Som are marcht already. I will be with you, or meet you, with 4000 Highlanders, Islanders, and Lochaber only, besyds all that will joyn us from Badenouch, Atholl, Mar and other loyall contries.

I have a boat goeing imediatlie for Irland, to acqueant the King of all this, and to heasten to por in troups on all hands, and advise himself to land in the west. I sent Mr Hay, to him who landed in Irland ten days agoe, to press his landing, which I am sure you will see imediatly: so you have a glorious occasion, and no great danger, and I will assure you I will bear testimony of all your good actions, and see you rewarded, I am, sir, your most humble servant.

[P.S.] I am resolved that whouever refuses, in any part of the kingdom, to joyn the kings standard, at my call, who have his Maiesties comission and authoritie to make war, I will hold them as traitors, and treat them as enemies, but I need not suspect any of you, and I designed not to have stirrd for som tym, had I not heard that Major-General Makay was to fall upon your contrey and Mar.

---

[257] The letter was addressed to two of the heritors, Leonard Robertson of Straloch and John Robertson of Bleattoun.

I

To Cluny Macpherson   'Gleanings', *TGSI*, xx, 222

Strone, 14 July 1689

Sir, I have just now received a letter from Colonell Cannon[258] then att the Castle of Dowart in Mull giving me ane account of his arrivall there the twelvth, and that the Kings shippes had brought along a great number of officers with a considerable body of men ammunition and armes—the particulars he refers till meeting, when he is to deliver me his Majesties letters.

He gives account of the defeat of the Scotes fleet. They fell upon the two Glasgow friggots killed both the Captains, taken the shippes and have all the rest of the men prisoners. He tells me likways that Dairie is certainly taken, and the French fleet is att sea, and the first newes we will hear will be the King's landing in the west. The men of warr are by this time in Ireland, to attend that service, so with the asistance of Almighty God we will now in a verie short time see our Gracious King restored to the Throne of his Ancestors.

Wherefore tis high time for you to draw to armes, which I desire you to do with all your men and folowers, and I shall give you notice where to join us. I am, sir, your humble servant.

[P.S.] Sir, this I wryt to you to be communicat to all the gentrey of Badenoch, so call them togither for from the head to the foot I will spair non that Joyns not. The gentrey must march themselves, and I expect 400 men and no expenses will be allowed. McIntosh, Grants, and all must come out.

To Lord Strathnaver[259]   Dundee, *Letters*, 69[260]

Strone, 15 July 1689

My Lord, Your Lordships, dated the 3d, I received the 13th, and would have returned an answer before now, had I not been called suddenly to Enverlochie, to give orders anent the forces, arms, ammunition sent from Irland.

---

[258] Alexander Cannon, Dundee's second in command.
[259] John Gordon (1661-1733), Lord Strathnaver, son of the 14th earl of Sutherland.
[260] This letter was reprinted by Napier from Sir John Dalrymple of Cranstoun, *Memoirs of Great Britain and Ireland*, i, appendix, 'The Sutherland Papers'.

My Lord, I am extreamly sensible of the obligation I have to you, for offering your endeavours for me, and giving me advice in the desperate estate you thought our affairs were in. I am persuaded it flows from your sincere goodness, and concern for me and mine, and in return, I assure your Lordship I have had no less concern for you, and was thinking of making the like address to you, but delayed till things should appear more clear to you. I am sorry your Lordship should be so far abused, as to think that there is any shadow of appearance of stability, in this new structure of government these men have framed to themselves; they made you, I doubt not, believe that Darie was relieved three weeks ago. By printed accounts, and I can assure you, it never was relieved, and now is taken. They told you, the English fleet and Dutch were masters of the sea. I know for certain the French is and in the Channel, in testimony whereof, they have defeated our Scots fleet. For, as they came alongst, they fell on the two frigats, killed the captains, and seised the ships, and brought the men prisoners to Mull. They tell you Shomberg[261] is going to Irland to carry the war thither. I assure you the king has landed a considerable body of forces there, and will land himself amongst our friends in the West, whom I am sorry for, very soon.

So, my Lord, having given you a clear and true prospect of affairs, which I am afraid among your folks you are not used with, I leave you to judge if I or you, your family or myn, be most in danger. However, I acknowledge francly, I am no less obliged to your Lor[d]ship, seeing you made me an offer of your assistance in a tyme when you thought I needed it. Wherein I can serve your Lordship or family, at any time you think convenient, you may freely employ me: for, as far as my duty will allow me in the circumstances we stand, I will study your well, as becomes, my Lord, your most humble servant.

To Cluny Macpherson   'Gleanings', *TGSI*, xx, 223

Strone, 18 July 1689

Sir, I need not say much because the bearer can tell you all the news. There is a regiment come from Yrland and severall other provisions with tou ships they have left to us. I have a letter all writen with the

---

[261] Friedrich Schomberg, 1st duke of Schomberg, William's general.

King's oun hand assuering me of mor assistance imediatly, and he is just ready to land. The French fleet having bate the Dutch and keeped the Inglish in. The French have 15,000 men aboard and 30,000 camped at Dunkerk waiting only if the King has use for them.

The parlements of Ingland and Scotland ar all by the ears amongst themselves—D[uke] Hamilton was cheased. D[uke] Gordon is treacherously imprisoned after all, and many other nobles, such opressiones were never heard of and must be shaken of. All mankynd almost nou beggs our asistance and you will see a great apearance. All behynd you ar here saive M'cklowd[262] who is coming—E[arl] Seaforth is to land in his own contry, and has undertaken to reas 3 regiments.

I dessein to march on Saturday or Munday. I would not have delayed so long had it not been that the Yrish forces could not conveniently cross from Mull because of the great wynds. I expect you will have all your contrey in armes on munday, and I shall send you word where to join us. Nobody offers to sit my sumonds so I expect that you will not. I am, sir, your most humble servant.

[P.S.] This I desyr you will comunicat to the rest of the gentry of the contrey and befor Sundays night. Lait me have your positive answer in wryt not by proxie and that signed or I will not notice it.

To Cluny Macpherson   'Gleanings', *TGSI*, xx, 224

[c. July 1689]

Sir, I send you here a proclamation and a copie of the King's instructions. You will see thereby hou you oght to walk. The French fleet is nou com betuixt Scotland and Yrland. We expect to hear from you what M[ajor] G[eneral] Makay is lyk to doe. I can be tuyce as strong as ever when I please. I am, sir, your most humble servant.

[P.S.] Any word you have a mynd to send to me you may cause delyver it to Alex[ander] McDonald[263] who will keep gaird in Glenroy. Lait the rest of your friends see this proclamation.

---

[262] Iain Breac Macleod of Dunvegan, chief of the Macleods of Raasay.
[263] Alexander MacDonald, brother of Coll MacDonald of Keppoch.

To Lord Murray[264]   Dundee, *Letters*, 71

Strone, 19 July 1689

My Lord, I was very glaid to hear that yow had appoynted a randevous of the Atholl men at Blair, knowing as I doe from your Lordships oune mouth your principles, and considering your educatione and the loyaltie of your people, I ame persuaded your appearance is in obedience to his Majesties commands by the letter I sent yow, which is the reasone why I give yow the trouble of this line, desiring that wee may meet, and concert what is fittest to be done for the good of our country and service of our lawfull King.

I doubt bot your Lordship knows that it hath pleased his Majestie to give me the command of his forces in this natione till his aryvall, and he is forced to putt in my hands many other trusts for want of other persones, many of his loyall subjects being imprisoned, or fled, or out of the way, so as he cannot know their inclinations.

Your Lordship is happy that is at liberty, and on the head of so considerable a body of loyall men; by declairing openly for the liberty of your country, and the lawfull right of your undoubted sovereigne, you may acquyre to yourself and family great honours and rewairds, and the everlasting blissing of Almighty God, which is above all. Yow are wiser then to thinke, tho yow were of other principles, that the Atholl men can be, conterary to their inclinatione, ever induced to fight against their King, no more then D[uke] Hamilton, were he never so loyall, could think to make his Streven and Lishmahaygoe men be for the King, notwithstanding all the power and interest he hes in that country.

I see nothing can hinder or scare any persone from serving the King in this occasione, unless it be that they think the people hes right to dethrone the King, and sett up ane other, which I ame sure a man of your sense can never be so fare foold as to believe. To satisfie the people as to their consciences, hes he not given his royall promise, in his declaratione, that he will secure the Protestant religion as by law established, and put them in possessione of all their priviledges they have at any time enjoyed since the restoratione of King Charles the Second, which should satisfie the Episcopall and Cavaleer party? He promises to all other dissenters liberty of conscience, which ought to

---

[264] John, Lord Murray (1660-1724), eldest son of 1st marquis of Atholl.

please the Presbitereans; and, in generall, he says he will secure our religione in Parliament to the satisfactione of his people. This he hes in reitterated letters under his hand and seall assured me of, and given me warrant in his name to signifie so much to all his loving subjects. E[arl] of Melfort hes written to me, fully signefeing his reall intentions to that purpose, which, may be, yow will have more to doe to believe; but, I will assure yow, it is true. His Majestie, in his declarations and his letters to me, as to our liberties and properties, says no less.

I ame persuaded every thing will be done to the content of all reasonable men in the next Parliament, which will be, so soon as the King in safety can hold it. Much of this was offered by Brydies letters, but keept up by these, who desyred not that the people should be satisfyed, but were resolved to dethrone their King at any rate, I pray God forgive them.

My Lord, if there be any thing more that yow think needfull the King should grant to satisfie his people, I begg you may let me know of it, for he wants advyce, and informatione, as yet, of things and tempers of men here. The indemnitie the King promises by his proclamatione, seems very gracious, and of great extent; nobody is excepted, except such as are come from Holland, who are supposed to be chiefly concerned in this usurpatione, and these who votted to dethrone the King and gett up ane other in his place; for my oune part, knowing the prosperous conditione the King's affairs were in, I would wonder he is so condescending, considering the great provocations he hes gote, but that he cannot alter the claimant temper that hes ever been found in the family, and hes emienently appeared in his persone.

Tho I have no warrant to say any thing further that he will doe that way, in particular, yet, in the generall, I ame desired to get advyce to him from his friends here, to whom the circumstances of persones are better knowne than to them who are beyond sea, how to draw ane indemnety, such as may be exact, and satisfeing to all honest men as to the exceptions. This is not done for want of the opinione of your Lordship, and others of your quality and capacity; I now desyre it of yow in the King's name, and assure yow that your proposalls, eather, in the generall, for the good of the natione, or in favour of any particular persone, shall be seconded by me with all the little interest I have; for, knowing yow so well, I need not fear yow will offer any thing unreasonable.

Now is the time these things ought to be treatted; for, if once the King enter on the head of a royall and alreddy victorious army, and insurections appear on all hands, and invasions on every side, there will be no more place for treating, but for fighting. I know ther are many persons of quality, and particularly my L[ord] Marques of Atholl, who is aprehensive of my L[ord] Melfort's ministry, and, for their satisfaction in that point, tho he hes solemnly declaired he will never remember past quarrels, bot enter on a new score, and live well with all the world, I have represented to him how much he hes the misfortune to be misliked, and, for that reasone, what hurt hes being at the helme may doe to the King's affaires; he asuers me the King will not pairt with him, but, however, that he is resolved to leave him against his will, if he see that his presence is in any way prejudiciall, and that with joy, he says, in good earnest, he would resigne his office of Secretarie for Scotland to any honest man, and bids me give him advyce, and this by three different letters, and I know that all I have written to him on that head was seen by the King himself. I ame sure it will be brought about. I know these things some months agoe would have satisfeid all that is good for any thing in this natione.

My Lord, consider if it be better to harken to these things in time, which is all we can ask, then let the King enter the conqueist, which in all humane probabilety he will assuredly doe. As I writt now to your Lo[rdship] so I have done to all others I can reach with letters. I am sure whatever evill befall the country, the King is innocent, and I have done my deuty.

I need tell yow no news; yow know all better then I doe, who dwell in deserts; yet I can tell yow that the French fleet consists of 80 capitall ships, and is at sea with 10 fire-ships and 400 tenders; that the Dutch, who designed against them, are beat back with loss; that the English dare not appeir; that the French have 15,000 of the old troops aboord to land in Ireland or Brittane; that ther are 3000 more campt at Dunkirk, waiting for our King's service; that the King is now maister of all Ireland, and hes ane army of 6000 men in good order rady to transport; that Shomberg knows not where to goe for defence of England, and is not thinking of Ireland for all hes being said. In a letter all written with the King's oune hand, I know we are imediatly to be releived. The Parliaments of England and Scotland are by the ears, and both nations in a flame. Use the time. I ame, my Lord, your most humble servant.

[P.S.] From France we are asuered by good hands, that now is the time the King's friends will declair openly, and their fleet is out.

To Murray   Dundee, *Letters*, 78

[19 July 1689]

My Lord, Since the writing my last, I hear Ballachen[265] hes obeyed the order I gave to possess that Castle of Blair for the King. I hope, since it was in obedience to the King's authority, you will not blame him. Your Lo[rdship] will see that it has pleased God to put me in that conditione, that your Lo[rdshi]p or any declairs for the King, will not need to fear; soe, for God's cause, doe now what you ought.[266]

To Cluny Macpherson   'Gleanings', *TGSI*, xx, 226

Strone, 20 July 1689

Sir, You hear what is fallen out in Breamar. The Atholl men ar resolved to stand by them and both have sent to me for relief. I am ready to asist all honest men. It is nou no mor time to look on when all your nighboors ar ingadged. I asseur you it will prove your uter ruin if you doe; so you will doe well to drawe to armes or be looked on as rebelles. If you sit this Sumonds you shall not be often troubled with mor letters from me so I desyr a positive answer and I requyr you to call the contrey and intimat this to them.

The man that comes from you is honest but I believe he mynds not what he says for I know a great many things he tells me not to be treu. Darie is certenly taken by storm last week. Shomberg has refused to head the P[rince] of Orange armey for fear of loosing his honor with new troops that will run for it. I expect the landing evry minut. I am, sir, your humble servant.

[P.S.] That McKintosh is a lying rogue. The D[uke] of Gordon gave no comision to forbid you to ryse. I spok with on that sawe [him] on Thursday last and was in the castle as well as McKintosh. This Sir I desyr you will acquaint the contrey of and when he came first he said no such thing.

---

265 Patrick Stewart of Ballechin, the factor of the Atholl estates.
266 This letter was unsigned, evidence of its hasty construction.

To Breadalbane   SRO, Breadalbane Muniments, GD112/39/145

Strone, 20 July 1689

My Lord, I dout not but your lordship has heared hou that after the seidge of Darie was over the Inglish frigats that lay befor that place hearing that the Glasgou frigats wer seised made after to saive them but missed them and gating information that the French fregats had taken towards Dowart they came thither and fyred at the castle but for oght I hear yet have don no hurt but dung doun som skleats. The French frigats wer long gon; there only remained two barkes that had been taken by the way. So soon as Bregadier Canon persaived the frigats he caused run them aground and took out the ammunition and provisions and ferryed over the men at ane other place so that all came from Yrland with them is yet saif and a great deall of provisions that wer in those barks for Darie. The regiment is nou ferrying at the Coran of Ardgour.

My Lord what was said by the officers of the kings opinion of you I dout no ways of and I hop evry day will confirm him mor for if things succeed [that] your lordship has in hand you will be the great ingyn of his business here.[267] I am very glaid to hear that the gentrey of Argyl shyr ar lyk to be wyse and take right measeurs for their oun good. All who joyn not shall be under the kings protection. I shall in the eyes of all the world make them inexcusable, and shall play to your hand all I can tho I dar tell it here to no body no not that I have so good opinion of you as I really have, for fear what you ar about be seen throu.

As to my Lord Lorn he has a good occasion to restor his family to its ancient honor and luster and to gaine to himself the kings favour and aplause of all man kind, and which is above all the blissing of Almighty God by this he restors and establishes his family in rightiusness which is the only lasting fundation.

Your lordship in the manifesto sent to the king and comunicat to me befor, did advise the restauration of that family[268] which I wondered of because there ar feu considerable cadets so just to their chief. If Argyl wer out of the way Bredalben would be all in those contreys and have the wholl name to follou him. You may remember I was willing the king should be advysed to doe it on conditions they should declair

---

[267] Breadalbane was one of the most substantial figures with whom Dundee was in regular correspondence.

[268] One of Breadalbane's motives was the restoration of Argyll; another was the dismissal of Melfort.

francly for him. I am still of the same opinion; the only difficulty we have nou is the exceptions of the indemnity he is excluded by both all benifit of it so that seing the king says he will pardon all but those it seems to import he will not pardon them. Therefor I dar not promise positively or undertake absolutly his remission and restauration but I doe declair upon my honor I shall indevor it and I dout no ways of it. I am perswaded the king will put him in the same condition his father was in befor the forfiture if there be any difficulty it will be anent the jurisdictions and superiority which was but a father in his caip.

The business of the M'cleans I fear too. They have been so fordward for the kings service and so francly joyned with me that I can not in honor indevor any thing to their prejudice but it will be easy for the king to make up that ane other way.[269] Unhappy he if he imbrace not this occasion to make himself and family for ever glorious and so rub af any steins that remain on them. His relations oght to abhor him if he loose this looky minut. For I will swear I am most sincer in the thing I rise not to disemble; nor have I any family or name piks as som may fancy; I lyk ane honest Cambel as well as a Grahame.

If your chief will follou your advice in a fourtnights time I lay lyf you get our enimys confounded. The thing he oght to doe is to push the business home, he should seise L[ieutenan]t Coll[onel] Clieland, Yong[270] and the considerablest officers but first devyd the regiments and disarme them after the officers ar secured and I shall answer upon my honor no hurt shall be fall them as to their lyves. And upon this we would all ryse and joyn and push to the heart of the kingdom the wholl north would ryse and most of the south. For what a glorious work you would bring about siting with soar foot at the fyr seyd[271] we would envy you and the world admyr you there is nothing wanting but that Lorn be so wyse as to set his good in time for I must be free after things have taken a turn which I think you will see however, lait them not dream that I will give the least ear to any such proposals so now or never.

---

[269] The Macleans were in dispute with Argyll, whom Breadalbane supported; hence Dundee's effort to tempt Breadalbane to usurp him.

[270] Lieutenant-Colonel William Cleland had been one of the Covenanters' leaders at Drumclog and was to die in victory at Dunkeld on 21 August; Captain William Young was in charge of the Kintyre detachment of the earl of Argyll.

[271] Breadalbane had declared that, due to gout, he would remain at home and would not involve himself with either side in the rebellion.

The landing in Kintyr needs not hinder for unless they should offer to attaque they will doe no hurt, and upon the least notice I shall if things goe send orders only to take free passadge. Or which is better send officers to receive them who shall take with them som of your gentrey in that caice. I could cause 1000 imediately land there and they confound the enemys in this nation befor the king land which would be mor honor for us and our contrey. If he goe to Edin[burgh] and desert lait me knou I shall follow your advice intyrly.

I am very well satisfyed with Lochnel[272] he is the first and oght to be the better used which I have wryten to him and he shall in dew time fynd. I shall lait no body knou of hes wryting to me. I give out I am going to Argyl shyr a purpose that it may not be perceived what is amongst us.

My lord I fear you will not read this for all our people ar nou in this contrey and I have a deal to doe with them so am in hury.

We will hear very soon again from the king; I shall not feall to lait your lordship knou all. I dout not but you have heared that Ballachen has posessed himself of the castle of Blair by my order for the king my lord Muray [sic] but got no entrance he said he would cause Balachen repent it whither in anger or earnest I knou not but I look on my Lord Muray as a man of honor and conscience so can not think ill of him whatever the apearances may be.

Adieu; I will be impatiant till I hear hou your great work goes. What you think fit I should wryt to L[or]d Lorn I will and further your lordship Dumfermling and I make a committy of councell with pouer of full councell we will grant him all the councel used to doe in lyk caices in caice of treaty it wer fit the officers horse were restored. I dar pand my lyf for gating my lord Lorn all he had and I am in good hopes we will not be refused to restor the family but he must be franc adieu.

To Patrick Stewart of Ballechin   Dundee, *Letters*, 78

Strone, 21 July 1689

Whereas his sainted Majesty King James the seventh did send a commission to the Marquess of Atholl to rais all his men and followers in that country for carrying on his service and makeing war ag[ain]st his

---

[272] Alexander Campbell of Lochnell, a chamberlain of Breadalbane and a zealous Jacobite.

rebellious subjects, and being disappointed of that assistance by the said Marquess being off the Kingdome, and non of his relations taking on them to supply that great duty, we by vertue of his Majestie's authority, takeing to our consideration your constant loyalty, and tryed couradge and conduct, w[i]t[h] your forwardness in this occasione for his Majestie's service, do appoint you Patrick Steuart of Balleachan to command es Collonell all men of Atholl, Vassalls, Tennants, neighbours, who have been in use to serve under the Marquess of Atholl, and heirby require them, all and every on of them, to receave your orders and obey you in every thing relating to his Majestie's service. For doing q[uhai]rof these shall be to you and them sufficient warrand.

Wee doe alsoe declair that a Commission of Collonell signed by his Ma[jes]tie, shall be sent to you soe shoon as it can come, it being already sent for.

To Cluny Macpherson   Atholl, *Chronicles*, i, 290

Strone, 22 July 1689

Sir, Our people coming from this countrey which doeth not abound in provisions will want meat when they come into Badinoch. I am unwilling that they should go loose in your countrey (to seek provisions as they did last) for fear of ruining it, wherefore I send yow this advertisment that you may cause provisions come in again to morous night near to the place of Clunie, for fifteen hunder men for two dayes. The rest of our men are provided.

If yow fail in this lett the blaim of all the dissorders that shall be comitted be upon yow. These who bring in the provisions shall be fully satisfyed for them.

I expect that the country will be raidy in arms to join us seeing Marr and Atholl are immediately to do it, and I may say almost all benorth Tay and a good pairt besouth, so now is the time if ever, for to show yourselves loyall men. I pray yow force me not, to do things to yow, against my inclination. I am, Sir, your assured freend and humble servant.

[P.S.] In answer to yours yow and your friends are to meet me tomorows night (without faill) at Garva.

Sir, bak these letters and send them to the most considerable of the gentrey of Badenoch.

To Murray   Dundee, *Letters*, 79

[Cluny Castle?,] 23 July 1689

My Lord, Tho ther be no body in the nation so much in my debt as y[ou]r Lo[rdship] having writen t[w]yce to yow without any return; yet, being concerned that yow should have [no] ground of offence that might in the least alienat your inclinations from the King's service, or discourage yow from joyning with us his faithful servants, I have thought fitt to venture this line more to yow, to let yow know that it was no distrust of your Lo[rdshi]p made me take possession of the Castle of Blair, but that I heard the rebells designed to require yow to deliver it up to them, which would have forced yow to declare before the time I thought yow designed. I thought it would oblige yow, to save yow from that lotche of either delivering up, or declairing; and for Ballachen, knowing him to be very loyall, I forced him to it, by requyring him in the King's name to do it. If, after all I have said in my former letters and this, I gette no return, my Lord, I most acknowledge I will be very sorry for your saike, for I am very sincerely, my Lord, your most humble servant.

[P.S.] My Lord, upon my word of honour, I can assure yow Derry was taken this day 8 dayes; they gote their lives.[273] There are 20 French frigatts at Carrickfergus, and 2000 men to transport from thence; 3 saill are at Dublin, the rest comes from thence; the great fleet is at sea. I have assurance of all the north. The great army is from Dublin. I believe this week the west will see strangers.

To Murray   Dundee, *Letters*, 80

[Cluny Castle?,] 25 July 1689

My Lord, I have written often to your Lo[rdshi]p and not only desired yow to declare for the King, but endeavoured by reasons to convince yow that now is the proper time, which the state of affairs may easily show yow; to all which I have never had any return from yow, by word

---

[273] There had been an offer of surrender by the Governor on 11 July, which led to a report in Scotland that the town had fallen.

or writ, tho I can tell yow there is none of the nation has used me so, and I have tryed all that have not already joyned Major Gen[eral] Mackay, on this said Tay, who have any command of men; yet, that I may leave nothing untryed that may free me from blame of what may fall out, I have sent these gentlemen to wait on your Lo[rdship] and receive your positive answer; for you know, my Lord, what it is to be in arms without the King's authoritie. Yow may have the honour of the whole turn of the King's affairs; for, I assure yow, in all humane probability, turn it will. Ther is nobody that is more a weelwisher of your father and family, nor desires more to continue, as I am, my Lord, your most humble servant.

To Cluny Macpherson   Atholl, *Chronicles*, i, 298

Blair Castle, 26 July 1689
Sir, My Lord Muray is retyred doun the contrey. All the Atholl men have left them saive Stratherel, Achintully, and Baron Read Straloch,[274] and they will not byd my doun coming to morou. The rest of the heritors will be here to morou. They will joyn us, and I supose to morou you will have ane answer so if you have a mynd to preserve yourself and to serve the King be in armes to morou that when the letter comes you may be here in a day. All the world will be with us blissed be God. I am, Sir, your most humble servant.
[P.S.] My service to all the loyall gentrey of Baddnoch.

---

[274] Possibly Leonard Robertson of Straloch.

APPENDIX

This appendix contains three documents which are of doubtful authenticity, and in the first case of uncertain date.

In a fictionalised biography of the wife of Graham of Claverhouse, *My Ladie Dundee* (1926), the author, Katherine Parker, quoted two short passages from a letter (in modernised orthography) apparently written by Claverhouse in the autumn of 1684 to his brother-in-law, Lord John Cochrane, congratulating him on his marriage to Lady Susannah, daughter of the duke of Hamilton. In a footnote to the text, the author states the source as 'Dundonald Letters'. The present editor has been unable to obtain this original letter or a transcript of it. An inventory of the Dundonald papers was published in *Charter Chest of the Earls of Dundonald*, edited by F.J. Grant (Scottish Record Society, 1910). This ends with an instrument of sasine dated 1662 and the 'Dundonald Papers', mostly nineteenth- and twentieth-century letters. The preface, however, notes that ten pages had been 'cut out of the inventory': this offers one possible solution to the mystery.

Another possibility is contained in a reference in Katherine Parker's preface to the 'friendship and help of ... the Earl of Dundonald ... for giving me ready access to the family pictures and papers'. The present, 14th, earl of Dundonald has assured me, however, that all family records are with the Scottish Record Office. If the letter is genuine, it may simply have been lost, or become part of a collection of autograph letters sold to a private buyer.

The Killiecrankie 'battle speech' and letter to King James have been the subjects of considerable controversy. They were discovered by James MacPherson among the Nairne Papers in the Bodleian Library, the speech on the back of the letter. MacPherson printed them both in his *Original Papers*, vol. i (1775). Neither were in Dundee's handwriting but both are generally acknowledged to be contemporary, though whether they are genuine is doubtful. Several of the biographies contribute to the debate, as do C.S. Terry and J. Anderson in 'Claverhouse's last letter', *Scottish Historical Review*, vi (1909), 63-70. Even if the letter and speech are contemporary forgeries, they are of interest as examples of Jacobite propaganda.

The texts follow.

To Lord John Cochrane   Parker, *My Ladie Dundee*, 147

[autumn 1684]

I who have so lately come off the irons, cannot but know how great a joy success yields to poor languishing lovers, so I might be thought very wanting in my duty if upon this occasion I did not congratulate with your Lordship on so honourable a match with so fine a lady, which will certainly contribute much to your happness; and, I'm thinking, my Lord, I need not tell you that nobody takes more share in your concerns nor rejoices more in all your prosperity than myself.... Your sister salutes you kindly, and complains you have forgot her, which I think unjust seeing that you have other ton on your rod.... It stirs up malice against you, so you must not think it strange that our statesmen are informed that you talk huffily and disobligingly of the Government. I did vindicate you all I could.

Speech to the army before battle   Dundee, *Letters,* 81

Killiecrankie, 27 July 1689

Gentlemen, you are come hither this day to fight, and that in the best of causes: for it is the battle of your King, your religion, and your country, against the foulest usurpation and rebellion; and having, therefore, so good a cause in your hands, I doubt not but it will inspire you with an equal courage to maintain it. For there is no proportion betwixt loyalty and treason; nor should be any betwixt the valour of good subjects and traitors.

Remember that to-day begins the fate of your King, your religion, and your country. Behave yourselves, therefore, like true Scotchmen: and let us, by this action, redeem the credit of this nation, that is laid low by the treacheries and cowardice of some of our countrymen; in which, I ask nothing of you, that you shall not see me do before you; and, if any of us shall fall upon this occasion, we shall have the honour of dying in our duty, and as becomes true men of valour and conscience: and such of us as shall live and win the battle, shall have the reward of a gracious King, and the praise of all good men. In God's name, then, let us go on, and let this be your word: King James and the Church of Scotland, which God long preserve.

To King James   Dundee, *Letters*, 82

Killiecrankie, 27 July 1689

S[i]r, It has pleased God to give yo[u]r fforces a great victory over the Rebels, in w[hi]t[c]h 3-4ths of them are fallen under the weight of our swords. I might say much of the Action iff I had not the honor to comand in it; but of 5000 men w[hi]t[c]h was the best computation I could make of the Rebels it is certain there can not have escaped above 1200 men: wee have not lost full out 900. This absolut Victory made us Masters of the ffield & the Enemy's Baggage w[hi]ch I gave to yo[u]r soldiers, who to doo them all right both officers and comon men, Highlands and Lowlands & Irish behaved themselves wi[t]h Equal Gallantry w[ha]t ever I saw in the hottest Batles fought abroad by disciplined armies, and this McKay's old soldiers felt on this Occasion.

I Can not now S[i]r be more particular but take leave to assure yo[u]r Ma[jes]tte the kingdom is generally disposed for yo[u]r service and impatiently wait for yo[u]r Coming: and this success will bring in the rest of the Nobility and Gentry having had all theyre assurances for it except the Notorious Rebels. Therefore S[i]r for God's sake assist us tho it be w[i]th such an other detachment of your Irish fforces as you sent us before especialy of horse and Dragoons & you will Crown our beginnings w[i]th a Compleat success & yo[u]rselfe w[i]th an entire possession of yo[u]r Ancient hereditary Kingdom of Scotland. My wounds forbid me to enlarge to yo[u]r Ma[jes]tie at this time, tho they tell me they are not mortall. However S[i]r I beseech yo[u]r Ma[jes]tie to believe whether I live or dye I am entirely yo[u]rs.

CHRONOLOGICAL TABLE

1648   Born at Glen Ogilvie near Glamis, between late June and early September.

1657   Matriculates at St Salvator's College, St Andrews University, in Faculty of Arts.

1660   Created a burgess of Dundee and a brother of the guild.

1661   Graduated MA, 27 July.

1667   Attains title of laird of Claverhouse.

1669   Commissioner of Excise and JP for Forfarshire, 11 February. Commission withdrawn on grounds of minority, 24 June; reinstated, 2 September.

1672   Commission as junior lieutenant in Sir William Lockhart's Scots regiment serving in the French army, 25 July.

1674   At battle of Senneffe, saves life of Prince of Orange, 14 August. At siege of Grave, October. Returns to Glen Ogilvie on death of his mother and remains for six months.

1676   Returns to Holland, and serves at the siege of Maastricht, April. Commission as captain of horse. Sudden decision to leave the service.

1678   Receives permission from privy council to travel abroad, 27 February, but offered commission as lieutenant in marquis of Montrose's new troop of horse, and subsequently rank of captain. Begins his service in south-west Scotland.

1679   Start of correspondence with Menteith over possible marriage to Helen Graham, which continues until end of 1681. Appointed sheriff depute of Dumfries and Annandale, 11 March. At battle of Drumclog, 29 May. Defends Glasgow, 30 May; returns to Stirling, then Edinburgh. At battle of Bothwell Bridge, 22 June. Goes to London with Linlithgow to see the king, 25 June.

1680   Petitions the king for return of fines confiscated by Queensberry, May. In skirmish at Aird's Moss, July. Travels to Scotland with Prince James. Is made a burgess of Stirling, 7 October. On the assize at the trial of Argyll, December. Narrowly escapes drowning in 'The Blessing'.

1681   Takes the Test oath, 22 September. Objects to Act for Securing the Peace. Becomes sheriff of Wigtown and bailie of Longlands. Brings a complaint against Viscount Stair, 14 December.

1682 Brings an action against Stair for libel. Thanked by privy council
      for his activity in Galloway, 15 May. Escapes assassination at
      Bellspool, 16 June. Promoted to colonel, 29 December.
1683 Imports cloth for his new regiment. Sent to London on delicate
      mission, 1 March. At Newmarket, 9 March; in London, 20
      March. Granted Dudhope estate and constabulary of Dundee,
      26 April. Becomes deputy commander of Scottish army and
      privy councillor. Holds circuit court in Stirling, 9 June. Dundee
      burgh council protests at his appointment.
1684 Obtains possession of Dudhope, 23 March. Woos Jean
      Cochrane; weds her in Paisley, 10 June. Letter to his brother, 9
      September, also commutes death penalty for Dundee prisoners.
      Holds court in Galloway with Queensberry and Drumlanrig,
      October. Assists in search of Edinburgh, 29 November.
1685 Appointed to visit Edinburgh Tolbooth. Is a 'delegate' to Fife
      and Kinross. Holds circuit court in Fife. Supports soldiers'
      claims against Colonel Douglas. Loses his temper in privy
      council and is suspended for three meetings. Promoted to
      major-general but loses precedence to Douglas. Made burgess
      of Aberdeen, 17 August. Escorts prisoners from the Bass. On
      commission of treasury and exchequer, 11 December.
1686 Nothing known of his activities, no surviving letters or records.
1687 Signs Declaration of Toleration, 17 February. In court against
      Lin of Larg, 16 June. In London with wife and Balcarres from 27
      June to late November, also a visit to Bath.
1688 Installed as provost of Dundee, 29 March. On Council for
      Advancement of Trade, 15 May. Presides at meeting of Dundee
      burgh council, 4 September. Warranted to receive weapons
      from Holland, 13 September. March to London, 11 October.
      Quartered in Westminster, 25 October. Meeting with king, 9
      November. Army rendezvous at Salisbury, 10 November.
      Visits king and is made viscount of Dundee. Attempts to
      persuade king to remain, 17 November. Similar meeting at
      Rochester, 21 November. Disbands his regiment, 22 Novem-
      ber. Sends reply to William of Orange, 24 November. Becomes
      commander of Scots army, 25 November, and returns to
      Scotland.
1689 Summons to Convention of Estates, 13 March. Discussion with

duke of Gordon in Edinburgh Castle. Interventions in debate. Reveals a plot to assassinate him. Announces rival Convention and quits chamber. Requests Convention reply to King James' letter. Requests permission to go to Ireland. Rides from Edinburgh. Parleys with Gordon at postern gate. Halts at Dunblane. Returns to Dudhope. Birth of his son, baptised 9 April. Declared an outlaw. Declares war on William of Orange on Dundee Law. Withdraws to Glen Ogilvie to elude capture. Receives commission as lieutenant-general of Jacobite army. Rides north. Halts at Huntly Castle. At Gordon Castle, Auldearn, Inverness, Fort Augustus. Raids Dunkeld. At Glamis. At Dundee. Raids Ruthven Castle. Pursues Mackay through Glen More. Halts at Edinglassie. Retreats to Strone. Attempts to recruit an army. Rendezvous with Colonel Cannon and the Irish. Marches to Blair Castle, 26 July; council of war. To Killiecrankie, 27 July.

SOME LATE SEVENTEENTH-CENTURY BUILDING CONTRACTS

edited by J. G. Dunbar, MA, FSA, HON.FRIAS and Katherine Davies, PH.D

INTRODUCTION

This group of documents relating to building operations has been selected from among the considerable number of such writs that were enrolled in the Register of Deeds[1] during a period of some thirty years towards the end of the seventeenth century. The practice of presenting deeds of various types before a court of law for the purpose of registration can be traced back to the medieval period; the main intention of the consenting parties was to obtain the force of a judicial decree for the document thus registered, so that prompt action might thereafter be taken by either party in the event of the other's failure to observe the agreed conditions. The existing Register was commenced in 1554, and is still in operation. The years c.1660–1690 were chosen for the purposes of this collection largely because this is the earliest period for which an adequate classified index is available. Within the period, an attempt has been made to select documents illustrative of a wide range of building activities in different parts of the country.

Most of the deeds are referred to as 'contracts', but some (nos. 3, 11, 13, 16 and 19) are described as 'agreements', and one (no. 21) as an 'indenture'. Although this variation in nomenclature reflects certain differences in earlier usage, it appears to have no significance in the present context. The documents also vary somewhat in style, but commonly take the form of an agreement between an employer and a craftsman, or contractor, for the execution of a specified building task

---

[1] Preserved in the Scottish Record Office, Edinburgh (Class RD).

at a fixed price payable by instalments or, in one instance, at a given wage rate. There is generally a penalty clause, binding upon both parties, but in the case of no. 18, where the employer seems to have paid for the work in advance, the craftsman alone is subject to this provision.

Contracts of this nature were evidently introduced into the building trade at an early period, and a comparison between the documents transcribed below and one of the earliest known Scottish examples, namely an indenture for the erection of chapels in the south aisle of St Giles Church, Edinburgh, in 1387,[2] shows that seventeenth-century practice closely followed medieval precedent. Not all such agreements were presented before a court for registration, however, and of those that were, not all were enrolled promptly, although the interval of thirty-one years that appears to have elapsed before registration in the case of no. 1 was no doubt exceptional. Scribal errors made during the process of enrolment occasionally led to discrepancies in wording between the original warrants and the register itself; the present transcripts have therefore been prepared from the warrants, except where these no longer survive, or are illegible.

As well as providing much detailed information about the erection and repair of individual buildings, these documents also throw a good deal of light upon the organisation of the building trade in Scotland.[3] It seems clear, for example, that by the end of the seventeenth century the direct labour system, although still sometimes adopted by the Crown, was little favoured by other employers, who almost invariably preferred to conduct operations by means of contracts entered into with one or more tradesmen.[4] Only in the case of no. 4, by which the laird of Strowan appears to have undertaken the entire responsibility for providing the labour force for the construction of a mill on his estate, does the direct labour system seem to have operated. However, it was not unusual for employers to furnish workmen for demolition and site clearance, and for the performance of certain menial tasks (cf. nos. 3, 5, 6, 23 and 24).

---

[2] Reproduced in L.F. Salzman, *Building in England down to 1540* (2nd edn., Oxford, 1967), 466-7.

[3] Cf. also J.G. Dunbar, 'The organisation of the building industry in Scotland during the 17th century', in *Building Construction in Scotland: Some Regional and Historical Aspects* (Scottish Vernacular Buildings Working Group, 1976), 7-15.

[4] For earlier practice see D. Knoop and G.P. Jones, *The Scottish Mason and the Mason Word* (Manchester, 1939), 9-14.

The practice of sub-contracting seems to have been fairly widespread in the case of large-scale operations. Nos. 14 and 17, for example, almost certainly relate to the erection of the same building (Gallery House, near Montrose), the first being the main contract between employer and master-mason, and the second, drawn up some two months later, a quarrying contract between the master-mason and two quarriers. Likewise the contract for leadwork at Drumlanrig Castle (no. 25) between William Lukup and William Waldhave, plumber, refers to what was evidently a general contract previously entered into between Lukup, in his capacity as Master of Works,[5] and the duke of Queensberry.

Two of the documents differ somewhat from the remainder. The contract between Stewart of Physgill and the burgh of Whithorn for the repair of the harbour and tolbooth (no. 7) seems to be a speculative financial agreement, in which Stewart assumed general responsibility for these tasks with the presumed intention of concluding a separate contract with a tradesman for the actual execution of the work. No. 26 provides evidence of a rather different type of speculative building, in which the Edinburgh architect and master-mason, Robert Mylne, appears in the dual role of building-contractor and property-developer in the erection of Mylne Square, High Street, one of the earliest improved housing schemes in the city.

The method of payment usually adopted was the allocation of a fixed sum of money, or a sum of money supplemented by a stated amount of food, for the performance of a particular task. Payment to slaters and quarriers, however, seems to have been calculated in relation to units of work done (cf. nos. 9 and 17), and there is one instance of a mason being recompensed in the same way (no. 23). Only in the case of the contract for the completion of Invergarry Castle (no. 11) was payment to be made by daily wages, and this document also stands apart from its neighbours by reason of its unusual wording and vague specification of works.

The arrangements made for the supply and carriage of materials were very varied. One or two prosperous building-contractors, such as Thomas Wilkie and Robert Mylne, were evidently able to assume

---

[5] He is so described on his tombstone in Durisdeer Churchyard: Royal Commission on the Ancient and Historical Monuments of Scotland, *Inventory of Dumfriesshire* (1920), 63.

complete responsibility in these matters (nos. 14 and 26), but it was more usual for the employer at least to assist with carriage (nos. 1 and 9), and he frequently undertook to supply certain materials as well (nos. 5 and 24). There are also a number of contracts, not all of them relating to small craftsmen, in which workmanship only was bespoken, the employer undertaking to supply and transport all materials (nos. 3 and 10). In one instance, an agreement for the construction of a bridge in a remote part of Upper Clydesdale (no. 20), the employer agreed to provide lodgings for the workmen and a separate room for the master-mason.

Much can also be learnt about the respective roles of master workman and employer in the formulation and execution of designs. It seems clear that in most instances the late seventeenth-century mason, like his medieval predecessor, was both designer and executant craftsman. Often he would carry out much of the task with his own hands, assisted by a partner or by a small group of workmen (nos. 1, 12 and 22). He was usually capable of making any drawings that might be required, as for example at the reconstruction of Logie Church (no. 21), which was to be rebuilt 'conforme to ane draught drawen be the said Tobias [Bachop][6] himself' (cf. also nos. 14 and 16). On the other hand the mason's responsibilities were sometimes limited by the appoint-ment of an overseer, who might be an experienced fellow-craftsman or an 'architector', whose task it was to ensure that the finished work reached a satisfactory standard (nos. 5, 18, 25 and 27).

In addition to their roles as craftsmen and designers, however, a number of the more skilful and prosperous master-masons also acted as building-contractors. Such, clearly, were Robert Mylne, the King's master-mason, and Thomas Wilkie, Deacon and Warden of the Edinburgh masons, who were able to undertake full responsibility for large-scale building operations involving several trades—sometimes at a considerable distance from their homes—and to engage their own sub-contractors (nos. 14, 20 and 26). Some master-masons, including Mylne and James Smith, possessed exceptional ability as designers and achieved reputations as 'architectors', in which capacity they might be called upon to supply plans and drawings and to exercise professional

[6] On whom see H.M. Colvin, *A Biographical Dictionary of British Architects, 1600-1840* (London, 1978), 79.

control over building operations. Invermay House, for example, was to be 'contrived be Sir William Bruce of Kinross or [Robert] Mill Architect or any other relevant architect that the laird shall think fit' (no. 24), while Smith evidently undertook a similar role at Drumlanrig (no. 25).

The employer's chief safeguard for ensuring that he got the sort of building he wanted was, of course, the provisions of the contract itself, together with the particulars shown in any accompanying design drawings. In one instance it was stipulated that such drawings were to be inspected and agreed by both parties before the keys of the new building were handed over (no. 14). The amount of detail recorded in the specifications varied greatly from one contract to another. Some were drawn up in the vaguest of terms, the craftsman simply undertaking to erect a building of a particular size, or one containing so many rooms and chimneys (nos. 10 and 23). Others, however, were extremely detailed, almost each item of work being precisely specified (nos. 3 and 26). In most cases, however, provision was made for consultation between employer and craftsman as work progressed so that minor adjustments could be made and unforeseen contingencies resolved to mutual advantage. At Gallery House (no. 14), for example, the entrance was to be 'of such hansome order of work as the said Sir John and the said Thomas Wilkie shall agree of', while the door to Mr Matthew Campbell's loft at Galston Church (no. 18) was to be 'in any place quher the said Mr. Mathew sall apoynt the samyn to be'. Once a building was completed in accordance with the agreed specification it seems to have been assumed that the craftsman's responsibilities were at an end, for only one of the contracts (no. 11) contains any provision for the remedy of defects that might come to light after work was finished.

One noticeable feature of late seventeenth-century building practice is the frequency with which craftsmen copied their own and one another's designs. Cullen market-cross, for example, was to be 'off ane perfyt figur cross neir wnto the cross of Banff' (no. 12), while the new battlements at Closeburn Castle (no. 27) were to be 'conforme to the height, breadeth, and workmanship of the Tower of Glencairne pertaining to Sir Robert Lawrie of Maxweltowne'. This custom, acceptable to employer and craftsman alike, was firmly grounded in medieval precedent, and it was not until the emergence of the

professional architect in the eighteenth century that originality in design came to be prized.

Finally something may be said about the main classes of building materials referred to in the documents. Most of the buildings were constructed of rubble and lime mortar, the stone usually being quarried locally. Freestone ashlar facings or dressings were frequently used in buildings of high quality (nos. 17, 20 and 26), and since supplies of suitable freestone were limited, these materials were often transported considerable distances (nos. 14 and 17). Stone and clay were used to build a dyke at Langton (no. 6), while the Edinburgh tenement referred to in no. 8 was of stone and timber-frame construction, the ground floor being of masonry and the upper storeys 'all timber work'.

The only building that may possibly have been entirely timber-framed was the mill at Kinloch (no. 4), but timber was, of course, widely employed for roofing and flooring, for scaffolding (nos. 12 and 25), and for many internal fittings. The roof of Coldingham Church (no. 5) was to be of fir, and fir was also specified for the rear of the loft at Galston Church (no. 18). The front of the loft, on the other hand, was to be of wainscot, a term which probably signifies the use of oak. The oak window-frames mentioned in no. 24 were probably hinged casements, but sash windows were evidently being installed at Drumlanrig Castle in 1686 (no. 25)—an early example of this type of fitting in Scotland. Internal wall-surfaces, when not lined with timber, were commonly plastered (nos. 13 and 26), while the plaster ceilings of the principal apartments might be enriched with relief decoration (no. 14).

Scone Palace, a late sixteenth- or early seventeenth-century structure, appears to have been equipped with fixed windows of leaded glass, such as were commonly installed in buildings of that period. These were to be repaired with French glass (no. 2), and the same material was specified for the new casement windows at Gallery (no. 14), but at Mylne Square, Edinburgh (no. 26), the somewhat coarser English glass was used. For reasons of security, windows, particularly those on the lower floors, were often provided with iron bars or grilles (nos. 14 and 24), and iron was also employed for locks, fastenings and nails. Lead was also widely used, as the Drumlanrig contract (no. 25) makes clear—not only as a roof covering, but also for the construction of cisterns and water pipes. The usual roof coverings were slate (nos. 7

and 9) and skaillie (nos. 21 and 24), this latter apparently being a superior and more expensive (no. 14) variety of blue slate. Stone slabs were also used, particularly in association with a masonry vault (no. 1).

In preparing the texts for publication the opening clauses of the contracts, which set out the date and place of the transaction and the names of the contracting parties, have been summarised, except in the case of no. 1, which may serve as an example. Likewise, the concluding sections, comprising formal clauses of registration followed by the signatures of the principal parties and of witnesses, have been omitted from all except no. 1. The documents are presented in their original spelling, but with the letters i/j, u/v and y/z modernised. Some punctuation and paragraphing has been added to clarify the sense, and capitalisation has been modernised.

J.G.D. & K.D.

1. *Contract for the reconstruction of an aisle at Fearn Abbey, Ross and Cromarty: made at Tain, 29 June 1637 (Dur. warrant no. 685, registered 1668).*

Ane mutuall contract betuix George Rois and David his brother, and Wm. Rois master meassone.

At Taine the penult day off Junii 1600 and threttie sewine yeiris: It is appoynted, agreit and finallie indentit betuix the pairties following, they ar to say: George Ros off Ballamukie and David Ros in Meddit his brother germane on the ane pairt, and Williame Ros maister meassoune on the wther pairt, in maner subsequent, that is to say:

The said Williame Ros maister meassoun binds and oblisses him be the fayt and treuthe of his bodie to cast ane sufficient watter ticht pend and wolt betuix the tua syd walles off the lytill iyill of the kirk off Ferne betuix geawell and geawell, and to theack the samen to the hicht with sufficient hewin theack staynes, withe ane bell hous hawing sewin foott within walls off the hicht of sextein foott with ane new hewin dore muillit in comllie fashione, and to mak herin ane hewin window in the east syd of the said iyill for schewing off guid licht.

Lyk as the said Williame oblisses him to furnishe to the said wark hewing stones, lyme and tymer with all wther necesessars requiseit for the said wark, the samen being allwayis transportit and carreit wppon the saids George and David Rossis thair awin proper chairgs and expenssis to the said iyill fra any sea port within the sea parrochine off Tarbat or fra the sands of Nige.

And the said Williame oblissis him, God willing, to enter and begine to the said wark at the feast and tearme off Mertimess nixto cum in anno 1600 and threttie sewine yeirs, and to conteinwe and abyd himselff and his compainie at the said wark till the finall compleiting thairoff, quhilk he oblissis him, God willing, to compleit affoir the terme of Mertimess in anno 1600 and threttie aucht yeirs.

And also obliss him effauldlie and trewlie to wark and finishe the said wark sufficientlie according to condiscending but froud or guyill.

For the quhilkis caussis the said George and David Rossis binds and oblissis them, ther airs and executors, conjunctlie and severallie, to thankfullie content, pay and deliver to the said William Ros maister meassoune, his airis, executors or assigneyis, all and haill the sowme off ane thousand merkis money off this realme proportionallie as followes, viz: thairoff the sowme of fyve hundrethe merks money at the begining

of the said wark, quhilk is at the feast and tearme of Mertimes nixtocum but any longer delay; and the sowme of wther fyve hundrethe merks money in compleitt payment of the said sowme of ane thousand merkis money at the feast and tearme off Mertimes nixt therefter in the yeir of God 1600 and threttie aucht yeiris but any longer delay; togidder with the sowme of ane hundrethe pundis money in name of penaltie for everie ane of the saids tua tearmes quherin it sall happine the saids George and David Rossis to failyie.

And sik lyk the saids George and David Ros binds and oblissis them and ther forsaids to content and pay to the said Williame Ros and his abowe nameit the number and quantitie off off [sic] seiwine bolls good and sufficient aite meall of the crope and yeir off God 1600 and threttie seiwine yeiris, at suche tymes and occationes in pairt and pairt as it sall happin the said Williame to requeir the samen.

And finallie it is mutuallie condiscendit betuix baithe the saids pairties off ther awine consent that the pairtie braiker and not willing to performe ther pairt of this present indentour, sall content and pay to the pairtie willing to the [sic] performe the samen the sowme of ane hundrethe punds money forsaid in name of penaltie, by and attour the performeing off the premissis.

And for the mair securetie heirin, baithe the saids pairteis ar content and consentis that thir presenttis be insert and registratt in the buiks of counsell and sessioune or commissor buiks of Ros to bear the strenthe of ane decreit of ather of ther judicatoreis, that letters and executorialls af horneing, poynding and warding on ane simpill chairge of ten dayis allanarlie may be directit heirwpoun, and thairfor constitutis [blank] thair procuratoris conjunctlie and severallie promittin derratto.

In witnes quheroff (wreittin be Donald Ros in Tayne) they have subscrivit thir presentts with ther hands, day, yeir and place forsaid, beffor this witnessis: Androw McCoulloche yunger, burges of Tayne; James McCoulloche bailyie, burges ther; and Donald Ros weritter heiroff.

2. *Contract for glazingwork at Scone Palace, Perthshire: made at Scone, 21 March 1660 (Dur. warrant no. 628, registered 1662).*

David, Viscount Stormont [and] Ninian Hadon, glazingwright, burgess of Stirling.

The said Ninian Hadon binds and obleidges him to put in new glasses sufficientlie leaded in the severall rowmes following (all of French glass), to witt: in the whole windowes of the great hall of the palace of Scone, the window of that chamber called the lobie, and the window opposite to the doore therof, the windowes of the dynning rowme, kings chamber and cabinat within the same, the haill windowes in the long gallery, dukes chamber at the north end therof, and thrie rowmes within the same, all of guid and sufficient work and weill leaded as said is.

And sicklyke he obleidges him to put in thrie new glasses in these windowes of the yll of Scone, guid and sufficient work as said is.

And farder the said Ninian obleidges him to mend and repair all the rest of the whole windowes high and laich of the said palace sufficiently with glasses and lead.

And wher it sall happen that any of the glasses therof is not removed and new ones put in the places therof, he binds and obleidges him to wash the samen and make them guid and sufficient strong work, weill leaded, and to do all wther things requisite and neidfull therto belonging to ane glassinwricht.

For the which causses the said noble lord binds and obleidges him to content, pey and delyver to the said Ninian Haddon the sowme of six hundreth merks guid and wsuall Scots money, in maner and at the termes underwritten, viz: the sowme of two hundreth merks at his entrie to the said work; and the sowme of other two hundreth merks at the midle therof; and the sowme of other two hundreth merks and in compleit peyment of the haill sowme at the finishing therof; together with four bolls sufficient oat meall.

And it is heirby declaired that the said Ninian shall have the whole old glass that he sall happen to take out of the windowes forsaid for his owne wse.

And he obleidges him to enter to the said work betwixt the daitt heirof and the fourteinth day of Apprill nixttocome.

And finallie both the saids pairties obleidges them to obtemper the premisses hinc inde each of them to others, and the pairtie failyiear to pey to the pairtie observer or willing to observe the sowme of ane hundreth punds money forsaid of liquidat expensses in caice of failyie, by and attouer the implement of the samen.

3. *Agreement for the erection of a manse (?) at Lasswade, Midlothian: made at Edinburgh, 2 May 1660 (Dal. warrant no. 382, registered 1661).*

Mr Robert Prestone of Prestone, Mr James Cunynghame, minister of Lasswad and Gilbert Hay of Bridgelands [and] Alexander Smaill, mason, portioner of Pleasants.

The saids Alexander Smaill binds and obliges him and his aires, executors and successors to big and build ane howss according to the fashione and in maner particularlie aftermentionet, viz: of length fiftie four foot of measure within the walls, twentie foot of breadth within the walls also, and twentie foot of hight for the sydewalls, with thrie gavells to the top and a midwall of stone to the first geasting, with a jame of sevine foot of wydnes north from the north wall of the hous towards the midle, and eightine foot of length alongs the said north wall of the hous: which jame is appointed for a scale stair for the entrie to the overrowmes, quherin is to be a hewing door, with a mullering and two hewing doores within the said jame wpon the north syde of the hous to serve for entries to the laigh rowmes.

Item, fyve windows to be in the laigh rowmes and two chimneys thairin and one of them to be pendit.

Item, the second storie to be divydit in thrie rowmes, in everie one of them a chimney, and eight large windows amongst them.

Item, in the thrid storie to be in [sic] two rowmes, with one chimney in one of them, and a window in each gavell.

Item, the two wtter gavells to be caried up with peat stones, and the gavells of the said jame to be carried wp also with peat stons, with sufficient lights in the jame to serve the stair, and to hew and lay the herthstones, and to hew the coapstons.

Item, a stone door to be on the north syde of the hous of the second storie, and a door in the midgavell of the second storie.

Which houss, of the quantitie, fashion and maner particularlie abovespecifeit, the saids Alexander Smaill as principal, and with him Williame Purves of Woodhouslie as cautioner for him, binds and obliges them, conjunctlie and severallie, and thair aires, executors and successors, to big and build in good and sufficient work betuixt the dait hearof and the first day of November 1600 and sixtie yeares instant, provyding the materialls after mentionet be furnished to him in maner wnderwrittine, wnder the pane of a hundreth pundis Scottis money as

liquidat expenssis in case of failyie or the said Alexander his deserting the work befor the compleating thairof throughe his default.

For the quhilk cawssis the saids Mr Robert Prestone, Mr James Cunynghame and Richert Hay binds and obliges them conjunctlie and severallie, and thair aires, executors and successors, to content, pay and delyver to the saids Alexander Smaill, his aires, executors or assignayes, the sowme of thrie hundreth and fiftie merks money forsaid at the termes after specifiet, viz: ane hundreth merks money within eight dayes of his entrie, quhilk is declared hearby to be at and wpon the first day of June nixtocum; and the sowme of ane uther hundreth merks within a month thair after; item, the thrid hundreth merks quhen the walls is sydewall heaght rownd about; and the sowme of fiftie merks in compleat payment of the saids thrie hundreth and fiftie merks at the closing of the said work: wnder the pane of twentie pundis money as liquidat expenssis for ilk terms failyie within eight days of the saids terms.

And in lyk maner the saids persons binds and obliges them and thair forsaids to caws cast the ground of the saids hous, and to lay to stones, lyme sand and all uther materialls necessarrie to the said work and for the building hairof.

And in case through the want of the saids materialls the saids Alexander and his workmen shall ly idle, the saids persons bind and obliges them and thair forsaids to delyver to the saids Alexander for ilk day that he himself shall ly idle twentie shillings Scottis, and for ilk maissone man threttine shillings four pennies, and for ilk barrow man sex shillings eight pennies money, by and attour the payment of the pryce abovewrittin.

4. *Contract for the erection of a mill at Kinloch, Perthshire: made at Dunkeld and Kinloch, 1 and 11 July 1660 (Mack. warrant no. 913, registered 1665).*

Alexander Robertsone of Strowan [and] James Hay in Cowlie.

Forsameikell as the said Allexander Robertsone is myndfull, God villing, to caus big up ane saw mylne and coarne mylne and ane valk mylne, all in ane stok upon the boundis of his lands of Kendloch whair the samen sall be thought maist convenientlie to stand, and for that effect the said Allexander Robertsone obleissis him to carrie timber, staines and all wther necessaris for bulding up of the forsaids mylnes,

dammis and water gangis therto, and sall furnisch the varkmen and servandis that sall work the said wark at the said mylnes, dammis and wattergangis, cutting and transporting of timber therto upon his awin charges: and that be the speciall advyse and derectione of the said James Hay as overseiar and maister of wark, and as he sall think meitt and expeidient in all thingis necessar for performing of the said wark, and thir thingis being sua done accordinglie as the said James Hay sall appoynt to be done for performing and prosecuting of the said wark as sall be thought necessar, and that befor the first day of Apryll nixttocome.

Than and in that caice the said James Hay sall, Godvilling, have the said wark perfyttit againe the first day of September therefter in the yeire of God 1600 and thriescoir ane yeires, and sall attend the samyn work himselff att all occaissioines neidfull to the full accomplischment and finisching therof.

For the quhilkis caussis the said Allexander Robertsone of Strowan bindis and obleissis him, his aires and successoris, to pay to the said James Hay, his aires and assignayes, sice sowmes of money as sall be modiefiet be the right honourable Sir James Drummond of Machanie knyt and Patrik Graham of Inchbrakie, to be payit to the said James Hay at the finisching of the said wark.

And what sowmes of money the said Allexander Robertsone in the meintyme sall advance to the said James Hay affoir hand for doeing of his necessar affaires for the tyme, the said James Hay sall be haldin to allowe the samyn to the said Allexander Robertsone in the first and [sic] of the sowmes of money that sall happin to be modiefiet to him be the persones abovenamit: and quhairupon he sall be haldin to give his tickatis off resaitt to the said Allexander Robertsone therupon at all occaissioines as the said James sall happin to ressaive the samyne.

And heirto and haill premissis baith the said parties obleissis them and ther forsaidis to observe, keipe and fulfill the haill premissis to utheris safare as concernis ther awain partis therof, and to content and pay the ane partie to the uther the sowme off twa hundreth pundis money Scottis of liquidat expenssis in caice of necessar regestratione heirof in any of the bookis wnderwretine and letters reasing heirupon.

5. *Contract for the partial reconstruction of Coldingham Church, Berwickshire: made at Coldingham, 20 August 1661 (Dal. warrant no. 1930, registered 1662).*

K

Heritors of the parish of Coldingham [and] George Wilsone, younger, mason, burgess and freeman of the Cannogate.

The said George Wilsone undertaks and obleidges him to build up and repair upon the old ground wall of the kirk of Coldingham, in the particular formes therof as is afterspecifeit, viz.

In the first, to tak doune the head and rooff of the said church and to tak doune the south sydwall and west gavill therof to the ground, and build them up in good and sufficient archler work in the utter syds: and to build the innersyds of the saids southwalls and westergavill also with archler work anserable in the hight to the northwalls of the said church.

And to tak doune the wholl walls by the root of the heigh halyware, and to mak a sufficient and compleat passage from the ground from [sic] asscending hence to the top of the platforme of the said church, in good and sufficient masone work.

And also to tak doune the northwall and eastergavill of the said church to the root of the uppermost halyware therof: and to repair and help quhat is faultie and deficient in the said eastergavill, and mak the same sufficient anserable to the rest of the work.

And to close up the angular turnpyks, the one in the southeast corner and the uther in the northwest corner, in rough work, in respect they ar to mak no uther use therof.

And also to close up the waistplaces betuixt evry halyware upon the northsyd and eastgavill in good and sufficient work.

And to mak all the said masonework sufficient, as is abovewryttin, by the sight of Johne Milne, master measone, or any uther they shall bring to visite the same efter finishing therof.

And to mak sufficient lyghts and windowes suteable to the roumes of the said church.

And to furnish and mak ane sufficient platforme timber rooff of firr, able to carie lead for covering therof.

And to furnish all tymber and tymberwork, yron, ironework, glass and glasswindowes necessar and requisit for compleating of the said work.

And to mak three sufficient doores, the one in the southwall, the uther in the westgavill, and the thrid in the northwall: and to mak the saids doores compleat with locks, keyes and snyks, and delyver the keyes therof to them or any they shall appoynt to receive the same.

And to have the tymber requisit for the said work in readines upon

the shoare of Eymouth or Coldinghame sands, readie to be transported to the said church in maner underwryttin.

And to enter to the said work betuixt the date heirof and the tuentie third day of August next to come, without further delay: and to continow constantlie therat, working by himselff or his servants, and not desert the same untill the compleating therof as is abovewryttin.

For the which causes and better advanceing of the said work, the saids heretors of Coldingham pariochin obleidges them and ilk ane of them, conjunctlie and severallie, ther aires, executors and successors, intrometters with ther goods and geir quhatsoever, in the first place to tak away the rubbish of the walls as the same shall happin to be cassin doune from tyme to tyme, and to clear the ground therof.

And next to buy, furnish and caus lead to the said kirk, lyme and sand sufficient for compleating the measonwork therof.

And to cause cary and transport from the said shoar of Eymouth and Coldinghame sands respective all such tymber requisit for the said work as the said George shall lay or caus be layd downe ther for transportatioun, and lay the same at the said church, and that upon ther awin proper charges and expensses, and free the said George altogether of the expensses of transporting therof.

And heirby gives and dispones to the said George Wilsone, his aires, executors and assigneyes, the wholl tymberwork of the said rooff present on the said church, quhilk is to be takin doun be him, to be made use of and disponed upon be him and his forsaids as he or they shall think fitt: provyding he doe not medele with the lead of the said church for his awin use, bot declaires heirby it shalbe made use of as the saids heretors shall think fit.

Lykas the saids heretors binds and obleidges them, conjunctly and severally, and ther forsaids, to content and pay to the said George Wilsone or his forsaids, for the full compleating of the said work and furnishing all necessars as afforsaid, the soume of four thousand tuo hundreth merks Scotts money in maner and at the termes following, to witt: the soume of fourteen hundreth merks as the first termes payment therof at the feast of Mertimas next to come; the soume of uther fourteen hundreth merks at the compleating of the middle or halff of the said work; and the soume of uther fourteen hundreth merks at the compleating and finishing of the said wholl work.

And that for all maner of uther payment, wages, meat, drink or

drinkmoney or quhatsoever els the said George can for himselff or his servands ask or crave of the saids heretors or ther forsaids for the said work, or materialls therto, any maner of way.

And heerunto and to the performance of the haill premissess and evry head and article therof abouewryttin, the said George Wilsone as principal and James Scott wright burges of the Cannogat as cautioner for him conjunctlie and severallie on the ane pairt, and the saids heretors of the said pariochin of Coldinghame on the uther pairt, obleidges them and ther forsaids, conjunctlie and severallie, respective hinc inde to uthers under the penalty of fyve hundreth punds Scotts money, quhilk the pairtie failyers obleidges them, conjunctlie and severally, and ther forsaids, to pay to the pairties observers and willing to observe ther pairts of the premisses, by and attour the fulfilling of the same.

And the saids heretors obleidges them and ther forsaids to free and releive evry one uthers of ther proportiouns of the soumes abovewryttin, and to bear equall and proportionall burthen with uthers theranent.

Lykas the said George Wilsone obleidges him and his forsaids to free and releive his said cautioner of his obleidgement for him anent the haill premisses, and of all hasard and danger he or his forsaids may sustain or incurr any maner of way theranent.

6. *Contract for the building of a dyke at Langton, Berwickshire: made at Langton, 26 February 1664 (Dál. warrant no. 1091, registered 1664).*

Sir Archbald Cokburne of Langton, knight and baronet [and] Thomas and James Temples and Alexander Duns, masons in Duns.

The saids Thomas and James Temples and Alexander Duns be thir presents binds and obleissis thame, ther airs, executors and intromitters quhatsumever, to big to the said Sir Archbald ane gude and sufficient dyke with stone and clay about the hauche in the wode, as it is takin in with the red cruiche that runes about the same.

And also they bind and obleidge thame and ther forsaids to win the stones thameselffes for that effect in any pairt of the ground they sall find most convenient, it being alwayes withane quarter of a myll of the forsaid ground that is to be incloased.

And also the forsaids massones binds and obleissis thame and thers abovewrittin to perfyte the said dyke sufficientlie in work full elne broad and full thrie elnes of hight, with squair hewine coynyies to the

cope, and that betuixt the dait heirof and the feist and terme of Lambes nixtocum in this instant yer of God 1000 sex hundreth thriescoir four yers, but longer delay.

For the quhilks causses the said Sir Archbald Cokburne binds and obleissis him, his airs, executors and intromitters quhatsumever, thankfullie to content, pay and delyvir to the saids Thomas and James Temples and Alexander Duns, ther airs, executors or assigneys, betuixt the dait heirof and the termes of payment following: all and haill the soume of eightscoir sevintene punds money of Scotland with twa bollis aitmeill and twa bollis beir, to witt: the sowme of fyftie sevin pund money forsaid in pairt of payment of the said sowme is presentlie payit at the dait herof, quherof they hald thame well satisffiet and dischargis the said Sir Archbald and his forsaids therof for ever; and the sowme of thriescoir punds money forsaid at such tyme as the said dyke sall be halff built about; and the sowme of thriescoir punds in compleit payment of the forsaid haill soume of eightscoir sevintene pund at the compleiting of the work.

And the forsaid four boll as followis, to wit: the ane halff therof at the dait herof, quherof they hald thaim well satisfiet and dischargis the said Sir Archbald therof; and the uther twa bolls quhen the half work is perfyted.

And farder the said Archbald binds and obleissis him to caus leid the stones quhen they are win, and lay them within sex quarter of the wall, as lykwayis to find ane barrowman quhen they are laying the dyke about, and to caus red the ground of the dyke.

And heirto baith the saids pairties binds and obleissis thame to uthers, and the pairtie failyeing obleissis tham to pay to the pairtie observand the sowme of ane hundreth merks money of Scotland, by and besyd the fulfilling of the premisses.

7. *Contract for repairs to the harbour and tolbooth of Whithorn, Wigtownshire: made at Whithorn, 24 October 1664 (Mack. warrant no. 1604, registered 1665).*

Alexander Stewart of Fishgill [Physgill], with Alexander Houston of Presterie [Prestrie] [and] Alexander Donaldsone, provost, James Stewart and John McBurnie, baillies of the burgh of Whithorn,

Alexander McCandlish in Owtown [Owton], burgess, and Wiliam Donaldson of Arbrok, with John Houson of Drummastown.

The said Alexander Stewart as principall and Alexander Houstown as cautioner binds and obliges them, conjunctlie and severallie, their heires, executors and successors, sufficientlie to build, finish and compleat the harbor, bulwork and kei at the Isle and port of Whithorn, according to the ancient longitude and latitud theirof, the height therof being three foot heigh above the floodwatter at any tydde, in all pairts therof being six ells broad above.

And whereas any of the poalls or stobbs are not sufficient or broaken, the said Alexander Stewart and his foresaids obliges them to fix sufficient poals or stobbs in place of such as are broken or unsufficient, and to build ane ramper or sconce upon the topp of the harbor or heaven of ane elle heigh, erected upon the toppsyd of the said kei.

Lykwayes the said Alexander Stewart as principall and Alexander Houstown as cautioner binds and obliges them, conjunctlie and severallie, and their foresaids, to build ane sufficient scleat rooff upon the old tolbuth from the midd geavill to the southwest end therof, and to furnish the same with window casements and leaves, and to hang ane sufficient leave upon the door thereof, and to loft and floor the same throughlie from the said geavill compleatly to the said door sufficientlie with jests and planks, the walls therof being compleated, rectified and amended be the said town cownsell and communitie of the said burgh and the pairties taking burden for them.

All which work and building of the said harbor and tolbuith the said Alexander Stewart as principall and the said Alexander Houstown as cautioner binds and obliges them, conjunctlie and severalie, to perfect, accomplish and compleatlie finish betuixt the deat hereof and the terme of Mairteinmasse in the year of God 1600 and threescore fyve years, wnder the paine of five hundereth pownds Scots money, by and atouer the fullfilling of the premisses.

For the which causes soe to be accomplished, perfytted and finished, the said Alexander Donaldson provest, James Stewart and John McBurnie ballies of the said burgh, Alexander McCandlish in Owtown burghes and Wiliam Donaldson in Arbrok, together with the said John Houstown of Drummastown as cautioner, suretie and full debtor for and with them as taking burden foresaid, binds and obliges them, conjunctlie and severallie, their heirs, executors and successors,

thankfullie to content and pay to the said Alexander Stewart and his foresaids, or his assigneyes, the swmme of two hundreth and fourtie pownds usuall money of Scotland in manner and at the termes aftermentioned, viz: the swmme of threescore pownds money foresaid at the terme of Mairteinmasse nixt in the instant year of God 1600 and threescore four years; and the swmme of other threescore pownds money foresaid at Beltaine nixt thereafter in the year of God 1600 and threescore five years; and the swmme of other threescore pownds money foresaid at the terme of Lambs masse nixt thereafter and year of God foresaid; and the swmme of other threescore pownds money foresaid, which compleats the whole swmme of two hundereth and fourtie pownds money, at the said terme of Martein masse 1600 and threescore five years: together with the swmme of twentie pownds money foresaid for each termes faillie, with the due annuall rent of the said principall swmme, yearlie, termelie and proportionallie, soe long as the same shall happen to be unpayed after the said termes respective.

Lykways the said pairties principall and their said cautioner, taking burden as said is, binds and obliges them to delyver to the said Alexander Stewart or his foresaids the Act of Parliament granted in favours of the said burgh of Whithorn for ane voluntar contribution to be collected furth of the respective shyres and others mentioned in the said act for repairing of the said harbor of the Isle of Whithorn.[1]

And to give warrand, power and commission to the said Alexander Stewart and his foresaids to uplift and receave the said contributiones from all persones and at all places within the bounds and limitts of the said Act.

Lyk as be the tenor hereof, the said Alexander Donaldson provest, James Stewart and John McBurnie ballies of the said burgh, with Wiliam Donaldson in Arbrok and Alexander McCandlish in Owtown burghes, as taking burden foresaid, gives warrant, power and commission to the said Alexander St_wart to intromett with, uplift and receave the said contributiones conforme to the said Act, within the said bounds therein limitted and in all other place wheresoever the said Alexander shall be recommended for supplie and contribution to the said work, with power to him to aply the same to the use of the said

---

[1] This act, passed in 1661, enjoined collections in all the churches of Galloway, Nithsdale, Teviotdale and Lanark: *Acts of the Parliaments of Scotland*, vii, ed. T. Thomson (Edinburgh, 1820), 28-9, c.44.

work or other wayes as he or his foresaids pleases, allwayes provyded the said harbor and tolbuth be compleated and finished as is above rehearsed.

Lyk as the said pairties, as taking burden foresaid, be the tenor hereof mak and constituts the said Alexander Stewart and his foresaids their verie lawfull, wndowbted and irrevocable sessioner and assigney in and to the conditions of ane indenter mad betuixt the deceast Harie Blaine meason indweller in Wigtown and the said magistrats, cownsell and communitie of the said burgh, which is of deat at Whithorn the eight day of Janwarii 1600 and threescore three years, together with all clauses of obligement therein contained, and in and to the swmme of fourtie pownds Scots money of penaltie contained in the said indenter incurred through the default of the said defunct, his heirs and executors.

With power with power [sic] to the said Alexander Stewart to persue the heirs and executors of the said defunct for performance of the said conditiones and for payment of the said penaltie before any judge or judges competent, sentences and decreets to recover, lift and rease, and to compone, transact and agree thereanent.

And generallie all and sundrie other things to do, use and exerce thereanent quhilk they might have doone before the making hereof, turning and transfering all right and clame quhilk they or their foresaids had hes or may pretend to have in and to the said indenter whole conditiones and and [sic] obligesments therof and swmmes of money therin contained to and in favours of the said Alexander Stewart and his foresaids, whome they have onlie surrogat in their full right and place thereof forever.

Declairing lykas it is hereby declaired that the said persones pairties cedents, as taking burden foresaid, shall be free of all conditiones of the said indenter, and that the said Alexander Stewart and his foresaids shall be obliged and lyable to performe and fulfill all clauses and articles thereof quhilk in any wayes may relaite to them as taking burden for the said burgh of Whithorn.

Lykas the said pairties, as taking burden foresaid, maks and constituts the said Alexander Stewart and his foresaids their sessioner and assigney in and to all and sundrie swmmes of money resting in the hands of John McCulloch, leat ballie of the said burgh, of the contributiones receaved be him in the kingdome of Irlande conforme to ane commission mad to him for that effect, with power to the said Alexander and his foresaids

to sutte for payment thereof, call, follow and persue therefore as accords of law, and generallie everie other thing to do quhilk they or their foresaids might have doon before the making hereof, promitting hereat to abyd ferme and stable.

More over it is hereby declaired that the foresaid swmme of two hundereth and fourtie pownds money foresaid granted to the said Alexander Stewart is in lew and satisfaction of the swmme of three hundereth merks money foresaid granted be the Estats of burrowghs as ane contribution toward the repairing of the said harbor, and the swmme of ane hundereth pownds money foresaid granted be Patrick Agnew of Wig be his obligation toward the repairing of the tolbuth, and that the said Alexander Stewart is not to creave repetition or payment of the said swmme of three hwendereth merks and the said swmme of ane hwndereth pound, or of any other swmes alreadie intrometted with and receaved be the said burgh, their commissioners or others in their name, be vertue of the said Act of Parliament or otherwayes, in satisfactione whereof the said swmme of two hundereth and fourtie pownds money foresaid is granted and accepted.

And lastlie both the said pairties and each of them obliges them and their foresaids to relive and skeathlesse keep their said cautioners, and each one of them and their foresaids, of all interest, coast, skeath and expences they or either of them shall happen to incurre throwgh their becomeing cautioners in manner above wrytten.

Lykas the said Alexander Donaldson provest, James Stewart, John McBurnie, Wiliam Donaldsone and Alexander McCandlish obliges them to releive each other pro rato.

8. *Contract for the wrightwork of a new tenement in the Cowgate, Edinburgh: made at Edinburgh, 1 July 1665 (Mack. warrant no. 1928, registered 1665).*

James Belsches, son to the late James Belsches, indweller in Edinburgh [and] George Herreis, wright, burgess of the said burgh.

The said George Herreis binds and obleissis him, his aires and successors, to build up ane tenement of land perteneing to the said James Belsches, lyand within the brugh of Edinburgh, at the foot of the Horswynd on the eist syd therof in the Cowgaitt, nixt adjacent to that tenement of land perteneing to Thomas Craufurd merchant on the eist syd therof, quhich tenement of land is to be fyftie sevin Inglisch foot of

lenth and sevinteine and ane halff of breadth iff the said tenement be als long and als bread, and thrie storie high off the ground.

The first storie is to be meassone work (quhich the said James Belsches is to furnisch himselff with all other meassone work therto belonging), and the tuo stories above is to be all timber work, quhich the said George is to build up and to furnisch materialles therto, to witt: tries, dailles, nailles, iron work, lockis, keyis, bandis, glass work and all otheris belonging therto, necessarie and expedient.

Conteneing tuelff roumes, and so many studies and pantries as sall be contryved, thoght fitt and convenient in the foir land.

And all the parple wallis and devisiones within the house to be syllered on both sydis.

And the jeastis and floireing to be dight beneath, and the roof therof to be ane pletforme, quhich the said George is also to doe, and furnisch all materialls therto with ballasteris turned about.

And generallie to furnisch and perfyt the said tenement of land, under and above, with the wholl workmanschip and furnitur therof, in everie thing necessarie and expedient quhatsumever, wpone his owine chairges and expenssis (exceptand onlie measone work quhilk the said James Belsches is to furnisch allenerly).

And quhich is to be done, furnisched and endit betuixt the dait heirof and the terme of Witsondey nixttocum.

And the said George Herreis obleissis him that the said tenement of land sall be whollie waterthight the haill winter seassone eftir the said terme of Witsondey nixttocum: and in caise it sall not be waterthight bot inlaicking, in that caise he obleissis him to mak the samen waterthight upone his owine expenssis.

For the quhilk cause the said James Belsches bindis and obleissis him, his aires, executors, successors and intromitters quhatsumever, to content and pay to the said George Herreis, his aires or assignais, the soume of tuo thousand merks money of this realme: and that at the finisching and compleitting of the said work.

And the said James Belsches bindis and obleissis him and his forsaids that ane hundreth dailles and threttie treis in his custodie sall properlie perteine and belong to the said George Herreis for effectuating of the said work, and that he sall mak the samen furthcomeand to them [sic] for that effect.

And both the saids parties binds and obleissis tham to performe the

premissis, aither of them to otheris, and the partie failyier to pay to the partie observer or willing to observe the soume of fyve hundreth merks, by and attour the fulfilling therof.

9. *Contract for the slating of Bourtie Church, Aberdeenshire: made at Aberdeen and (blank), (blank) July 1666 (Mack. warrant no. 1728, registered 1669).*

Sir John Keith of Caskiben, Walter Ogilvie of Bankheid, tutor to Margaret and Elizabeth Seatons, heirs portioners of the lands of Blair, for two parts of the said lands of Blair, Alexander Gordone of Kinguidie [Kingoodie], for the third part therof, William Pantone and John Fraser, for the lands of Blackhouse, John Reid of Barra, John Andersone of Bourtie, Alexander Simpsone of Thorntowne and Patrick Ross of Collihill [and] Oliver Yong, slater in Bogfechill.

The said Oliver Yong binds and obleidges him to winn and prepair eleven thowsand sklaitts out of the quarrie of Tillimorgane immediatelie eftir his entrie therto, quhilk shall bee and begin, God willing, upon the sexteint day of July instant.

And eftir transportatione therof to the kirkyard of Bowrtie, therwith to build and thatch the rooff of the said kirk of Bowrtie, and to compleit the same in all things requisit belonging to sklaitterwork.

And not to tak any uther work in hand fra his entrie to the quarrie till the rooff bee accomplished.

And dureing his abode at the said quarrie and rooff, to mantaine himself and his servands upoun his owne proper chairges and expenses.

For the quhilk causes the said Sir John Keith and the remanent heretors, lyfrenters and wodsetters abovementionat binds and obleidges them and ther aires to cause transport the forsaid number of eleven thowsand sklaits to the said kirkyard of Bowrtie upoun ther owne horss chairges and expenss.

And to pay and delyver to the said Oliver Yong, for winning ilk thowsand of the forsaid number, the sowme of ten merks Scots money and half a boll of meall: the one half of the said victuall and money at his entrie to the quarrie, and the uther half therof at his depairtur therfra.

And sicklyk they obleidges them and ther forsaids to pay to the said Oliver Yong the sowme of eight pounds Scots money and half a boll of meall for everie rood of sklait work upoun the said rooff, and proportionallie the one half of the said money and victuall at his entrie

to the said rooff, and the uther half at his accomplishment of the work.

And heirto both pairties binds and obleiss them and ther forsaids under the failyie of threttie pounds Scots money to be payit bee the pairtie falyier to the pairtie observer or willing to observe, by and attour performance of the premiss.

10. *Contract for the erection of a house at Auchenbowie, Stirlingshire: made at Stirling, 17 September 1666 (Mack. warrant no. 1100, registered 1667).*

John Simsone, mason, burgess of Glasgow, and George Simsone, his brother [and] Robert Bruce, younger, of Auchinbowie.

The saids John and George Simsone faithfullie bindis and oblisse them, conjunctlie and severallie, with all possible dilligence to build ane sufficient house of nynteine foots in breid within the lands of Auchinbowie, as the samen is presentlie boundit, with tuo ston gavells and tuo syd walls of tuentie sex foot high and thrie foot in breid, by and attour quhat boundis the joists sall take upe of the said wall, with sex ventis or chimneyes, quherof on of them to be on the syd wall, togither with ane pin turnpyke conforme to the said house, with alse many windowes as the said pairties sall think convenient the tyme of the building, togither also with four hewen stone dors.

And also the said John and George Simsone binds and obleissis them to pavement the laich floore of the said hous, and also to build therin ane hewen timber table upon the wall syd therof, and siclyke to make up hewen chimney heidis.

For the quhilks causse, the said Robert Bruce younger of Auchinbowie bindis and oblissis him to furnish to the said John and George Simpsones alsmany stones and alse much lyme, sand and watter as will sufficientlie build the said house, and to cause lay the samen to them at the eist gate of Auchbowie.

And lykewayes to furnish barrow tubes, tries and uther neccessrs for carieing up of the samen, and also to delyver to them four bollis good and sufficient oat meall at ther entrie to the said work.

And farder binds and oblissis him, his aires and executors, to pay to the said John and George Simpsones the sowme of fyve hundreth merks Scotis money, and that within ane moneth space efter the compleiting of the said worke.

And heirto both the saids pairties binds and oblisses them to uthers in the most sure forme of contract that can be devysit, and the pairtie failyier to pay to the pairtie observer the sowme of ane hundreth punds money forsaid, by and attour the fulfilling of the premissis.

11. *Agreement for the completion of Invergarry Castle, Inverness-shire: made at Invergarry, 9 November 1670 (Dal. warrant no. 878, registered 1671).*

Aenas Lord Mcdonell [and] Robert Nicolsone, mason.

I the said Robert Nicolsone binds and oblidges me, and my aires, executors and asigness, to come to Invergary upon the first day of Aprill nixt 1671 yeirs, haveing other tuo sufficient measones alongs with me, and that to acommpleice and fully commpleit such as is wnperfytted of the bodie of the newe hous of Invergary.

Lykways I be thir presents binds [and] oblidges me and my forsaids to enter and begin at the forsaid day the rest of the work condescended upon, or requisit to be in or about the house or close of Invergary, and to finish and compleitlie outreike the same.

And if ther shall hapen any defect or imperfection to be in the forsaids measone work after the acommplishment of it, than in that caice I bind and oblidge myself to mak up the said defect and perfytly compleit the same, upon my owne expenses.

And to all thes forsads I doe bind myself wnder the failyie of fyve hundreth merks Scots money.

And we the said Lord Mcdonell binds and oblidges us and our aires to content and pay the said Robert Nicolsone and the forsaid measones in daily wages dureing the time they shall be working at the forsaid work, and that to be as use and wont formerly, and that wnder the failyie forsaid.

12. *Contract for the erection of a market-cross at Cullen, Banffshire: made at Cullen, 9 December 1674 (Mack. warrant no. 116, registered 1678).*

Georg Leslie off Badse [Bauds] and John Bard, baillies of the said burgh, Georg Lawtie off Tochieneill [Tochieneal], John Loriemer, town clerk of Cullen [and] Daniel Ross, master mason in Gellon [Cullen?].

The said Daniel Rosse be ther presents binds and oblissis him, be himself and his servants, to build and erect ane cross off frie stone and wtherwayes off ane perfyt figur cross, neir wnto the cross off Banff, without King or tounes armes, only two houseings for erecting the same heirefter, with all wther thinges that are convenient and requisit to ane perfyt cross.

Quhilk cross is to be hewen and builded betwixt this and Lambes nixt cumming in the yeir off God 1600 and sevintie fyve yeires.

And the said Daniel being aluayes provyded be the fornamed persones in matter of frie stone, rucgh stone, lyme, clay, leid and iron, with skaffelin reqwisit.

For the quhilk work, swa to be perfyted be the said Daniel and his servants abow specifeit, the said Georg Leslie, John Baird, George Lawtie and John Lorimer clerk binds and oblidges them, ther aires, executors and successors, to pey and delyver to the said Daniell Ross, his aires, executors [and] assigneyis, out off the common guid off the said brucgh, the soume off two hundreth twentie fyve merks money at thrie sevirall tearmes efter mentionat (viz:) fourtie nyne pounds elevin shilling Scotts money theroff at Candlemese nixt comeing in the yeir off God 1600 and sevintie fyve yeires; with fourtie nyne pounds elevin shillings at Witsonday nixt therefter; with fiftie pounds aughtein shilling, quhilk comp[l]eits the said soume, at Lambes nixt following in the forsaid yeir off God: by and atour the annualrent off the saids sevirall soumes, efter the termes off peyement abowe mentionat.

And finallie the saids parties oblissis them and ther forsaids to performe the premissis, ilk ane to others, wnder the pain of fiftie pounds money to be payed be the partie braker to the partie willing to performe the samen.

13. *Agreement for plasterwork at Nuick, Stirlingshire: made at Nuick, 6 February 1675 (Mack. warrant no. 297, registered 1676).*

Andro Ross of Nuick [and] Andrew Elies, plasterer.

I Andro Elies plesterer oblidges my self to plaister to Andro Ross of Nuick his uholl hous of Nuick, both all quhat is presently built and lykuyse that chamber on the east end of the hall quhich is to be built, it being nothing augmented in lenth to uhat it is at present, to wit:

All the walls of his uholl hous and the roof of his hall and the roof of
the high chamber of the sam, uith ane cornish round about the roof of
the forsaid hall, and lykuayse about the roof of the said high chamber of
the sam, and morover to plaister the uholl skaile stare and starekaise
quhich he is to putt up to serve the entries to the chambers above, and
the wardrops.

For the quhilk cause the said Andro Ross oblidges himself thankfully
to content and pay to the said Andro Elies the soume of fyftie ane pound
eight shilling six pennies Scots, and that in full contentatioune and
satisfactioune to me, the said Andro Elies, for plestering the uholls
walls, skaile stare and kaise and rooft work of his hous uith the kornish,
according as it is above expresht.

And the said Andro Elies is to plester on of the high roomes again the
tuintie tuo day of this month, and all the rest according as the said
Andro Ross desyres, proveiding he give me tymous advertisment by
any person, and the said Andro Ross is [to] pay me proportionably as I
work his work.

For the quhich cause we both undersubscrybing binds and oblidges
ourselfs to fulfill each of our pairts to other thankfully, under the pain of
tuiintie pound by and attour the fulfilling of the premisses, as witnes
our hands at Nuick the six of February 1600 and seaventie five, befor
thir witnesses: Robert Rainie wright in Falkirk and Alexander Peticroe
masson at Parkhall.

14. *Contract for the erection of Gallery House, Angus: made at Montrose, 30
April 1677 (Dal. warrant no. 1152, registered 1680).*

Sir John Falconer of Bollmakellie [Balmakellie], Master of His
Majesty's Mint, [and] Thomas Wilkie, mason, burgess of Edinburgh.

The said Thomas Wilkie binds and obleidges him with all convenient
dilligence by himselfe and his servants to go about the founding,
building and perfect finishing to the said Sir John Falconar, upon his
lands and within the precinct of the Gallraw (according as he shall mark
the place for the fundatione therof), ane compleit house consisting of
ane double house, threttie eight foote over walls in breadth and
seavintie foote in lenth, with tuo jams joineing to the said bodie being
eightein foote squair over walls of the said jams, to be of equall height

and to answer to the floores and communicate with each storie of the said double house.

The said bodie and jams to be caryed up thrie storie hie besyds garrotts, the lowest of which stories, being ten foote and one halfe hie betuixt floores, is to containe seavine roumes of a floor, wherof fyve are to be fyre roumes, one of which as it shall be placed in the draught heireftirmentioned is to have one large pended chimney for ane kitchine.

And under the first storie of each of the saids jams he obleidges him to found and build tuo cellars, with convenient lights in each the saids cellars, being seavine foote hie: and in the second storie the lyke number of fyre roumes with closetts: and in [the] thrid storie the equivalent number of fyre roumes.

And also ane galleryie the full lenth of the said house, upon the fore syde therof, or in such other place of the said house wher it shall be designed in the draught, with tuo chimneys therin convenientlie situate, with closets wher they can be had.

And above the said thrid storie to frame sufficient garrotts betuixt upper and lower balks, floored, secket and grubbed, with sufficient storme windowes through the whole house and jams.

The saids thrie stories he obleidges him to edefie with a sufficient number of windowes and chimneys in each roume, as they shall be found necessare, and placed in the draught eftermentioned: and to jeast and floore the saids thrie stories with sufficient jeasting, timber and dealls, laid broken joynted efter the best maner.

And to provyde the saids haill windowes, viz: the undermost storie with irone stenchells, kneed and crossed, with sole and lintell of irone and mid bares and double caisements of wainscote, with glass above and under, with bands, snecks, rings and other necessars for the saids caisements: and to lyne the saids windowes of bed chamber, nursarie, closet.

And the dynning roume to be lyned with pannelled joyned worke quyte through.

And in the second storie to lyne the windowes of the whole roumes and closets therin.

And four of the chimneys to be planted with four severall sorts of mouldries of timber, eftir the forme of marble chimney peices.

And in lyke maner to furnish for the said haill second storie, for the

haill number of windowes therin, sufficient double wainscot caisements and broads, placed and filled up with French glass, with bands, snecks, rings and other necessars above mentioned, and the windowes in the thrid storie to be lykewayes provyded with caisements, broads, glass snecks etc, efter the maner above written.

And to build, place and carry up ane large scale staire of good and sufficient stone work to the whole thrie stories, the steps therof fyve foote of measoure in lenth and twelve inches breadth in the treade, hewen, dinted and botled, the plait theroff to be fyve foote, conforme to the steps: and the entrie front and partition of the said staire to be decored in a hansome maner as shall be found necessare.

And also obleidges him to plaister the whole roumes in the saids thrie stories and stair caise, roofe and syde walls, with sufficient plaine plaister with a large hansome cornice of good order, except the upper dynning roume which is to be decored with some raised freatt worke and a large cornice and freeze of good order.

And to divyde the haill forsaids roumes with partitiones and transes as they shall happen to fall out through the haill house: the saids partitiones to be lyned with full dealls upon the one syde of the branders and laith and plaister on the other syde.

And to furnish doores for the haill entries [and?] so many of them double and pannelled as shall be found necessare.

[The entrie] to the said house to be of such hansome order of [work] as the said Sir John and the said Thomas Wilkie shall agree of, with a housen therupon: the entrie gaite [to] be of double wainscot, lyned with firre and planted with globb or losen nailes with tuo leaves.

And also to furnish for the said whole house all maner of locks, keys, bends, slotts and other irone worke that is necessare therto.

The haill materialls of stone, lyme, sand, timber, irone, glass, lead and other furnitor necessar for the buildings, plaistering, jeasting, flooreing and all other maner of maissone, wright, sclait, glass and smiths worke, the said Thomas obleidges him to furnish, provyde, transport and carye upon his oune proper charge.

And to worke the same upon his oune accountt and to bear the expense of the workemenship, and to pay maissons, wrights, plaisterers, glassiers, sclaitters, smiths, servants and barrowmen, and all furnitor and necessars belonging to the said building, without any

maner of charge or expensses to the said Sir John except the pryce underwritten.

And its heirby provyded that the haill soles, lintells and raebetts of the said house shall be of a whitte stone from the Qweens Ferrie.

And the roofe of the said haill house and jams to be sarked with dealls, and the jams sclaitted with scaillie (The said Sir John alloweing the difference betwixt scaillie and sclaitts), and the saids jams to be raised be way of pavilion from the house.

And the said worke and building to be compleit and furnished conforme to the draught therof to be subscriveit and keeped by each partie, which is to be observed and full filled and to be produced and compaired by the said Thomas Wilkie at all occasiones necessare, and at the finishing of the said work by both the saids parties: which is to be compleitt and finished, and the keys of the haill doores delivered up by the said Thomas to the said Sir Johne or his order, betuixt and the first day of November 1600 and seavintie eight yeares.

And in caice any parte of the building shall happen to be altered from the said draught by consent of both parties, the samen shall not inferre any further payment then the pryce under wri[tti]ne.

For the which causes the said Sir John Falconar binds and obleidges him, his aires, executors and successors, to content and pay to the said Thomas Wilkie, his aires, executors or assigneys, as the pryce and worth of the said haill worke, workmanship, furnitor and haill other charges and expensses therof, the soume of ten thousand merks Scots money in maner and at the termes following, viz: the soume of tuo thousand and fyve hundreth merks money therof as ane equal forth pairt betuixt and the first day of July nixt to come; and the soume of other tuo thousand fyve hundreth merks betuixt and the first of October nixt therefter; and the lyke soume of other tuo thousand and fyve hundreth merks betuixt and the first of Februarii 1600 and seavintie eight yeares; and the lyke soume of tuo thousand and fyve hundreth merks in full and compleitt payment of the forsaid principall soume of ten thousand merks, as the compleit pryce agreed on for the saids buildings, at the compleitting and finishing of the said worke.

And also to deliver on his demand the quantitie of eleavine chalders of meall at the toune of Montrose, with the mett and measure therof: and also one hundreth stone of irone or tuo hundreth merks money forsaid, in his optione.

And heirto both the saids parties binds and obleidges them hinc inde to observe, keep and fulfill the premisses to others under the penaltie of tuo thousand merks money forsaid, to be paid by the partie failyier to the partie observer, by and attour the full filling of the premisses.

15. *Contract for the construction of an oven in Todrig's Wynd, Edinburgh: made at Edinburgh, 16 May 1677 (Dal. warrant no. 86, registered 1678).*

James Stainhous, baxter, burgess of Edinburgh [and] John Harroway, mason, burgess of the said burgh.

The said John Harroway faithfullie obleisses him, be himself and servands such as massones and borrowmen, to build in good and sufficient massone worke ane ovin in ane bake voult within the head of Todrigs Wynd, in the land or tenement perteining heretablie to the said James Stainhous, the circumferrence quheroff is to be eight foott large within the walls, and in everie respect in sufficiencie, larges and roundnes to be conforme to Patrick Wallace baxter his ovin.

And to that effect to furnisch not only all sort off worke men therto and working instruments therfor, butt alsoe all wther materiells suitable for the same, such as stones for soll, pending, lyme, sand and what els belongeth to the said work.

And to make the same ane sufficient ovin at the sight off twa honest tradsmen betwixt and the sixtein day off Junii nixtocume.

And likewayes the said John binds and obleisses him to make to the said James of compleat massone worke ane chimney above in his chopt, but not to carry the brig farder then his working tuolles can reach.

And to that end to furnish him with ane massone and a borrowman ane wholl weik, for accomplishing therof after the work is done.

For the whilkes causses the said James Stainhous binds and obleisses him, his aires and executors, to make good and thankfull payment to the said John Harroway, his aires, executors or assigneyes, off the soume of twa hundreth and thertie merkes Scottes money, and that att the respective termes following [viz:] the soume off sevintie six merkes 6s 8d money forsaid as being a third pairt of the forsaid soume, imediatly att his entrie to the said worke; and ane second pairt therof when the same is half finisched; and a third and last pairt off the forsaid soume off twa hundreth and thertie merkes, whilk is in full and compleit payment off the same, within ane month preceisly after the

compleiting and building off the said ovin and chimney foresaid at the sight and to the satisfactione off twa honest tradsmen in maner abovewritten, to be indifferrently choysine be both pairties, with the soume off sevin pound money abovespecifeit for ilk termes failyie.

And lastly both pairties binds and obleisses them to wtheres, and the pairtie failyier to pay to the pairtie observer or willing to observe the soume of tuentie pound money forsaid, by and attour the fulfilling off the premisses.

16. *Agreement for wrightwork and plasterwork of a tenement in Leith: made at Leith, 20 June 1677 (Dal. warrant no. 1306, registered 1678).*

John Tailyeor, skipper in Leith [and] John Cleugh, wright in Leith.

The said John Clewgh for the soumes of money wnderwrittin hes wndertacken and oblidged himself, and be the tennor heirof wndertackes and oblidges himself, not onlie to work the heall wright work proposed for the rebuilding of the tennement of land bellonging to the said John Tailyeor, leying in the toune of Leith neir the heid of the hill, as flouring, leying leying [sic] of jeastes, makeing partitiones, putteing on the rooff, makeing of the doors, windowes, window caices and uthers necessry, conforme to the draught subscriveit be them theranent, and to dight the heall dealles to be made use of in floaring, quhich ar fyve upon on syde, but also he oblidges himself to plaister the tuo wpmost stories and heall partitiones therof, or otherwayes to lyne them on both sydes as the said John Tailyeor sall think fitt.

And to plaister the lowest stories and the heall stone walles and partitiones therof.

And to lyne the chop in the lowest storie with deales abowt the walles.

And to plaister or syller tuo in the rooff storie or wardrop, as the said John Tailzeor sall direct.

Item, the said John Clewgh oblidges himself to make ane handsome cornish in evrey roume of the saids wpmost stories, and in each of the saids upper stories to make a studie and pantrie.

And to this effect the said John Clewgh oblidges himself to furnish all manner of nailles necessar and reqwiseit for the said building, upon his owne chairges and expensses (except sclaitt nailles), ane able workman for workeing of the said work, and to use the wtmost of his airt and skill

in makeing of the same handsome and substentieall, and to have the same compleitlie feinished and perfyted against the firsth day of February nixtocome.

For which causses the said John Tailyeor oblidges himself not onlie to furnish all manner of dealls, trees, jeasts, lyme, hair and sawers for sawing of the timber and dealls upon his owne propper chairges and expensses, but also to pay or causs be payed to the said John Clewgh the soume of tuo thousand markes Scots money, as the pryce of the said workmanshyp heirby agried upon betuixt them, in manner following, viz: the soume of six hundreth sixtiesix merks nyn shiling, as the just thrid pairt therof, within tuentie dayes nixtefter the dait heirof; the lyke soume of six hundreth sixtie six merks nyn shiling at the putting on of the rooff; and the soume of uther six hundreth sixtie six merkes nyn shiling, in complet payment of the soume forsaid, imedieatlie efter the perfyteing of the said work.

Declairing heirby the tuo upper floarings ar to be of broken joynt work, and that the said John sall be oblidged for to plaister the turnpyck within the walles.

And feinallie both pairties oblidges them to observe the premisses, ather of them to utheres, and the pairtie failyeor to pay to the pairtie observer the soume of fyve hundreth merkes Scots, over and above the fulfilling therof.

17. *Contract for stone quarrying at Limekilns, Fife: made at Edinburgh, 5 July 1677 (Dal. warrant no. 1351, registered 1677).*

Thomas Weilkie, mason, burgess of Edinburgh [and] Mungo Dow and Thomas Smith, quarriers at Lyme Killines.

The saids Mungo Dow and Thomas Smith binds and obliege them, ther aires and executors, conjunctlie and seaverallie, to work and wine att the stone quarrie of Lyme Kilines al and haill the number of ane thowsand peace of ruch stones for heweing, accompting fyvescore and ten peaice of good and suficent singell eixylyrs and ten peaice of lang stones, being of four foots and fyve foots stones, to ilk hundreth:[2] And

---

[2] This is evidently a case of the 'long hundred', denoting six score or 120 stones. Cf. P. Gouldesbrough, 'The long hundred in the exchequer rolls', *Scottish Historical Review*, xlvi (1967), 79-82.

to imbargwe the samen upon ther owen expensses att the port and herbower of Lyme Kilines, and to caus transport and cairie abowt the samen, upon ther haizerd and expensses, as said is, to the port and shore of Montroise.

And to deliver the said number of ane thowsand peaice of ruch stones of the quallatie and quantatie forsaid wpon the said shore of Montroise to the said Thomas Weilkie or any haveing his order in meaner followeing, to witt: one boats loadeing of the saids stones betwixt the dait heirof and the tweintie fourth day of Jully instant, and the rest of the saids stones betwixt and the first day of November nixt to come, but langer delay, winde and wather serveing.

For the quhilks caussis the said Thomas Weilkie bind[s] and obliesses him, his airs, executors and intrometters with his goods and geir whosumever, to thankfulie content, pay and deliver to the saids Mungo Dow and Thomasses [sic] Smith and ther forsaids the soume of thretie twa punds Scotts money for ilk hunderth stones of the saids thowsands stones.

And to pay ilk skiper ther fraght that shall bring abowt the saids stones out of the first and readiest of the said sphyes [sic] conform to the order or letter of advyce that shall be sent be the saids Mungo Dow and Thomas Smith to the said Thomas Welkie for that efect, and that within tweintie four houers efter ilk skipers lifrerie.

And to pay the rest And to pay the rest [sic] of the pryce of the said stones within eight days efter the delivery of the samen.

And lastly booth the saids pairtes binds and obliesses them and ther forsaids to performe ther pairts of the premisses to others, under the paine of threscore punds Scotts money of liquidatt pennalltie for ilk fallyie, tottius quoties, by and attour the fullfilling of the premisses.

18. *Contract for the erection of a loft in Galston Church, Ayrshire: made at Galston, 8 October 1678 (Dal. warrant no. 1131, registered 1679).*

Mr Mathew Campbell of Waterhalse [Waterhaughs?] [and] James Muir, carpenter at Crucksmylne.

The said James Muir is to buld ane loft to the said Mr Mathew, for his acomandatoune in the east end of the church of Galstoune, betuxt sevin and eight footts in breadth and sextin footts in lenth, with thrie pewes in

the foir frontt inclosed with ane cower abow ther head, and the cower to stand wpon wainscot pillers, and the head of said peller to be cut out of the samyn, and the foir front and the syd of the said loft sua farr as the pewes goes to be all of wainscot, weill cutt out and good timber and bund in the best fashoune, confforme to any other seatt the said Mr Mathew pleases to pitch wpon within the shereffdome of Air.

And the rest of the said loft bakward from the said pewes as both to the front therof, and the rest of the loft to be all of good and suficent firr, and of alse good fashoune of work as any seatt or loft buldit of firr will allow.

And the loft benath to be sylloured with firr and fogged betuxt.

As alse the said James Muir is to buld wp ane heun dore wpon the south syd of the church, with ane plaine stairr of brotched work being four foott in bredth at least, in any place quher the said Mr Mathew sall apoynt the samen to be, as ane entrie to the said loft.

And the said Mr Mathew is bund to furnish and provyd the materialls belanging to stone, lyme and sand for the dore and stairr, and run jests and warrping for the pewes and iron work only, and the said James is to furnesh and provyd all other nesesars for the wholl work, both wainscot, firr and maine jests, and pillers wherwpon the maine jest stands.

And is to doe the said work and perfyt the same betuxt and the first day of May nextocum, and that wpon his oune proper charge and expensses.

The quhilk conditounes abowwrittin the said James Muir binds and oblssis him, his aires, executors and succssors, to doe and perfyt the same betuxt and the forsaid day, and that be sight of Sir Hew Campbell of Cessnock knight and Sir Georg Campbell younger of Cessnock his sone, or ather of them, and any good trodsman that they sall pitch wpon.

And that wnder the penultie of thretie punds Scots, ower and abow the perfformance of the premissis.

For the quhilk cause the said Mr Mathew hes contented and peyit to me, the said James Muir, the soume of ane hundreth punds Scots and tuo bolls meill and ane boll malt, quherof I grant the reseat, renuncand all exceptounes in the contrar.

Thairffor wit ye me to have exonered, quytclamed and simpliciter discharged, lyk as I be thir presents for me, my aires, executors and

succssors, exoners, quytclames and simpliciter discharghes the said Mr
Mathew, his aires, executors and succssors of the samyn for ever.

19. *Agreement for the construction of a dovecot at Nether Liberton, Midlothian:*
made at Liberton, 19 April 1680 (Dal. warrant no. 608, registered 1681).

Alexander Gilmour of Craigmiller [and] Patrick Huntar, mason in
Edinburgh.

The said Patrick Huntar binds and obleidges him, his airs and
successors, to build ane doucat to the said Alexander Gilmoure upon
the ground of his lands of Natherlibbertoun, in that yaird therof
presentlie possest be George Peacock elder, and which doucat shall be
of the dementione and forme following, to witt: ane double doucat
with ane wall in the midle therof and tuo ston hewen enteries, four
cornerd, all hewen corners being in lenth threttie sex foot and in breith
nyntein foott over the walls, the back wall therof being tuentie sex foot
hight and the foorwall fyftein foot.

And to mak the samyne ane sufficient doucat as to the mason work
efter the forme, paterne, and als good as Mortounhall doucat.

And als to tak doun the said Alexander Gilmoure his old doucat
standing upon the place.

And for that effect to furnish workmen for building of the said
masone work and taking doun of the said old doucat, upon his own
proper charges.

And which work he obleidges him to compleit betuixt the dait heirof
and the first day of September nixt to come.

And on the other pairt the said Alexander Gilmoure binds and
obleidges him, upon his own proper charges, to furnish all materialls
for building of the said doucat, as ston, lyme, sand, skaftling and others
convenient therto, and to cause lay the samyne upon the said ground,
and what shall be found necessar over and above the stons of the old
doucat alreadie upon the ground.

And als to mak payment to the said Patrick Huntar of the soume of
thrie hundreth and fyftie merks Scots money for his and his workmens
work, at the terms following, to witt: the soume of ane hundreth
pounds Scots therof at Witsonday nixt to come; and the soume of tuo
hundreth merks in compleit payment imediatlie efter the compleiting
of the said work.

And which soume is in satisfactione of the said workmanship and all other dewes relaiting therto.

And both pairties obleidges them to fulfill the premisses to others, and the pairtie failyier to pay to the pairtie observer the soume of ane hundreth merks, by and attoure the fulfilling of the premisses.

20. *Contract for the erection of a bridge over the river Clyde at Littlegill, near Abington, Lanarkshire: made at Edinburgh and (blank), 30 March and (blank) April 1682 (Mack. warrant no. 1336, registered 1682).*

William Baillie of Litlegill [and] Robert Mylne of Balfarge, His Majesty's Master-mason.

The said Robert Mylne, for the sowme of money wnderwriten to be payed to him as followes, binds and obleidges him, his aires, executors, intromittores with his lands, rents, goods, gear and successores whatsomever, to found, build and erect ane bridge over and wpon the watter of Clyd, at that pairt theroff wher the rock and craige commonly called Ramellweill Craiges are situat.

Which bridge is to consist of ane arch of fourtie fyve foot day light fifteen foot bread betwixt sumer and sumer, and thirtie two foot from the bottome of the runing of the water to the tope of the bridge, and is all to be wrowght and done in substantiall aistler work in landstaills, arch and raile therof: the landstaill runing back one each syde twentie foot and of aistler work as said is: and the haill soliditie of the worke of this bridge to be made up off solid stone and lyme, and to calsay the same the lenth of ane hundred foot.

And lykwayes to build ane ledgement, one each syde, cut in the tope with a semicircle, thrie foot above the said calsay, myttered each joynt to ane other, which thrie foot is included in the former thirty two foot.

Lykas the said Robert Mylne binds and obleidges him and his forsaids be thir presents to build and erect upon the midle of the said bridge, or at either end, two pillasters for ane raised gate or chainyie to stope the passadge at the said bridge: the said William Baillie furnishing iron and lead therto.

As also the said Robert Mylne hearby binds and obleidges him and his forsaids to build, fownd and erect ane houss off two storie height for a change at the west end of the bridge, consisting of fourtie foot of lenth and eighteen foot within the waalls, and thirteen foot from the

foundatione to the levelling for the cowples, with a scale stair to the first storie without the said howse: which house is to have therein two hewen dorres only, with sex hewen windowes and four hewen chimneyes.

And in lyke maner the said Robert Mylne binds and obleidges him and his forsaids to furnish all timber, short and longe, for the use of the forsaid bridge alanerlie, and to transport the same to the place upon his own proper charges and expensses.

And to enter to the building of the bridge and house betwixt and the tenth day of the said moneth of Apryll, and finish and perfyte the same in the massone worke compleitly betwixt the day and date hearoff and the terme of Mertmes nixt to come in this instant year of God 1600 fourscor two yeares, but longer delay.

And heirunto the said Robert Mylne binds and obleidges him and his forsaids in the most sure and ample forme that cane be devysed.

And in caice it happen him to failyie in perfyting of the said bridge and house betwixt and the terme above mentioned, in that caice he by thir presents binds and obleidges him and his forsaids to content and pay to the said William Baillie, his aires or assigneyes, the soume of thriescor pounds sterleing money forsaid, as liquidat expensses, damnadge and intrest to be susteined ther anent, by and attowr the perfyting of the said work in maner abovewritten.

Lykas at the ending and perfyting of the samen work the said Robert Mylne binds and obleidges him and his abovewritten by thir presents to delyver to the said William Baillie, or any others in his name, the haill timber to be made use for building of the said bridge: in leiw and compensatione wharof the said William shall be obleidged, and be thir presents binds and obleidges him and his eftermentioned, to fornish and provyde to the said Robert ane qwelified wreight, as also to furnish nailes to the said work wpon his own proper charges and expensses.

And on the other pairt the said William Baillie of Litlegill be the tenor hearof faithfullie binds and obleidges him, his aires, executors, intromitters with his lands, rents, goods, gear and successores whatsomever, to make good and thankfull payment to the said Robert Mylne, his aires, executors or assigneyes, of all and haill the sowme of thrie hundred pownds good and usewall money of England, with four chalders good and sufficent oat meall, with twentie wedders wnder the wooll, in maner and at the termes following, viz: the sowme of fiftie

pownd sterleing money forsaid, quhich the said William Baillie hes instantlie advanced to the said Robert Mylne at the subscriveing hearof, and quherof the said Robert grants the recept and for him and his forsaids discharges the said William Baillie therof for now and ever; and the lyke sowme of fiftie pownd sterleing money forsaid betwixt and the first day of Jullii nixt to come in this instant year of God 1600 fourscor and two yeares; and the sowme of ane hundred pownd sterleing money forsaid wpon the compleiting of the landstaills for the arche; and the lyke sowme of ane hundred pownd sterleing money abovewritten, in compleat payment of the said haill principall sowme of thrie hundred pownds sterleing money forsaid, at the finishing and compleating of the said haill work.

And in caice that the said William Baillie and his forsaids shall failyie in payment of the said last hundred pownd sterleing at the finishing of the said work, in that caice he as principall and with him [blank] who be the tenor hearof becomes caationr, souertie and full debtor for and with him, faithfullie binds and obleidges them and ilk ane of them, conjunctlie and severallie, ther aires, executors, intromittores with ther lands, rents, goods, geir, and successores whatsomever, to make good and thankfull payment to the said Robert Mylne and his forsaids of the said sowme of ane hundreth pownd sterleing money forsaid, within the space of two full yeirs nixt efter the finishing and perfyting of the said haill work abovewritten, with the dew and ordinar annualrent theroff, conforme to the Act of Parlament, fra the tyme of the finishing of the samen work wntill the compleit payment theroff.

And sicklyke the said William Baillie be thir presents binds and obleidges him and his forsaids to make payment and delyverence to the said Robert Mylne and his forsaids of the said four chalders oat meill and twentie wedders, in maner and at the tymes following, viz: ane chalder and ane half of the said victuall with the said twentie wedders att and upon the first day of June nixt to come in this instant yeir of God; and ane other chalder and a halfe thairof at and upon the first day of August also nixt to come; and the last chalder thairoff, in compleit payment of the same, att the finishing and compleiting of the said work.

And farder the said William Baillie be thir presents binds and obleidges them [sic] and his forsaids to furnish to the said Robert Mylne and his forsaids ane sufficent dry qwarrie for wining of stone for the said

bridge allanerly, quhich the said Robert is to winn wpon his own proper charges and expensses.

And the said William heirby obleidges him and his forsaids to winn the stones for the forsaid houss himselfe, and to carrie and transport the same, with the haill sand, lyme, stone and water necessar for the said bridge, to the place forsaid wher the same is to be built, upon his own proper charges and expensses.

And lykwayes to delyver to the said Robert the haill stones, hewen and unhewen, for advancement of the said work, lying aither at the place or qwarrie, and to transport the samen in maner forsaid.

And lykwayes the said William Baillie be the tenor hearof binds and obleidges him and his abovewritten to provyde the said Robert ane sufficent chamber for his comeing and goeing to the forsaid work, with ane houss neir the place for his servents to ly inn, they allwayes furnishing them selfes beds, meat, drink and other furnitor for themselves, upon ther own charges and expensses.

And failyieing of the fulfilling of any of the said William Baillie his obleidgements abovewritten heirin conteined, in that caice he be thir presents binds and obleidges him and his forsaids to content and pay to the said Robert Mylne and his forsaids the sowme of ten pownd sterleing money forsaid as liquidat expensses, damnadge and intrest, presentlie modified and agried upon, to be susteined be them theranent for ilk failyie therof, by and attour performance and fullfilling the samen.

And finallie the said William Baillie be tenor heirof binds and obleidges him and his forsaids to warrand, frie, releive and skaithles keep the said [blank] his cautioner abovenamed and his forsaids of ther cautionrie above written heirin contained, and of all and fra all payment of the sowmes of money abovespecifiet wherfor they stand obleidged for him in maner abovementioned: and off all and fra all losse, skaith, damnadge and expensses they shall happen to sustein or incurr ther throw, in any maner of way at all hands and against all deidlie as law will.[3]

21. *Indenture for the reconstruction of Logie Church, Stirlingshire: made at (blank), (blank) 1684 (Mack. warrant no. 356, registered 1687).*

George Stirling of Herbertsheir, John and Mr John Keiries of Gogar for

[3] This contract has previously been printed by R.S. Mylne in *The Master Masons to the Crown of Scotland* (Edinburgh, 1893), 221ff.

themselves and in the name of the Earle of Mar for his lordship's lands within the parish of Logie, James Steivnsonson [sic] of Spitall, Alexander Christie, merchant in Stirling, for the laird of Blair, John Christie, portioner of Coarntoun for his own interest and the feuar of Coarntoune, and John Wordie of Torbrex for the laird of Hoptoune his lands of Aithray within the said parish, persons appointed by the visitation of the church of Logie kept at the said church the [blank] day of February last, and the rest of the heritors of the said parish, to settle and agree with workmen for re-edifying and building of the said church of Logie [and] Tobias Bachop, mason in Alloway [Alloa].

The said Tobias Bachop, for the causes afterspecifiet, binds and obleidges him, his airs, executors, successors and intrometters with his goods and geir whatsomever, to take doune the said kirk, both walls, skaillie, ruffe and timber, and read the ground therof sufficientlie, and to rebuild the samen of new againe, conforme to ane draught drawen be the said Tobias himself and depositat in the hands of the said James Steinsone till the said work be perfected, in walls, hight, bread and leanth, windowes, doors, ruffs, theicking, glasing, glassbands and other necessars.

And to make steicked and lockfast doors conforme to the said draught.

And to putt one ane new rooff one the said church, of good and sufficient double sparrs of threttie couple, and ane bake laigh to everie couple of double sparrs, and ane high of single sparrs, sark the same with new dealls and theick it sufficientlie with skaillie, and the place for hinging of the bell conforme, and to furnish, buy and pey for the said timber, skaillie, lyme, nails, and all other necessars for rebuilding of the said church, ridle the sand and winn al the stones neidfull for rebuilding therof, putting wp the said windowes with glass, glassbands, making the doors, hinging the samen sufficientlie with crooks, bands and others necessars belonging therto, and to doe everie thing for perfecting and rebuilding the said church in maner abovexprest.

And to rebuild, perfyt and compleit the said work betuixt and the first day of August nixt to come.

For the whilkes causes abovwritten the saids George Stirling, John and Mr John Keiries, James Steivinson, Allexander Christison, John

Christison and John Wordie, for themselves and takand burding in and wpon them in maner forsaid, binds and obleidges them, ther airs and successors, to content, pey and deliver to the said Tobias Bachop the soume of ane thousand fyve hundereth and fiftie merks Scotts money at and again the terme of Wheitsonday nixt to come.

And shall cause the tennants, possessors and wthers within the said parish lead and carie to him the said timber from Stirling, Alloway, or the Maner Neock, and the lyme from the Maner Neock or Suallihall Glen, the skaillie from the Skaillie Craig, and lead and carie the heall sand, hewen stone and other stones neidfull to the said work, where the samen may be most convenientlie hade near to the said church, wpon advertisment when he stands in nead of any of the saids necessars to be given to him to the said John Christison who is appoynted overseer therto.

And the said Tobias Bachop, for the better performance of his pairt of the premisses, hes found the said Mr John Keirie cautioner and souertie for him and his forsaids as cautioner and souertie for him for that effect.

And the said Mr John Keirie binds and obleidges him and his forsaids as cautioner and souertie for the said Tobias that he shall perfyt and compleit the said work, in maner abovexprest, again the said first day of August nixt.

And both pairties and cautioner forsaid binds and obleidges them and ther forsaids to performe the heall premisses to others, wnder the paine of thrie hundereth merks money forsaid as ane liquidat soume, modified of ther oun consent, to be peyed be the pairtie failyier to the pairtie observer and keeper of ther pairts of the same in the heall heads, articles, and conditions abovspecified, and that by and attour the doing therof.

And the said Tobias Bachop binds and obleidges him and his forsaids to frieth, releive and skaithless keep the said Mr John Keirie and his forsaids of ther cautionrie and souertie abovwreaten, and of all coast, skaith, damnadge and expenses that they shall sustaine or incurr therthrow any maner of way.

22. *Contract for the erection of a summerhouse at Prestonhall, Midlothian: made at Prestonhall, 24 October 1684 (Mack. warrant no. 1021, registered 1686).*

Mr Rorie Mkenzie of Prestonhall [and] Hugh Kirkland, mason in Portsburgh.

The said Hugh Kirkland binds and obleidges him, betuixt and the first of August next 1600 and eightie five years, to build a summerhous on the northeast corner of the yaird dyke of Prestonhall of tuo storie hight, the first storie being eight foot high below the floor, and the second storie nyn foot high of wall, of which summerhous the south syd and eastend ar to be uale heughen worke.

The first storie haveing a door on the west gavell, thrie foot wyd and six foot high, and tuo windous to the south, each tuo foot and nyn inches wyd and five foot and six inches high.

The second storie to have a door in the midle of the south syd, thrie foot wyd and six foot high, and on each syde of the door a window tuo foot and nyn inches wyd and five foot and ane halfe high, with a window on each gavele of the [said] bread and hight raised with stormonds.

As lykewys to build a scale stair up to the said door consisting of sixteen steps, each halfe ane foot high and five foot longe, with ane hinging botle with pillesters and ballesters upon the said stair and plat on the head of the stair to the number of fourtie with bass and rale.

And on the other pairt the said Mr Rorie binds and obleidges him, his airs and successors, to pay to the said Hugh Kirkfield for building of the summerhouse and stair, as said is, all and haill the soume of thrie hundereth merks Scots, the said summerhous being alwys tuentie foot long and tuelve foot wid within walls: as lykwys tuo bolls of oatmeall.

And halfe of the price to be payed when the house is geast hight, and the other halfe when it is ended.

And both pairties obleidges themselves to performe the premisses, under the failyie of fourtie punds Scots, by and attour performance.

23. *Contract for the erection of a house at Leys, Kincardineshire: made at Leys, 15 May 1686 (Mack. warrant no. 1048, registered 1686).*

The laird of Leyis [Sir Thomas Burnett] [and] Francis Rosse, mason.

The said Francis Ross bynds and oblidges hime to build ane house of three storie hight, and to hew the ston work therof, to bynde the roofe and to sark the samen with dales: heirby oblidging himselfe to enter to

his work the first of Jully in this instant yeare, and to perfect the said house against the last of August 1600 and eightie six.

As also the laird of Leyis is heirby bound and lykwyse bynds and oblisses himselfe to pay to the said Francis Rosse tenne pound Scots and ane bolle of meale for ilke roode of work, and fyve shilling six pennies for ilke foot of hewen stone, and eighteine shilling Scotts for each couple, and his morning drink and four houres to hime and his men.

Lykuyse the laird of Leyis is to furnish hime with barowmen to giwe stons and morter, and to giwe hime ready service uthrwayes, to pay hime wages quhen he keepes hime idle, either for wont of such materials as are fitt for the work or men to serve hime.

And sicklyk it is heirby declaired that if the said Francis shall leave the work, except in caice of sicknes, he shall be lyable to the laird of Leyis for his oune and all his mens wages that workes at the work with hime, and that ay and sua longe as he stayes from it after the tyme of entrie theirto abovespecifiet.

And both pairties are to stand to this condescendence and agreement under the failyie of two hundereth merkes, which the pairtie breaker must paye to the pairtie observer and willing to observe.

24. *Contract for the erection of a house at Invermay, Perthshire: made at Invermay, 19 May 1686 (Dal. warrant no. 879, registered 1686).*

The Lairds of Innermay Elder and younger [James and David Drummond] [and] John Craigie of Dumbarnie.

Imprimis John Craigie of Dumbarnie binds and obleidges him, his airs, executors and successors, to edifie and build ane good and sufficient double house of fourtie eight foots of lentgh and thrittie six foot of breadth, or less ass the contriver underwritten shall think fitt.

The said house having a mid wall, and the chimneys and closetts upon the first, second and thride stories to be placed at Innermays pleasure, with three vaults in the neathermost storie, viz: the kitching with ane ovin in the chimney thereof, with the cellar and ladener, with garretts above the thride storie: the first, second and thride stories to be sufficientlie plaistered with wall plates quher is necessar, the vaulted roumes only excepted.

The said house, in breadth, height and lentgh, is to be built at the expensses of John Craigie of Dumbarnie and divided [sic] and contrived

be Sir William Bruce of Kinross or [blank: Robert?] Mill architector, or any other relevant architector that the laird shall think fitt.

The forsaid house is to be roofed, theiked with skaillie, sarked with deals, rigging, stoned, jeasted and lofted, the whole windows glassed, caised and broaded with oak, the first and second stories to be sufficientlie stenchered with iron.

The whole house having such doors, windows, chimneys, locks, keyes and passing snackes for the haill chambers and closetts and other doors necessar, togither also with such sufficient and fasshionable scail stairs and others as is necessar for the said house.

As also the said John Craigie binds and obleidges him to throw doune the houses on the north and south sides of the close, and to furnish the whole casters doune and cariage men in meat and drink as is usuall.

Item, the house is to be extended six foot furder to the lentgh, if the Contriver shall think necessar.

For the whilks causes the lairds of Innermay, elder and younger, binds and obleidges them, there airs, executors and successors, to pay to the said John Craigie of Dumbarnie, his airs, executors or assigneys, the soume of tuo thousand and five hundreth merks Scots money, with ane chalder of meall, viz: five hundreth merks Scots from the old laird, and the soume of tuo thousand merks Scots and ane chalder of meal from the young laird, payable at the termes underwritten, viz: ane thride pairt of the whole money and victual abovewritten at and against the first day of July 1686, which is declaired to be his entrie and begining of the said work; and ane other thride pairt at Candlemess 1600 and eightie seven; and the last thride pairt, in full and compleit payment, at and against the the [sic] terme of Lambas 1600 and eightie seven.

Att and again the which terme the said John Craigie and his forsaids are hereby obleidged to build, end and perfite the said house in maner forsaid, he having always the whole houses in the north and south sides of the closs (the insight, moveable houshold plenishing being excepted) to be disposed be him at his pleasure.

As also he hes to have ane days work of ane hundreth and twenty men from the said laird of Innermay for casting doune of the forsaids houses, with the cariage of the whole lime, stone, timber, skaillie, rigging, stone and iron what is necessar more then the old houses above disponed can affoord.

The carrage of the timber being only from the bridge of Ern and the

L

stones from Innermays ordinar quarrie: the lime from the Lomonds or Pitlessie, or any other place nearer if it can be had: the iron from Perth or the bridge of Ern, and skaillie from Logiealmond or any other craige quher the Laird of Innermay shall gett ine [sic] quarrie libertie.

As also the Lairds of Innermay, elder and younger, dispones to the said John Craigie and his forsaids the firr trees growing on the west forgainst the stable doors, being of the number of twenty one trees or thereby, the expenssis of the said additionall six foot to be referred to the contriver and the Lady [sc. Laird?] and in caice of variance the laird of Orchell as oversman.

This above written minute is to be extended in ample form betwixt and the fifteenth day of June.

And both pairties binds and obleidges them and ther forsaids hinc inde to others, for the performance of the haill premisses, under the pain of five hundreth merks Scots in caice of faylie, by and attour the fullfilling of the premisses.

25. *Contract for leadwork and waterworks at Drumlanrig Castle, Dumfries-shire: made at Drumlanrig, 6 November 1686 (Mack. warrant no. 877, registered 1690).*

William Lukup [and] William Waldhave, plumber.

The said William Waldhave plumber binds and oblidges him to cast leid and cover the north quarter and north west tour and the thrie torrets on the tope of it, and to mak and put wpe all pypes and sistrens to carie away the watter from the rooffes of the north quarter and tour, conform to thes that is allredy mad, and in the sam form and fasion everie way.

As allso the said William Waldhave binds and oblidges him to cast and cover with leid a cloak hous or cupillo above the entrie on the north quarter sufficiently with leid, as shall be ordered and as the said William Lukup is oblidged to cover it in his contrack, and to tak aff the leid rooffe aff the north east turnpyk and put it on againe, conform to the other turnpyks that he hes doone all redy on the other syd of the court.

As allso he oblidges him to cast and cover suficiently with leid the sixe pavillions with bellcast roofs, conform to ther proporsions, and to put wp scaffolds for them and all other leid work that he is oblidged to doe, in and about the castell of Drumlanrig.

As allso the said William Waldhave binds and oblidges him to cast and lay all the pyps for bringing in the watter from a great sistren above the Horss Know, and to order the bringing in the watter to it from all the springs about Auchenskrigh and Castell Hill (be advice only), and to carie the watter from that sisteren to another sisteren on the wnder syd of the Horss Know, and from that to the gardein, wher he is to mak a clanging coke, and from that the said William Waldhave is to carie the watter throw the gardeins and courts and stavells and geats, and to carie the said watter to the inner court to on or twa sisterens ther, and to mak them spring handsomly ther, and to carie the said watter throw all the said office houses that the said William Lukup is oblidged to in his contrack.

And the said William Waldhave obliges him to cast allsmany leid paisses as will serve all the chess windows in the castell, as allso he is to furnish all soudder for the haille forsaid leid work, and that on his own charges and expence.

As allso he is to furnish all sorts of brass coaks and all sort of moulds for casting all sorts of pyps for the watter works for the haill watter works [sic] above mensioned, and to furnish labourers for himself during the holle work on his own charges.

And feinily he is to doe all mainer of leid work sufficently everie way as the said William Lukup stands obliged in his last contrack with his grace the duke of Queinsberrie, and conform to the synd draughts, and that at the sight of Mr James Smith or any his Grace is pleased to apoynt for survaying the said work.

And the said William Waldhave obliges him to perfyt this and what he is to doe of the last contrack for the south and west quarters.

And for the said work the said William Lukup is to pay to the said William Waldhave the sowme of ane hundereth pownds sterling, wher of he is to have in hand the sowme of fyfein pown sterling, and is discharged in this present contrack, and the rest proporsionally as the work goes on; allway the said William Lukup is to keipe in his own hand tuentie pound sterling till the haill work be finished and compleit.

And the said William Lukup is to furnish to the said William Waldhave all leid and coalls for casting or smelting of it, and timber for scaffolding and naills therto, and all measons work for the watter works and others, and to help to carie the webe leid to the rooffes and the pyps

to the watter works, and cast or ditch the said ground for the haill watter work.

And the said William Waldhave oblidges him to perfyt all this above said work, and that betwixt this and the first of November 1600 and eighty and nyne years, and that wnder the peneltie of tuentie pounds sterling, to be payd be the pairtie breaker to the pairtie observer or willing to observe.

26. *Contract for the completion and purchase of a flat in Mylne's Square, High Street, Edinburgh: made at Edinburgh, 6 April 1688 (Dal. warrant no. 556, registered 1688).*

Mr William Cunningham, younger, of Enterkine, and Mistris Kathrin Hamiltoun, his lady [and] Robert Milne of Balfarg, His Majesty's Master-mason, and Androw Patersone, wright, burgess of Edinburgh.

Forsameikleas the said Robert Milne hes bought and acquired the right of the two tenements of land lyand upon the north syde of the High Streit of Edinburgh over against the Tron Church at the heid of Sclaitters Closs, lately belonging to Alexander Hamiltoun late baillie of the said burgh, and hes demolished the samen and is rebuilding them in the front with polished aisler stone work consisting in lenth of fourtie foot of measure within the walls east and west to the front, and twenty foot of breadth to the midle wall and nyne foot hight betuixt floor and plaister, haveing ane midle wall for chimneys of three foot breadth, and benorth the said midle wall eightein foot breadth and twenty four foot long within walls, which faces to the north to ane large court.

Therfore and for the caussis aftermentioned, the said Robert Milne binds and oblidges him, his airs and successors, to purshass and obtaine valid and sufficient dispositiones and rights to the saids tuo tenements of land in his favours, bearing procuratories of resignatione, absolut warrandice and all other claussis requisit in due and compitent forme.

And obtaine himself infeft in the samen old tenements and new building erecting theron, and the right therof legallie established in his persone.

And the said Robert Milne binds and oblidges him and his forsaids to carie on and compleit the forsaid fabrick, the front quherof of polished aisler of compitent thicknes and the back work nixt to the court of good-roch massone work of two foots and ane half thicknes, each storie

of which fabrick is to consist in lenth, breadth and hight as is above mentioned.

And the entry to the samen is to be in the midle of the said fourtie foot by ane pavemented walk of six foot breidth and fourtie eight foot long, levell with the High Streit, off the east syde quherof, to the north of the midle wall, ther is ane entrie to ane handsome scalestair consisting of four foot goeing by tuo scails and two plats to the first storie, and so to continow on to the second, third and fourth stories above stairs: the steps of quhich scalestair consists of four foots in lenth within the walls, six inshes thick and thertein inches broad, haveing stone plaits, and each plate haveing ane handsome hungbotle weill polished turneing scale-wayes, and each plait nixt to the court haveing tuo large lights to be weill glassed in so far as the entry belongs to the said fourth storie, with ane double jamm betuixt them of hewen work, and the entry to the sellars is to be by the foot of the said scailstairs.

And into which fabrick or new building the said Mr Wm. Cuninghame is to have the fourth storie within the scaile stairs above the shops and cellars, being the fyfth storie above the ground.

And the said Robert Milne binds and oblidges him to build and compleit the samen in stone work, and furnish therunto all stones great and small, lyme, sand, watter, and other necessars for the said stone building, upon his oune expenssis.

And quhich fourth storie is to containe fyve roumes, one of them dark, as follows, viz: the entrie therto to be from the said scale stairs by two dores, one going foreward, and the other turneing to the west from the scalestair.

And to enter by the forsaid dore forward to ane litle lobie of five foot square, from which ther is to be ane roume of twenty foot long south and north, and fyftein foot breadth east and west, which roume is to have ane concave chimney in the midle wall of three foots day light, with two windows to the High Streit, each of them five foot hight and three foot broad, from which roume ther is to be ane bedchamber to the east of thertein foot long and fyftein foot broad, with ane litle closset to the north therof and ane small window to the scalestair, which chamber is to have ane hansome concave chimney and two windows to the streit of the hight and bredth forsaid.

As also to the west of the said large roume ther is to be ane other bed chamber of twelve foot broad and fyftein foot long with ane concave

chimney to the west and tuo windows to the streit, of the hight and bread of the former.

And sicklyke on the north ther is to be ane other chamber of fyftein foot long and thertein foot broad with ane concave chimney in the west gavell therof, with tuo windowes to the north of the hight and breidth forsaid, togither with ane dark roume which intercepts betuixt the westmost fore chamer and bedchamber to the north, with ane chimney in the west gavell therof.

And lykewayes ane kitching lying nixt to the scailestairs, of eight foot wyde and fyftein foot long, with ane large pended chimney therin on the east gavill of six foot day-light and tuo foot and ane half betuixt back and bossome, and ane window to the north with ane pantrie of three foots which interveins betuixt the kitching and bed chamber.

And the said Robert Milne binds and oblidges him to carie up all the chimney heids ten foot above the roof and kape the samen with hewen kape, and make the chimneys good and sufficient work of ane foot and ane half at the lintilling betuixt the back and bosome.

And build the haill forsaids chimneys with fashonable concaved jamms and hansome stone moulding on the jamms and lintills (except the kitching and dark roume).

And to lay the haill hearthstones both of the kitching and other chimneys with sufficient polished pavement, all levell with the floors.

As also the said Mr Wm. Cuninghame is to have ane cellar beneath the court of [blank] foots of breadth and lenth.

And when the said court is to be calsayed, the said Robert Milne binds and oblidges him to put ane iron-grate for the light of the said cellar, fyftein inshes square.

And sicklyke the said Mr William Cuninghame is to have ane pass key to the platforme, for quhich he is to mentaine his proportion of the lead with the rest of the heritors, and the said Robert Milne and the rest of the acquirers is to oblidge themselves to mentaine ther pairts of the samen roof, effeiring to ther respective proportiones.

And the said Robert Milne binds and oblidges him to erect ane batlement of aisler-work round about the said plateforme and roof of the haill lodgeing.

And the said Robert Milne binds and oblidges him to make ane studie, with ane squant light to the forestreit, in the south west corner of the forsaid westmost fore chamber.

And finish and compleit the said stone work and lay the batts, alse many as shall be fund convenient, with hewen dores and windowes.

And that betuixt the date heirof and the terme of Mertimis nixttocome, and that under the penaltie of two hundereth merks Scots money in the caice of failyie, to be payed to the said Mr Wm. Cuninghame by and attour performance of the premisses.

And inlykemaner the said Robert Milne binds and oblidges him and his forsaids to make, subscrive and deliver to and in favours of the said Mr William Cunnghame and his said Lady, his airs or assigneys, ane valid and sufficient dispositione of the forsaid fourth storie above the chops, being the fyfth from the ground, consisting of the roumes abovementioned with the cellar abovespecified, containing procuratories of resignatione with other claussis requisit and absolut warrandice, and that whensoever the said Robert Milne shall be required therto.

And to purchass and procure ane sufficient progress of originall wryts of the saids tuo tenements, and therafter to deliver the samen at the sight and be the speciall advice of the said Mr William Cuninghame and consent of the most part of the other persones who hes acquired or who shall acquire right to the other stories, to any one the saids acquirers shall nominat and elect to have the keeping of the saids originall wryts, and that at the subscriveing of the forsaid dispositione, the receivers of the saids originall wryts allwayes subscriveing and delivering to ilk ane of the saids acquirers ane inventar therof containing ane oblidgement to give authentick transumpts of the samen, and that upon the said Mr William Cuningham and other acquirers ther proper charges and expenssis.

And to make the saids originall wryts furthcomeing to the saids acquirers or other of them wher the transumpts therof shall not prove sufficient, upon the requirers oblidgements for redeliverie to the persone nominat and elected for keeping therof.

And sicklyke the said Andrew Patersone binds and oblidges him, his airs, executors and successors, to furnish and work the haill wright work of the forsaid fourth storie and cellar, and jest and roof the samen storie, and furnish therunto good and sufficient fourtein ell-trees in the fore and back pairts therof.

And to place the saids jests within tuelve inches of one another, and

furnish good and sufficent weill seasoned daills, and other timber, for floreing, lathing, dores, and windowes.

And to lath and plaister the haill roofs and partitiones on both syds, and to put up the saids partitiones with wall plaits and washing boards, daill broad, alse weill about the stone walls as the plaistered devisiones, in what place the said Mr William Cuningham shall disyre, not exceeding the roumes abovementioned, conforme to ane draught therof subscrivit be both parties of the date heirof.

And to floor all the roumes sufficiently with broken-joynt-flooring, and to plaister the saids haill roumes sufficently with plain plaister, and put ane handsome cornish round in the principall roumes and ane litle gaula in the kitching and dark roume, and furnish all lyme, hair, timber, naills and other necessars for jesting, floreing and plaistering as said is.

And sicklyke to furnish and put up the haill glass windowes in caises and caisements, weill bund, of compitent thicknes, of weill seasoned wainscot, and sufficent bands, slots, snecks, and rings therto in the haill roumes, and glass the haill windows with good new Inglish glass, both for high windows and casements, with glasbands of wainscot.

And to make and furnish weill bund dores in each roume of the said storie (except the kitching, dark-roume and pantrie), with two strong double dores upon the entries and ane dore to the cellar.

And he binds and oblidges him to furnish the locks and keys to the utter dores and cellar with slots, snecks, and calls, the best lock therof not within four pund Scots, and the cellar dore eightein shilling Scots, and lykewayes to hing all the dores of the house and cellar with sufficient cruicks and bands (all lyning, pass locks and pass keys being expressly excepted).

Which haill work the said Androw Patersone binds and oblidges him to finish and compleit to the said Mr William Cuningham and his forsaids, and deliver the keys therof to him, betuixt the date heirof and the terme of Whytsonday 1600 and eightie nyne years, under the penaltie of two hundereth merks money forsaid to be payed be him to the said Mr Wm. Cuningham and his forsaids in caice of failye, by and attour the performance heirof.

For the which caussis the said Mr William Cunnhame [and] his said spouse as factrix as principalls, and [blank] as cautioner, bind and oblidge them, conjunctlie and severallie, ther airs, executors, success-ors and intromitters whatsomever, thankfully to content and pay to the

said Robert Milne and Androw Patersone, ther airs, executors or assigneys, the soume of six thousand merks Scots money as the agreed worth and pryce of the forsaid fourth storie, and that in maner and att the termes following, viz: the soume of four thousand merks therof at the terme of Whytsonday nixttocome, and the soume of two thousand merks, in compleit payment of the forsaid principall soume, att the finishing of the haill work abovewrytten and deliverie of the keyes of the said fourth storie: with the soume of five hundereth merks money abovementioned of liquidate expenssis for ilk one of the saids termes failyies, and annualrent of the saids two moyeties so long as the samen shall happen to be due after ther respective termes of payment abovespecifeit.

And the said [blank] to warrand, free and releive ther said cautioner and his forsaids of his cautionrie in the premissis, and of all coast, skaith and damnage he shall happen to sustaine or incurr therthrow in any maner of way.

27. *Contract for the demolition of the old hall of Closeburn, Dumfriesshire, and for alterations to Closeburn Tower: made at Closeburn, 18 April 1689 (Mack. warrant no. 544, registered 1690).*

Sir Thomas Kirkpatrick of Closeburne, knight and baronet [and] James Alisone, mason, indweller in Keir-moss, and Alexander Cooke in Clonegaite of Glencairne, wright, in the sheriffdom of Nethsdaile.

The said James Alisone and Alexander Cooke binds and obleidges them, conjunctlie and severallie, and failying of the one be decease the other survivand, is [sic] to take downe the old hall of Closeburne, timber worke and sklaite therof, with als litle damnage and prejudice to the timber and sklaite therof as is possible by airt and industrie.

And lykewayes to build, putt up and perfite ane square battelment round the old tower of Closeburne, conforme to the height, breadeth, and workmanship of the tower of Glencairne pertaining to Sir Robert Lawrie of Maxweltowne.

As also to flagg and cover the said tower and topp vault therof with freithstone, sufficiently wrought, with bond and cover according to the forme of capestone worke, quherby the house may be water and wind-tight.

And lykewayes to raise ane chimney vent upon the south-syde of the said tower, from the middle vault therof to the topp and rooff forsaid, and to raise and cleare the chimneys therof to a sufficient hight for venting, conforme to the caperooffe, and ordinary standard of chimney heads above the rooffe.

And lykewayes to raise the stoneworke of the turnepeick head or jamb of the said tower upon the northe side with two sufficient hewen doores, one therof to goe off the plate of the staire to the battelment, and ane other in to the cape[house] or upermost vault of the said tower, with ane window of hewen stone adjoyning to the said turnepeick head or jamb for giving light to the cape-house or uppermost vault, and a litle slittwindow upon the head of the turnepeickstaire to give light downewards, with a sufficient plateforme of freithstones and spoutestones round the said house and tower for carying of the water from the cope rooffe and off the said house.

Whilk worke forsaid, both in downetaking and upputting therof, the forsaid James Alisone and Alexander Cooke binds and obleidges them, conjunctlie and severallie, and failying be decease of the one, the surviver or longest liver, to performe, perfite and end the said worke betwixt the daite hereof and the last day of October nixt in the instant yeare of God 1600 and eightie nyne yeares, and that sufficiently and honestly wrought to the said Sir Thomas his contentment, and that be the sight of two judicious workemen to be chosen be him for that effect.

For the whilke cause, and for compleating and perfyting the said worke, the said Sir Thomas Kirkpatrick binds and obleidges him, his aires and successors, to pay to the said James Alisone and Alexander Cooke aequallie betwixt them, and failying be decease of the one to the other, the sowme of three hundreth and twentieth markes Scotts money with ane boll of sufficient oatmeall, measure of Neith, and that according to the advancement and progresse of the forsaid worke; the last part and moyetie of the forsaid sowme and victuall to be payed at the ending and perfyting of the forsaid worke.

And further the said Sir Thomas binds and obleidges him to lay in, cause lead and carry stone from the quarries, lyme and other materialls to the said house and tower of Closeburne for performing of the said worke, as the workemen shall require.

And the said James Alisone and Alexander Cooke are to furnish all

necessary workers therto, except quhat helpe the said Sir Thomas shall make to them of his free will upon urgent occassiones.

To all and sundrie the premises both parties obleidges them to others hinc inde, and the partie failyier to pay to the partie observer the sowme of ane hundreth markes money forsaid, by and attour fullfilling of the premisses.

GLOSSARY

aisler, aistler, archler, eixzlyr ashlar, building stone cut into rectangular blocks and tooled on the external face. The terms 'single ashlar' and 'double ashlar' were commonly used to distinguish standard blocks of different sizes

bake laich and ... *high* low and high balks; the lower and upper collars of a collar-rafter roof (?)

balk wooden beam

ballaster baluster

batt iron batten or bar

bellcast roof roof having a bell-shaped profile

bond and cover overlapping joints (?)

bosome, bossome breast of a chimney, etc

botled wrought with a convex moulding

brander brandreth, timber framework

brig bridge, connecting portion of masonry

broken-joynt flooring flooring in which the boards are so laid that their joints do not appear continuous throughout the length of the floor

brotched work broached work, tooled stonework

call part of a door-catch (?)

calsay pave

chainyie chain

chess window sash-window

chop, chopt shop

clanging coke scouring-cock

coak, coke cock

cornish, kornish cornice

couple, cowple a pair of rafters, or one of a pair

coynyies quoins

daill, dale, deale, deall, dealle plank or board of fir or pine wood

dight planed, to plane

dinted worked, dressed

double house a house two rooms in breadth

eixzlyr see *ashlar*

fogged packed with moss

freatt worke fretwork

freithstone freestone
gaula a moulding of two members, one concave the other convex
gavell, gavill, geavill, geawell gable
geast see *jeast*
geasting joisting
geavill see *gavell*
geawell see *gavell*
globb nailes round-headed nails
grubbed see *secket and grubbed*
halyware wall arcade (?)
heughen hewn
hinging botle, hungbotle a type of convex moulding
housen housing, niche or recess
hungbotle see *hinging botle*
inlaicking leaking
iyill, yll aisle, projecting wing
jame, jam, jamm jamb, wing
jeast, geast, jest, jeaste, jost joist
kaise case, the surrounding wall of a stair
kape cope, coping
kneed bent to an angular shape
kornish see *cornish*
ladener larder
landstaill abutment
leid lead
losen nailes lozenge-headed nails
mouldries mouldings
muillit moulded
mullering moulding
paisse weight for a sash window
parple wall partition wall
peat stone coping stone
pended, pendit arched
pending arch construction, arching
pin turnpyke a spiral staircase having a newel (?)
plat, plait landing of a stair, platform
platforme, pletforme flat roof
raebetts rybats, dressed stones forming the sides of an opening

ramper rampart
red, read to clear
rigging stone ridge stone for a roof
roch massone work unwrought stonework
rucgh stone, ruch stones unwrought stone, stone unsuitable for dressing
sark board
scaillie see *skaillie*
scale stair, scail stair, skaile stare stair composed of one or more straight
    flights
scleat see *sklaitt*
sconce protective screen, shelter
secket and grubbed tongued and grooved
sistren, sisteren cistern
skaffelin, skaftling scaffolding
skaile stare see *scale stair*
skaillie, scaillie a superior quality of blue roofing-slate
sklaitt, scleat, sklaite common roofing-slate
snacke, snyk sneck, door-latch
soll sole, base
soudder solder
squant light an obliquely aligned window (?)
stands upright supports
steicked secure
stenchell stanchion
stenchered stanchioned
stobbs poles, stakes
stok timber framework
storme windowe a window raised above the roof, dormer window
stormonds gable copings, pediments (?)
sumer bedwork of an arch
syllered, sylloured covered, lined with boards
theack to roof
theiked roofed, covered
transe passage
tuolle tool
uale heughen well-hewn
valk mylne walk-mill, fulling-mill
voult, wolt vault

wainscot, wainscote superior quality of timber, usually oak, used for
   panelling, etc
washing board skirting board
webe leid lead sheeting
wolt see *voult*
yll see *iyill*

CORRESPONDENCE RELATING TO MILLBURN TOWER AND ITS GARDEN, 1804-1829

edited by Clare Taylor, PH.D

INTRODUCTION

Millburn Tower, Gogar, eight miles west of Edinburgh, was the home of Sir Robert Liston of Kirkliston. Born in 1742, he became a diplomat, an unusual career for a self-made man, although a good linguist. His wife, Henrietta, was the daughter of Dr Nathaniel Marchant of Antigua; he had trained at Glasgow University, and before 1770 Henrietta came with her brothers to live with a step-uncle, James Jackson, the postmaster of Glasgow. She married Sir Robert over twenty years later. Both were middle-aged, and planned to live on his Millburn estate when he retired.[1]

The Listons married in 1796 before leaving for the United States, where Robert Liston served as British Minister until 1800. They visited Antigua in 1800, by which time their ideas for a new house at Millburn had formed. The American architect, Benjamin Latrobe, submitted a plan for a circular building;[2] but Henrietta's Caribbean journal showed her liking for a picturesque landscape, for 'a fairy castle', 'on a small

[1] For Sir Robert Liston (1742-1836) see *Dictionary of National Biography*; *Gentleman's Magazine*, 1836, ii, 539; E. Wright, 'Robert Liston, second British Minister to the United States', *History Today*, xi, 2 (February 1961), 118-27. For Henrietta Liston (1752-1828) see J.C. Nicholls (ed.), 'Lady Henrietta Liston's journal of Washington's resignation, retirement, and death,' *Pennsylvania Magazine of History and Biography*, xcv, 4 (October 1971), 511-20; B. Perkins, 'A diplomat's wife in Philadelphia: letters of Henrietta Liston, 1796-1800', *William and Mary Quarterly*, 3rd ser., xi, 4 (October 1984), 592-632; V.L. Oliver, *History of the Island of Antigua* (3 vols., London, 1894-9); J.A. Mackay, *The Postal History of Glasgow* (n.p., 1984).
[2] A.A. Tait, 'The American garden at Millburn Tower', *Eighteenth Century Life*, viii, n.s. 2 (January 1983), 84-91. Benjamin Latrobe was regarded as the John Nash of America.

Millburn Tower from the east in 1815, showing the lake (perhaps somewhat idealised). The American garden lay to the north-east, the conservatory and walled garden to the west. The engraving by Brydges is reproduced by courtesy of Mr & Mrs W. Bayard.

scale but enchanting', with *jets d'eau*.[3] This vision became the model for their new home and garden, and owed much to Welsh friends, Thomas and Jane Johnes.[4] The Listons visited Johnes' Gothic mansion, Hafod in Cardiganshire, in 1802 and in 1805. Johnes' wife and Mariamne, their invalid daughter, planted an American garden, and the Listons followed their example, in memory, too, of American friends, including President George Washington. Their first gardener was George Ishmael Parkyns, an Englishman who had worked on Washington's estate.[5]

The policies of Millburn, then as now, were about twenty-seven acres, and included a thatched cottage and working mill. Other features were the south drive to the house, at the end of which Latrobe's circular gatehouse was built; the straight drive from the north, along which a line of beech trees was later planted; and a stone bridge across the burn. Parkyns laid out gravelled paths, and trenches for shrubs, probably at the north end of the garden. There were fruit trees and a kitchen garden at the southern end, later enclosed by a circular wall. Shrubberies and a holly hedge were later planted, and still exist, to link the garden, north to south, in front of the house, and separate it from the park. Liston described his work as 'smoothing the face of nature and embellishing the landscape'; and in the park he planted thousands of trees, refusing to farm lest he fall into debt.[6]

The building of the new house and garden began simultaneously. The Listons were not rich; Liston relied on Coutts the bankers, for his pension was often in arrears, and with a dowry of only £2,000 Mrs Liston was not a major West Indian heiress;[7] but Liston wished to live like a gentleman, and not sink in retirement 'to the level of a Scottish

---

[3] C. Taylor, 'Lady Liston's West Indian journal', *Barbados Museum and Historical Journal*, xxxvii, 4 (1986), 321-36, and xxxviii, 1 (1987), 92-106; or MS 5704.

[4] E. Inglis-Jones, *Peacocks in Paradise* (Shoreham-by-Sea, 1971); *DNB*; C. Hussey, *The Picturesque* (London, 1927); Sir Uvedale Price, *Essays on the Picturesque* (3 vols., London, 1794); M. Clarke & N. Penny (eds.), *The Arrogant Connoisseur: Richard Payne Knight, 1751-1824* (Manchester, 1982). The Liston Papers contain many letters from the Johnes family.

[5] American gardens were fairly common: see Tait, 'The American garden at Millburn Tower,' and A.A. Tait, *The Landscape Garden in Scotland, 1735-1835* (Edinburgh, 1980), 200-01, which gives an account of Parkyns' career. Henrietta described talks with George Washington in her journals, but dismissed his attempts to beautify Mount Vernon as tasteless: MSS.5696-5703. C. Taylor, 'The Liston Papers, 1796-1800' (Microform Academic Publishers, n.d.).

[6] MS 5681 ff. 13, 20.

[7] Thomas Coutts, the banker, wrote often about Liston's pension and Henrietta's dowry.

peasant'.[8] No record exists for the commission given the architect, William Atkinson, for a two-storey tower, built between 1804 and 1806.[9] Letters noted that they were 'ornamenting the cottage and improving the country' in July 1805, and Mrs Liston mentioned 'the slow progress of the tower', saying 'it is not yet time to see Millburn to advantage'; but in 1806 her sister in law, Mary Marchant, wrote from Antigua: 'I am delighted to hear your tower is so nearly being finished and I do not wonder at you having so little inclination to leave it; in my opinion it is one of the most charming places in the world & all day long I wish myself with you to wander about & admire'.[10]

The charm of the tower is still apparent; Atkinson was fashionable in his day, succeeding James Wyatt as architect to the Board of Ordnance. He is best known for designing Sir Walter Scott's home, Abbotsford in Roxburghshire; in 1804 he rebuilt Scone Palace and was asked by the future fourth earl of Rosebery to plan a new house at Dalmeny. This idea was scrapped, possibly because the third earl, known for his parsimony, thought little of him, and noted in a letter to his wife: 'I fancy the Architect, Atkinson I think his name, and who I always thought wanted taste has teazed him [our son] into that Gothic Idea'.[11] Posterity endorsed Lord Rosebery's view, but Atkinson was also the inventor of an efficient form of cement, and advocated a picturesque setting. He must have pleased the Listons by combining the practical with the romantic: the tower at Millburn is elegant, and seen on approach has lightness and grace. Henrietta Liston's enthusiasm for the sublime was tempered by her common sense, and she needed all her diplomatic skills to smooth out the difficulties arising between her husband and his family over money.

The two-storey tower with a single chamber on each flight was the first addition to the thatched cottage. Liston invited the earl of

[8] MS 5621 f. 35.

[9] William Atkinson was an English architect, a pupil of James Wyatt; see J.M. Robinson, *The Wyatts: An Architectural Dynasty* (Oxford, 1979).

[10] MS 5608 ff. 48, 161; 5609 ff. 86, 132; 5610 f. 109.

[11] *Country Life*, 17 August 1989 and 24 August 1989. *Country Life* also ran a feature on the *cottage orné* on 31 August 1989; but the thatched cottage at Millburn was an old farm cottage, not a fashionable retreat, though Liston followed contemporary and royal custom by enlarging his house, as at Royal Lodge, Windsor. For Atkinson's work on Scone and Abbotsfords, see *Country Life*, 11 August 1988, 18 August 1988, and 8 June 1989. At Scone a tower and a wing were added to existing buildings. I am indebted to John Gifford and the staff of *The Buildings of Scotland*, and to the present owners, Walter Scott & Partners, for accounts of the building of Millburn Tower.

Hopetoun to visit in 1809, hoping that he would forgive their simple cottage and admire the new tower.[12] Another building, probably the kitchen, was soon added to the rear of the tower. This caused worry, and was noted as 'smoking away', or causing alarm when wrights built too large a fire near the vents of the tower.[13] The Johnes made a memorable visit in 1809 and it was Thomas Johnes who first used the name, Millburn Tower, in 1807.[14]

The garden proved a social attraction. Parkyns arrived in June 1804 and left early in the following year, his services having cost £100.[15] He deepened the burn at the rear of the house, which helped create an island, used as a sanctuary for ducks and swans. A print of 1815 shows that the artificial lake thus formed gave real elegance, but when Sir Walter Scott visited the garden in 1828 he was critical, as the lake had silted up and become overgrown.[16] Scott preferred a natural landscape retaining the historic features of the country; he disliked walled gardens, and made no comment on the clever planting of trees to hide the house until the visitor was close upon it.

There is no trace today of the American garden, except for a maple and a sumach, and we find few references in the Liston correspondence to plants native to North America, though a list was made, now unfortunately lost.[17] Kalmias and clethras are mentioned; Liston received plants from the East Indies, and japonicas and camellias thrived in such a warm, sheltered spot; whilst mimosas were the glory of the greenhouse. Mrs Liston acquired American plants, 'some for love, some for money'. In 1804 Edward Thornton, who had succeeded Liston as British Minister in America, spoke of sending plants and mocking-birds, a red one for Mrs Johnes.[18] Plants and seeds sent from Antigua, including a coconut tree, a guava and an oleander, were prized by the head gardener of the Royal Botanic Garden at Inverleith in

---

[12] MS 5622 f. 33.
[13] MS 5620 f. 98.
[14] MS 5611 f. 82.
[15] MS 5609 f. 1.
[16] *The Journal of Sir Walter Scott*, ed. W.E.K. Anderson (Oxford, 1972), 493. Scott had his own views: 'Landscape Gardening', *Quarterly Review*, xxxvii (March 1828). See also J. Reed, *Sir Walter Scott: Landscape and Locality* (London, 1980). The print made of Millburn Tower about 1815 was by Brydges, an itinerant artist: MS 5645 f.140.
[17] MS 5621 f.35.
[18] MS 5608 f. 27; 5609 f. 132; 5610 f. 48.

Edinburgh, William McNab, and the botanist, Robert Falconer; they were regular visitors, and looked after rare specimens.[19]

By 1812, yellow roses and ivy grew round the tower, and white primroses flourished in the flora Britannica. A conservatory was built in 1811 by the Carron Iron Works for under £100, with help from John Hay, an Edinburgh seedsman who specialised in such work.[20] The conservatory was invaluable, taking the place of a simple pit for wintering special plants. A glass house on the top of the tower was condemned for causing leakage and water rot.[21]

Parkyns was succeeded by Joseph Smeal, probably a Quaker like many Scots gardeners.[22] In 1809 Robert Liston was elected a member of the Caledonian Horticultural Society, and described as a gentleman who took 'an interest, or pleasure in Horticultural pursuits'.[23] In fact he left gardening to his wife, who corresponded widely over the exchange of plants. She and Jane Johnes discussed gardening long after Hafod was destroyed by fire in 1807; they exchanged rare plants like the strawberry plant and tiger lily ('a tyger plant'), and both visited a West Indian friend in London, Mrs George Hibbert, whose husband had a plant nursery.[24] Henrietta's Creole background stood her in good stead when Glasgow friends, the Dunlops, collected plants sent to her from Antigua via Greenock.

Her Creole links probably pleased Thomas Johnes, who cultivated the West India interest politically and artistically.[25] Liston depended on Johnes to advance his career; but as Whigs they lacked the goodwill of the Tory government. Retirement had advantages, and brought the

---

[19] For William McNab see H.R. Fletcher & W.H. Brown, *The Royal Botanic Garden, Edinburgh, 1670-1970* (Edinburgh, 1970). Robert Falconer of Carlowrie was a botanist.

[20] MS 5615-16, passim; Tait, *The Landscape GARDEN IN Scotland*. J. Harris (ed.), *The Garden: A Celebration of One Thousand Years of British Gardening* (London, 1979), discusses the importance of conservatories.

[21] MS 5637 f. 91.

[22] See Catalogue of 'Gardening', 1988 Exhibition at NLS, and J. Reid, *The Scots Gard'ner* (Edinburgh, 1683).

[23] MS 5615 f.114.

[24] The Liston-Johnes correspondence is filled with news of exchange of plants. MS 5613 f. 205 mentions Mrs Hibbert. *The Nursery Garden* (Museum of London pamphlet, 1990) notes that James Knight was employed by Alderman George Hibbert, member of an important Jamaican family, to run his private botanical garden in Clapham, and to found a nursery in 1808, the Chelsea Exotic Nursery. Knight specialised in rareties from America, Australia and the Cape of Good Hope.

[25] MS 5611 f. 82; D. Hall, 'Absentee proprietorship in the British West Indies, to about 1850,' *Jamaican Historical Review*, iv (1964), 15-35.

Listons closer to friends and neighbours: Cumberland Reid at Ratho house, Thomas MacKnight at Gogar Bank and Dr Duncan, the parish minister. Amongst Liston's kin, the Ramages and Wilkies farmed nearby, or lived outside Edinburgh, like the Trotters of Dreghorn, the Coutts and the Hamilton Dundases of Corstorphine or Duddingston, an established circle, joined on occasion by David Wilkie, the artist.[26]

Liston's family pedigree dates from William Listoun of Kirkliston who died in 1633.[27] The Listons were mainly churchmen, and Liston had been expected to take holy orders. His elder brother, a writer to the signet, died young without issue; and an only sister, Henrietta, married Alexander Ramage, captain of the port of Leith. Their sons became Liston's heirs, but only two married, and only one left legitimate issue. A step-aunt, Janet Liston, married William Wilkie of Bonnington. Other Listons mentioned in correspondence were step-aunts, or from another branch. Henrietta's family was scattered; she was closest to her brother Nathaniel, and after his death in 1804, she remained in correspondence with his widow, Mary, and her son by another marriage.

Robert Liston enjoyed good living; he commissioned David Wilkie to paint his portrait, and in America he had Gilbert Stuart paint Henrietta and himself.[28] At Millburn he entertained nearby gentry: Lord Morton of Dalmahoy, a leading Whig and an ally in politics; the earl of Hopetoun; Lord Douglas of Bothwell Castle; Lord Torphichen of Calder House near Edinburgh; and Lord Haddington of Tyninghame. He also moved among Whig lawyers in Edinburgh. Liston's family arms, which he had created in 1816 when he received his title, are surmounted by a plough with the motto, 'Poco a Poco'; but though he was prepared to build his house 'little by little', he waged war with his nephews over money, and their desire to farm the estate. He insisted

[26] For David Wilkie see *DNB*.

[27] H.B. McCall, *Pedigree of the family of Liston* (n.p., 1889). The Ramage nephews were: Edward, a post captain, RN, who died unmarried in 1806; Patrick, in the Honourable East India Company, who died without issue; Robert Ramage Liston, who died in 1824 and had issue who inherited; Alexander (Sandy) Liston Ramage, WS, who died in 1814; and Dick, who farmed Scotston Park and died unmarried in 1815. Sandy left £6 per annum to a woman who had borne him an illegitimate child, to the scorn of his lawyer who thought it a pitiful allowance for the aliment of any gentleman's child. MS 5645 f. 63.

[28] Gilbert Stuart's portraits of the Listons are in the Chester Dale Collection, National Gallery of Art, Washington, DC; David Wilkie's portrait of Liston is in the National Portrait Gallery, Edinburgh.

that a few cows be kept, but wished to live as a gentleman off his slender income without incurring debts. He even charged his gardener, Joseph Smeal, with dishonesty, an unhappy episode.[29]

A need for money probably led him to accept another diplomatic post in 1811, when he was nearly seventy. Typically he left no reason for his actions, though expensive plans to build a new wing to the Tower would have ended his ambitious social life. As Ambassador to Constantinople, he succeeded the art lover, Lord Elgin; whilst Henrietta, whose habit was to keep a travel diary, was a worthy successor of Lady Mary Wortley Montagu.[30]

The Listons' departure marked a new stage in the history of Millburn Tower. Henrietta sent plants from the Mediterranean, shipped to London to be forwarded to Leith. Smeal was able to cultivate carnations and lilies, grapes and citrus trees; but McNab warned that some plants sent were fairly common annuals. The Ramage nephews began planting a shrubbery, a thorn and a holly hedge; thinning out the trees in the park; building a wall to enclose the conservatory and the kitchen garden; ploughing a field for oats; ditching, dredging and building roads outside; and improving the domestic water supply.

Between 1811 and 1815 they built domestic offices some way from the house; a cottage for William Gray, who probably managed the animals; and a smaller one for 'Lilly', who helped with the poultry but whose chief function seems to have been to produce babies. A byre, stables and a pigeon loft were built, and a single-storey wing added to the tower, and castellated; although the thatched cottage may not have been demolished before 1821. Sandy Ramage, and then Dick, developed consumption; Sandy was dead by 1814, and Dick left in 1815 for Lisbon, to die on arrival.

The Listons returned briefly in 1816, concerned about the debts incurred through Sandy Ramage's neglect, and the factorship passed to Robert Ramage. He continued to improve the public rooms where the chimneys smoked and darkened the rooms, and completed the building with additions to the south end.

---

[29] Liston may have been confused when he made this accusation, for not long after he was declared senile; he had earlier been pestered by Parkyns' family for money. MS 5613 f. 71; MS 5616 ff. 63–4; MS 5618 f. 223. However, Liston had been accused of taking bribes in America: F.J. Turner, 'Documents on the Blount Conspiracy', *American Historical Review*, x (1904–05), 574–606.

[30] Lady Mary Wortley Montagu's *Letters*, published in 1763, are famous.

The chief authorities for these years are the letters of the housekeeper, Henrietta Ramage, another family connection. They are a mine of information about life on the outskirts of Edinburgh. She gave a detailed account of domestic affairs, showing her high standards of housekeeping, her strict morality and belief in temperance. As a record of domestic servants her correspondence is a valuable and amusing one. Mrs Ramage was a busybody; but she gave a detailed description of the garden and the visitors to it. Her letters, preserved by the family of David Wilkie who painted the poor and simple, are a memorial to the staff. Sir Robert was no radical, in an age when the common man was respected, but he was held in regard; and Henrietta Liston, who had been left four slaves in her father's will, showed black slaves in America the same kindness she showed the bread man or her poultry maid at Millburn Tower.

The Listons returned to Scotland by 1822, but they were aged and spent several months of each year in warmer climates. They visited or corresponded with friends: Eliza Fletcher of Edinburgh, married to a Whig lawyer and herself a radical; Anne Mackenzie; Jane Johnes; and Robina Craig Millar, daughter-in-law of John Millar, Professor of Law at Glasgow University.[31]

The Listons' monument stands in the churchyard at Gogar with the inscription: 'They are remembered here'. It is a fitting one: Robert and Henrietta Liston achieved much in their life, not least the creation of a fine house and garden. A contemporary called it 'a neat house',[32] but there is no evidence that it influenced the earl of Rosebery in 1816 to build in the Gothic style, though William Atkinson was connected with both houses. Parsimony was the common characteristic of the owners of Hopetoun, Dalmeny and Millburn, and though Rosebery gave the commission to build to a Cambridge friend, William Wilkins, he cleverly acknowledged the influence of the master builder, James Wyatt, and Atkinson's name seems to have been tacitly avoided at Dalmeny as at Millburn.

[31] Eliza Fletcher was a well-known bluestocking: *Autobiography* (Edinburgh, 1876). Anne Mackenzie was an old friend: C. Taylor, 'Waiting on Mrs Mackenzie: A Bromley doctor and his patient in the early nineteenth century', *Beckenham Historian*, no. 212 (October 1988). Robina Craig Millar's husband died trying to found an idealistic community in America, and left his widow a charge on the Listons.

[32] W. Park, 'Extracts from the journal of Jessy Allan', *Book of the Old Edinburgh Club*, xiii (1959), cited in Tait, 'The American Garden at Millburn Tower', 90.

It is a pity that Millburn Tower was never compared with Rosebery's grand mansion. Brydges' print of Millburn Tower, made in 1815, is a conventional work, while Alexander Nasmyth's painting of Dalmeny shows the house in a romantic light. In reality Dalmeny is heavy, whilst Millburn Tower is light and elegant, even if the single-storey wing gives the building a truncated appearance. In recent years the furnishings of Dalmeny have been embellished, as have those of Millburn Tower, so that the two houses, so nearly contemporary, can at last stand comparison.

Dalmeny and Hopetoun were grand mansions. Everyone remarked on the small scale of Millburn; and there were no comparisons with houses at Ratho or Gogar. The exotic plants at Millburn Tower attracted visitors, and contemporaries recorded the fame of Sir Robert Liston: Eliza Fletcher said that he reminded her of Pope's lines:

Polite as all his life in Courts had been;

Yet good, as he the world had never seen;[33]

and neighbours wept when 'the ambassador' drove away.

Millburn Tower was a suburban villa, though Liston preserved some of the trappings of a farm, and improved his small park; but the city was visible from the roof of his tower. The house compared well with similar homes: when Lady Liston visited Charles and Amelia Long in Bromley, she saw a house grander than her own, and a garden in which every artifice had been used to create an appearance of space in a small, confined holding. Some traces of the old farm also remained at Bromley Hill, but the idea, as at Millburn Tower, was to create a residence where everything was on a small scale, but magnificent.[34]

The aim of the present work is to describe the building of Millburn Tower and its garden; to illustrate the domestic economy of a house on the outskirts of Edinburgh in the early nineteenth century; and to indicate the social life of the Listons during their stay there. The original spelling of the letters has been retained, although punctuation has been modernised in some cases; square brackets indicate the editor's reading of a doubtful or abbreviated word or passage. Thanks go to the

[33] E. Fletcher, *Autobiography*, 157.
[34] The nineteenth-century suburban villa and garden were increasingly fashionable. See S. Margetson, *St John's Wood: An Abode of love and the Arts* (pamphlet, London, 1988); R. Strong & M. Galinou (eds.), *London's Pride* (London, 1990). For the Longs of Bromley Hill, see C. Taylor, 'Charles and Amelia Long, Lord and Lady Farnborough,' *Beckenham Historian*, nos. 198-9 (April-May 1987).

National Library of Scotland for permission to use the Liston Papers; to Walter Scott Partnership, the present owners of Millburn Tower; to Mr and Mrs Walter Bayard of Lesser Millburn; and to the Scottish History Society. The selections here presented form a small portion of the Liston Papers in the National Library of Scotland (to which all MS references relate), deposited by the family in the 1930s, but the correspondence indicates the importance for the Listons of their house and garden, which became the centre of their social life. Their letters, so carefully preserved, remind, then as now, of the 'pleasuer' the beautiful estate gave to everyone.

C. T.

George Parkyns[1] to Robert Liston   MS 5608 f. 35

Grange, 24 May 1804

My dear Sir, Be assured your wish to see me in Scotland, affords me the highest gratification, my mind is capable of receiving; an excursion into that part of Britain, I have always anticipated with pleasure; at this moment, as it will afford me an opportunity of devoting to your service the little ability I possess, it will, in a twofold degree, be rendered more agreable; for which purpose, I shall not lose a single moment making preparations, to join you, and dear Mrs Liston in the North.

Lord Henry Stuart,[2] informs me, your residence in London cannot be protracted beyond the first of June; I am sorry it will not be in my power to reach Town by that day, but if I am favoured with your approbation, in regard to my following you, in the course of the ensuing week, it will render me inexpressibly happy.

With every sentiment, of the most perfect esteem and regard, & most respectful compts to Mrs Liston, I remain my dear Sir Your truly obedient and sincere.

Henrietta Liston to Captain Edward Ramage[3]   MS 5609 f. 132

Millburn, 21 December 1805

My dear Sir, Mr Liston & I were extremely pleased at your good fortune in obtaining the situation you wished, & glad that you had *humility enough to ask it*. Little has been done here, but what is of course the slow progress of the Tower, except deepening & almost *forming* the piece of water in the front. I observe that in this small spot every alteration is, not only an improvement, but changes in some degree the character of the place, & nothing has more completely affected this than the appearance of this *tranquil River*; the island we propose to fit up for the accomodation of the ducks. My American garden has received a great accession of Plants, some for *love* some for Money. The ground is

---

[1] See Introduction.
[2] A son of John Stuart, 1st marquis of Bute, he accompanied Liston to America.
[3] See Introduction for the Ramage family.

all trenched & the gravel walks partly made ready for the complete forming in the Spring.

The Winter, which has set in the first of the Month, has pretty well cleared us of workmen, & on Monday the 23d we intend to set out for Glasgow where we shall keep our Christmas, & probably remain a fortnight, after returning home to see how things are, we shall continue to pay gradually all the visits we owe in the Neighbourhood, for in Summer it is impossible to move Mr Liston. Amongst our promised visits Lord Haddington's[4] still remains unpaid. He and his family were here lately & the promise was renewed. I think it likely that sometime in the month of February we may set about discharging this debt, &, as we shall then be halfway to Berwick, it is not impossible, if the weather is tolerable, but that we may eat a Beef-stake with you: I'll give you timely notice that you may have it tender, & bespeak a bed in a good Inn.

Mr Liston received a letter from Verdun dated about the middle of October. Bob poor fellow,[5] seems to make the best of it, & is in excellent spirits. He says he hopes your hundred pounds will see him out of France without the addition of Mr Liston's fifty. I am not sure of that, the Devil seems to be exerting himself in behalf of his Protege Bonaparte, for, if he succeeds in what appears to be his present intention of, dethroning the Emperor of Germany, we may all be in Verdun for what I know. But for Nelson's victory I verily believe half the good people here would have been packing up, nor, indeed, do I see what even with it, can be the end of all this, at *best* I fear a *bad* peace.

Mrs Ramage has heard from Patrick &, availing herself of her brother's offer of carrying her as far as Manchester, she seems preparing to set out; I dont know if she goes your road. I hope in God Patrick w[ill] escape Linois' Squadron,[6] which has already been very successful against India ships. Adieu, I am just recovering from a bad cold & severe headache. Mr Liston's affectionate remembrance. Believe me yours faithfully.

---

[4] Charles Hamilton, 8th earl of Haddington, lived at Tyninghame.
[5] Robert Ramage was held prisoner at Verdun by Napoleon.
[6] The French under Admiral Linois threatened ships of the East India Company, by whom Patrick Ramage was employed.

Earl of Torphichen[7] to Henrietta Liston   MS 5612 f. 21

Edinburgh, 16 February 1808

Dear Madam, My gardener has, very naturally a great desire to see your collection of Plants, and I therefore take the liberty of sending him to Millburn. He is very far from being a first rate genious, but is a very worthy, sober good man, and anxious to learn. Nobody understands the kitchen garden better than he does, but that is not quite enough, and I think that in seeing your American garden, and the order in which it is kept, will be of great service to him, and, par consequent, to *me*.

You cannot reasonably expect that I should make you any apology for this trouble I now give you. You are only reaping the fruits of your kindness, which I fear you will think has taught me the usual lesson of presumption. With our best Respects to Mr Liston, believe me Dear Madam Your most obliged & faithful servant.

Earl of Hopetoun[8] to Robert Liston   MS 5614 f. 104

Hopetoun House, 14 June 1809

My dear Sir, We rejoice to learn that Mrs Liston & you are return safe from the bustle of the great world to your delightful farm & garden at Millburn, and we hope in improved health. I made a narrow escape the morning after you left us at Arnistoun Hall, whence we return here end of last week, and if you can would be glad to see Mrs Liston & you here next Saturday till Monday, or that day fortnight July 1st, Sunday June 25th, being our Sacrament Sunday here at Abercorn. With best wishes remain your faithful Johnstone Hopetoun. Pray answer by post. We dine at half past three.

Earl of Hopetoun to Henrietta Liston   MS 5614 f. 106

Hopetoun House, 16 June 1809

Roses to be returned to Mrs Liston from Lord Hopetoun. 1 Rosa multiflora. 1 infernal Rose. & a mimosa.

---

[7] James Sandilands, 9th earl of Torphichen, of Calder House near Edinburgh.
[8] James Johnstone Hopetoun, 3rd earl of Hopetoun, a parsimonious, devout man, had known Liston for years. William Adam and his sons built Hopetoun House, as they did Arniston for the Dundas family.

Earl of Hopetoun to Henrietta Liston   MS 5614 f. 108

Hopetoun House, 16 June 1809
Dear Madam, Accept my best thanks for your kind attention in
procuring me the new roses, and for your prudence in saving my
money which being scarce now, for lead does not sell at present. We
will refer the japonicas and all other high priced plants however
beautiful till cash flows in more abundance. The severe winter bore
hard on us here too.

I hope your two camellias & guava will arrive safe, and beg you will
accept two of the 4 roses you have had from me.

Have the goodness to order Lee and Kennedy's acct.[9] to be paid: it is
£5. 8. I remain Madam your faithful servt.

Thomas MacKnight[10] to Robert Liston   MS 5614 f. 148

Ratho House, 17 July 1809
Dear Sir, If my health had permitted I would have paid my respects to
you at Millburn Tower before this time, and I am particularly sorry that
this is not yet in my power because it would have given me an
opportunity of learning from your Friend something of the modes
practiced in Wales for reclaiming and improving Bogs, and at the same
time of inviting him to see my *whin butter*, and *threshing mills*, the last
name of which is I believe the most powerful in Britain.

If Mr Johnes[11] thinks it worth his while in the course of your
forenoons' airings in this neighbourhood, to ask at Ratho House, my
son will be in the way to shew, these agricultural machines, provided
you will be so good as give me a little previous notice of the time when
we may have that honour.

I know that you laugh at my Mania for agricultural Employment,
and differ widely from me respecting the *Utility* of persons in my
situation (that is to say not regularly bred to the Business, and of
consequence under the necessity of carrying it on by committing the

[9] Lee and Kennedy were Edinburgh seed merchants, as were Walter Nichol and the nurseryman, John
Hay. All were used by the Listons.

[10] Thomas MacKnight of Ratho House was probably kin of Samuel MacKnight WS, who handled
Liston's affairs in the 1790s.

[11] See Introduction for the Johnes family. Thomas Johnes (1748-1816), noted for his fashionable
interest in agricultural improvements, visited Millburn Tower in 1809.

management to an overseer) [?] engaging in such pursuits, in so far at least as the hope of profit is their Motive. But notwithstanding the more than common disadvantages under which I have carried on the business of *Farming* for more than 20 years I have not changed my opinion that of all the *staple manufactures* in Britain wherein capital is employed under the management of proper Overseers, there is none *so profitable* to the Undertaker (taking into account the safety of the speculation) as the *manufacture of Bread corn*; and that there is no business in which a Gentleman can engage with a *view* to profit, requires personal attention in that it is pleasant pursuit; is generally admitted and profitable to the Public, whatever it may be to individuals is seldom denied; it should therefore be encouraged by every friend to this country.

The want of capital in the hands of those who in general cultivate the soil, I am convinced is of the greatest if not the greatest obstacle to the improve of our own soil, and rendering Britain independent of foreign supplies for *Bread Corn*. Whatever tends to encourage the employment of capital in this way must be useful, for which reason I miss no opportunity of *'propating'* my opinions respecting the profit attending this Employment of Capital. Even when employed by Men *ignorant* themselves of the knowledge necessary to conduct the Detail of the farming Operations for which their capital is to be employed. You will pardon *an old man*, for troubling you with this long harangue on a subject which he thinks of great importance. I remain with sincere respect dear Sir Your most obedient humble servant.

Benjamin Rush[12] to Robert Liston   MS 5614 f. 138

Philadelphia, 4 July 1809
Dear Sir, Permit me to introduce to your acquaintance my third son Dr James Rush who goes to Edinr. (the birth place of his father in the profession of Medecine) in order to prosecute his studies in our science. He is accompanied by a young gentleman Dr Thomas Fuller, the son of a wealthy and respectable planter in South Carolina, for whom I beg the same honour that I have solicited for my son. They have both graduated in the University of Pennsylvania.

[12] A distinguished Philadelphia physician, trained in Edinburgh, Benjamin Rush (1745-1813) was a close friend of the Listons, introducing them to leading political figures in America, including the Presidents George Washington, John Adams, Thomas Jefferson and James Madison.

My dear Mrs Rush has done herself the honour of addressing a few lines to Mrs Liston. She is now, with my youngest daughter on the way to take a final leave of my British daughter Mrs Manners before she sails from Canada to England.

My son will inform you how much joy the renewal of the intercourse of the United States with Great Britain diffused through all classes and citizens.

Our new President Mr Madison is trying a bold experiment, and that is, whether our people will submit to the administration of our government by a regard to its principles, in extending its honours and offices to men of both the great parties that have long divided our country. Hitherto the experiment has succeeded, for he is alike popular with all classes of our citizens. With uncommon talents, and attainments, he possesses in an imminent degree the prominence and common sense of one of his predecessors, General Washington, from the want of which Mr A[dams] and Mr J[efferson] have retired, without being followed with the affection or attachment of the respective parties to which they were devoted. I do not mention this fact as a mark of their want of integrity. On the contrary, it was probably the effect of this adhering to dictates of their judgments and consciousness, for I am sure they both deserved well.

Mr Adams has lately appeared in our public papers in defence of his peace with France. He writes sensibly and eloquently, but every now & then, discovers that he is in the 75th year of his age.

Should any of your friends visit Philadelphia I beg you would honour me with a draft for Civilities to them.

With respectful compliments to your excellent lady I am dear Sir with great regard Your sincere & affectionate friend.

A. Munro[13] to Henrietta Liston   MS 5616 f. 142

Livingstone, 21 May 1810
My Dear Madam, I was favoured this morning with your most kind letter of the 19th inst. and my gardener in compliance with your desire shall await upon you with this tomorrow morning.

---

[13] A close neighbour and probably the diplomat, Sir Alexander Munro, who had served in Spain as Consul General.

M

I shall highly prize such of your American plants or seeds as you can easily spare me and I doubt not but those you term common will also prove an acquisition. I have not enough of Botanic knowledge to boast of being partial to *rare* more than beautiful plants, and the latter are too often despised because they are common. At one time I felt some little ambition to emulate my predecessor at Livingstone, for you must know it was here that the first Botanic Garden in Scotland was formed, and to it that of Edinburgh owes its origin, but I found I was too old to begin a new science. My gardener convinces me of this daily for the name he gives to the plants today I forget most completely before tomorrow. I have heard them a thousand times over from Mr Erskine and him and do not now remember one Botanic name.

I saw the Erskines yesterday in fine health.[14] They went to town last night.

Mrs Munro joins me in best wishes to you and Mr Liston and I remain with sincere esteem. My Dear Madam Your faithful friend.

J. Stanton, Manager for Carron Company,   MS 5617 f. 94
to Robert Liston

Carron, 9 October 1810

Sir, We beg leave to annex you an Invoice of the Supporters of Mrs Liston's Conservatory amounting to £95. 15. 6. which sum may be paid at your own convenience to Messrs Ramsay Bonars & Co on our own Account, and their Receipt shall be equally valid to you as our own. We have made no charge for Patterns, Boxes, or other preparatory articles, being anxious to execute this work on the most moderate terms possible. It will afford us much pleasure to learn that these supporters answer the purpose. I have the Honour to be with the highest Respect, Sir, Your very obedient humble servant.

Earl of Torphichen to Henrietta Liston   MS 5617 f. 115

Calder House, 8 November 1810

Dear Madam, I had the Honor of receiving your letter of the 6th yesterday and according to your desire I send a Cart. It may have a formidable appearance to be sure, but I could not send by any other

14 Probably the family of Henry Erskine, a noted Whig advocate.

conveyance my plants intended for you. Inclosed in this is a list of the names of them all, except of 4 plants, which we do not know, and among them you will find two of the Evergreen of which we were ignorant of the name. I have found it out however by Cormacks means, and it is the *Clethra Alnifolia*. He says it is a very fine plant. I only wish that these plants were more worthy of your acceptance. Our establishments here are all in their infancy as you know, but I hope that now we are on the way of improvement.

I have no Patience with Cormack for his stupidity in arriving at Millburn at so unseasonable an Hour, & the more especially as I apprized him well of what he would see there. Your American Garden is unquestionably without Rival in this country, with the choices of the plants, in their arrangement, and above all, in their wonderful beauty and thriving Condition. I have ordered a large collection of flowering shrubs for our little Garden; and flatter myself that with care, and with the benefit of Instruction from you, we shall ere long make a tolerable figure.

A thousand thanks for your goodness in bestowing upon us the American plants. You may remember that by your desire, I wrote down the names of several, and I transcribe them on the opposite leaf to save you the Trouble of recollection. I particularly beg however that that list may not fetter you in any Degree: whatever you can spare without Inconvenience to yourself, will be most acceptable to us.

We shall be happy at all times to pay our respects to you and Mr Liston, but meanwhile we shall hope for the Honor of your Company to pass a Night *at least*, here. Could you not make a stage of us on your Return from the West?

We offer our best wishes to you and to Mr Liston and believe me Dear Madam, with much Respect and Regard, Your most obedient & most humble servant.

1. Broad leaved oak. 2. Sumachs. 3. Viburnum. 4. Cherries. 5. Jessamine. 6. Broadleaved Spirea. 7. Napaea. 8. Rudbeckia Hirta. 9. Diervilla-Honeysuckle. 10. Bladder Nut. 11. Dwarf Horse Chestnut. 12. Tall Phlox. 13. Persimmon. 14. Black stalk Sunflower. 15. Blue Lobelia. 16. Caucasus Honeysuckle.[15] 17. Castor Oil Nut. 18. Fringe tree also perhaps seed of the Dahlia Purpurea.

---

[15] Previously thought to have been introduced into Britain in 1825. Information from the Royal Botanic Garden, Edinburgh.

John Hay to Robert Liston   MS 5617 f. 157

Edinburgh, 22 December 1810
Sir, I received your card and by the time you will have received the
columns. I would have wrote by the servant but he had to call at my
house as I have been confined for some days and he could not leave his
Horses long. The Iron Roods which are to connect the columns, with
the Front [mountin?] of the conservatory are the Circular ones which
were standing in the Barn the last time I was at Millburn, everything is
now sent that you ordered, there is only the wires now wanting to
compleat the whole so as to be ready for the creepers, and they shall be
sent so soon as you please to order them. There are if I remember right
13 small holes in the arches through which the wire is to pass and in
ordering them you have only to send the length in full from north to the
south column with a small round pin of wood that will pass easily
through the whole in the Iron and how many wires you want in each
side. If James the Mason is with you when they go up I explained the
whole of my ideas to him. I have the Honour to remain Sir your most
obed. Humble Servt.

Alexander Liston Ramage to Henrietta Liston   MS 5620 f. 36

Edinburgh, 28 September 1811
My dear Madam, I have laid out the road between ye kitchen garden
and the Evergreen shrubbery south of the conservatory, but it does not
by any means please me. The square plot on ye west side of the
conservatory, the straight walk on ye west & south of *it*, makes it look
awkward. But the shrubs are planted & you can remedy the defect
yourself. You, who never was in my situation, cannot conceive how
much disagreeableness I have felt about Millburn, because you never
acted for any body except yourself, & you never acted for *Mr Liston*.

The front of ye servants Room has been, for some time finished. *I
wish you saw it*. I wish you heard what people say about it. It is truly
everything you or Mr Liston could wish.

I should like to know whether Mr Liston means the Holly Hedge
west from the kitchen court to grow up as it pleases, or whether it is
intended to be pruned low or allowed to grow up in single trees. You
know my opinion is that every man is entitled to do with his own as he

pleases, and *you know* also that I am sometimes, perhaps you will say always, inclined to give my opinion in a decided manner. It is a pity that so much fine mason work should be *entirely* screened from the view.

William Henderson[16] has been [un]able to undertake the Pigeon House, and the Birds must *all* be killed. They sit upon the cottage all night & they will not enter their own House. Even if it was *properly* fitted up, they have acquired a bad habit, and these, we all know, are not easily got rid of. The Pidgeons are I can see a favourite object with you, and you may rest assured that it shall be attained before your return.

The entrance road at Gogar is formed & ye *mound* made round the two Beech trees. It does not look quite as well as I expected, as Mr T. has made it too narrow on ye west side. I have a reluctance again to ask him to make both sides alike, but I must do it.

I am quite vexed at your last letter to Mrs Ramage. If you *insist* on the cows being kept for Lilly's sake, I will not be able to let a single grass park next April. You must really write me to do *in this matter* as I please, otherwise you will derange all my plans.

The two orange trees as you enter at ye south Conservatory Door have not grown. May I take them out & put in two new young ones? Believe me yours in great affection.

Henrietta Ramage to Henrietta Liston   MS 5620 f. 64

Millburn Tower, 18 October 1811
My Dear Madam, I have just now received your letter by Mr Thomson. Many people indeed came to see Millburn Tower. I sometimes tyre when three parties come one After another in one day, but I can pick up some amusement from their remarks, and it makes me look forward with pleasuer to the quait of winter nights. Its a very great enjoyment to me having so much of Sandie Ramages company. The corns will be all in this week. I think of giving the servants a dinner some day next week. Its so common in this part of the country there would be a good deal of grumbling if it were not done. Keeping the people in good humer commonly makes things go well on. Ill take care

---

[16] For the staff at Millburn Tower see Introduction. The men servants included William Henderson, a mason or carpenter, William Gray, the cow man, and David; the women, Lilly, the poultry maid, Bell, a house maid, and various cooks and housekeepers.

of Jamie; he is just the same ceevil attentive lad as when you were at home.

James Wilkie's[17] death was indeed a very shocking one. His Brother Mr Matthew was living in East Southing looking at a farm for him & James was living at Bonnington to take care of the Harvest. Mr C. Reid[18] with a Band of his sheerers were the first who came to his assistance: was so much disfigured that no person could know him: they were proposing to carry him to Ratho, upon which he Named himself and pronounced the word Bonnington: never spock more. Mr C. Reid acted a very freindly part; remained with Mrs Wilkie till 10 oclock at Night. She was taken very ill; has kept her bed ever since. The poor widow expects some of these days to Ly in of her tenth chile.

Old Mrs Young is in a very feeble state but upon the whole in tolerable health. Mrs Duncan[19] died very soon after you left Scotland. I hear she left something conciderable to her Brothers familie. Charles Richie[20] was here yesterday. I asked him if John had ever made amends for his fault: he said he doubted he had not. I cant give you his Address. His letters are all sent to the Jerusalem Coffee House.[21] Harry Liston[22] came home just at the beginning of Harvest. His mother came here [and] stayd two days with me about midsummer; have heard nothing of her since.

Bell is still at her mothers from what I hear. I hope she will be the better of these medecines she got from London. Never saw Lillie in better health than at this time. Her children are all of them very industerous Creatures. Have amongst them gleen'd a [Boll?] of wheat, and she herself has made a piece of linnin cloath. Mr Falconer of Carlowrie[23] has been very much indisposed all Summer; he is now getting better, & means to come and look at your plants some day soon. A lady upon seeing the American garden lately observed that everything in it was in the paint stile everything so large & vigerous, not a weed to be seen. Joseph[24] is to answer your letter himself. Mrs P.

---

[17] See Introduction for the Wilkie family.

[18] See Introduction; Cumberland Reid lived at nearby Ratho House.

[19] See Introduction; Dr Andrew Duncan was minister of Ratho from 1803 to 1827.

[20] The Richies seem to have been distant kin of Robert Liston.

[21] A London tavern used by members of the East India Company.

[22] See Introduction for other members of the Liston family.

[23] His son became a leading member of the Botanical Society of Edinburgh.

[24] See Introduction for the head gardener at Millburn, Joseph Smeal.

Ramage has been once seeing me, and I have been once in her house where I had the pleasure to see her acting as she should do, as really mistress of the house. Mr Cumberland Reid is in his ordinary health, com[ing] here now and then and looks at what is going on. I now have I think answered your questions, & shall be happy to do so again, when ever you favour me with a letter. I beg Mr Liston and you to accept of my best respects.

Alexander Liston Ramage to Robert Liston   MS 5620 f. 66

Edinburgh, 19 October 1811

My dear Uncle, I received your very welcome letter this morning. Some time ago I was so much surprised at not hearing from you or Mrs Liston that I caused a friend of mine in London call at the Royal Hotel to enquire if you were in good health, or whether you were *really* gone, & I got an answer to both.

I will mention to Mrs Shireff what you write; but will she not think, (whether she says so or not) that the sooner the application is made the better.

I mentioned to Mrs Liston in a late letter that Wm. Henderson had *not* been able to undertake the Pidgeon House; and even yet it remains *in status quo*, so that you have an opporty. of either altering it, or allowing it to remain as it is, or of fitting it up as you please.

You appear of late, my good sir, to have taken aversion to sketching or drawing; otherwise I think you would have given me *in pencil*, some notion of your Dutch Pidgeon House. I shall try my hand at it before I dispatch this letter. I suppose it ought not to be placed in the middle of the Stable Yard, but about six feet from the Door east from the washing House, and should be so high as to be seen from the green trees. The first, that it may not be in the way in the court yard, and the second that it may have the House (itself) placed out of the reach of cats, and be seen from the north, peeping over the washing House &c. The size of it I have today ascertained ought to be four feet square and about six high with a small door on the north side, and the whole made as warm as possible for a thing of that sort. It must be devoted to house Jane Pidgeons only.

The Barn and mill, Lilly's cottage and the Henhouse, and William Gray's thatched House are all Built. The three latter are roofed, and

partly thatched. The Roof of the Mill goes on next week, and the Heather is nearly ready. The two cottages and Hen house will be plastered week after next, & the servants will remove when they please, or rather when I think it safe for them to do so.

Wm. Gray's byre! That is a matter I never thought of untill I was just [put] in mind of it by, I need not tell who. He and his wife wish it placed to their House on the North. I say no; because that would defeat all our object as to neatness, cleanliness &c after the old cottages are down and untill that is done I cannot put the ground & about them in the state you mentioned. Think the best way would be to continue the north wall of the Hen house eastward & put a [too fall?] to the South of it for Wm.'s cow. The wall would answer the stable or whatever afterwards you may build here. If you differ from me please inform me; I shall pay attention to G. and ye Book when necessary. We have commenced cutting ye Hedges, and I clean them and the Ditches as we go along. It will prove a very tedious operation, but it is a very useful one. I do not mean to make the new enclosure till next Feby., or March.

The Hedge round the South kitchen garden: ought it not to be sliced up, & made straight at the top, and about six feet high? On the east side there are two rows of trees, one Scotch fir next the garden, and close behind it one of spruces. The Scotch are destroying the spruces by their branches. These last must, one time or another, fall off; & then you have only a naked stem. But before this happens the lower part, & indeed all the stems of the spruces will be destroyed, & they never recover; whereas were the Scotch firs all taken away now, or even half of them, the spruces would be covered to the bottom, & *ultimately*, as well as at present, give shelter. You will see I think this ought to be done, but you will say aye or no.

Mr Crawford of Ratho spoke to me about the re-division & alteration in the West Loft! An Entail I suppose of this ancient subject! I wish you to say what I am to do if again applied to.

I have ordered young Hollys to be planted at the bottom of the Holly hedge, and in the gaps of it.

You know perhaps that Miss Liston agreed to go to Mr Johnston's House West of & *out of* the town of Corstorphine, if it could be procured. Now ye tenant has gone away Mr Johnstone has offered it to her with garden cows grass etc. free of all Taxes & completely furnished at £10 per annum, but she declined going! oh that you had never given

any place to her! or that I had never meddled with it! Yours faithfully &
affectly.
P.S. Anything to be done about paying ye Debt to Mavisbank?[25]

Henrietta Ramage to Henrietta Liston   MS 5620 f. 96

        Millburn Tower, 10 November 1811
My Dear Madam, It gave me great pleasuer last week to learn by a letter
from Mr Morell to one of the Servants here, that Mr Liston and you
were in perfect good health. Mr and Mrs Dunlop[26] called here some
days ago, on their way to Edinburgh with two sons for the Collage.
Mrs Dunlop seemed to take much interest in the American garden,
looked at & examined everything in it. The Rose on the East side of the
Octticon door is just now in great beauty and also the sweat brier tree in
the flower garden. These two atrack the Attintion of every person who
see them.

 Everything without doors is now beginning to put on the sober
saddness of a winter appearance. The curtains in the Conservitory are
all put up; the plants in a thriving state. We have got the carrots potatoes
and yams all in before any froast has come on. The cott houses are really
pretty things. The Porticos at the door give them to look altogether out
of the common road; there insides have a snug comfortable
Appearance. The thatcher went from this to Dreghorn; Mr Trotter[27]
wants all his Cot-hous to be done in the same manner as the Barn here.
The dry rot has got into the fine new house there. I hear people who
understand these matters say it is a very bad affair.

 Miss McKinsie has left Gogar Loge. Dr. Stuart has got a Lady Oddly
to live with them, a little disordered in her mind I understand. Mr
Granger's son John is very soon to be married to a Miss Henderson.
Said to be good and bonny with £50 of Portion. Miss Liston is to
remove from Newgardens; is to come to a house in Corstorphine.
There is a vile dispute going on betwixt Mr Osburn and Robert Hyslop
the Mason. Mr Osburn thinks himself overcharged about £100. There
is a Building Erecting at Perth intended as a depot for French prisoners

[25] The Listons often visited Mavisbank, designed by William Adam for Sir John Clerk of Penicuik in
the 1720s.
[26] See Introduction for the Dunlops of Greenock.
[27] See Introduction for the Trotters of Dreghorn.

will cost Government 1800£. 400 Masons are working at it, which occasions a scarcity of men of that profechin over the length of Edinburgh. These French people are like to eat us all up; those at Pennycook alone consume 20 Bolls of potatoes every week. Oh that they were all away home and our own dear youth return'd.

Mr Gardner's familie have left this part of the country for good's all. Dr Duncan has sent his oldest son to the College this winter. Mr William Wilkie has also sent his son. Poor Mrs James Wilkie was delivered of a daughter some days ago. The Reverend Mr Olivers oldest son died on Sunday last. Joseph desires me to say he has raird a Snake-plant from the seed you gave him, and it is stronger and handsomer, than the one that came from London. Mr Cumberland Reid is frequently enquiring for Mr Liston and you. He enjoys pretty good health at precent. I wish to know what ship is Appointed to take you out. May everything that is good Attend Mr Liston and you by sea or by land. I ever am My Dear Madam most respectfully & most Affectly yours.

Alexander Liston Ramage to Robert Liston   MS 5637 f. 91

25 February 1812

My dear Uncle, You never even hinted to me that you wished the vestible wall to be tarrassed, but it is now done similar to the front of the servants Rooms. It will answer both yr. objects you had in view; but the fact is that a great part of the damp in the servants rooms comes from the ground, and it was from the stupid way Thomson had hung the Bells (running the wires perpendicularly thro' the roof) which will allow the water to get down, but this has been remedied.

I wrap round this Letter my Plan for castellating all the west of Millburn, even altho' you seem to disapprove of *any* thing of that sort. It was made many months ago to be sent to you, if you asked for it; and it will at least show you *how* the servants rooms are actually finished, of which you have never, I suspect, had a very accurate idea. After looking at the mode of finishing above the Door, you will observe that the *Pediment* is no longer visible in front. Indeed, after much puzzling I found it impossible to put embrasures on the level walls, as you directed, and retain the Pediment, the one being inconsistent with the other. I hope you will approve of the Breaks, which have a good effect.

If a Belfry is erected, and you wish a tarrassed one, (in speaking of tarrasse I mean Roman cement not Dav. Richie's Roof comp.)[28] it must be of Brick or rough stone; for the Cement, altho' it stands well on either, will not do on wood. It cracks wherever they come in contact, and common plaster will not do. I have tried my hand upon two or three, but am really at a loss what kind of a thing you would wish. My own idea is that its erection would greatly improve the elevation of the servants Rooms, because it would take off the bad effect of that lengthened and straight appearance which they still have, and which is their only defect. You may therefore return me any one of the sketches you like best; only I would much rather that it had come from you. Before concluding this subject I may suggest that altho' the tarrassing the Belfrey all over is infinitely superior, and in unison with the rest of the Building; yet a wooden one may be repainted with white lead, and splashed over with sand, but the Roof will never be sufficient, and will always be giving you trouble.

I cannot leave *my Plan* without remarking that I have frequently altered my ideas upon hearing yours; and I now think the place would more *like itself,* were it finished as on the Sketch B. But the square Tower appears to be *indispensible* to close the castellation properly. I could finish all of that plan for £40 or £50.

The wood house partly tumbled down, and great part of the Roof was blown away. I therefore was glad of the excuse, & removed it altogether. I was shocked at your writing you *intended* to remove all the rubbish thereabouts, dress up &c why there is not a spot about the Place (Policy I mean) that is not as neat as the little Lawn before the cottage Door, and you do not now see anything or anywhere, out of order; but we have sad battles with the Docks, the dainty Lion, and the still more detestable Bishops weed.

The east gable of the cottage will be done next week precisely in the way you wish it.

The very day after I wrote you about the octagon roof standing so well, a deluge of water destroyed the whole of the west side of the Room. After getting the lead mended I caused size it exactly as you did before.

The green House was the cause of the Rain getting thro' the Roof of the Tower. Upon taking off the Boarding not only were they *completely*

---

[28] See Introduction. William Atkinson invented Roman cement.

rotten, but even half an inch of the Beams was in the same state. It was the moss which had caused this. I began the tarrasse about three inches under the Lead apron on the walls, and raised it on the green house five inches, then covered that with painted boarding as you did before, so that you can perceive no difference. If there is *not* too much elasticity in the joisting I am confident we shall never be troubled again with water. I have found out that the damp in the easter turret does not come thro' the Roof, but between the interstices of the stones of the wall (where the Embrasures join to it) and which you know is very thin. The inside is grown greenish, but when the Painter was there he said that a Putty of a certain kind, put in carefully between the stone would remedy the defect. It is not easy to get at, but I'm going to try it myself.

In writing to you about the island I by no means intended anything like *finicality*. I merely proposed that the edges of the Island ought to be made something like the edges of the Canal, that is that the grass should grow to the water's edge, which you know it does not do in some places, particularly to the South where there are two feet of perpendicular *red* soil; and which is not the case in *small* natural Islands. The Evergreens planted on it were four or five of the yews which were in the garden at New gardens. They will never obstruct our view, whatever they may do in a few centuries.

The Bridge to be made to the Island is to be at the south end of it, and will be of spruce or other trees with the bark on, and will only go to the Island: and never ought there to be a Bridge into the sheep park at all. Such must have a gate that may be left open, and then everything is at the mercy of the sheep, and they have done no little harm during last winter.

Until I received your Letter I never had any idea how the Drawing Room was to be finished. On speaking to Mr Henderson I find you gave him dimensions and instructions; taking it for granted that he is correct, these shall be attended to in the course of this month.

I am sorry my motions respecting the east Hedge of the kitchen garden were more rapid than you could have wished. My idea was that whatever directions you might afterwards give as to the *Rise* of the new fence, still the Thorns must have been taken up. I could show you, on your own Estate, evident proofs that a transplanted thorn Hedge (much younger) does not thrive. The Hedge was planted according to the curve or bend you returned in my sketch, from the northwest corner of

the coach house; altho' this was not consistent with an after part of your letter where you speak about its being awkward to look into the back of a Hedge. But it can be taken up at a future time in half an Hour. Some of the large thorns *were* planted at full length, as well as a number of Firs (silver when to be had and young ones intermixed) between the west American garden Hedge and the Planting, and many of the tall Thorns have been planted in several other places, so that all is nearly as you originally wished. The Road from the Coach House to the north west corner of the American garden is up, as you proposed, and makes a good *fence* on the north of the newly transplanted Hedge, and will be covered with creepers of sorts next year. All the Spruce whose tops were broken off (and of course never would grow well) were rooted out, and others and silvers put in their place; except those close to the east of the conservatory which were not replaced, because more elbow room was wanted there. I did exactly as you wished as to the spruces and the Scotch firs, sacrificing such only as were least precious, and which injured others. All the heights in the planting between the Conservatory and kitchen garden on the west, & American garden in the east are levelled, all the hollows filled up with good earth and all smoothed and sown with grass seeds, and the change is very great indeed. Im not good at drawing ground Plans, but I'll try and get some good natured person to make one of all these things for me, that you may see exactly how all is finished; and I am very much mistaken if you are not perfectly satisfied.

A course close slab rail is put up between the north east corner of the coach House and the south east corner of the East Stable seven feet high with a small Door and a swans Hole, and a similar one with a large and small Door between the S. west corner of the shop, so there is much shelter afforded, much snugness obtained, and the view excluded on both sides, which has a good effect.

You never said any more about W. Gray's cow I therefore acted upon that part of your letter where you say and also no cows but our own that it therefore stand upon this footing, for she is gone long ago; and we have now (thank God) no animals, except what are of use in one way or another.

The new line of the public Road, having been approved of at a General Meeting of Trustees, is lined off, with a lesser & very natural curve and the Hedges planted all south of the Thrashing Mill, and all the

young trees put in. There will be a great quantity of earth to remove, for I have kept the Road as low as possible. I do not think there will be anything done this season as to making it.

John King and his wife remove at Whity. from Callerstane to Comiston. I may again repeat my thanks, more especially as it is of their own accord, of their own wish, and without Complaint of any kind. I need not add that I take no person in his stead. George Kerr goes to his House, and Tibby Forrest to George's. This was my arrangement, for poor Tibby was turned out of his House, and otherwise must have gone to some other part of the country.

Newgardens is let to an Advocate, son of Miller of Dalswinton at £90 partially furnished by me. Again, and more than ever, are my thanks due. The tenant keeps the Gardener, so the place is quite safe.

If this and my last reach you, then every subject (except about the farm) is exhausted, but I shall continue to write however little I may have to say. My next shall be to Mrs Liston and I am always Your very affecte. nephew.

William McNab[29] to Henrietta Liston   MS 5641 f. 62

                              Botanic Garden, Edinburgh, 19 February 1814
Madam, I had the Honour to receive yours of the 29 Dec. 1812. I am happy to have it in my power to give you a favourable report of the state of the plants in your conservatory at Millburn, which are (with very few exceptions) in a very luxuriant state; I need not mention the increase in number since you went off that has not been communicated to you already, I cannot help however, remarking that they are very considerable, and I trust with the attentions & exertions of Joseph that you will find a select collection at Millburn on your return. The following are among the finest specimens now in your concervatory, and several of them the finest specimens of the kind I have ever seen viz. *Mimosa decurrens longifolia v. suaveolens. Melaleuca hypericifolia. Sparmannia africana. Corchorus japonicus. [Pyrus paperius?].* with many others though not equal in size yet in very great perfection. A few of them in the Pit. *Joseph* & I intend to consult with *Mr Falconar* (who is particular anxious as to their success) about moving one or two pretty large

[29] See Introduction for William McNab.

plants, as soon as the season is a little farther advanced, as some of them now near the edge of the Bed has overgrown some of the Dwarfer ones in the centre. *Sparmannia africana* for me I think will be better near the centre; I hope this you will not object to when we consult *Mr Falconar*, and another season would make the plants so large that they would not be so easy moved without injury. The little stove (which is in a very forward state) will be a great acquisition for keeping some of the more tender plants through the winter or spring; which though they will live in the conservatory yet you can never see them in perfection without a little more heat during winter than what is necessary to keep the conservatory at—[sic]. The *Passiflora* at the end of the House of course you have been made acquainted with; although it keeps alive and grows a little in the summer, yet it loses nearly as much in winter, and I have no hope of seeing it flower where it is. It will however I expect do well in the stove. *Joseph* mentioned that you wished it sent here, but upon considering it, we concluded that it would injure it less, to let it remain where it is till the stove is ready, and take it up and plant it in the stove at once than run the risk of injuring it by moving here & back again. The *papyrus* has not done well in the cistern: I hope however yet to see it ornament a part in the concervatory as I saw it lately in a fine state in Mr Hopkirk's green House; which is a reason in heating the conservatory in severe weather, since it has been altered it draws well and he can keep the house this winter to any heat he wants with care.

Everything in the American garden is in a very luxuriant state and it has been kept in very neat order, some of the larger rarest trees and the commoner sorts, which you know would so completely fill the garden to the great injury of the better plants, and as they are yet in a size fit to be moved without injury, it appears necessary to move some of the commoner ones elsewhere, & let them grow to what size the climate will wish them to do. Nor has the *Flora Britannica* been neglected, but it will require some time to get it filled and properly arranged; the soil & situation is well calculated for the purpose, as everything that has been put in thrives well. I shall find a pleasure in contributing my mite towards getting it filled up from time to time *Joseph* can get it done. Of course you have been made acquaint with the loss of the [?] *Pine* which you left in my care.

The seeds which you sent last season and which you so liberally ordered a part of them for me, I cannot give you a very flattering report

of them. They have turned out principally common Plants such as *French Marigold; Wallflower; Candytuft; French Honeysuckle; Sow thistle* &c. &c. One small species of *Hypericum* a species of *Cistus* & a *Sonchus* have not yet flowered and perhaps may prove new. *Joseph* has raised exactly the same sorts as I have done. The *Mimosa* has come on very well; I have several plants of it. Joseph has the same. I hope it will prove new; it has much the habit of *Mimosa julibrissin* a species not common in this country, but it has red flowers: you describe this as having yellow. It will be very desirable to procure plants of seeds of it & likewise some dried *specimens* of the flowers & leaves. Indeed this would be very desirable in most cases where you have an opportunity of procuring dried specimens of any of the plants you can get. It is difficult for me to name anything particular that would be more desirable than another, as Plants which I never saw nor heard off would be most acceptable; however we shall be very thankfull for any thing which we can get either in *seeds* or *Bulbs* of any sort and among them (particularly among the Bulbs) many new ones to this country may reasonably be expected. Seeds of any of the good sorts of ornamental flowers will be a treasure.

As you mentioned the great difficulty you have had in getting seeds of any of the common plants collected, I fear it will be of little use to mention not using too much freedom that I should be particularly obliged to you if you can promise seeds of any of the native *grasses*, or any [plants?] that can be got and also any of the *grains* cultivated, but perhaps the latter may not differ much from those cultivated in Britain. Should the [country?] be rich in acquatic plants I need not remind you that seeds of any of them will be valuable. One plant I shall mention which I am in favour &c. &c. [sic] grows in *Malta* but not native there, the *Upas gloriosa*, which is said to be a most beautiful plant should you call there on your return Home perhaps you may have an opportunity procuring some of it should it prove new to you.

I fear Madam, I have already trespassed too long on your valuable time. I hope Mr Liston & yourself are well. Permit me to wish you Health & Happiness and with true respect do I sincerely pray for your safe arrival again in this Happy Island. I have the Honour to be Madam with great respect, Your most Obedient and Humble Servant.

Henrietta Ramage to Henrietta Liston   MS 5641 f. 218

Millburn Tower, 30 May 1814

My Dear Madam, I have to acknowledge the receipt of two letters from you of the 15th February and 7 of March, the last came first which I no sooner received that I sett about exciting your commissions. Called on Mr Laing; he told me Mr Trotter had taken it upon him to do everything about Mrs Polson's[30] affairs, that all her papers he believed to be in Miss Donaldson's possession; sent his daughter Miss Laing with me to Miss Donaldson who showd me a Trunk seald up with all Mrs Polson's letters & papers said she could not open it unless Mr Trotter were precent. Upon my reporting all this to Sandie Ramage, he said would go out to Dreghorn and see about it, which he did. Found Mr Trotter had sett off the day before for London where he was to remain for the three months, wrot him upon the subject, but as yet has no return to his letter. You will perceive by all this that everything was done that could be done.

Our Winter here has been very severe indeed; the ever greens have suffered saddly. I mean over all the country; those in the American garden, particularly at the South part of it have been less injured than anywhere else. Every plant and shrub in it are in good health. The Flora Britanica is really very pleasant, in every wind enjoys shelter. There is a great deal of flower upon all the fruit trees this season. The concervitory is in great beauty just now, everything in it strong and vigerous. Lord Seaforth[31] was here last week, a very frail old man indeed, but perfectly alive to all the pleasuers of a Botanist, greatly pleased with the variety and condition of the plants. It was Amusing to see Joseph: he was in a Maner enchanted with finding a person of so much knewledge. Lord Rosebery[32] died in March last; the precent Lord means to Build a new house.

We were all in a Hubbub of joy upon the late success of the Alied Powers: Bonfires and iluminations of vairous kinds throut the whole Country. Mr Reid had a 130 candles lighted up in his House. The white cockade was universally worn, it even came down to Thom Torrance,

[30] Ann Polson, an old friend, introduced Henrietta to Robert Liston.
[31] Francis Humbertson Mackenzie, Lord Seaforth (1754–1815), Governor of Barbados at the end of the eighteenth century.
[32] Neil Primrose, 3rd earl of Rosebery (1729–1814) was succeeded by his son, Archibald Primrose, 4th earl of Rosebery (1783–1868).

not a bit of white ribband was left in Edinbr. When it was spent, the people had recourse to paper.

Miss Mackenzie is gone to Durome. I hear she got well there and was pleased with her situation. Bob Ramage is in London, busieing himself with his Indian affairs. We have had many arraivals from France of late. You may believe it gives me great pleasuer to hear it again and again repeated that Mr Robert Ramage is a very respectable man. I make no doubt he has wrot to Mr Liston or you since he came to London. I look for him now and every day. I called upon Dr Cochran's widow shortly after his death, but did not see her; she is living in the same house, & enjoys the same sort of health as formerly. I shall call first time am in Town and let her know you enquair for her. Wm. Grey has got two Brids in his Familie: both his Daughters are to be wedded in a few days. Sandie is considerably better than he was in winter. I cant say so much for Dick; he is still complaining a good deal. Mr William Wilkie has again had a very severe affliction in his familie: his second daughter died very suddenly in April last. Miss Liston is gone to Town, and I hear findes herself very comfortable in her ludgings. Mr Reid is at precent in pretty good health. Dick will remember anything I may have forgot. My memory now plays me many a slippery trick, among others am affraid makes me repeat to you the same thing over and over again. I must trust to your goodness to overlook these mistakes. I ever am my Dear Madam Your most Affecteinot humble Sernt.

Henrietta Liston to Dick Ramage   MS 5643 f. 38

Constantinople, 10 March 1815

My Dear Dick, I had the pleasure to receive yours of the 4 Jany. some days ago. Sandys account reach'd us at the same time.

You have probably heard ere this that Mr Liston has asked a leave of absence, in order to arrange his private affairs & you will naturally conclude that Sandy's *first account* & the truly alarming paragraphs of his accompanying letter, that Millburn lost yearly hundreds more than the rents produced together with the unexpected burthen of the Interest of Mrs P. Ramages two thousand pounds, induced him to anticipate his return, yet we cannot quit this country earlier than the end of the summer, or reach England probably sooner than next Spring, provided the leave be granted, of which there is, indeed, little doubt.

The produce of Millburn, or the price of grain, seem to concern Mr Liston very little. His wish was to pass throught the short remainder of life in easy circumstances & indolent enjoyment, to clear his land entirely of debt; & if I outlived him, to leave me such an income as might support me decently without my being forced to *beg of* Government (for I presume you know that these things are *never offered*). He now dreads to find that the Land has been cultivated & enriched for *Posterity* without a thought of the ease & comfort of his probably short life. I should be sorry that Sandy, in his present sad situation, should know the disappointment & complicated misery he has occasioned, & to what purpose my Dear Dick. God knows I grieve to say that none of you promise to live or have families to enjoy it. To whom then is this ruinous expense to fall in future? to distant connections who may not even thank either of you for your trouble?

Mr Liston seems now to have taken the resolution to do what he says he had at his departure wished you & Sandy to do for him. Turn the whole farm into grass, & do not expend during his life another half penny on it. & indeed I fear that should he at his return find himself deeply *involved*, he may be tempted to sell his land, pay his debts, & perhaps seek a happier clime.

Altho' part of his distress appears to be the destitute situation in which he may be obliged to leave me, at his Death, (for entre nous, He made me promise on the day of our *marriage* that I was never to ask assistance from Government at his Death,) yet my hopes are more sanguine, first that you & Sandy may both get well, that by strict economy the debts may be paid, or at worst that I shall not live long enough after him to feel the pressure of want in any degree. I have only now to entreat that you will put an end to every possible expence & with these prospects, I conclude this truly painful subject.

I must trouble you with one paragraph more on business. Mrs Ramage's last letter gives a sad account of the present state of the roof of the Tower, & seems to impute it to the small Green House at the top. Mr Liston says, that if that is the case the room must be taken down immediately, & the roof completely mended; the expence he fears may be considerable but the *roof must be watertight*.

I have said to Mrs Ramage that no expence must be gone into as preparation for us, particularly no Carriage Horses, or Coachman; the

Garden, the Poultry yard, & a good Cow are the most important points in the present uncertainty of our motions.

Now many thanks for your news, especially that which concerns the Dunlops at Greenock. I very sincerely regret Mrs Liston, old Cathy, & my friend Mrs Napier. Mr Liston felt the loss of Mr McCormick; Sir Alexr. Seton's is not great to any one.

I shall hope as the season advances to hear better accounts of you & your Brother, if he weathers the three Spring months I shall have hopes from the Summer. Pray take care of yourself, & give us early information of Sandy; Mr L. had a letter from poor Bob; do me the favour to send the inclosed letter & note *immediately*, without *putting* them *into a Drawer or anywhere*.

Mr Liston joins me in love to you & Sandy, to Miss L., Miss Ramage &c. &c. Believe me yours very affectionately.

Dick Ramage to Robert Liston   MS 5643 f. 145

Millburn Tower, July 1815

My dear Uncle, I find that where houses or land are concerned it is much easier to lay down resolutions with respect to expenditure than to keep them. The West gable of the Cottage has been in a very shattered state for years, & has been frequently patched up. I have found it necessary to give it hewn stone corners &c., so that it now looks much better, & being well bound together, will I hope give no more trouble. The east end stands the weather most beautifully being rough-cast, over the Roman cement.

The Roof, that is the ceiling of the Dining Room fell down this Spring, in the night time, with a tremendous crash, to the great alarm of Mrs R. It look'd very ill before, being much blistered, crack'd, and out of shape, and the quantity fallen was so great that I have caused the whole to be finish'd and present no *eye sore* on your arrival. We have managed to preserve the *cornice* entire. This Room is very dirty; I mean to cause the wood work to be well wash'd, and to re-paint the walls of the same sombre size colour as before. The Drawing room has remained as you left it to this day, only that it is much blacker and dirtier. It smokes ocasionally and Mrs R. had made a sleeping place of the closet. I cannot tell you what a kennel it is & has been. And many a time I have blushed to see it exposed to strangers.

I observed on reading some of your letters to Sandy, written on the passage out, that you wished it put into *decent* order. This, combined with my own feelings on the subject and the desire that you should find things tolerably comfortable on your return, and not to involve you almost instantly with Tradesmen but to give you some time to look about you, has induced me to cause Mr Henderson put up the wainscot doors and lining, which will be a trifling expence, and a few pounds will make it clean and comfortable, by painting (in size colour) the walls in a temporary way, leaving it to you to finish with the cloth in the way originally proposed when you find it convenient. With the help of an old carpet, some green baize and the old Turkey carpet in the House, it may be made to have a tolerable appearance. But this never can be the case as long as it is used as a sleeping place, probably Mrs L. might give a hint as to this.

The Green-House is removed from the Roof of the Tower. I had a regular survey on it & it was unanimously condemned as already rotten dangerous & at all times prejudicial. Altho' taken to pieces with great care by Mr Henderson himself, I do not think it will ever go together again. The under part is quite decayed, and the upper part was so firmly put together, that it required to be torn to pieces, and the glass snapp-crack'd in every direction as soon as it began to shake. Mrs L. does not seem aware that the *windows* of this place are used in the stove or Hot house created for the conservatory two years ago. The *frames* of the windows, and other woodwork, are carefully put aside in a corner of the Barn, where I *hope* you will find them safe. Now that the roof is relieved of this extra weight, and the numerous cracks & flairs soldered up, I am anxious to try it another season, as it is tight at present. But chiefly that if it must be renewed (the lead), you may have an opportunity of doing it in your own way, as I learn from Mr Henderson, you was particularly anxious to have it free from protuberances. I am my dear Uncle your affe. nephew.

Robert Ramage to Henrietta Liston   MS 5644 f. 10

London, 10 September 1815
My Dear Madam, A short time after I last wrote Mr Liston (19 July) I received your favour of the 29th June; since that time nothing material has happened. I had a letter from Dick a few days ago; he has

determined on going to Lisbon, to take shipping from Glasgow if he can. It would be much better to go from here as by so doing he will avoid the long round of the English Channel, which is often very tedious. I have written him that if he thinks I can be of any service in assisting him in getting off, that I would go down for that purpose.

I have frequently been out of Sydenham lately. Miss Elliot and George have been complaining a little, but are now quite well; they come to Town the end of this month, and Robert goes soon afterwards to Cambridge.

Mr Laing Senior and family have been in London this some time past. He has been unwell, but is now on the recovery. Capt. Robertson (his son in law) arrived from church about three weeks ago. Francis tells me that he does not intend to return to Malta; he has got a small pension in lieu of it. I find I was wrong in saying that Mr Dalzel was going to Algiers; he is settled at Malta, with a place under Government.

As for my prospects here, they are not very bright. I have had some offers, but as yet they have been such as are unacceptable.

I am afraid I may perhaps have given my uncle unnecessary trouble on a subject I wrote him upon in my last, at least nothing *as yet* has been determined upon respecting the India Packets, the company & Post office are not a good understanding upon that point, altho' its generally supposed that the latter will carry it.

Mr Stodart & family are well. I do not know whether you may have heard that about three years ago he took a large farm (600 acres) for his eldest son in the county of Kent. Mrs S. constantly resides there. I fear it is rather a bad concern, as the value of land has decreased greatly of late, on account of the low price of grain, and the farmers in general are complaining much. You will see great alterations and improvements in London on your arrival; there is a fine new street to be made from Carlton House to the new Road, Portland Place making the heart of it. They have already begun to pull down the houses; at the north end of this is a very large piece of ground (extending from Paddington on the west, to Tottenham Court Road on the east and almost surrounded by a canal) converted into a park, and call'd the Regents. There are also three new Bridges building, one of Iron between London and Blackfryars, another of stone between Blackfryars and Westminster, & a third at Vauxhall. A new Post Office on a great scale is about to be built at the

top of Cheapside, and a large street to be opened from that into Aldersgate street &c.

Edinburgh is also increasing fast, particularly at the north & south sides, and the new Road (Wellington entrance) which is to go along the South Brae of the Calton hill, with a Bridge thrown over from the end of Princes Street to the Calton will be a very great improvement. I have not heard anything lately about the canal.

We have had an extraordinary fine summer, and the crops throughout have been very abundant. The fine weather still continues, and Rain is now much wanted for the grass. Trade is dull; everybody afraid of speculating in the present state of affairs. By the last accounts, all at home, are in their ordinary, with my kind compliments to Mr Liston I am ever My Dear Madam Yours most affectionately.

Henrietta Ramage to Henrietta Liston   MS 5644 f. 77

Millburn Tower, 9 November 1815
My Dear Madam, Your letters of 26 July and 10 August came both to my hand about the end of September; ten days ago I received one dated 12th of January. What you wish for is indeed very hard to be found, viz. a sober cook maid. The vice of drunkeness has like a mighty torrent overrun the land, and its not only the old and the infirm but the young and the happy and the gay & what is more unpardonable, the accomplished and well informed spend there time & attention in the vile employment of drinking whisky. By what you say I perceive its a cook and housekeeper would answer your purpose. I shall be upon the lookout for such a one. Bell can really dress a shirt very well, not so expedicious perhaps as some other folks, but she does it clean and well. I know this from haveing Dick with me all summer. The precent dairy Maid is one who was long with Sandy and Miss Ramage. She does everything very well about the Milk and butter and can dress a plain dinner, is perfectly sober. With regard to myself I'll never think of leaving Millburn, till you fix at home for good and all. The cook & house keeper I think should be able to handle every sort of Needle.

Dick left this for London in October; when Robert saw how very weakly & distressed his only Brother was, he resolved to go with him to Lisbon, and will return in one of the English ships in two or three months. And now I am left a widow indeed, not one to comfort one.

Dick did not gain any strength all summer, for all the good things he had at Millburn. The grapes were a great treat to him; when sick feverish and distress'd a bunsh never fail'd to cool and relieve him.

I went in to Leith and Apply'd to Mr T. Richie to take care of your Boxes with the Bulbs. He wrot down the names of the ship and Captain in his pocket-book; said he would examine Loids list every day by which he would see when the Tiger arrives in the Thames, and will then calculate when they may be expected to be in Leith. And will then make enquairy at all the smaks and this all that can be done at this time. Joseph beg you may be told that the American garden is all dress'd up for the winter; every plant in it is in a thriving state. The same may be said of the Concervitory. I must say Mr Smail as we call him now does his duty to everything. I had a visit lately from the Duddingstone familie all in good health, rejoying greatly in the prospect of your return home. I saw Miss Liston & Jeannie Ramage today. Miss Liston is become very feeble. There are some little attentions I have paid them tho' not instructed so to do, takein it for granted that both Mr Liston and you would reather be pleased than otherwais. The weekly allowance of butter continued, and some help in the matter of coals driveing. Mr Reid is pretty well just now but oh much changed since you saw him. I remain My Dear Madam Most respectfully & affectionately yours.

Henrietta Ramage to Henrietta Liston   MS 5647 f. 85

Millburn Tower, 14 December 1816
My Dear Madam, Two days ago I received your letter of the 10th from Glasgow for which I return you many thanks. Robert received your first by post. The fur foot bag is wrapt in linen & put in the place where it lay safely for five years. We have made every possable search for the key of the Book press, but cant find it nor indeed any key for the Drawers or Bunker. I read over to Mr Smail the part of your letter about the marble-table.

Mr Reid had a sever attack of pain and distress immediately after Sir Robert left him. Had in some measuer recovered his ease & tranquility when some person told him they had seen the Ambassadores carriage drive from the door upon which he burst into tears, & could not refrain for above an hour. Mr Wm. Wilkie call'd here the day after you left us.

He had been ill very ill indeed with a Bealld throat sadly disappointed at missing his freinds. He & his familie are feeling themselves more comfortable than at Kinpoint. Jeannie Ramage is recovering, delighted with the Books.

I have got everything in the low Bedchamber arranged as you wished. The piannaforde is covered up. Robert and I do now sleep in the Tower, so when you return in Spring you will find your own rooms in season and everything I hope in good order & condition. At least if I enjoy my ordinary good health, no endeavours shall be wanting on my part. I'll stay where I can *out of sight* not otherwais. Oh what sad weather this is. I think with much anxiety about your health. Will you have the goodness when you write, as to say how you are.

December 23d. Nothing remarkable has occurred here since writing the above. Robert and I are liveing together very quaitly and peaceably our most frequent visiters are the Black birds and Robins. I have got the Soffa in the Octagon room all covered with the Reid stuff and as much of it over as will cover the sofa in the drawing room. we have had very cold stormy weather. All from the west as you are advanceing to the East we hope you may have escapeted it and all its ill consequences to your health.

Great exercions are made in this country to relive the Labouring poor. In Edinh. about 300 men are sett to work at Publick works at one shilling a day with libberty to go away if they can find higher wadges. Lord Hopetoun is employing a great many work people at Hopetoun House. Mrs Dundas is giveing out yarn to spin. Everyboddy who is able is doing something to lessen the generall distress. We are to have a Meeting of the Heritors of the Parish on Thursday to consider what is to done for the poor. The managers of the Theatre at Edinburgh are to give the profits of one Night to the fund for the Labouring poor.

May I take the libberty to offer most affectionate compliments to Miss Bond[33] and Miss Travours. Mr Falkener was here today; poor McNab's much worse, is now become apprehensive of his danger. The Measels are radgeing at Edinr. I see by the newspapers there is a son of Mr Monrows dead. You will remember how he talked of his children. Mr Reid is just as he was. Jeannie Ramage continues to recover. I ever am My Dear Madam yours most faithfully.

---

[33] The sister of Phineas Bond, a British Consul in America during Liston's term of office there.

Henrietta Ramage to Henrietta Liston MS 5648 f. 72

Millburn Tower, 9 February [1817]

My Dear Madam, Some days ago the wood pigeons and several others of the fether'd tribe have proclaimed it at Millburn that the time of the singing of birds is come. The snow drops & Polianthesis are beginning to peep out; everything in the concervitory and stove are in high good health.

Mary Gray has lost her aunt, and got her Eighteen years services rewarded by a settlement of ten pounds a year. The sons thought it too little; they have added five pounds to it. She is in very poor health. I have seen Mrs Wm. Crawford: if her countenance is to be believed she is everything that is good. The old lady I hear is very much pleased with her daughter-in-law. Last Sunday Dr Duncan took noteis in prayer of the insult offered to the Prince Regent.[34] Lord Hopetoun is becoming very popeler here; sent 48 Bolls of Meal to the poor of Kirkliston Parish. Two of his farms were reported to him as in fameis good order. He lett the tenants have them at something less than what they offer'd.

17th. Your letter of the 1st to Robert came here in due course of post. Mr Falconar was with us one day last week. The list of plants was not finish'd.[35] He says he could push the Printer to make more dispatch, but they are very apt to make mistakes when they are hurried. They send over the sheets to Mr Falconar to be corrected. Says he has as yet had very little to do with it in that way. There will be about 37 pages in it.

Mr McNab is considerably better in his general health, but no change at all upon his voice. The Doctors now think the disorder is upon his windpipe & not upon the lungs. The makein of footpaths is going on here with some spirit. I hear the parish of Kirknewton intend to follow the good example sett before them. Do you remember a miserable looking wretch like a Beggar who used to go about here. She fell sick lately at the house of Laird Smeal. It was thought needful to make her clean an opperation to which she submitted with much reluctance. There was found about her person £3 sterling in silver, and many parcels unexamined.

Lord Torphichen calld here today. Most unfortunately Robert was in Town. His Lordship left a pressing invitation for him to come and see

---

[34] A mob stoned his coach as he returned from opening Parliament in January.
[35] This catalogue of the plants at Millburn is unfortunately lost.

them at Calderhouse. I hope he will go some day very soon. Mr Smail seems very well content with the young man he has got for an Asistant in the garden. I think him a very indurstes person. Mr Reid continues much in the same state he has been for some months past. The parcel you sent by Mr Robert Liston is come to hand, but no letter is yet come by him. Jeanie Ramage is now upon her feet again, but complaining saddly of weakness. Dr S. has sent away the insain gentilman as incurable; says he will have nothing more to do with people in that state. The first peas is above the ground. The wheat which was planted in the west garden is looking very well. John Douglas is in Raptures with the Drawing of Millburn.[36] I can think of nothing more to write at precent. I remain as ever most faithfully and Affectionately yours.

Henrietta Ramage to Henrietta Liston   MS 5651 f. 15

Millburn Tower, 23 November 1817

My Dear Madam, This day's post brought me your most wellcome letter of the 10th of October. I had been grieving' over the uncomfortable circumstance of your not hearing from us.

Again am at the old business, writing of the death of freinds. On the 8th of October the Hon Henry Erskine died at Ammondell.[37] I hear Mrs Erskine is going to resied at Edinr.; some of your Glasgow correspondents would mention Mrs Balfour's death. I have never been able to lear any particulers about it. Mr Reid was better during the summer months, is rather worse, restless & in great measuer lost his realish for conversation. Mrs Grant of Lagan[38] & a coachful of ladys were here in June; one of them wished to make me believe that she was intimately aquainted with Sir Robert and you said all Sir R.'s near relations were gone to settle in America. I had a letter from John Douglas, a very kind enquairy after your health. He was alarmed by seeing in the Newspapers that the Plague had appeared in Constantinople.

The strelitz Regina was sent to Lady Morton[39] to take a drawing of it.

[36] Reproduced on p. 330.
[37] Hon. Henry Erskine (1746-1817), a leading Whig advocate.
[38] Mrs Anne Grant of Laggan, *née* MacVicar (1755-1835), author of the *Memoirs of an American Lady* (1808).
[39] Susan Elizabeth Yarde-Buller, wife of George Douglas, 15th earl of Morton, a noted Whig.

I dare say you will have a letter from her ladyship, at the same time with this. The Rev. Mr Torrance has his son settled his assistant and successor. Miss Margaret Liston has recovered her health. Young Robert Liston is sett up a surgeon in Edinr. & is getting into repute as an operator.[40] Lord Rosebery has made good his promise to the Queensferry People: brought in watter to their Town.

The carnations were not in flower at the time Joseph wrot. They were very showy & pretty, with many different coulers and shades. The stocks made a fine appearance; two of them much admired as rare. Lilly has got an unexpected addition to her family; her oldest daughter has got a husband. Dr Stuart's son Alexr is going out to America, to his uncle who is to receive him as a son & heir. A Gas light company is Erected in Edinburgh. 1000000£ was the sum requaired; the subscription was filled up in the course of *one month*. I was glad to hear about Miss Bond; shall tell Charles Richie all you say about him.

Alace, Alace, our young Princess; the grief that is express's for her is very general.[41] On the funerall day the shopes were all shut, and the churches opened in the afternoon. Two or three of the ministers refused to open there churches; you will wonder to hear that Sir Henry Moncrieff was one who refused.

[The] Books in the drawing room closet are [?]; we had them all out & exposed to [?] for two days. Robert helps with these sort of operations. The ivy is cut from the window, so that it admits more aire. The mimosas are cut more & look very well. Mrs Crawford at Ratho-house is now for the most part confined to Bed; no hope of recovery. A young Heir or Heires is expected there some of these days. Dr Dunkan has got five lady Boarders. The canal is begun. I can think of nothing more to say excedpt that I ever am Sir Robert & your very affectinot and most humble servant.

Robert Ramage Liston to Henrietta Liston   MS 5655 f. 116

Millburn Tower, 13 December 1819
My Dear Madam, I take the opportunity of Joseph's writing to enclose this at the same time, altho' I have but little to say. I have received your

---

[40] Robert Liston (1794–1849), later professor of clinical surgery, University College, London; Fellow of the Royal Society.
[41] Princess Charlotte, daughter of the Prince Regent, died in childbirth in 1817.

favour of the 25 Nov. enclosing the seeds and a letter for Mr Hopkirk. The seeds appear to be in good order.

The circumstances which occasioned Mr Wilkie's death were these. He had been riding out in the fields and on his return in putting up his horse in the stable he was shifting the bridle for a halter when the animal turned round and bit him in the side, which caused him great pain. He walked into the house, but a mortification soon ensued and he died the night of the following day. He had been in possession of the horse for a considerable length of time and it was never known to bite before.

This is something like the shape of the garden wall at present, tho' you will easily see that no proportion is observed, but you will recollect it perfectly as it is done nearly as possible according to Sir Robert's directions. The only fault which I hear people speak of in making their observations is, that it may look a little awkward the west side being an oblong circle and the east a straight line.

We have had an uncommon mild winter: as yet the Pentland hills have never had the least white upon them, but a good deal of rain of late. Mrs Ramage and all friends are well. I beg kind respects to Sir Robert and am my dear madam yours most affectionately.

Robert Ramage to Robert Liston   MS 5657 f. 32

Millburn Tower, 14 February 1820
Honoured Uncle, I received your letters of the 27th & 28th Decr. last yesterday, and am rejoiced to find that you and Lady Liston are pleased with my marriage, and the many kind things you both say on the occasion, are very grateful to my feelings. She is indeed a very fine young woman, and I am convinced that you will both be satisfied with her in every respect.

Your offer of my living here till you return and of them removing to New Gardens, I will accept with pleasure, as also the fifty Pounds for factorship, which I shall set down at the end of your account for the present year only. As for your other generous offers, I beg leave to decline accepting them at present as I think I shall manage very well without.

Having laid out so much money in bringing the Marylands purchase into good order, has as yet prevented me reaping any profit; on the contrary, but I think as the principal expenditure is now nearly over, I

may look forward to make at least legal interest. Having laid out a good deal upon it, and having to pay Interest on the greater part of the purchase money, the £500 lately got comes a propos enough; but if I could get Mr Hunter to settle accounts with me, I should have plenty. He seems however very dilatory.

The coach house stable, & Byre, we have finished, as also the flooring over the coach House, and stable, and were proceeding to lay the flooring over the Byre and other rooms, so that your letter has just come in good time to prevent us going on. As Mr Henderson has all the flooring prepared, we can let it by till wanted. I shall lose no time in getting the necessary information respecting the stones for the new building, and begin to drive as soon as possible. I fear we shall not be able to accomplish driving them all with our own horses as they will be busy for some time in ploughing and laying down the North Callerstone field for grain, grass seeds &c. &c. We shall however do as much as we can without them.

Liston Shiels. I some time ago asked Mr Henderson to give me a statement of what he thought a building would cost as you proposed at Liston Shiels. My question was, what would a square plan building of two storeys, with a flat roof, 18 feet square (that is a little larger than the new Room at the west end of the Barn) with 4 windows, decently fitted up, amount to. I enclose his answer, but I should suppose a head Roof with a parapet wall like the new building at the west side of the Barn would answer equally well, and the expence would be trifling in comparison. It would be difficult to say what the expence of making alterations or improvements on the old House might come to, but when Aitken gets the new addition, he might be allowed to fit up the old House in the way he thinks best, at his own expence. We could not get the Dyke above two thirds finished before the winter set in, from the seasons being so far advanced before we began to it. Lord Morton has not yet begun to his side; it might not be amiss should you have occasion to write him soon, to give him a hint, as we cannot commence planting untill both sides are up, and we have a quantity of young plants raised ready.

I mentioned to you in a former letter that I had a disagreement with John Anderson respecting the garden wall. He wishes to charge a large sum (sixty or seventy pounds) in addition, for its being built circular altho' he took the measure and knew perfectly well in giving his

Estimate that it was to be so; and I told him all the time, that you wished to know as nearly as possible what the *whole* amount would be, in order that you might determine whether you would build it, or not. I am determined not to pay him, and several architects who I have consulted, agree that I am quite right. I am therefore not upon good terms with him at present, but as he does his work well, and as I know on that account you would prefer employing him about the new Buildings I shall speak to him, tomorrow, and if he chooses to give up the point, shall consult with him about the stones &c.

I enclose a rough sketch of the ground plan of the Buildings as they now are, as also the different measurements which I took yesterday.

You will observe by the yearly account which I sent about the middle of last month, that I gave Miss Gray the ten Pounds in the month of December. She looked better at that time than I had seen her for a long time before.

I do not think Mr Hopkirk has failed. I imagine he had only found it necessary to stop payment for a time; at least I hope that is the case, as I have not heard any more of it lately.

Mrs Hamilton continues always well. Miss Liston joins me in kind respects to you & Lady Liston. I am Honoured Uncle Your most affectionate nephew.

Robert Ramage to Robert Liston   MS 5657 f. 140

Millburn Tower, 29 May 1820
Honoured Uncle, Your favours of the 12th & 13th April does not lessen the embarrassment I lay under with respect to the plan I ought to adopt regarding the easter rooms, as I find by the present sketch which you enclose, that you still suppose *were we* to make the middle wall the Gable (that is excluding the small north room) the outside walls would measure Thirty six feet nine inches, whereas they only actually measure about thirty feet and a half. In this dilemma I am very much at a loss how to act; whether to build it up to the length you suppose it to be, or to build it up to the length it really is. Doing it in the first way might hazard its being in the way of the rooms you are projecting on the west side. If done in the other manner, the space would be too small for three rooms. Yet from your saying, that from the sketch I sent you, your recollection of the situation of the washing house &c., induced you to

think they might be left standing, I am inclined to Follow the first plan, by making the wall of the gable as thin as possible at the north end, and lessening the length of the wall from 36 feet 9 in to say 35 feet 9, and taking in that proportion.

By doing this, the Gable would stand about three feet and a half further south than the north side of the wall of the Bath, wash house &c., the north side of which wall stands four feet three inches farther south than the south side of the wall which divides the mangle room & laundry from the old stable, so that altogether in that case, the north end of the eastern row would stand about seven feet and a half further south than the line of direction of that wall which divides the mangle room from the old stable. I think this is the plan I must follow, deferring it however for some time in hopes of hearing further from you, and in the meantime be getting the stones hewn, and everything ready. I am sorry to say that the Ivy was taken down some time ago, as upon receiving your letter of the 28th Feby. I immediately consulted Joseph upon what would be the best time to remove it, with a certainty of its growing, and it was his opinion that we had no time to delay. We therefore cut it up in flakes, and planted it about the garden wall, & old pigeon house. As the saving of it seemed to be your only motive for not pulling down the north gable, I shall not now hesitate in doing so, as the stones will be useful to us. I wrote yesterday to Mr Johnston, stating to him your wish respecting the fences at Listonshiels, but I am doubtful whether he will readily comply. I am told he is a strange character, and penurious in the extreme.

I have at last settled accounts with John Anderson *in my own way*, that is, without making any allowance for the walls being built circular. He was however so long in coming forward, that I had previously engaged a young man at upper Gogar for the Easter stables, who I have no doubt will do the business as well, altho' a young beginner, and I have every reason to believe at a cheaper rate. I think the sketch you enclose for the addition to the house at Liston Shiels will look extremely well, and will be much better adopted for that part of the country than a flat roof.

I saw Lord Morton's factor lately, and he says his Lordship has given directions to proceed with the March Dyke on his side, so that I hope we shall be able to begin planting a part at least in the autumn. The Edinburgh new water company have I understand found a spring more convenient for them than that at Listonshiels.

I doubt whether this will reach you at Constantinople, but hope should you have left it, it will be forwarded to you.

All friends in this part of the country are in their usual health. Mrs Ramage and Miss Liston join me in best wishes to you and Lady Liston and I am Honoured Uncle Your most affectionate nephew.

Robert Ramage to Robert Liston   MS 5657 f. 207

Millburn Tower, 6 November 1820

Honoured Uncle, I have received your favour of the 23d Octr. I wrote to you on the 10th, and to Lady Liston on the 17th Ult. I am uncertain whether this last may have reached [you] before your departure from Geneva. It was giving her the sad news of Mr J.H. Dundas' death on the 8th Ult. and informing her that Mrs Liston was delivered of a Daughter on the 16th Ult.

We had made all the pitts for the trees at Liston Shiels, and had intended to let the planting of them stand till the spring, as I had been advised, but as you seem to prefer planting in the autumn we shall set about it soon.

By your speaking of the plantations interrupting the road up to the top of the hill, I apprehend there is some misunderstanding respecting the distance which the Dykes are carried south, as they only extend about half way from the northern towards the southern boundary, Mr Aitken not having asked to carry them further. The ground above them is so excessively wet & swampy that I suspect no trees would grow without a great expense of draining previous to planting, and after this follows a steep rocky hill. We have made the pitts at three feet distance from each other, but shall make them nearer, particularly in the clumps of spruce firs which you mention. All the trees you speak of were included in our arrangements except the Hornbeam and Silver firs, some of which we shall get from Edinburgh. As Lord Morton proposed that the Burn should still be the March, it would not do to plant a *single* hedge, but one I think might be planted on each side of the Burn. We have sown a quantity of Haw which may be used for that purpose when ready. We plant all our side of the Burn, and Lord Morton on his side. Mr Aitken has made an open drain near the back of the dyke to prevent the water rushing down from the hill into the plantation and to keep his sheep dry under lee of the dyke. The contract

N

is signed between Mr Johnstone's man of business, the contractor, & myself, for building the East march Dyke, which is to be finished next year under a penalty of £50, at the rate of 8/11 pr. Rood. By measuring the length of the map I think the expense will amount to about £300 in whole.

I forgot to mention to you before, that I found it absolutely necessary to paint the outside of the conservatory this summer, as the paint was quite worn off, and the wood in some parts showing symptoms of decay.

The wrights are busy about the new building; the cornices, battlements, &c. are made exactly to the plan, and look extremely handsome. The only deviations from the plan are, two additional embrasures, the walls four inches higher, the windows a little larger, and the north gable of aisler. I also forgot to speak of the coat of arms. I consulted Mr Fairbairn (a nephew of the Professors, who has the management of the building of the College)[42] about it, and he very obligingly extended the drawing from the arms upon the Lyon clerks [? and ?] recommended a man who has done all the [?] work about the college. He has been at work on it these three or four weeks, and he appears to be doing it very neatly but it will cost I imagine nine or ten Pounds. I thought I had formerly mentioned that Mr Hamilton & Mr Wrench had called here three or four months ago. Mrs Hamilton I am told supports her loss much better than might have been expected. All other friends are well. Miss Liston is almost quite well, and the child is in the best of health.

Mrs Ramage writes Lady Liston about Mrs Shirreff. I intend going to Leith today to see about the chimney pieces for the easter Rooms. I am ever Honoured Uncle Your most affectionate nephew.

Henrietta Ramage to Henrietta Liston   MS 5664 f. 19

Millburn Tower, 29 February 1821
My Dear Madam, The postscript to your letter of the 4th of this month

---

[42] James Fairbairn, later the author of *Crests of the Families of Great Britain and Ireland*, (2 vols., London, 1860).

gave me very sincere concern indead. Well do I know what it is to lose an only and much loved sister.[43] These sorrows is a tax we must all pay for the length of our lives in this world.

There is a Miss Rainnie a candidat for the place of Housekeeper at Millburn Tower; has been 14 years in place as a Governess, was accationally left with the charge of the house for a month or two at a time in the Ladys absence, which is all the experiance she has got in the Housekeeping line; was taught dress making in the early part of her life, understands the makeing of wines jellys &c. Her father was a once wealthy farmer in East Lothian, but faild in his circumstances, so that his familie were all obliged to do for themselves. I think her a good looking serviceable kind of person. Evendently much better Educated than is common for one in that line, refers herself to a Mrs Hossak at Newington, the widow of a West India gentilman. I shall make enquairy there as to sobriyty and temper.

We were all inlived this morning by Sir Roberts letter from London. God be praised you are once more upon English ground. Robert & his wife sett off this forenoon for New Gardens. They are to return the day after tomorrow and take away the child. One of the cows has brought a femal calf: shall I rear or sell it? The [verds?] in East-row are going most fameously; there is a camelia in the concervitory fourteen inches in circumference of a most beautiful white but this is not all its Excellence. Its so healthy & vigorous as delights one to look at it. Indeed everything in the place is in high health & good order. Miss M. Stuart at Queensferry has got a Legacy of £700 left her by a freind. I shall wait for your instructions about the calf and the Housekeeper. The wages she had in her last place was £30 a year.

A considerable change has takein upon me within the last six or eight months; many of the weaknesses of old-age have come raipidly on. I can still move about a little in the morning, but by midday am just a feeble good for nothing old woman, so much so that I can't sit up a whole day. Ever my dear Madam your most affecy.

---

[43] Mary Marchant, the wife of Lady Liston's brother Nathaniel, died in Antigua in 1820. She and her son sent plants and seeds from Antigua.

Sir Robert Liston to the Rev. Dr Jamieson[44]   MS 5681 f. 20

Millburn, 22 November 1821

My dear Sir, You have my thanks for the gift of your *Gothick* structure, & for the flattering mode in which the present was made.

The nature of the edifice is not such as to attract the attentions of *the many*; and of the few that may notice it there may well be a large portion of half informed cricks who may be less inclined to praise than to find fault. I am one of small number who will take a warm interest in the system of architecture, and in the manner in which the building is executed. But I will not promise even to look at the structure, till my own erection be completed, which I hope may be at no distant time; it is indeed already so far advanced as to put it in your power to judge of the stile of the Fabrick, which I flatter myself will not displease you. And I hope that, while you spend your leisure in illustrating to the learned the depths of philological science, you will not contemn or disapprove the man who employs a portion of his time and his means (with a view to the enjoyment of the traveller and the lover of rural sciences) in smoothing the face of nature and embellishing the landscape, within the narrow sphere that surrounds his retreat.

I have felt disappointment at having seen so little of you during the past summer. I endeavoured to find you in Edinburgh, but was misled by a Blunder of the Directory, which had placed you in George's Street, and immediately after I was told you were at Paris. I trusted that at your return, you would give us *signe de vie*.

Like you, I prefer sunshine & long days for paying visits, but, I rejoice that you have resolved to brave the advanced Season and come to us even now. And though in the midst of great confusion, in consequence of having pulled down our old accomodation, & not completed the new, we can, notwithstanding, give you a warm and comfortable Bedchamber. But we are so much engaged, with company at home and dinners abroad, that the only days on which we can receive you with perfect convenience and pleasure are *Tuesday* and *Wednesday of next week*, when I hope it may suit you to come to us, and if so, I hope you will permit me to call on *Tuesday forenoon* & bring you out, and we can with perfect ease carry you into town on *Thursday*.

[44] Rev. Dr John Jamieson (1759-1838), philologist and Minister at Nicholson Street Chapel, Edinburgh.

In consequence of our present want of acomodation, we have not yet unpacked our Turkish Baggages, and Lady Liston cannot for the moment lay her hand on the few medals she had destined for you, but she will make an effort for that purpose before Tuesday. Believe me &c.

Henrietta Ramage to Henrietta Liston MS 5667 f. 48

Millburn Tower, 9 April 1822
My Dear Madam, This day past brought me your letter of the 4th. I am very much at a loss what to say about David. He has undoubtedly lost that respect which a superior servant ought to have, from the other servants in a familie. Yet I dont think any of them would use him ill, & if he is in better health he will be able to Act his own part. [Mrs?] McDougal says the people about the place were very often asking for a dram from him and he was so simple as to give it. It appeared he never paid the whisky account, which amounted to £16 some shillings. McDougall says he was so poor as not to have one shilling in pocket, but borrowing from her and from Joan. Said he had so many things to Attend to that he was not able to keep accounts: had he told me this I never would have lett the whisky accounts run on.

One Sunday evening he went in the twilight backward & foreward past the Housekeepers windows, with a Pistol in his hand. I am not a pet to be frightened with trifels, but I must confess a drunk man going about with fire-arms in his hand Alarmed me very much. The excuse he made for it was that he overheard Mrs McDougall say, where is that old wretch going now, and he resolved to give her a fright.

One of the Ewes has brought two lambs; we have made a cheese. Lilly has been going about in seartch of a topted Drake; she found one but the People it belong to would not sell it, but promised to give her some of the Eggs.

McDougall has got both a Dairy Maid & cook: is perfectly satisfied with the recommendation she got of them. The cook is a stout looking person, is out of place & will come home Eight days before the term. Mrs Wilkie has sent six Goose-eggs, which Lilly says she will get hatcht. There has been a great stealing of Hens about us, one of your bonny gees went too. We have made some marmelade; the oranges

were beginning to turn very scarce, and I was affraid you might lose the Opertunity. I ever am My Dear Madam Most faithfully yours.
P.S. David marked all the diffrent wines ere he went away.

Henrietta Liston to Lady Morton   MS 5667 f. 197

Millburn Tower, 23 July 1822
My dear Lady Morton, I shall be highly gratified to join in paying a compliment to the King & I esteem myself obliged by the honor & kindness of your remembrance of me on so flattering an occasion. We must indeed esteem ourselves indebted to Sir Walter Scott for his suggestion.[45]

If your Ladyship will have the goodness to subscribe for me we will settle the matter at meeting. With best wishes to the family at Dalmahoy. I remain yours very faithfully.

Henrietta Ramage to Henrietta Liston   MS 5675 f. 45

Millburn Tower, 16 December 1825
My Dear Madam, Your letter from Tiningham arraived in due course; very wellcome it was to Miss Ramage and me. The account you give of your health tho not equal to our wishes was at least up to our hopes. We have been lamenting over the bad weather every day. Sir William and Lady Fitiss have had a long letter of inquairy from Mrs Lindsay. The Clifton hall Familie are in deep distress by the sudden death of Mrs White. The Bell is put upon the Door; the cover is ready for the cairrage; the carpets and window-curtains are all laid up & cover'd with pact-sheets.

The vilage of Ratho is freed from one of its Irish Inhabitants; fled from the Land of justice, after comiting an Enormise crime—Rape.

16 Decem. Miss White Melvil called here today; med many kind enquairys about your health. Mrs Troter Dreghorn sent today to enquear anenet your health. Mr Hil[l] a Builder in Edin. has fail'd for 30000£; several other Bankrupciss in the same time are dayly expected.

[45] The visit of George IV to Edinburgh in 1822.

December 22d. I received your letter from London yesterday; glad to have such favourable accounts of the weather and your health. I hope you may be able to send us still better news from Devonshair. We are all going on here very Peasably and quaitly. Nothing but good humer in every department of the familie. You will see by this letter that my sight is nothing mended, if it should please God to affect me with blindness, I trust & hope he will also grant the grace of resignation to bear it. I have got Eight Letters I know not how to get them convay'd to you. I feel very gratfull for Miss Bonds kind remembrance. I ever am My Dear Lady Liston Yours most faithfully & affectinotly.

Henrietta Ramage to Henrietta Liston   MS 5676 f. 71

Millburn Tower, 1 June 1826
My Dear Madam, Your letter of the 21st and 25 of May made me happy some days ago. A thousand thanks for the postcript. No person who knows so much of Col. Brown[46] as I do but must take an interest in everything that concerns him. We have got Plumbers and glaisers puting everything to rights in there diffrent lines. The floar cloaths in Sir Roberts dressing room and yours are in a very bad condition; absolute rags indeed. They have turned out so worthless that [I] am unwilling to buy anything of the same kind. Why should not you have the comfort of a carpet upon these chambers? but I'll not do anything in it till I hear from you again. We have got home the new cow; a very handsome Animale not very large. I dar say a Month or a little more may pas over ere she calf. Five young turkeys are come out & a large familie of Duklings. The Watter-hen is come back. Robin is singing most chearfully. Dr Stuart has lost his oldest Brother.

June 2. Sir William & Lady Fitis were here today inquering after your welfare. They took a look of the concervitory, were charmed with its various beautys, and the high order in which everything about it is. I feel gratified with Miss Bonds kind remembrance. I see by the last Newspaper that Sir Walter Scott has lost his Lady and Mr Finley has got a son. I can think of nothing more worth writing to you. Miss Ramage joins me in respectfull & affectionate compliments.

[46] Frank Fynes Brown, Mary Marchant's son by a previous marriage.

Henrietta Ramage to Henrietta Liston   MS 5677 f. 26

Millburn Tower, 16 March 1827

My Dear Madam, I think it is now time I should begin another letter. We have had a most dreadfull storm, such as has not been seen since 1796; the snow fell incessantly for two days & nights. Its consequences was severely felt here; the new well over-flowed in the night time; about five in the morning we had a foot and a half water over all the under parte of the House. With good deal of labour and some expence of coals & whisky we have now got everything put to rights again.

I have got home the glass cloathe web 56 yards, so you wont need to buy anything of that sort for a long time to come. The Hams are makein today; they look very well. One of the Animals wighed 10 stone, the other 9 stone 10 lb. Mrs Liston spent a day with me this week, for all the bad roads; she is very good & kind to me comes and sees me frequently. Little Robert is going on very well with his leasons; if he does not turn out a good speller it won't be for want of practice; he now spells every word that he speaks. All the familie are in good health. Mr Hogg of New Liston died last week. Lord Buchan is so much better as to be again in the Liveing room; Lord Morton is still alive & that is all that can be said. I hear there are very few parties in Edinr. this winter. The Ladys are busieing themselves in working for the poor. There last last [sic] sale produced £300.

March 19. I was very sorrie to see the Estate of Westburn in the newspapers, to be sold on the first of June. Mr Burns the Architect[47] sent two men here tother day beging the favour to let them take the dementions of the living room Chimney pice. He is to put one of the same at Rickerton. Mrs P. Ramage is about buying a House; there are pennyworths of that sort to be got just now, so many Builders have failed. Robert Liston[48] has lately performed a cure upon a person who was poisoned, by means of a pump. We have got Wilkies diner with all the speaches into the Mercury; its amusing to see how much Mr Smail is delighted with it. Sir Robert's speatch he has read over & over and over again. I think he has been fortunate in his two youn[g] gardeners; they

---

[47] William Burn (1789-1870) built Riccarton for Sir William Gibson-Craig, and rebuilt Tyninghame for the earl of Haddington.
[48] The famous surgeon; see above.

are both of them sober attentive lads. We are to have the sacrament dispenced at Ratho on Sunday next. It will give you pleasuer to hear that Mr Aitkin has not suffered by the late storm.

March 21st. This has been a week of increas; the large cow has brough a fine calf, and 18 chickens are hatched. One of the christmas familie is alive, a stout little fellow. We have also had deaths, yesterday Vulcan killed 14 Ratts. I was just returned from church when yours of the 21 Feby. was put in to my hand; very glad I am that you can say, you are both in good health. Harriot is employed in the way you wish. I hope your servant is now recovered. I have been sympathizing with you in that kind of trouble; George had a violent illness. Bell was for 12 days little out of Bed; the cook fell sick at her Mother's house, & was away two weeks; we are now all of us perfectly well. I am My Dear Madam Most sincerely & Affectionately yours.

David Wilkie[49] to Sir Robert Liston   MS 5678 f. 37

7 Terrace Kensington, London, 18 July 1828
Dear Sir Robert, I was gratified in hearing lately from Mr Hamilton that both Lady Liston and yourself are in pretty good health, and at present enjoying the beauties of the season at Milburn. I had great pleasure in receiving your own & Lady Liston's letter from Madrid, from which place after making a journey to Seville I have returned here about 3 weeks ago.

My friends here have shown much kindness to me since my return and one instance of this is a very distinguished one I cannot help mentioning to you. The king on hearing of my arrival, of himself, sent for me to come to him, at St James' & to bring whatever Pictures I had made on my travels. I went and was very graciously received. Of the pictures I had made in Italy he selected two for himself, and gave me strict injunctions to come to him with those I have made in Spain the moment they should arrive, and reminded me of various works he had formerly commended of me.

This favourable disposition in such a quarter unabated by absence, appears to set me up a good deal in my own mind. My malady retards

---

[49] See Introduction.

me much in what I am doing, but if the Pictures I made in Spain were arrived I still count upon being able to make some show of work.

Private. Whether the mark of His Majesty's condescending remembrance of me may have originated in a circumstance in which you have yourself, with much kindness towards me, had a share I cannot altogether determine but its effect, (it is but proper I should state to you), will make what we had in contemplation less necessary to be urged. Or at all events I think it right that you should be informed of this as you can judge much better than I what should or should not be done in that matter.

The king I had not seen for 4 years, he is but little changed: appeared hale hearty & in high spirits. He introduced me to the Duke of Clarence[50] who was with him who asked me several questions about my travels. May I present my respectful regards to Lady Liston in which my sister heartily begs to join me I am now again settled in my house here my brother & sister with me. Mrs Wilkie of Fowlden with her son were here & this way to pass the summer in Scotland after an absence of 5 years. Of Miss Mackenzie's return I have not yet heard.

With high esteem & respect I have the honour to subscribe myself Your most devoted Servant.

Eliza Fletcher[51] to Sir Robert Liston   MS 5678 f. 105

Auchendinny, 14 November 1828
My dear Sir, I have not ventured to intrude upon you since your sad bereavement. But we have often heard of you from your grateful and attach'd young sculptor, and I cannot deny myself the satisfaction of assuring you that the kind encouragement he met with at Millburn Tower this summer, has had the happiest effect in exciting his hope of professional success, and consequently in stimulating his industry. I owe this acknowledgment no less to the memory of the kind friend he has lost, than to yourself and if (as *she* predicted) He should one day become an eminent artist; I hope he will never forget to whose early, and most friendly notice he was so much indebted. I heard the other day

---

[50] William Henry, duke of Clarence (1765-1837), later William IV.
[51] See Introduction.

from our friend Mrs Craig Millar;[52] she mentiones Miss Cullens improved health, but the chief subject of her letter is Lady Liston's death and while she does no more than justice to the many rare and excellent qualities she preferred, she adds 'how fortunate for herself and her survivor that her sufferings were not protracted but that she enjoyed life almost to the very last'.

Mr Fletcher altho' confined to a sick bed desires me offer you his sincere and grateful respects, and I am my dear Sir Your truly obliged and sincerely Respectful.

Jane Johnes[53] to Sir Robert Liston   MS 5680 f. 41

Hill Court, Exeter, 28 May [1829]

My Dear Friend, I had the pleasure of receiving your very kind letter last night. How good was you in writing to me not having heard from me but indeed I never received your first letter & the first intelligence I had was from the publick paper. The shock I felt very severely & for several days I was confined to my bed. Till I lost her I knew not how very dear she was to me & oh what a loss is yours but you have nobly born it but we must be mourners all our lives but not like those who have no hope. A short time will unite us to those dear friends never again to be separated.

I have been very unwell all the winter & have such a weakness in my right arm that I can scarce hold a pen; this must be my excuse for a sad scrawl & a short letter. God bless & comfort you. Believe me to be my dear Sir Robert Your grateful & ever sincere friend.

[52] See Introduction.
[53] See Introduction. Jane Johnes (1757-1833) died soon after.

INDEX

Numbers in **bold** refer to numbered cases in the 'Plea roll of Edward I's army'. All other numbers refer to pages.

SCOTTISH HISTORY SOCIETY

OFFICE-BEARERS AND COUNCIL
1989-1990

President

PROFESSOR D.E.R. WATT

Chairman of Council

DR JEAN MUNRO

Honorary Treasurer

PROFESSOR IAN B. COWAN

Honorary Secretary

DR NORMAN A. T. MACDOUGALL
Department of Scottish History
University of St Andrews
St Andrews, Fife KY16 9AL

Honorary Publication Secretaries

DR JULIAN GOODARE   DR MICHAEL LYNCH
Department of Scottish History
University of Edinburgh
17 Buccleuch Place, Edinburgh EH8 9LN

Council

MR GEORGE DALGLEISH
MR C. J. DAVEY
DR JAMES KIRK
DR ALLAN MACINNES
DR FARQUHAR MACINTOSH
MR IAN MACIVER
DR ROGER MASON
DR CHARLES MUNN
DR ATHOL MURRAY
MRS MAIRI ROBINSON
DR E. P. D. TORRIE
MRS VIRGINIA WILLS

Corresponding Members of Council

PROFESSOR MICHEL DE BOÜARD, *France*
PROFESSOR MAURICE LEE, JR, *USA*

MEMBERSHIP

Membership of the Scottish History Society
is open to all who are interested in the history of Scotland.
For an annual subscription of £15.00
members normally receive one volume each year.
Enquiries should be addressed to
the Honorary Secretary, whose address
is given overleaf.

SCOTTISH HISTORY SOCIETY

103rd ANNUAL REPORT

*Presented to the Annual General Meeting
by the Council, 9 December 1989.*

The second volume of the new Fifth Series, *Letters of George Lockhart of Carnwath, 1698-1732*, edited by Dr Daniel Szechi, was issued to members in August. With documents relative to the union of the parliaments and the Jacobite movement, this publication is expected to arouse considerable interest. Its issue was, however, overshadowed by the sudden death in London on 7 July of the Publication Secretary, Dr T. I. Rae, who had finalised arrangements for its distribution only days before his decease. As Secretary of the Society from 1969 to 1976 and Publication Secretary from 1976, Dr Rae had worked unstintingly in the service of the Society and was responsible not only for the new style and appearance of the Fifth Series, but also, in conjunction with the printers, Pillans & Wilson, for the new system of printing which has produced considerable financial savings for the Society. It is hoped that a fuller appreciation of Dr Rae's many services to Scottish history in general and the Society in particular will appear in a subsequent volume.

The choice of a successor to Dr Rae has not been an easy one, but Council is pleased to announce that they have appointed Dr Julian Goodare and Dr Michael Lynch as joint Publication Secretaries. Inevitably the processing of future publications has been somewhat disrupted, but it is still hoped that Professor Adam's edition of the *Calendar of Fearn, 1471-1667* will appear on schedule, while two of the items for the proposed *Miscellany* volume are already to hand. Unfortunately other proposed volumes are in jeopardy. The future of the *Cupar Town Council Minutes, 1640-1655*, which were to have been co-edited by Dr Rae, is questionable, and preparation of the *Minutes of the Mid and East Lothian Miners' Association, 1894-1914* has been suspended. Council would welcome proposals for future publications.

In financial terms, the cost of producing volumes, despite recent economies, continues to rise. In this respect a very generous

benefaction of £12,500 from the late Godfrey W. Iredell will offset the cost of the *Letters of George Lockhart of Carnwath*, while the balance will be applied to the reserve fund established during the course of the year. If in consequence the balance sheet looks unusually healthy, Council believes that the rise in subscription agreed at the last Annual General Meeting and implemented this November was a necessary safeguard for the future. Even after the rise of subscription, income will only equal expenditure if finance can be generated from other sources. In this respect members are urged to purchase past publications while stocks remain available and also to consider covenanting for their subscription payments. Administratively, alteration of existing bankers' orders is a time-consuming exercise, but our bankers have advised against direct debiting which, because of the small number of members involved, would not be cost-effective.

Mr Stuart Maxwell retires as Chairman of Council after a busy and energetic term of office which included our centenary celebrations and the launching of the Fifth Series of publications. Council nominates as his successor Dr Jean Munro.

The three members of Council who now retire by rotation are J. D. Galbraith, J. B. Hume and H. L. MacQueen. To replace them and Dr Munro, Council nominates the following for election by the Annual Meeting: Dr J. Kirk, Dr F. MacIntosh, Dr Athol Murray and Mrs M. Robinson. Any other nominations made by at least two other members of the Society should reach the Honorary Secretary not less than seven days before the meeting at which this election is to be held.

During the past year eight members of the Society have died, seven have resigned and ten have been removed for non-payment of subscription. Fifteen new members have joined. The total membership, including thirty-one joint members and 200 libraries, is now 735 compared with 745 in 1988.

ABSTRACT ACCOUNT OF CHARGE AND DISCHARGE OF THE
INTROMISSIONS OF THE HONORARY TREASURER

1 October, 1988 to 30 September, 1989

I. GENERAL ACCOUNT

CHARGE

I. Cash in Bank at 1 October, 1988:

    1. Sum at credit of Savings Account with Bank of
       Scotland   £12,800.00

    2. Sum at credit of Current Account with Bank of
       Scotland   251.58

                 13,051.58

II. Subscriptions received   7,486.68

III. Past Publications sold   2,088.52

IV. Reprints sold   50.00

V. Interest on Savings Accounts with Bank of Scotland 1,572.78

VI. Income Tax Refund, 1987–88   587.23

VII. Royalties and fees   138.27

VIII. Grant from Carnegie Trust   600.00

IX. Sums drawn from Bank Current
     Account   £21,039.10

X. Sums drawn from Bank Savings
    Account   £9,900.00

                £25,575.06

DISCHARGE

I. Cost of publication during year
  Government and Social Conditions £2,532.28
  Letters of Lockhart of Carnwarth 10,698.88
 Cost of printing Annual Reports,
  Notices and Postage etc. 120.00

             £13,351.16

II. Insurance   67.60

III. Postage on past publications   363.00

IV. Bank Charges   221.16

V. Miscellaneous Payments   270.85

VI. Sums lodged in Bank Current Account £21,102.28

VII. Sums lodged in Bank Savings Account £21,138.11

VIII. Funds at close of this Account:

 1. Balance at credit of Savings Account
  with Bank of Scotland   £400.00

 2. Balance at credit of Premium Account
  with Bank of Scotland   £10,838.11

 3. Balance at credit of Current Account
  with Bank of Scotland   £63.18

             11,301.29

             £25,575.06

GLASGOW, *19 October, 1989.* I have examined the General Account of the Honorary Treasurer of the Scottish History Society for the year from 1 October, 1988 to 30 September, 1989, and find the same to be correctly stated and sufficiently vouched.

JOHN A. SMITH
Auditor